Horace Holley

HORACE HOLLEY

Transylvania University
and the Making of
Liberal Education
in the Early
American Republic

James P. Cousins

UNIVERSITY PRESS OF KENTUCKY

Cover: Portrait of Horace Holley by Matthew Harris Jouett (1788–1827), 1827.
Courtesy Transylvania University Special Collections and Archives.

Editorial and Sales Offices: The University Press of Kentucky
663 South Limestone Street, Lexington, Kentucky 40508-4008
www.kentuckypress.com

Library of Congress Cataloging-in-Publication Data

Names: Cousins, James, 1976– author.
Title: Horace Holley: Transylvania University and the making of liberal
   education in the early American republic / James P. Cousins.
Description: Lexington, Kentucky: The University Press of Kentucky, 2016. |
   Includes bibliographical references and index.
Identifiers: LCCN 2016031617| ISBN 9780813168579 (hardcover: alk. paper) |
   ISBN 9780813168586 (pdf) | ISBN 9780813168593 (epub)
Subjects: LCSH: Holley, Horace, 1781–1827. | College presidents—United
   States—Biography. | Transylvania University—Presidents—Biography. |
   Transylvania University—History.
Classification: LCC LA2317.H633 C68 2016 | DDC 378.0092 [B]—dc23
LC record available at https://lccn.loc.gov/2016031617

This book is printed on acid-free paper meeting the requirements of the American
National Standard for Permanence in Paper for Printed Library Materials.

∞

Manufactured in the United States of America.

Member of the Association of
American University Presses

For Carrie Anne

CONTENTS

Illustrations follow page 148

Introduction

The heat and humidity of that late-spring morning in Kentucky must have seemed all the more oppressive in the fifty-six-by-thirty-six-foot, windowless chapel now filled to overflowing with local dignitaries, curious bystanders, and a retinue of nearly one hundred students. Outside, an even larger group waited; a semicircle of finely dressed young women fronted the crowd and surrounded the building's entrance in a display meant to sharpen an already impressive ceremonial effect. As the procession of General Marquis de Lafayette (Gilbert du Motier) advanced on the main building of Transylvania University on May 17, 1825, its president, the Reverend Dr. Horace Holley, took his place behind the pulpit and readied the opening address of his "literary repast," a showcase of student talent prepared in honor of the "distinguished and excellent" hero of the revolution. The general was no doubt already flattered. He had arrived in Lexington the previous evening at the head of a lavish procession and amid celebratory cannon fire and adoring throngs of cheering Kentuckians, most wearing medallions inscribed with Lafayette's likeness pinned to their shirts. That night he had retired to a room adorned with fresh flowers and baskets of fruit, gifts of Mary Austin, Horace's publicly reserved yet privately charismatic wife.[1]

President Holley began the ceremony with honorifics and ended with a rhetorical flourish worthy of Pericles. "Your presence is making impressions upon the ardent and ingenuous minds of the young men around you, which they will never forget. They and their children will dwell upon the recollection as a most interesting era, and will, should duty call, shed the last drop of their blood in defending the cause, for which Washington and LaFayette hazarded all they held dear, wealth, freedom, life, and fame."[2] Student orations followed: short, carefully scripted odes to patriotism and liberty delivered in English, Latin, and French, their guest's *langue maternelle*. The event was by all accounts a success. Lafayette appeared gratified by the display, and those in attendance

1

were almost certain to reaffirm President Holley's intelligence and charisma. If it is true that Horace Holley's years at Transylvania (1818–1827) carried a tide of educational progress to early Kentucky, then Lafayette's visit was almost certainly the cresting wave of that success.

Recognition seemed well deserved. In the years since Horace Holley's appointment, the school had risen above its forbears' loftiest expectations. State financial assistance and extravagant private donations mixed with the enigmatic charm and ambition of its newly elected president to breathe new life into old plans. The law program, an innovation yet to be fully developed in many eastern schools, now presented a more accessible path to legal licensure; the "Academical" Department was as rigorous as it was experimental, benefiting from the exotic genius of its faculty; the university library contained more works of science, medicine, law, and theology than most other colleges of the day. The Medical Department, the first of its kind west of the Appalachians, was Horace's crowning glory. Here were assembled some of the most distinguished scientific minds of early America. Enrollment soared under Horace's oversight and 400 students from sixteen states counted themselves among the matriculates by the spring of 1825 —a number on par with Harvard (407), slightly below Yale (471), but well above Dartmouth (277), Bowdoin (134), and Columbia (34).[3]

Yet accolades from Lafayette's visit, like most successes of Horace's administration, were short-lived. In mid-November of that year, newly elected Kentucky governor, Joseph Desha, presented a scathing rebuke of the university to the Kentucky state legislature. Transylvania, Desha warned, profited only the rich. Though drawing liberally from state coffers, it never met "the reasonable expectations of the public." Its overpaid president earned more than twice the salary of the highest-paid state employee, donated resources were criminally mismanaged, and the entire enterprise, Desha concluded, contributed to an illiberal "aristocracy of wealth."[4] Horace might have anticipated this response. His personal letter to Desha, sent just three weeks earlier, detailed the recent successes of Transylvania and lobbied for further state assistance. Desha's letter of reply no longer exists; perhaps it never did. Horace, now threatened with a severely reduced salary and an end of public assistance, delivered his letter of resignation to university trustees a short time later. Though he agreed to delay his departure so as to allow time to locate a replacement, the Holley era at Transylvania University had come to an end.

The Historiography of Horace Holley

Horace Holley breathes rarefied air in histories of the early American West. Narratives paint him as the embodiment of an intellectual golden age; never before had the region enjoyed so great a reputation for educational achievement. Horace is also taken as a symbol of an emerging but constrained liberalism; bigotry, partisanship, and religious division form a background to his accomplishments and set the foundations for more than a century of educational apathy. But despite his recognized historical value, only a few comprehensive studies of him and his time at Transylvania have been published, and, to date, no modern book-length biography of him exists. Charles Caldwell's *A Discourse on the Genius and Character of the Rev. Horace Holley* (1828), a panegyric eulogy assembled with considerable input from Mary Austin Holley, remains the unquestioned primary source of choice for later authors. Mattie Austin Hatcher's *Letters of an Early American Traveller* (1933), Romie D. Judd's *The Educational Contributions of Horace Holley* (1936), Niles Sonne's *Liberal Kentucky* (1938), and Rebecca Smith Lee's *Mary Austin Holley: A Biography* (1962) are the only comprehensive accounts of Holley's life. More recent descriptions of Holley—in narratives, biographical sketches, historical asides, and one coauthored chapter—draw heavily and often exclusively from these works.[5]

In *Discourse on the Genius and Character of the Rev. Horace Holley*, Caldwell mingles intimate recollections with reconstructed private letters, extracted writings, and other artifacts to form an intimate personal history. It is a heroic remembrance of a recently departed colleague and husband; letters and other pieces of evidence are carefully selected or taken out of context to present Horace in the most flattering light. The story itself is built around unqualified overtures to his "vigorous and glowing thoughts," "lofty philosophical disquisitions," "famed discourses," and near mystical powers of intellect and erudition. He never tired, never questioned his purpose, and never lessened his resolve. When he arrived in Lexington, Transylvania was "but a grammar school." Horace was the "master spirit" and sole author of all good things to come.[6]

Educational Contributions and *Mary Austin Holley* give few additions to and no qualifications of this view. Both draw heavily from *Discourse* and present equally flattering, uncritical biographical overviews. In the former, Judd provides little more than a summary of Caldwell's *Discourse*. In the latter, Smith Lee incorporates new evidence—letters, official documents, pamphlets, and other published materials—but favors poetic license over historical accuracy. The result is a compelling yet quasi-fictional and anachronistic account of Horace's background and time in Kentucky.

Liberal Kentucky is the most historically rigorous and often cited account of Horace's presidency. Here, Horace is presented as the protector of moral liberalism—a champion of unrestricted freedom who struggled against a rising tide of sectarian jealousy. A spirit of liberality embedded itself within the minds of Kentuckians at an early date. Existing alongside, Sonne argues, was an equally determined Presbyterian elite who were committed to the "ruthless destruction of every vestige of independent theological thought" and who shunned innovation at every opportunity. Long-running debates extracted from regional periodicals trace the major lines of argument between Horace's liberal supporters and Presbyterian opponents. According to Sonne, Horace was the chief architect of success, an "example of vigorous activity" and "intellectual achievement." He was persecuted for his liberal beliefs and forced out by conservative bigots—his successes, although brief, are significant because of his illiberal surroundings.

The argument is oversimplified and reductionist; disputes between competing factions subsume the entire political, economic, religious, intellectual, and cultural climate of early Kentucky. Horace's legacy is intimately tied to the destiny of Transylvania University, so that events leading up to his presidency are of tangential importance, and events after his departure are inconsequential.[7] Although more than seventy years have passed since the publication of *Liberal Kentucky*, it remains the standard account of Horace's presidency for local and state histories as well as for institutional histories of education.[8] But reducing Horace's life and contributions to education in this way undermines his wider significance, not only to the history of Kentucky but also to the ultimate shape of higher learning in America. A new perspective on Horace is required, one that takes advantage of historical understanding and hundreds of previously available but unapplied primary sources. In this retelling, events and circumstances from Horace's early life—his relationships, education, and ministerial career—are not colorful asides but details that deepen our understanding of his influence and contain meaningful historical value.

Horace's story is best told and most useful when filtered through the methods of the "biographical turn," a recent historiographic shift away from uncritical or superficial personal histories. Here, biography becomes a means to much larger ends; historical actors reflect but also complicate our appreciation of historical change while adding a new perspective of society and culture. Horace is significant to the history of Kentucky, and Lexington in particular, but he is equally significant to the history of American education.

Historians now conclude that the migration of colleges from the settled East to the frontier West was neither linear nor progressive. Colleges of the late eighteenth and early nineteenth centuries developed in an unwieldy mass of personal choices, local circumstances, and national ambitions.[9] A "higher" education was different things to different people at different times but became a coherent ideal in the early 1800s. The relationship between education and religion was fundamental to this arrangement, but religion was less significant than political and cultural influences. Professional academics—college presidents and professors—both guided and followed these developments. In doing so, they created a unique brand of scholar, one divorced from the pretenses of the Old World and the prejudices of the New. They coordinated with one another and shaped their opinions in light of prevailing trends; however, the creation of the American academic only crystalized under the dual pressures of local religion and national politics.

Horace, molded by the dreams of a liberal capitalist and conditioned by the fame of an intellectual, positioned himself at the vanguard of this transition and made education the focus of his ambitions for prestige and influence. As the son of a rising New England merchant family, a student at Yale, a Calvinist minister in a rural New England town, a Unitarian urbanite of national acclaim, a self-appointed critic of higher education, a relocated Yankee, a member of an elite scholarly network, and a president of the first and most prosperous university of the early American West, he personifies this transformation. He grew to maturity in the early republic, a time when America was made and remade by expanding opportunities and limitless potentials. Towns began to see colleges as a means toward reinvention, a way to rejuvenate or build economic opportunity and increase their share of political influence. Education also made personal reinvention possible, and those of Horace's generation came to see themselves as both inheritors and suppressors of revolutionary ideals. His personal experiences make these developments both less opaque and more easily tied to larger trends in American history. His formal and informal education, successes and defeats, personal connections, and bitter adversaries make him an important figure in the evolution not only of an emerging state university but also of the emerging state of education in America.

Lessons from Horace's life and career also resonate within modern contexts. His personal inconsistencies reflect all-too-familiar struggles between habit and aspiration, character and desire. He possessed a talent for reinvention yet maintained unshakable devotion to his ideals. His relationships with influential figures—national characters, state and local officials, American presidents, and others—were built around relatable patterns of mutual benefit and reciprocal exchange. He was both client and patron, protégé and power broker. His difficulties in unfamiliar social surroundings reflect distinctions among still-significant cultural identifiers, the regional differences now fixed within American historical memory. Finally, his educational career calls attention to unresolved challenges in American higher education. Modern theories of learning, questions regarding academics' professional responsibilities, debates over state funding, and arguments for or against liberal education are contemporary outgrowths of issues that developed during the time of his presidency at Transylvania. His rise and fall illustrate the promises and disappointments inherent in higher learning in America.

Life and Learning

Horace Holley, the fourth son of a wealthy Connecticut merchant family, enjoyed all the benefits of an elite, well-funded education. He was tutored privately in childhood, prepared for higher learning at Williams College, and completed his preparations for the ministry under Yale president Timothy Dwight. Chapter 1 considers these and other educational influences but within the context of a postrevolutionary intellectual and religious climate. The colleges of New England expected students to exhibit the right blend of Christian piety and political virtue. The goal was stability through inculcated conservatism, and so Horace, like many of his peers, came to see the world outside New England as a violent, chaotic, and uncivilized place where democracy had been corrupted by vulgar politics and despicable avarice. The details of his education give insight into his developing character but also speak to developing intellectual trends in the young nation.[10]

After Yale, Horace spent four years as pastor of Greenfield Hill, a Congregational church near the town of Fairfield, Connecticut. He resigned after only four years and became the minister of Boston's Hollis Street Church—serving there from 1809 to 1818. His oratorical skill and associations there led to wider circles of influence, first within elite gentlemen's clubs and charitable organizations and later in the Boston School Committee, Harvard's Board of Overseers, and the Massachusetts House of Representatives. Chapter 2 investigates Holley's pastoral career with an eye to his emerging educational, political, and spiritual views. In early-nineteenth-century Boston, church affiliation and public office were sometimes by-products of larger concerns; the city's moneyed newcomers found identity in Christian liberalism, and these associations often determined access to cultural opportunities and civic office. Horace's perception of utility, reputation, and ambition were shaped in this climate and helps explain the motivations behind his academic leadership in the early nineteenth century.[11]

His background made him an ideal candidate for the presidency of Transylvania University, a school recently incorporated by state authorities and in search of a religiously neutral, nationally recognized educational leader. Trustees offered him the position in November 1817, and he set out the following year to investigate the proposition. The journey from Boston to Lexington gave him the opportunity to visit the most notable institutions of higher education in America, inspect their programs, tour their campuses, and meet their presidents and professors. His impressions of these institutions—their curricula, holdings, campuses, and faculties—would form the basis of his educational philosophy and create a context for his work at Transylvania. Chapter 3 narrates Horace's journeys to Harvard, Yale, Dartmouth, Columbia, the University of Pennsylvania, and finally Monticello, the home of former president Thomas Jefferson, where he hoped to discuss ideas for a regional college and a national university. His reflections on the state of science, literature, and medicine in the late 1810s provide insight into shared expectations for higher learning in early America.

Horace—along with his wife, Mary; his daughter, Harriette; and his newborn son, Horace Jr.—arrived in Lexington in the fall of 1818. New surroundings made for a difficult transition—Mary was strongly against the move and remained inconsolable for months. Horace relished the change, however, seeing it as a necessary sacrifice, and consoled Mary with visions of bringing education and culture to an untamed wilderness. Science and literature were means to this end, and Holley recruited a slate of eastern intellectuals to staff his college. Charles Caldwell, Constantine Rafinesque, John Everett, and others helped him carry out his ideas and, in the process, melded eastern sensibilities with western aspirations. Chapter 4 examines the roots and trajectory of Holley's early plans, along with his attempts to distinguish Transylvania as a preeminent American university. Student medical theses, an improved curriculum, and essays in the *Western Review,* his short-lived periodical, gave flight to his best hopes.

Horace's skin thickened during his time in Lexington. Loath to accept him in his role as university president, local Presbyterians attacked his character, theological leanings, educational ideas, and personal habits. Of equal concern was the growing number of western colleges and universities, all of which looked at Transylvania with a mixture of jealousy and admiration. Horace, the most recognizable educational authority in the state, provided a natural point of convergence for competing positions. Chapter 5 considers the dual pressures of religious dissent and regional competition—how these forces shaped Horace's opinions of education and how they directed a larger trend toward the secularization of academics.

Horace's final years at Transylvania were also some of the last of his short life. He enjoyed a national prestige but suffered local indignities and in the end fell victim to the vicissitudes of American politics. This was also a period of dramatic change for Kentuckians, who suffered from the same economic troubles experienced nationally but lashed out in unexpected ways. The management of debt and a depreciating currency germinated the seeds of a populism that rampaged through the state and ended Horace's ambitions for public support. As an intellectual, Horace personified the type of elitism that, some believed, had precipitated Kentucky's financial debacle.[12]

The Holleys departed Lexington for New Orleans in March 1827 with the idea of heading a "traveling academy," a privately funded student excursion through Europe with Horace acting as headmaster to the sons of wealthy New Orleanians. When these schemes came to nothing, the Holleys elected to escape the Louisiana summer heat and return once again to New England. Their voyage from New Orleans to New York was ill fated. En route, an outbreak of yellow fever brought him and Mary to the brink of death; Mary survived, only to see her husband's lifeless body deposited off the western coast of Florida. Chapter 6 places Horace in the context of larger political trends and posits a different interpretation of the years of decline that succeeded his administration. His removal from Lexington is best understood as the product of excessive, not restrained, liberalism. The same democratic impulse that carried Horace Holley into Kentucky now frustrated his conservative ambitions and set the agenda for years of neglecting education.

1

"GREAT TRUTHS"

Forests of white birch, weeping beech, and craggy maple grow thick along the uplands of western Connecticut. In the town of Salisbury, at the northwestern reaches of the state, meandering creeks empty into ponds set low among rising foothills. Crooked lakes dapple the terrain and help isolate a place already removed from urban scenes. In the mid–eighteenth century, British colonists found red ore and the means of forging it in quantity; creeks powered their bellows, wooded hills turned to coal heated their furnaces. Settlements were carved deep into the landscape. Farmers uncovered an ancient lakebed, clearcut pastureland, and harvested grain from limestone soils. Salisbury and its adjoining hamlet, Lakeville, swelled from increase and matured. Brick replaced clapboard, trampled country paths became durable roads, bridges eased passage between neighboring communities, and by the start of the American Revolution the town counted nearly two thousand souls.[1]

Congregationalism added a resistive quality to Salisbury's social order. Church membership, here as in most parts of Connecticut, was exclusive to the elect, yet attendance at Sunday service as well as tax support for the church were mandatory for all. Colonial law, grounded in biblical precedent, blended Puritan morality with civil procedure and gave harsh punishments for adultery, lying, profanity, and laboring on the Sabbath. Influence was buttressed by clerics of long standing; the Reverend Jonathan Lee assumed responsibilities for Salisbury's Congregational church in 1744 and remained there for almost half a century. In addition to his spiritual leadership, Lee, a member of Yale's class of 1742, provided advanced tutoring for college-bound youths.[2]

The iron trade complicated Salisbury's timeless order, providing social mobility and enticing new settlers. New England's families needed nails, cutlery, and cookware; shipbuilders required cast iron for fasteners, ballasts, and anchors; the Connecticut militia needed shot and cannon of various sizes.

Blooming forges and blast furnaces spread quickly as demand surged. Some settlers succeeded, but most struggled to survive cycles of boom and bust inspired by capricious demand and intercontinental politics. Ethan Allen's furnace just south of Lakeville became a draining liability soon after its purchase. When the brothers Charles and George Caldwell assumed Allen's shares, they met a similar fate, and George went to prison over furnace-related debts. Richard Smith, a wealthy Boston shipping magnate, purchased a controlling interest in the furnace in 1770, only to offer the same property for sale three years later.[3]

For the Holley family, with roots planted deep in neighboring Sharon, farming seemed a more reasonable occupation. Joseph Holly,[4] one of the area's original lot holders, prospered after some initial difficulties. Joseph's son John, the second of twelve children, expanded these holdings but suffered when the family home was destroyed by fire in 1771. Enfeebled by apathy or illness or both, John left his sixteen-year-old son Luther, the youngest of four children, with the responsibility of providing for the farm as well as for his mother, sisters, and sickly father.

By day, the fair-haired, blue-eyed Luther worked the fields; by night, he traveled eight or nine miles to the nearest doctor in search of medicine, often falling asleep in the saddle and snapping awake in the dark quiet of a lonesome wooded path. He found comfort in books and took to them with zealous attention. Armed with only days of formal schooling—five, by his estimation—he learned numbers by drawing figures in coal on the floor of the barn. Luther then struggled with and conquered volumes of George Sale's immense work *Universal History,* memorized large sections of John Milton's *Paradise Lost,* and read widely so as to become useful in the art of pleasant conversation.[5]

Daily struggles became manageable over time, and with the "persevering industry" of his mother and sisters the family was maintained. Misfortune returned, however, when Luther suffered a deep cut to his leg while working at the plough. An infection in the wound left him bedridden for about ten weeks, and only with a good bleeding was the leg saved. Healed but now with one leg too stiff for farmwork, Luther turned again to his books, this time to qualify as a local schoolteacher. Connecticut's laws would have made this opportunity possible even to a novice since schoolmasters were responsible only for achieving basic literacy among their students, enough to read the scriptures and "other good and profitable books." Legal codes mandated instruction and secured employment for the willing in even the most remote Connecticut towns. Luther succeeded in his new occupation, increasing the number of students and soon winning the notice of Salisbury's town committee, which offered him a position in one of its schools. A salary of £5 a month, paid during the winter, added to farm revenues from the summer, allowed him to court a wife, buy a home, and raise a family.[6]

The terms, length, and even origins of Luther's negotiations for the hand of Sarah Dankin, the plump, black-haired, brown-eyed daughter of one of the region's earliest Baptist ministers, are either lost or unrecorded. Her father, Simon, was part of a larger wave of Baptist conversions that New Light Calvinists of New England attracted to the evangelical impulse of the 1740s. In 1773, the Dankin family settled in nearby North East, New York, when Simon took a position as the town's first Baptist minister. It is likely that his religious enthusiasm made Luther's courtship of Sarah challenging. Engraved on Simon's tombstone is this eternal testament of severity: "Stranger . . . think on the dread state of morality and pause, for here rests proof that affection, however strong, . . . piety . . . integrity and benevolence . . . cannot stand the invincibility of death." Attempts to win Sarah's approval and her father's blessing probably required no small amount of religious assurance and most likely baptism and confirmation. This was perhaps an uncomplicated matter for Luther, a man later described as "reverenced [of] the great truths of religion" but liberal in his understanding of God's blessings. Luther had been taught the Commandments, the Lord's Prayer, and the Apostle's Creed as a child but developed a religion mostly apart from Sunday services. By the time he reached adulthood, he had largely given up on prayer for want of concentration and a failure to ward off wicked thoughts. Theology baffled him, and so spiritual pursuits for him would always remain simple. Sarah took matters more seriously and became the family's religious ballast, leading her husband and children in the daily observance of Christian piety.[7]

Newly married and with bright prospects, Sarah and Luther settled in the Furnace Neighborhood of Lakeville and had four sons in quick succession. Milton, named for the author of *Paradise Lost,* died shortly after his birth in 1776; John Milton was born in 1777; Myron, born two years later, was named for the fifth-century Athenian sculptor; and in February 1781 the couple welcomed Horace, his name suggesting an affinity for the first-century Roman poet. After three years as a schoolteacher, Luther grew restless and began looking for more interesting and lucrative opportunities. A career in mercantilism was a natural choice. During the revolution, Connecticut remained largely untouched by British forces, leaving area merchants free to provision American soldiers and thus earn small fortunes. Luther, unable to enlist because of his leg injury, joined the fray as a seller's agent, taking commissions on goods purchased in Connecticut and sold in New York. In 1777, he purchased the general store across the street from his home for £60. In 1783, he and his partner, William Davis, made enough to risk a $300 purchase of gunpowder from a supplier in Holland. But when prices bottomed out in a postwar depression, Luther was pushed to the edge of bankruptcy. His partner abandoned his share and left Luther to sell the remainder of the supply at a loss. Later ventures were more profitable, and Luther developed an active trade in goods for the farmers, merchants, and craftsmen of the Connecticut and New York countryside. He was frequently away on business, purchasing goods—rum and molasses in particular—in New York for resale in Poughkeepsie, Red Hook, and any number of towns along the Hudson River. For a time, the family lived in Dover, New York, closer to mercantile concerns and Sarah's family. And here Luther held a position as representative to the New York state legislature. But in 1799 the Holley's returned to Salisbury, and Luther's accumulated earnings allowed him to enter Salisbury's lucrative iron business with the purchase of eighteen hundred acres, cannon-boring mills, water privileges, and a large blast furnace.[8]

And so in the span of twenty years Luther went from farmer to schoolteacher to merchant to entrepreneur. Self-education, industry, and a measure of good fortune brought profit from the boom years of the republic. His sons were well acquainted with these travails, learning that "Dada" succeeded because of a learned vocabulary and access to ancient wisdom. With trained minds, they, too, could take roles in public life and business. It was a popular narrative for the day. New England's merchants of the 1790s and 1800s earned vast fortunes in expanding American markets, while their sons attended Harvard, Yale, Bowdoin, and Williams to learn gentlemanly behavior and the skills of professional men. In the decades following the revolution, education became one of the fastest routes to social improvement, and the number of colleges in America nearly tripled; those unable to afford the luxuries of a higher education gladly paid the more affordable costs of a local day school or evening academy.[9]

The performative nature of Luther's education, his ability to recite memorized material, made this transition possible. It is difficult to judge the quality of his understanding or how his knowledge differed from that of men with access to formal instruction, but it is likely that displays of learning helped Luther and other aspiring mercantilists negotiate unfamiliar relationships. Quoting entire stanzas of *Paradise Lost*, recalling the legislative functions of the Roman Senate, and impressing associates with obscure knowledge or interesting anecdotes hinted at elite status and gave confidence to potential associates, men otherwise unknown to Luther. The abundance of self-improvement manuals from this period suggests the scope of a wider phenomenon. Handbooks, courtesy books, and pamphlets described the characteristics of genteel society and gave practical advice on "useful knowledge" and "polite conversation." The intention was to improve opportunities for social and professional advancement.[10]

On to Williams

The perceived usefulness of education forced more than a few awkward exchanges between well-meaning parents and well-worn teachers. Citizens of Connecticut often complained of programs that were focused on "branches of education which are the best fitted to feed parental vanity" and "in a great degree superficial, and useless." Parents scrutinized these programs' offerings, questioning the cost of tuition, grumbling when their children made inadequate progress, and otherwise harassing instructors whenever the chance arose. "He who is to lay the foundation for future usefulness and greatness must be in his own person and manners, little and obsequious," one anonymous schoolteacher lamented in the December 1790 issue of the *Litchfield Monitor*. The author sarcastically instructed parents to check the "growing influence and opulence" of instructors. "Frequently find fault with the masters and their mode of government and instruction; charge them with partiality, and ignorance, not forgetting to compare them with the great masters from which you received a knowledge of the alphabet."[11]

Luther's decision to send sons Milton, Myron, and Horace to the recently chartered Williams College, some sixty miles north of Salisbury, was likely born of these same concerns. Williams, nestled in the Berkshire foothills of western Massachusetts, was a "Yale in miniature," staffed and supervised almost entirely by Yale graduates, with a single, four-story brick building, and a library of around 360 volumes. Its lone wooden telescope constituted the entirety of its "scientific apparatus." However, low tuition—nearly half that of Yale—and lower entry requirements made Williams a popular choice. In the 1790s, Harvard, Yale, Rhode Island College, the College of New Jersey (later Princeton), and Columbia expected entering students to "read, translate, and parse" Cicero, Virgil, and books of the Greek New Testament, write "true Latin in prose," and demonstrate a knowledge of grammatical and mathematical rules. At Williams, applicants needed only a rudimentary knowledge of grammar and "vulgar Arithmetic" as well as the ability to translate passages of commonly used Latin and Greek authors. Students with knowledge of French were exempted from examination in a dead language in order to attract Canadian students. Moreover, Williams did not have the same expectations for religious observance found elsewhere, something that might have appealed to Luther's more liberal theology. The college's articles of incorporation provided no mandate for religious observance, unsurprising given that Williams's namesake, Colonel Ephraim Williams (1715–1755), had donated monies with the hope of building a school for the sons of militia men. Whereas Yale dedicated an entire chapter of its student law code to Christian regulations, Williams requested only that the student "be a Christian and a scholar" and uphold "manners of politeness." Williams's curriculum also suggested a focus on more practical subjects that would most likely be of professional utility. The scheme worked, and by 1800 Williams's enrollment rivaled or surpassed that of most other New England colleges.[12]

The number of new matriculates presented certain challenges for the president and his subordinates and created the need for an expansive list of rules and penalties. But because expulsions robbed the school of tuition, the Williams trustees elected to curb youthful malfeasance with an elaborate system of student fines and a rigorous daily schedule. The severity of the misconduct determined its cost: firing a gun on college property cost a student two shillings; drunkenness three shillings; setting fireworks, fighting, or acting in a play five shillings. Expulsion was reserved for the most odious offense of all: dressing in women's clothing.[13]

A rigorous daily schedule and other self-imposed restrictions also helped to reign in youthful enthusiasms. Horace's older brother Milton, the first Holley to attend Williams, and his friends were vexed by the chapel bell's monastic order and the rigor of their coursework. "The first thing in the [morning] ding

ding ding goes the bell then to prayers, finally the whole day is spent in prayers recitations, & meals," Milton's friend Thomas Fitch complained. The best remedy for student merriment was the year-end exam. Passing from one class to the next required a successful completion of a single oral test covering every subject, lecture, and reading from the year. Failure brought personal shame and possibly the end to a young man's college ambitions. Preparations began early, usually months ahead of time, and were all consuming. "We have been so much engaged in reviewing our studies for examinations that I have scarcely had time to think of any thing else," another friend grumbled. As exams approached, students grew more apprehensive. "A week from yesterday our examination begins," lamented another classmate. "I tremble; a still small voice declares to me the day awful and terrible."[14]

Troublemaking and manic study punctuated but did not define Williams, and throughout the 1790s the campus kept pace with regional trends. Francophilia and deistic sympathies swept the college in the early part of the decade as French revolutionaries began their preemptive war against monarchical Europe. The revolutionary spirit had, one of the college's first graduates recalled, "a commanding influence" as it "bore the multitude onward in its course." A spirit of French impiety affected no small number of students, and professors bore the brunt of "wicked" ridicule. Later, as America prepared for war with France and New England's politicians rallied around President John Adams, Milton and his peers demonstrated Federalist loyalties. Student commencement orations on the benefits of national unity, the security of the federal government, and "the spirit of Enterprise in society" became public displays of partisanship. In the summer of 1798, while President Adams considered his response to seditious personal attacks from Republican editors, Williams students sent a letter of support praising him for the "moderation, candor, and firmness which have uniformly characterized your administration." Adams responded with a simple note of appreciation for the "respectable sample of . . . literary talents."[15]

Williams College president Ebenezer Fitch encouraged these influences. His commencement address of 1799, delivered before Horace and brother Myron, implored graduates to defend the country's virtue against a "raging torrent" of "VANDALISM" now present on the European continent. It would be better, he argued, to "stand . . . at your posts and die like men" than to be "sacrificed at the unhallowed shrine of atheism and French philosophy." But

Fitch appeared somewhat more interested in preparing students for lives of professional fulfillment. Education in the arts and sciences was, he argued, "for the good of others," so Williams graduates might become "the blessing and the ornament of society." Divine favor bestowed men of "leisure and opportunity" with uncommon abilities and the capacity for "endless progressive improvement in knowledge and virtue." With the receipt of these gifts came an obligation to fulfill "higher and nobler" destinies to improve humanity's temporal and eternal well-being. "Learned Professions"—medicine, law, and the ministry—best suited these ends. Physicians provided physical comforts and preserved health through a skilled understanding of healing arts; attorneys protected and defended the rights of the just against the wicked through diligent study and precise application of law. The Christian ministry, the "highest and noblest" profession, required the greatest efforts but carried the greatest value. As Christ's chosen ambassadors, ministers had the solemn duty to proclaim the truth of God's atoning grace. Professionals were society's most esteemed representatives, possessing the respect and admiration of their families, the accolades of friends, and the ability to "acquire influence" in public life as well as the "supports, comforts, accommodations, and, perhaps, elegancies of life." Fitch's message left an impression. Many were unsure where their adult lives would take them, but nearly all were convinced of professional virtues. In a letter to Milton, Williams senior Ephraim A. Judson lamented his inevitable entry into one of the "learned profession[s] in life."[16]

Brothers

The Holley brothers grew along with their adopted academic home. In the fall of 1793, Milton, age sixteen, and younger brother Horace, age twelve, joined the college's first matriculates—Milton as a member of Williams's inaugural freshman class, Horace as an "affiliate," tutored apart from regular students and taught languages in preparation for admission. Milton set out on the first-year course of study with an intensive review of English grammar and dead languages. Horace returned to Salisbury before the year was over, evidently disappointed by his experiences. "I suppose it to be a good place to study anything but writing & Arithmetic," brother Milton explained to their father. "I do not think [Horace] has received any material benefit from this School."[17]

For the next few years, Horace remained with Salisbury tutors and under his father's supervision traveled to Poughkeepsie, Redhook, Genesee, and other New York towns on matters related to the family business. The experience, as Mary Austin Holley later recalled, was meant to "aid in giving firmness and tone to character" while educating Horace in the ways of the world. If the liberal arts could not engage him, perhaps a life of mercantile trade could. When plans to apprentice Horace at a respected New York trade house came to nothing, Luther agreed to duplicate the experience at his general store. However, time in the shop—filling orders, taking stock, and managing accounts on credit—convinced Horace of the need to complete a less hands-on course of instruction.[18]

But returning to Williams was no mean feat. English composition was a challenge that Horace found difficult to overcome. Writing to brother Milton, he complained of the hours spent attempting to compose letters. Long overdue responses were produced with great struggle and considerable amounts of pain. Milton remained encouraging: "what we expect, or think is within our reach, we are emulous to obtain, and for this reason you . . . ought to expect to write good letters." Milton echoed President Fitch's message of obligatory self-sacrifice, writing, "Expectation inspires us with ambition; and if it was not for this passion, genius would never have entered itself; mankind would not have been roused from the sleep of indolence, and civilization and refinement would never have illumined the world."[19]

Handbooks may have guided the early development of the Holley brothers. *The New Universal Letter-Writer, Juvenile Correspondence, The American Teacher's Assistant,* and other introductions to practical prose, all found in the Williams College library, taught through example. By adapting letters on business, on love and courtship, of advice and friendship, young men, one author claimed, might outdo even "masters of languages," who, guided by native ability alone, could not express the necessary elegance or dignity required by men and women of gentility. Chapters from *The New Universal Letter-Writer* featured sample letters of introduction as well as likely responses; an example, "From a father to a Son, on his negligence in his affairs," was followed by "The Son's grateful Answer." These and other models helped the unlearned articulate complex ideas while communicating elite sensibilities. The samples themselves—"Recommending a man servant," "From a trades-man requesting a Letter of License," and letters passed between friends on happiness, the "immortality of the soul," and other ideas—addressed topics of adult concern. Content reinforced behavior, conditioning students in the ways of polite society.[20]

Cultivating a learned style required practice, and even the best guides were no substitute for practical experience. Sharing letters was considered the best method of improvement, and the Holley brothers exchanged scores of them with each other, their parents, and friends. Milton hoped to maintain his skills by corresponding with classmates long after his departure; he wrote to continue his refinement, and his brothers thanked him for the chance to polish theirs. For Milton's friend Thomas Fitch, son of the Williams college president, letters offered a productive retreat from study, allowing him to "pass over that time with pleasure and instruction" and to refresh his mind to begin studies anew. Martin Field, a member of the Williams class of 1798, tested the limits of his prose with flowery recollections of past adventures and bawdy reminders of present frivolities. "Holley," he wrote to Milton, "what are you doing, do you study divinity, so do I, do you drink brandy, so do I, do you stroke the girls so do I, finally do you calculate to spend your days happily, so do I."[21]

Milton raised the level of discourse in the family out of necessity. After Williams, he replaced Horace in the family store. The dullness of his situation, made more difficult by the "Two legged unfeathered animals" that surrounded him, left him struggling to re-create the elevated conversation of his college days.[22] Friends were helpful but too busy to fill more than a page in their missives to him, so Milton's brothers carried most of the weight. Just as Horace now enjoyed the benefit of Milton's philosophical encouragement, brother Myron found himself ensnared in lengthy debates over how to remedy the "prevalence of foreign manners in America."[23]

Horace continued to write and continued to improve. In the spring of 1798, he was joined at Williams by Myron, whose early preparation allowed him to enter Williams as a member of the junior class, and his writing began to show learned polish. "I look forward with a pleasing anxiety to that moment, which will sit me down at the door of a beloved family . . . where from you, and the rest of the family I shall receive the more solid embrace of friendship," Horace wrote to Milton. Writing came more easily with time and was an opportunity to practice the acquired habits and useful knowledge. Horace and Myron remained focused—staying on campus during their recesses to read history, philosophy, and geography. "Horace," Myron reported to their father, "has made rapid progress in geography" and, despite contracting a "considerable fever," was committed to his studies. Myron, who carried the burden of corresponding with their father, set a fine example, reading eight books of Virgil, the first and second volumes of Horace, and Telemachus in French translation. These literary pursuits were in addition to his studies of English grammar, chemistry, navigation, arithmetic, and the sciences.[24] Luther was a generous benefactor but expressed at least a few doubts about the curriculum, feeling perhaps that memorization was a surer path to erudition. He was also unsure that someone so young—Horace was sixteen in 1797—could benefit from any of it.[25]

But it was at Williams that Horace began his life-long appreciation of poetic verse, a love perhaps inspired by his father's own devotion to *Paradise Lost.* Horace learned poetry as he did the art of genteel correspondence: by reading and imitating ancient and modern elegies, sonnets, and soliloquies in instructional manuals before composing his own. He learned the importance of proportion, the limitations of "low and vulgar" subjects, the power of emotional language, and he discovered that comparisons "mightily strengthen and beautify" one's work. Included within Williams's small library were the poetry collections *Elegant Extracts in Verse* and *The Muse's Pocket Companion,* the collected works of Alexander Pope, James Thompson's *Seasons,* and Timothy Dwight's epic *Conquest of Cannae.*[26] Horace's earliest attempts show evidence not only of these influences in their rhyming schemes and imagery but also his creative capacity.

Myron graduated in the fall of 1799 and with the help of his father became a legal apprentice to a judge in Cooperstown, New York. For Horace, Myron's absence was undoubtedly a difficult transition. A consolatory letter from his mother, written a short time after Myron's departure, chided Horace, "Keep up a strict watch over all your actions, that you may end your studies with as much credit as you have begun them." Horace, now eighteen, was ready to enter Williams as a regular student. His decision to leave Williams for Yale is unclear. He might have received encouragement from Williams's tutors—all of whom had attended Yale. His father's recent business acquisitions might also have allowed more extravagant educational expenses, considering that the cost of tuition at Yale was nearly double that of Williams.[27]

Raucous Yale

At the turn of the nineteenth century, Yale was a fantastic cacophony, a motley collection of young men who, as Horace's classmate Nathaniel Willis later recalled, hailed from parts of the country known only from books. At his first chapel service, Lewis noted the "berry brown tan" of a Georgian, the "Herculean" proportions of a young Carolinian, and the well-tailored New Yorker, "with a firm belief in his tailor and him-self written on his effeminate lip." In contrast to these figures was the self-possessed young Puritan, either from Vermont or New Hampshire, with a pale complexion and "stiff black coat." The vulgarity of the New England dialect challenged the uninitiated, but raucous youthful behavior was a more universal trait. Pranks, brawls, and general rowdiness punctuated an otherwise regimented daily schedule, a rhythm set to the chime of the chapel bells. Much like Williams, bells called students to morning and evening prayers, began class, marked periods of free and study time, and signaled meals three times a day.[28]

Despite the presence of tutors on elevated platforms, the Yale dining hall was a scene of remarkable incivility and unhygienic barbarity. Frivolity and lewd behavior forced the staff to remove all glassware and china and to institute a pewter-only policy to curb breakage. The meals themselves were generally of poor quality and became something of legend. The students' frequent remedy was to order food from one of New Haven's establishments—a frequent enough occurrence to merit codification in the college laws and a fifteen-cent penalty. This and other punishments, however, seem to have done little to squelch undercurrents of youthful exuberance. More than once during Horace's undergraduate years did students cut the rope of the chapel bell. They fired guns from dormitory windows, skipped classes, fought, and hung dead ducks over classroom doors with signs reading, "Turkeys for sale, 3 pence per pound." When punished, students rebelled openly, in one instance demolishing one of the first college buildings. Low behavior and high jinks became all too common, and tutors—the younger and lesser-paid assistants of more respected professors—were all too frequently singled out for the worst of it, having their windowpanes broken and barrels smashed against their dormitory doors.[29]

By the late eighteenth century, however, Yale also became synonymous with men of national standing and semimysterious intellect. Those who passed through its halls were repositories of the holy wisdoms of the Hebrew Bible and the ancient but profane teachings of Demosthenes, Plato, and Cicero. Some applied themselves with such intensity that they permanently damaged their eyesight. By 1800, the college could count an impressive list of distinguished alumni, attorneys, politicians, ministers, and men of business, all of whom framed their accomplishments and defended their intellectual pedigrees by reference to Yale.[30]

The Wisdom of Dr. Dwight

Though already significant by the time of his arrival, college president Timothy Dwight established Yale as one of the country's most politically relevant, theologically important, and esteemed institutions. Dwight, a member of Yale's class of 1769, returned to the campus as a tutor only two years after he graduated. Here, he earned a reputation for austerity and discipline but also sociability and teaching. Despite his popularity, Dwight was later forced to resign by Yale's governing board when he and his fellow tutors, charged with the lion's share of teaching and supervision, felt it necessary to modify the curriculum—adding belles lettres and rhetoric to the traditional offerings in theology, mathematics, dead languages, and logic. The additions were not as controversial as their decision to institute these and other changes without the board's approval. When in 1777 the board voted to suspend commencement following an invasion of British soldiers, Dwight and his fellow tutors ignored their injunctions and held it anyway.[31]

In the years following his departure from Yale, Dwight won acclaim for his teaching, his poetry, and, beginning in 1783, his spiritual leadership of Greenfield Hill, a Congregational church outside Fairfield, Connecticut. In addition to regular pastoral duties, Dwight was also charged with the management of the attached school. His enthusiasm for pastoral duties was matched only by his desire to celebrate the new American nation in passionate essays, poems, and songs that memorialized the country's origins, brilliant constructs, and ultimate destiny. In *America: Or, A Poem on the Settlement of the British Colonies*, published in 1780, he revered America's colonial past and predicted a glorious future. His epic *The Conquest of Canäan*, completed over a period of fourteen years, allegorically linked George Washington's triumph over the

British to Joshua's victory over the Canaanites. The central tenets of Calvinism supported emergent nationalism. America was, in a sense, predestined to overcome the innate depravity of Europe; divine grace speeded its emergence and solidified its standing.

In time, Dwight's literary productions extended beyond nationalism to attacks on infidelity and moral decline, a basis for the defense of Federalist interests. In "Essay on the Judgment of History Concerning America" and "Address on the Genius of Columbia," both published in 1787 and addressed to the members of the Constitutional Convention, he excoriated those "freaks of human nature" who with "selfish passions" and "baleful influence" made mockery of the inherited gifts of democracy. Jealousy, licentiousness, and a "train of follies and vices" could be expected with an abundance of unrestrained freedom, and Dwight urged caution in extending the franchise.[32]

Dwight was neither alone nor exceptional in his criticisms of privilege unrestrained; by the mid-1780s, a counterrevolutionary trend in New England attempted to bring order from disorder and narrow the scope of unrestrained democratic privilege. By attaching morality to the political health of the republic, Dwight confirmed the worst fears of New England Federalists while offering a Puritan hierarchical structure as a model for improvement that added political relevancy to the Congregational Church. The impression was strong enough to warrant the notice of the College of New Jersey trustees, who, because of these efforts, awarded Dwight an honorary doctorate of divinity in 1787.[33]

Dwight, who could now add the title "Dr." to his name, preached a message of moral rectitude and restrained liberality. In an essay published the following year and directed to "Ministers of the Gospel of Every Denomination," he raged against "spirituous liquors," militia musters, state fairs, lawsuits, the press, horse racing, clubs "of all kinds," and amusements "of every kind." Diversions, he argued, promoted immoral behaviors in otherwise moral men—turpitude placed not only the man but the entire republic in jeopardy. In his poem *The Triumph of Infidelity*, a work sardonically dedicated to Voltaire, Dwight lamented the intrusions of European deists, who with "learning vast, and deep research" were blind to "gospel truths." The answer was a strong central government directly influenced by ministers of the Christian gospel, a body whose influence could assign "reason over the passions of men."[34]

For America to avoid the same fate as France, where a revolutionary movement had metamorphosed into unrestrained terror by 1794, it needed nothing less than complete rehabilitation. *Greenfield Hill* (1794), the most popular of Dwight's early works, suggested that his local Connecticut parish and by extension all of New England might form the basis of this change. The simple values of the Puritan village—the selfless toil, unpretentious spirit, and collective good celebrated in the Connecticut countryside—were undergirded by a sturdy devotion to God. Here, parents modeled emulative examples of a shared commitment to austerity and industry. New England could, by extension, provide the same enlightened precedent for America, a shining example of unified interest extending "[f]rom yon blue wave, to that far distant shore," with "God's own Word the structure, and the base."[35]

Intermingled with Dwight's portrait of corporate concern and divine guidance were more significant calls for Federalist-style reforms. *Greenfield Hill* and other of Dwight's writings from the 1790s repeated and expanded on this premise. The revolution, he argued, had let loose unrestrained democratic liberality and had pushed America dangerously close to the edge of ruin. Christian ministers, the safeguards of morality, could inspire a less-complicated piety patterned after New England examples. Their influence, both with political leaders and the public at large, would staunch the rise of degenerating influences and return God's promise for a brilliant future. "Connecticut," Dwight concluded in his address before the Society of Cincinnati in 1795, "appears to hold . . . the first station." Men of "distinguished rectitude of disposition," supported by virtuous citizens committed to God and their fellow man, assured a long history of unrivaled happiness. Education, either for the ministry or for secular ambitions, conditioned the mind for worship; worship reinforced a community's devotion to God's Word. Ministers, "persons of knowledge, virtue and dignity," buttressed the whole.[36]

President Dwight

By the age of forty-three, Dwight had established himself as a theologian and educator at Greenfield Hill, enjoyed notoriety attached to his poetry, and grew confident in a political influence that spread throughout New England. His election to the presidency of Yale in 1795 was somewhat ironic given the manner of his earlier departure from that institution but nonetheless welcome. Despite his steadily weakening eyesight, said to have been acquired from years of intensive morning reading, Dwight remained enthusiastic and had a self-possessed dignity, and students revered him.[37] Immoral pursuits ceased, and students were transformed into scholars as Dwight fought back against the tide of liberality he so long grieved.[38] Student Benjamin Silliman found the changing atmosphere a tonic to the otherwise ill-tempered campus.[39]

Revised student laws enforced the austere Puritan solemnity of Dwight's Yale and groomed students for lives of obligatory self-sacrifice. New fines penalized students for missing lectures (three cents); excessive frivolity; playing "hand or foot-ball" in the yard (eight cents); singing, "hallooing," and general disruption (thirty-four cents); keeping a firearm (fifty cents); attending a dance (fifty cents); picking a lock (eighty cents); and acting in a play (eighty cents).[40] More fundamental to Dwight's moral order were regulations regarding divine worship. Undergraduates were required to attend morning prayers and sermons delivered throughout the week, with nonattendance holding a "penalty of two cents." Daily worship was, of course, in addition to their mandatory attendance at Sunday worship—and absence there cost a student six cents. Sermons were systematic, part of a separate four-year course of theological study based on the scriptures and expounding on those parts of divine worship most necessary for a pious life.[41]

In other ways, Dwight's Yale was similar to what former Yale president Ezra Stiles inherited from President Naphtali Daggett in 1780. Entry requirements at Yale remained what they were before Dwight became president, with admission granted only to students who could "read, translate, and parse Tully (Cicero), Virgil, and the Greek Testament and to write true Latin in prose."[42] The curriculum and required readings remained similarly unchanged. Classical languages dominated freshman and sophomore years, but as students moved through the curriculum, they were introduced to geography, history, algebra, plane geometry, trigonometry, and rhetoric. Juniors added logic, ethics, rhetoric, and biweekly "disputation"—debates around issues of political significance. Seniors came under the direct supervision of the president and a yearlong course in moral philosophy.[43]

Administrative responsibilities rested largely on the president and a handful of subordinates. In 1799, the year of Horace's admission to Yale's freshman class, five tutors—Benjamin Silliman, Ebenezer Grant Marsh, Jeremiah Day, Charles

Denisen, and Henry Davis—were responsible for the oversight and instruction of all four academic classes. The size of the sophomore class was so large it was divided in two, one group placed under the care of Jeremiah Day, the second under Henry Davis.[44] The challenges inherent in administering Horace's class alone—twenty-seven students at an average age of seventeen—were not trivial. But where the watchful eyes of tutors and professors went dark, students assumed responsibility, and Horace became initiated into a world controlled by an elaborate and unwritten code of freshman student conduct.

Connecticut Hall

Upperclassmen took charge as they always had, administering what Benjamin Silliman later called the "feudal laws" of the college. Soon after his arrival, Horace stood shoulder to shoulder with his fellow freshmen in the college chapel. Arrayed before them were Yale seniors and an elected member of their own class, who proceeded to go through a list of "peculiar customs."[45] That class member recited a list of unrecorded student-enforced rules against wearing hats or gowns, carrying canes, and other behaviors and gave more overt reminders of freshman obeisance. They were to approach doors and gates cautiously and give way to upperclassmen. They were barred from running in the yard or in the stairwells and prohibited from playing with or entering into "acts of familiarity" with upperclassmen.[46]

Freshmen were also at the beck and call of upperclassmen, made to fetch items, send messages, and perform other tasks throughout campus and the whole of New Haven. The use of freshmen as errand boys, clearly the single most insulting obligation, was the cause of considerable angst despite official rules against using students on "needless, unreasonable, or vexatious errand, or errands."[47] Punishments for violations, typically enforced by cocksure sophomores, might bring fines or gentle chiding but most often entailed a "trimming," a catchall term for physical abuse meted out to frightened lowerclassmen. Near the end of his freshman year, Horace rejoiced in the knowledge that the "practice of sending and lecturing freshmen" was nearly at an end and a "perfect harmony" was restored to the classes.[48]

Yale's injunctions against off-campus housing meant Horace was likely placed in one of the college's two dormitories: Union or Connecticut Hall. Connecticut, a building nearly fifty years old, was older but more commodious than newly built Union, with large shared chambers for sleeping and smaller rooms for private study. Private studies were unique but often went unused, being too hot in the summer and too cold in the winter.[49]

Horace thrived despite physical and mental discomforts, taking well to his first year's course in "learned languages"—Virgil, Cicero, and the Greek New Testament—and even assisting slower or less-industrious peers in the process. He negotiated byzantine student codes and mandates of religious observance with aplomb, never attracting sanction from teachers or upperclassmen. "My body," he confirmed early in his freshman year, "is indeed now subject to the law of this institution, and obliged regularly to attend its numerous religious exercises."[50] He accepted his position but struggled with the ceremony of it all. His mind wandered during Dwight's early-morning sermons. His classmates might have increased his concentration; included among them was Miles Day, the brother of future Yale president Jeremiah Day and a superior scholar in his own right; Noah Porter, eventual class valedictorian and Berkley Scholarship recipient; and Serino Dwight, the president's own son.[51]

Horace admitted to feeling out of place in his freshman year, but he also announced changes in his opinions and ideas. In letters home, he boasted about how Yale enhanced his mind and increased his usefulness, described a personal transformation, and claimed to have a clearer understanding of purpose.[52] He put aside childish things and cherished a scholar's life.[53] But most of all, Horace bragged about his school, the increasing student body (up to 217 by November 1800), the brilliance of his professors, and the difficulty of his course of study. He was especially sanguine about President Dwight, whose reputation was "very much increasing" nationally.[54] Dwight was "unexceptionable," with a keen, energetic mind.[55] All of this was meant to impress his family with the necessity of his education—perhaps because he was worried that his stay could be cut short with a downturn in his father's business. Luther responded only to calm Horace's concerns. "Go on, my son, and prosper," he cautioned. "Let no thoughts of the kind alluded to retard your progress."[56] He took special pride in his son's "path of science" and appeared pleased at Horace's ambitions to become "an ornament" to his country.[57]

The frequency of Horace's correspondence grew in proportion to his abilities. Letters to John Milton, whom he addressed simply as "Milton," became composition exercises written in the stilted prose style of a petulant youth. If, as Horace argued, the path to true usefulness was paved with good conversation and a practiced pen, then it would be necessary for Milton to absorb and respond to as many of his letters as possible. And throughout his first years at Yale, Horace did just that, writing Milton to proclaim the benefits of self-learning, to attack the pretentions of aristocratic authority, to emphasize the necessity of industry and the importance of a liberal education, and to flatter his brother, now a shopkeeper at the family store, with a prolix defense of a merchant's life.[58] The mercantile man, although less significant than a scholar or politician, was no less important to public good, and this would "always insure [sic] him respect and emolument."[59] Milton could hardly keep his end of the bargain, sending letters only sporadically but always with apologies for tardiness. The life of a merchant might have been useful, but it kept him taxed beyond present obligations. Letters would start and then stop because of haranguing customers or indiscriminate tasks.[60] Horace's skills improved, of this Milton had little doubt. Horace's letters attained a level of sophistication and gentility that confirmed the value of his education. Yale, Milton confided to brother Myron, was doing much to enlarge Horace's talents and magnify his ambitions.[61]

Horace complained about Milton's inattention but also about the lack of interest from others. "I can find nobody," he lamented, "who will write to me as often as I do to him."[62] He would write "half a dozen letters a day" if his friends would return the same kindness.[63] Horace admitted that some of this was his own fault; his personality left him with "but few friends" and not much else to do beyond writing letters and study. For a time, letters from Milton and his father were his best sources of comfort. His father was his "constant associate," brother Milton a friendly companion who filled him with "divine enthusiasm."[64] Horace's "versatility of temper," something he described as a propensity to unintentionally injure the feelings of others, was likely evidence of self-conscious inferiority. His family was of moderate but not excessive wealth. The ability to pay the price of tuition and board was one thing, but to live in the style of a New England scholar another, and Horace knew the difference.

At times, he channeled this sense of inferiority into impassioned statements of ambition that laid out the terms of his future success. Horace hoped to find distinction outside the "blood thirsty passion" of military heroes and to win public acclaim as either a lawyer or a statesman by improving his prose and mastering the art of disputation.[65] He hoped to write useful works to be "read with astonishment" and to ready himself for public service through vigorous study, cultivating the "habit of combining and separating ideas on the moment, of making nice distinctions between that which is applicable & illustrative, and other wise."[66] But in time he enthusiastically embraced the habits and appearances of a Connecticut gentleman. Near the end of his sophomore year, he proposed cutting off communication with Milton because the two were growing apart, mentally and occupationally. Milton, a mere shopkeeper, had little knowledge of the world of philosophers and men of great public character. The provincial charms of Salisbury were nothing compared to the urbane sophistication of New Haven, and Horace wondered how the two would get on in later years. Improvement required one to "live amongst continual noise" and to expose oneself to different ways of thinking and different impressions.[67] Summer visitors to the city, wealthy plantation families of the South who traveled north to escape oppressive heat, were open to similar criticism. The rusticity of their manners, the vulgarity of their expressions, and their superstitious religious views were no doubt the result of rural isolation. Horace wondered how the country could manage to remain whole with such wholly irreconcilable differences.[68]

The Classical Scholar

Advanced preparation in dead languages gave Horace an advantage. At Williams, years of conjugations and declensions had led to increasingly complex translation exercises, first in artificially constructed Latin prose, then in unadapted originals.[69] Grounding in ancient authors was necessary because the classical world formed the basis of Yale's curriculum. This is not to say that entering students easily connected grammar with abstract thought. In 1780, Princeton's president John Witherspoon criticized the skills of his entering students, finding many without the ability to speak more than a few lines of Latin.[70] President Dwight almost certainly agreed. Dwight's own youthful habit of studying fourteen hours a day and reading Homer each morning by candlelight likely guided his expectations. At Yale, Roman and Greek heroes became historical character lessons. Classical illustrations enlivened orations, a required part of the junior and senior curriculum. Students looked to these works for examples of oratorical brilliance and for insight to modern political debate.[71] Horace advanced quickly in languages, proudly reporting his success at recitation and then incorporating classical illustrations into his personal correspondence.[72] For him, ambition was fueled by noble examples from the ancient world. Philosophers were heroic in their virtue and had strong, well-reasoned minds as well as a preternatural commitment to useful knowledge.

Classical language study also supported the ideals of Yale's conservative, Federalist president. Dwight's publications and sermons linked Francophilia with excessive liberality and moral decline. Appreciation for the classical world promised to reverse the trend. If Jefferson's unrestrained democracy, patterned on French examples, threatened the moral and political health of the country, then classical ethics—promoted by Greek and Latin authors—might inspire a reversion to the structure of ancient republics and, by extension, federalism.[73] Freshman-year readings in Virgil, Cicero, and the Greek New Testament extolled these virtues. Virgil's *Aeneid* celebrated duty and self-sacrifice while reinforcing the unity between republican ideals and central authority. Cicero's *Orations* condemned base self-interest and argued for stability in the face of open rebellion. Passages from the Greek New Testament placed these ideas in a moralizing Christian context. In their sophomore year, students extended these readings and scrutinized the philosophical strands of the Roman poet Horace, whose blend of Epicurean modesty and Stoic integrity fortified the whole. Absent from the curriculum were those works considered philosophically vulgar or potentially confusing. Satires of the second-century Roman poet Juvenile were too critical of authority; Virgil, Homer, and Hesiod were too pagan for Christian scholars.[74]

The steady retreat of Federalist influence following the election of 1800 presented a special challenge to these standards. Federalist stalwarts were now openly criticized for their part in inspiring an ecclesiastical state, governed and controlled by the wily "Pope Dwight."[75] According to "A True Whig," the unnamed contributor to the April 1801 edition of the New York periodical *Gazette of the United States,* Dwight was a secessionist, a papal ambassador, and a false prophet who labored to spread a lecherous influence over weak minds.[76] A contributor to the *Impartial Observer* of Cooperstown, New York, believed Dwight to be the American equivalent of a Russian emperor, the enemy of free thinkers everywhere, whose imperiousness, corruption, and ability to corrupt young minds made him dangerous. At Yale, this author reported, students were "forbidden and restrained from attachment to republican principles," told to mimic the responses of their instructors or be exiled.[77] The *American Mercury* of Hartford claimed Yale men were "converted into party engines" and inculcated in the arts of a dissension so malevolent as to propel the country toward civil war. For proof, Republicans looked to Yale's commencement exercises of 1798 and 1799 and the "monstrous," Federalist-inspired student orations. It was clear, the author noted, that these ceremonies had become expressions of Dwight's own frustrated political leanings. His party ambitions destroyed Yale, defamed those in attendance, and besmirched the reputation of young participants.[78] When New Haven Republicans gathered for a "democratic festival" in the spring of 1803, they marched in procession past Dwight's house with the intention of harassing him.[79]

Dwight remained steadfast. In 1800, he and fellow New England educator Jedidiah Morse published the *New England Palladium,* a newspaper that vigorously defended federalism against emergent radicalism and supported the right of ministers to discuss politics in the pulpit. "A clergyman," Dwight countered, "is as much a free citizen as any other man, and therefore as naturally, and deeply interested in the political concerns of his country."[80] His students also rallied to his defense. They were not, as was argued, forcibly inculcated in Dwight's beliefs. Much the contrary, they were urged to reach their own conclusions; as the *Gazette of the United States* claimed, he "uniformly and earnestly cautions them against receiving his sentiment and opinions because they are his; and frequently reminds them that youth are naturally prone to take the opinions of their instructors upon truth." Ever-reserved Dwight reminded them to base their arguments on reasoned fact, not on mimicry.[81]

Horace drank deep of Dwight's influence. In his freshman year, he attended the trial of Samuel Holt, the editor of the Republican newspaper *New London Bee,* who had been arrested on charges of sedition when he republished an anonymous letter criticizing Federalist president Adams's military policies. He was found guilty under the Sedition Act, fined $200, and sentenced to three months in jail. Horace recorded the events in a letter to Milton and believed the sentence entirely satisfactory, for citizenship, he argued, was much like a family and required the wholehearted commitment of each part.[82] The government acted as benevolent parent, distributing goods, encouraging prosperity, and otherwise protecting its children from foreign invasion and domestic slander, "malevolence, & misrepresentation." To reap the benefits of government but undermine governance was ungracious in the extreme.[83] But in the fall of his sophomore year, Horace applauded similar attacks on Republican president Thomas Jefferson by brother Myron. Jefferson and his "undecisive deluded Republicans" held only the worst of tyrannical intentions.[84]

A poem Horace composed during his junior year betrayed an affinity for Dwight's poem *The Triumph of Infidelity*, resembling it in both form and content. Like Dwight, Horace connected excessive liberty with moral decline—when we are left to our own devices, anarchy reigns.

> When revolution its career began,
> And France commenc'd the cry for "Rights of Man,"
> With sounds so sweet and promises so fair . . .
> We soon discover'd, in this fair disguise,
> Fraud, rapine, lust, and violence and lies;
> Names were perverted, language was abus'd,
> Old truths attack'd, and ignorance amus'd;
> Vices to virtues rose by magic art,
> Virtues to vices sunk in every heart

Horace also mirrored Dwight's belief that the durability of American liberty relies not on individuals, but on the resolute force of a strong government.

> It is indeed of Nature the decree,
> That all are equal, and that all are free,
> But equal, not in gifts, nor power, nor wealth,
> Nor size, nor strength, nor beauty, nor in health.
> No rights to office and command we show,
> But such as others lawfully bestow.
> What folly to assert our means the same
> For learning, science, eloquence, or fame!

And like Dwight, Horace lauded the shared obligations of democracy. Men and women work for the collective good by shunning evil and embracing spiritual gifts; parents have the responsibility to cultivate godly children.

The right to use our talents and our skill
To gain the good and wisely shun the ill,
To raise the soul by knowledge and by truth,
With just and generous thoughts to guide our youth,
Of men of worth the confidence to seek,
To think with freedom, and with freedom speak.[85]

By the spring of his junior year, Horace demonstrated a vigorous mind, a defined political outlook, and expenses appropriate to his sense of worth. His confidence in his skills in poetry, composition, and especially the art of public debate increased his vanity but also attracted his classmates' scorn. The "thousand little envious sayings" that passed the lips of his rivals or of the "malignant sycophants" who roused him to anger may have been few, but they were persistent. Milton counseled restraint on both counts, to trim his "haughty or domineering" tendencies and to ignore the aspersions from others. "The great difficulty," Milton added, "lies in being just yourself, while others around you are unjust."[86]

Being a scholar now meant more than simple ambition, and in time Horace grew unapologetic about his pecuniary situation. "I acknowledge there are many scholars who live with very little," he wrote father Luther in February 1802. "The greater part do. But I am not among that greater part." He would rather "be a dog & bey the moon" than live the life of a scholarly wretch.[87] Visits to nearby New York, new clothing, and other amenities, all funded by Luther, offered him the chance to mix in polite circles and embrace the life of an aristocratic scholar. Now growing less magnanimous and increasingly more aggressive in his politics, Horace became critical of farmers and of the idea that farming, as conceived of by President Jefferson, was the backbone of the republic. Farmers were, after all, without the education needed to be either citizens or representatives of citizens. His sentiments were no doubt insulting; Holley family origins were tied to the land. "Look round, my son," Luther cautioned, "and carefully examine the causes by which the United States are thus rapidly increasing in wealth and improvement. Is it not because we are habituated to, and not ashamed of labor?" Horace was, after all, fed and dressed by the labor of others, common men who, "though less informed in science[,] . . . are yet the most meritorious citizens." Luther urged modesty for his son, who would soon need to converse with both the wealthy and the common in professional life.[88]

Thomas Paine's first "Letter to the Citizens of the United States," published in late 1802, offered Horace a chance to demonstrate these emerging political attitudes. Paine's attack on Federalists, whom he labeled "despotic" scoundrels who considered government the best means to their own ends,[89] aroused Horace's enmity. "I think it is written in such a way that it will produce mischief," he noted in a letter to his father. Though written with the appearance of moderation, Paine's letter, he opined, was replete with self-serving arrogance—an obvious but dangerous fact that might indirectly influence the "undiscriminating." Worst of all were Paine's comments "on the licentiousness of federal peoples," laughably contemptible statements that roused the young scholar with anger. "He says they are the disgrace of our country. Composition of this kind, from a man so completely abandoned as Tom Paine, must raise a smile of contempt, indignation, and pity." Paine, along with radical Jeffersonian Thomas Cooper, Republican newspapermen William Duane and James Cheetham, "and the whole train of these most filthy foreign scoundrels" escaped European jails only to exalt themselves above the country's rightful rulers. Their intrigues made Horace ashamed to be an American.[90] When a twenty-one-year-old Horace returned home for the winter break, cocksure and ready for debate, the resulting conflict with his father nearly ended his education. Luther, upset over some unnamed slight, claimed the money spent on Horace's education was "folley."[91] Milton believed his father treated Horace too harshly and agreed to fund the rest of his senior year.[92]

Revival

Throughout the 1790s and early 1800s, Christian leaders of New England took up the cause against deistic sympathies and the threat of widespread moral corruption. By the fall of 1802, Horace was swept up by the currents of theological conservatism swirling about Yale's campus. Revivals and the revivalist message of personal salvation and revelation whisked across New England and into Yale, a college now dominated by Dwight's enthusiastic conservatism. "New converts in the freshness of their illumination under these influences of the Holy Spirit," as one witness remarked, were drawn to Dwight's energetic preaching and refreshed theology.[93] Horace believed Dwight had "more energy" than most literary men in the country.[94] Students and faculty took the message to heart. Horace's classmate Noah Porter described students' weekly meetings in an upper room for prayer and religious reflection.[95] Tutor Benjamin Silliman wrote his mother to explain how the "trophies of the Cross" were multiplied and how Yale had become a "little temple," with most becoming awakened to a new respect for religion and others cowed into a "respectful silence."[96]

Private meetings led to increased membership in the college church. In the summer of 1802, the *Connecticut Evangelical Magazine* reported that students were becoming "particularly inclined to divine things" and "uncommonly serious" about religion. "With respect to religion," the author continued, "all of them are greatly desirous to be taught, but none to assume the office of teaching. No spirit of self sufficiency, no inclination to distribute censures, no appearance of arrogance, no flights of a wild imagination, have hitherto been discovered." In the closing days of the spring semester, fifty students had become members of Yale's church; another thirty, including Horace, joined that fall. Solemnity permeated the campus. Students took their classes more seriously, treated their instructors with greater respect, and were otherwise prevailed by "a distinguishable serenity." "On the whole," the author concluded, "the state of Yale-College is, in the view of the Instructors, more pleasing and desirable than at any former period within their knowledge."[97]

Armed with religious conviction, Horace now engaged in loving but at times heated spiritual dialogues with his family. When mother Sarah wrote to correct his dour, overzealous commitment to Christian purity, he responded with an apology culled from Dwight's sermons. "I almost fear to mention the subject of religion again, lest you should either think me enthusiastic, or given to boasting," he began. "You may expect that I shall be sad, and gloomy in the present world, given to mournful thinking, and out cast from pleasure, but this is by no means the case." As a Christian, he enjoyed life "to the highest," recognizing the true beauty of creation in a way not understood by others.[98] True happiness came from the fulfillment of his obligations to God; material pleasures were ephemeral or illusionary.

He smirked at the charming rusticity of his mother's religious spirit. "Your ideas of regeneration I thought rather indeterminate," he admonished. She was unrefined, he "more conversant with the instructions of theologians" and therefore more mature in his understandings.[99] At her request, Horace wrote to clarify points of doctrine; the result was a point-for-point review of Dwight's interpreted Calvinism. Salvation, Horace began, depended on a redeemer, and "none but god" could be that redeemer. "Repentance" required the prayerful acknowledgment of sin. "Adoption," membership in a church, required baptism. Man was "justified" not because God expunged sins but because Christ "has imparted to us his righteousness." "Sanctification" grows over time because the tendency away from sin is gradual. "Christ's mediation," Horace concluded, is "the only door of happiness." For his father, however, the content of one's theology mattered less than the style of one's presentation. "One essential thing with me," he wrote to Horace, "in every part of divine worship, is, that the preacher should feel what he says, and that he be hurried on at times, with increased energy, by the warmth of his own affections."[100]

Horace's father and brother received similar treatment. In the summer of 1803, Horace warned his father about favoring the "cavils of infidels" over the Bible. Intensive scriptural study had lifted the clouds from his own mind, and he asked his father to consider a similar commitment.[101] Horace counseled brother Milton on the dangers of vice by way of illustration. A boat ride from New Haven to New York City had introduced him to a group of "ignorant, unprincipled, illbred universalists" who played cards on the Sabbath. He had recoiled in anger and then shamed them into orthodoxy with an argument from Plato's dialogues.[102] And when he had crossed paths with "Birch," a longtime family friend, he had pointed out defects in Birch's religious character. "His heart," Horace opined, "has become too corrupt; and the restraints of Religion he knows nothing of."[103]

Debate

Horace's senior year was "worth the other three." He still had difficulty affording the style, but the life of a scholar suited him, and he reveled in thoughts of a career devoted to these pursuits.[104] He and fellow seniors spent the year under the direct supervision of President Dwight, working through a course of moral philosophy by expounding on John Locke's *Essay on Human Understanding*, William Wollistone's *The Religion of Nature Delineated*, Guiliel Amesii's *Medulla Theologica*, and Dwight's own writings. Together they dissected, critiqued, and applied these works to in-class questions and biweekly disputation exercises.[105] Forensic disputations were first practiced at Yale in the late 1740s but became the dominant form of student debate in most colleges by century's end.[106] Sessions began with Dwight posing a broadly based question of ethical or political significance. Students then took turns formulating and answering rebuttals. Success required advanced preparation, close readings of the material, and the rehearsal of potentially useful pieces of evidence. Assisting them in the pursuit of oratorical glory were Cicero's Orations and Hugh Blair's *Lectures on Rhetoric*, a three-volume compendium of everything from basic sentence structure to the use of figurative language, metaphor, and hyperbole. For Blair, all deliberative discourse followed the same "natural train of speaking"—the introduction, division of subject, explication, arguments, "pathetic," and conclusion. Each part included elaborate explanations of proper use and examples.[107]

Dwight touted these exercises as a necessary part of one's professional life. Where reading and observations presented facts, "conversation furnishes you with truths which were never written, and awakens in you valuable ideas, which otherwise would never be entertained." The rapid exchange of ideas, experienced in disputation, taught students the importance of a flexible mind and a resourceful tongue. Debates were also the most practical means of preparation for careers in law or the ministry. For aspiring attorneys, Dwight suggested a plain style, stating facts "nakedly" and presenting exhibits not to alarm or astound, but from a sincere desire to represent the truth. Ministers, he believed, should vary the subject and style of their preaching. Illustrations by way of personal examples were acceptable and worth the sacrifice of literary perfection. "To compensate this loss, you will gain the attention, the esteem, and not improbably the souls of your hearers." He recommended "a chaste, manly, energetic style" and simple statements, concentrating on the substance, not affectations or unnecessarily florid language. Earnestness, the emotional certitude based on godly devotion, was "the soul of eloquence." "All men," Dwight added, "when engaged and earnest, are eloquent."[108]

Horace took to oratory with special vigor, considering it the best way for a common man to display uncommon abilities. The greatest men in history were, in Horace's mind, not distinguished on the battlefield, but on the rostrum in courts or assemblies—perfection, insomuch as it was possible for men, could be reached only by those in public office.[109] Oratory was also a skill that could not be studied, or studied effectively, in rural isolation. A "real orator" was one who crafted his style amid crowded assemblies and among diverse audiences.[110] Exercises in disputation therefore became his favorite because they were "peculiarly gratifying" to his ambition.[111] There was no greater calling than that of public office and no better way to prepare for that calling than debate; Yale's Society for Brothers in Unity and the Phi Beta Kappa society offered the best out-of-class opportunity for practice.[112] Horace believed that both organizations carried public speaking "almost to as high perfection as the Bar or in the Pulpit," and he considered his membership in them a unique honor.[113] Students had created the Society for Brothers in Unity, one of two literary societies on campus, to enhance their skills in debate and oratory in preparation for professional lives. Throughout much of Yale's early history, membership in either the Brothers, established in 1768, or the Linonian Society, founded in 1758, was exclusive to "those possessing the requisite personal qualifications."[114] Exclusivity enhanced their ability to refine their speaking styles apart from the critical eye of their professors and away from the student body. Regular meetings and secret rituals bonded members in the need for shared improvement but also in an implied elite status.[115] Yale's chapter of Phi Beta Kappa reinforced these feelings through emotionally charged initiation rites. The minutes from the induction ceremony of 1787 record: "Language would fail, should we attempt to describe the nameless emotions of the Fraternity."[116] Initiation oaths promised a safe environment: "Here you may disengage yourselves from scholastic cares and communicate without reserve whatever observations you have made upon a variety of objects. . . . Here too you may indulge in Speculation, that freedom of inquiry."[117]

Horace beamed with pride when the Brothers asked him to prepare an oration for an upcoming meeting, considering the honor a "publick declaration . . . of my scholarship." His confidence approached the point of vanity and convinced him to spend the winter vacation on campus so he could be near his books.[118] When classes resumed, he addressed the question "Do the pursuits of ambition contribute more to happiness than those of domestic life?" His response followed the precepts of oratory set forth by Blair. After a proper introduction, Horace divided the subject, parsing the meaning and use of the term *happiness*. If happiness were a simple negation of sadness, "sticks and stones are to be envied." Happiness, he remarked, is thus an activity, specifically the pursuit of improvement. In his explication, Horace worked through the consequences of his definition—the body is susceptible to torpor and infirmity, so individuals are unreliable agents of their own happiness. "We must," he continued, "follow our nature into its social character, for it is in the relations of society that we find the most effectual stimulants to action." Happiness is, as such, impossible in isolation. His central argument then began with a question: Are the actions of domestic affairs as important as the pursuit of ambition? If the galvanizing force of ambition is dignity, and if by achieving dignity we increase the scope and quantity of our responsibilities, then, yes, he argued, a greater share of happiness is enjoyed by those who seek out authority. "Such men there are, men of gigantic minds, whose strong-limbed intellects and heroic hearts love to grapple with difficulties, and who are stimulated by opposition, and fired by peril."

The "pathetic," or conclusion, reinforced the connections between happiness and ambition by way of patriotic examples. Fighting against almost insurmountable odds, the Founding Fathers reached ahead of themselves, envisioning a new standard of freedom and opportunity. When the war was won, their charge extended to the creation of a unified system of governance; fractious party spirit confounded their efforts, but in this, too, they were victorious. These ambitions, Horace concluded, brought them happiness, "like the sun in the firmament, above and beyond the intervening clouds, they moved in majesty, and descended refulgent in glory." In his closing remarks, Horace made plain the association between public office, private happiness, and moral rectitude. Those who served in positions of political importance were heavily scrutinized, more accountable to the public, and thus less likely to harm their virtue, for "[n]o man wishes to be spoken of, or remembered, with contempt or execration." The ambitious thus promoted the highest good and enjoyed the most significant share of happiness in this life and for eternity.[119]

"Activity Makes the Man"

Horace passed the final months of his senior year in Poughkeepsie, New York, at the home of brother Milton, a decision that had everything to do with filial resentment. Classes ended in June, but final exams and graduation exercises were scheduled for early October. Time away from New Haven allowed Horace the quiet needed to complete his fall commencement address and mull over postgraduate plans. He was committed to the law but had doubts about where he might learn his trade and how he might afford it. After all, legal apprenticeships were not inexpensive; clerks did not draw a salary and in fact had to pay for the attentions of a master attorney. Apprenticeships were also long, stretching from between three and five years.[120] Some law students supported themselves by teaching, but this alternative, at least as Horace saw it, was a "tedious, gloomy road to law." Success required his wholehearted attention, and he begged his father to continue his full support, including room, board, and other assistance. In return, Horace promised the "first fruits" of his professional labor.[121]

Costs could be reduced by apprenticing somewhere near his parents' home, as some of his classmates proposed to do. Friend George Strong recommended Horace return with him to Long Island and clerk under a circuit court judge; another pressed him to go to Charleston, where he could become rich in a short time. His father suggested he remain in New Haven or work under a family friend in Albany. None of these suggestions made sense to Horace. The climate and habits of the South were unacceptable; the thought of practicing law in the country even worse. "I had much rather farm it," Horace scoffed. The only acceptable alternative was New York City; a "better opportunity for the exhibition of talents and industry" did not exist.[122] He was too comfortable with city living to consider anything else.[123]

His father remained unconvinced. "The advantages of going to New York to study law, do not strike me as being very great," he cautioned. The city was too expensive, and the potential benefits too small to warrant relocation. "Self-invention, and an independent mind resting on its own powers for support" were a stronger and more affordable foundation. Committing himself to a rigorous study in a smaller town would provide the same benefit as practice in a large city.[124] Horace answered these objections with assurances. A great many lawyers of Connecticut were of a singular opinion that New York City was "perfectly incomparable as to advantages in the law profession." Support was near, and expenses would be kept low; he would room with classmate Peter Dewitt and clerk for the well-respected Jacob Radcliff.[125] He also assured his father that he possessed the energy and character necessary to succeed. "Activity makes the man, both the mind and body," he wrote in early August 1803. Leisure created apathy; only in the midst of the "multiplied cares and the hurry of life" could one accomplish anything of worth.[126]

Seventy-three students graduated from Yale in September 1803.[127] Horace dressed in a dark-blue "nine coat" made specially for the occasion.[128] The *American Mercury*, a Connecticut paper with ties to Jeffersonian Republicans, claimed that public attendance at the commencement was less than half the normal number. The "ebullitions of scurrility" and "political trash . . . vomited on the Commencement stage" were, the author suggested, enough to keep good Connecticut Republicans from visiting their campus.[129] Horace was one of several graduation orators that day, and his piece, titled "On the Slavery of Free Thinking," might have justified these attacks. Although the text no longer survives, the title suggests Horace drew inspiration from Dwight's published works. "Free thinking," a phrase Dwight associated with Voltaire, Rousseau, Montesquieu, and other Enlightenment philosophers, compromised the integrity of otherwise moral men. Liberal thought encouraged the pursuit of earthly rewards and lives of moral turpitude; the want of material possessions enslaved men to fear and corruption.[130] Connections between free thought and unrestrained Jeffersonian liberalism were likely mirrored by student orations with similarly provocative titles: "On the Superiority of Moral over External Refinement," "Ought the Right of Suffrage to Be Confined to Land-holders?" and "Ought the Emigration of Foreigners to Be Encouraged by the United States?"[131]

President Dwight's address was less overt but no less political. He extolled the virtues of ministers, the happiest of men who experienced the full brilliance of God's love, took satisfaction in their mastery over base impulses, and lived the noblest of lives. He rejoiced in the knowledge that more than half the senior class had made public professions of faith and that the spirit of Christian observance now permeated the campus. He enjoined them to carry this devotion into the world and reminded them of their sacred obligations: "the vows of the Lord your God are upon you . . . you cannot go back." And he implored them to love their country, to pursue "its real interests," but to abhor political or monetary ambition and to treat with indifference the charms or repulsions of the mob. The path to political office was fraught with dangers and wholly incompatible with a righteous life. "In the wretched pursuit of office you will find temptations, and snares, and sins at every step; will," he continued, "turn your backs upon your God, and wander every day farther and farther from virtue, and hope, and heaven."[132]

The ceremony ended with the graduates' tearful good-byes to each other and heartfelt promises to continue their prayers and correspondence.[133] Most returned home to begin professional lives in either business or the law. At least a dozen, perhaps convinced by Dwight's energetic pleas, returned to Yale for ministerial training. Horace arrived in New York in December 1803 and, true to his promises, joined friend Peter in the law office of Riggs and Radcliff. But the adventure was troubled from the start. Horace's father backed out of his agreement to fund him or, at least, to provide as much funding as he had promised. Shortly after his arrival in New York, Horace asked brother Milton to assume a share of his expenses; the lack of support, he complained, threatened more than just his immediate goals—without money he would be without prospects and "late on the stage of action."[134] Letters to his father were more histrionic. Everything was going according to plan, "excepting in pecuniary concerns."[135] What little money he had was insufficient for living.[136] When the price of lodging in the boardinghouse became too expensive, Horace took a room in the house of Dr. Birch, the same family friend Horace had previously chastised for wrongheaded morality.[137]

But Horace's opinions of the place and the profession changed dramatically less than a month after he arrived in New York. In mid-January 1804, he wrote his father to complain of New York's low morality and to voice his low opinion of lawyers. "The multitudinous mass of corruption," he began, "which this city breathes, could it once be collectively held up to view, would make the bolder wretch on earth, however deep he may have plunged into infamy, shrink back with horror."[138] Too many "puppies" now flocked to the law, and the life of a lawyer was incompatible with Christianity. "The greatest danger," he complained in an apologetic letter to Peter Dewitt, "is that you will not naturally be lead [sic] to be better than you are, in the Evangelical sense." Lawyers neglected public worship, favoring their cases and their accumulated fees over spiritual obligations. He regretted the "bad state of affections" that consumed him. At the boardinghouse at 16 Beekman Street, he fell victim to "loose conversations" and "bent too far to the customs of the place." Too often did he find himself in the theater and engaged in destructive habits. His colleagues were detestable, and their clients, bankrupt cheats and swindlers, were repellent. He no longer trusted himself and, being forever stamped with "human imbecility," would almost certainly return to debauchery, "like the dog to his vomit."[139]

The situation convinced Horace to seek an alternate path, and he committed to the study of theology, where the mission was greater and the rewards more durable. Ministers were more necessary and more respected, even above the highest statesmen. Indeed, Horace concluded, "no man can be so useful as a

Divine."[140] He would return to Yale and prepare to fight the "overwhelming torrent of corruption" that flooded America and the "contemptible ignoramuses" that claimed to preach God's word. His education, his search for philosophic truth, his temperament, and his need for usefulness, honor, and happiness made the law a poor choice. "The profession of Law," he concluded, "could never give me self approbation, nor ever encourage me. . . . I now feel free, but in Law I felt a slave."[141]

Luther was well pleased by the news. "Happiness, my son, is the great pursuit of all. If you found it was not to be obtained by the study and practice of the law, you were perfectly right to quit it for the study of theology." "The ardent wish of my heart," he continued, "is, that you may be finally established in that course of life which will render you most happy, and where you will be most useful to mankind."[142] Brother Myron concurred, adding that the practice of law required too much moral flexibility; he himself had left the practice to launch a bookstore and a newspaper in New York.[143]

Mary Austin

Restored now to the bosom of his adopted home, Yale, Horace found his situation "extremely pleasant."[144] New responsibilities likely added to the charm of graduate study; Dwight placed William Jay, the fifteen-year-old son of Chief Justice John Jay, in Horace's care, assigning them as roommates. The boy, "a fine little fellow" in Horace's opinion, was much preferred to another graduate.[145] Horace's experiences were made all the more lively with the attentions of Mary Austin, the daughter of a once wealthy shipping family of New Haven. The Austins were as peripatetic as they were industrious. Mary's father, Elijah, had made his fortune through foreign trade, and his brothers, Moses and Stephen, found riches, first in Virginia's lead mines and later in Texas.[146] Elijah succumbed to yellow fever when Mary was ten, but her mother remarried quickly, so that Mary and her six brothers and sisters could continue to live in the style, if not the wealth, of their birth. Mary attended one of New Haven's many schools for young women, taking in enough grammar, mathematics, and useful knowledge to allow genteel pursuits in adulthood.[147]

It is unclear when or under what circumstances Mary and Horace met. Mary may have been the unnamed subject of Horace's letter to his parents from his first years at Yale when he told them of schemes to win the notice of a certain young lady who sat by the window of a New Haven home. A friend suggested he attempt an introduction by throwing a "brickbat" through her window, approaching the front of the house, and offering to pay for the window.[148] The only other mention of a female is the reference to a certain "Miss ——," but in general Horace denied any romantic attachments.[149] Their courtship may have been complicated by Horace's decision to leave New Haven for a legal apprenticeship but was certainly interrupted by his wandering affections; he had, on at least one occasion, called her by the another's name and had to proffer a poetic apology:

> And is it a crime, when thus lost in thy charms,
> When the eye with thy beauty entrances the soul . . .
> Say, is it a crime, with emotions so sweet,
> If my memory's power a moment depart,
> If the name of another my tongue should repeat[150]

Their affection grew strong in the months that followed his return from New York. Their initial attraction might have been more intellectual than physical; whenever Horace wrote about her, it was to express his admiration for her mind and conversation.[151] They shared a love of poetry, literature, and polite conversation. When he challenged her to defend her love of music, she agreed with only a moment of apprehension. "I am," she began, "unused to a systematic expression of my opinions and feelings, and may expose to your scrutinizing eye and correct judgment many errors both of thought and style. When you make the request however, I cannot hesitate to comply." Music was too frivolous and too effeminate for Horace, distracting from more godly and scholastic pursuits. Mary rebutted each of these misgivings, lauding the "genuine influence of music," "the most delightful of all arts." Music, she continued, "refines while it elevates and expands the mind; it increases the social and benevolent affections; and it calls forth the liveliest feelings of gratitude to God, particularly when it is associated with the pious sentiments of our sacred songs."[152] It was an impressive display of erudition and evidence of Mary's sharp mind.

She was, Horace wrote to his mother in April 1804, "all that my fondest wishes could portray," and she staved off his melancholy spirit.[153] His joy in finding Mary, however, mixed with the unpalatable chore of notifying fellow suitor

"G. Wiffile" of his affections. The two were longtime friends, but, unbeknownst to Wiffile, both pursued Mary. Wiffile's last letter to Horace spoke of both his "invincible attachment" to Mary and his sacrosanct attachment to Horace.[154] By May, Horace claimed that he and Mary shared a powerful attachment and that he could not live without her. In June, the twenty-three-year-old Horace wrote his mother to announce their engagement. Although he found it hard to live without her, a wedding would have to wait. A "proper" union required him to complete his studies and find a position.[155] Horace's father objected to the marriage and with good reason: unlike Milton and Myron, who had already achieved financial stability, Horace seemed destined for perpetual insolvency. His ability to support a family on the wages of a minister seemed a stretch, especially with his extravagant spending habits. Even during his theological training at Yale, Horace complained that he lacked the money necessary to live in the admittedly "enlarged" style of his peers.[156] "Be not alarmed, my dear Father," Horace pleaded in a letter home six months later. "I have weighted, maturely weighted, the consequences." But after outlining his prospects and explaining the "sober calculation" guiding his decision, he ended the letter by declaring that he was once again out of money.[157]

The Hopkinsian

A review of Horace's theological education at Yale is complicated by his habit of destroying notes, sermons, and anything else related to religious matters, for reasons known only to him.[158] It is clear his training began in May 1804, ended in September that year, and was under the personal supervision of Timothy Dwight.[159] Beyond this general description, the work of reconstructing this period falls on Mary, who later reflected on Horace's early infatuation with the work of Samuel Hopkins. Throughout the eighteenth century, Hopkins, along with fellow Yale graduates Joseph Bellemy and Jonathan Edwards Jr., attempted to reconstruct a more authentic version of Puritan doctrine. Their critics styled them adherents of a "New Divinity," an artificial, heterodox construct of their own making.

Key to this theology were definitions of regeneration and human agency as well as a more austere interpretation of moral obligation. The Holy Spirit, working through scripture, regenerates the corrupt soul. This regeneration occurs irrespective of our will, inclination, or desire; in point of fact, every part of the human body works against salvation. For Hopkins, it was delusional to believe that humans could affect regeneration. Election, however, was still subject to God's will; "means," Hopkins argued, were "necessary in order to convert and save the elect . . . as they would be if they were not elected."[160] Revelation, even if acted out according to divine sanction, relieved some of the emotional dullness and spiritual passivity associated with Calvin.[161] New Divinity was also more restrictive, both in qualifications for membership and in tolerance for the lapsed. The "visible" church was by its very nature impure, so its foundations must rest on a firm, unwavering commitment to moral purity.[162]

Hopkins's idea of "disinterested benevolence," the desire to serve God's divine plan regardless of personal benefit, entailed a more complete understanding of Calvinist redemption. Love of community above oneself was important, but virtue, Hopkins claimed, resided in those who sacrificed their mortal souls for the greater cosmic good. There was an ascetic purity to his theology, a complete abandonment of self-love or "eternal interest," the promise of heaven or threat of hell. Slave owners epitomized the destructive nature of greed; they elevated personal interest above the good of others and thus worked against God's eternal plan.[163]

Like Dwight, Hopkins had elevated his significance by connecting theology to pressing temporal concerns. His address *A Dialogue Concerning the Slavery of the Africans* was dedicated to members of the Continental Congress in 1776 and called for an immediate cessation of the slave trade in America. Here, Hopkins underscored the irony of America's intentions to win freedom while holding "so many hundreds of thousands" of enslaved Africans.[164] In his essay "The Slave Trade and Slavery" (1787), he looked warily at the culture of greed and avarice now unleashed upon America. The revolution, he warned, had opened a world of opportunity for trade and commerce but had also reaped the fruits of selfish intent, intemperance, and blasphemy. Those seeking "foreign luxuries or unnecessaries" were to blame as they encouraged jealousies and a spirit of corruption. The result was "insurrection, and open, violent opposition to government."[165]

The severity of his theology, the abstruse, metaphysical nature of his work, and his condemnation of the slave trade in particular saw Hopkins relieved of his first ministerial position in Massachusetts but later rewarded with a pastorate in Newport, Rhode Island. His message was especially well received among scriptural purists, who appreciated his more comprehensive understanding of God's ultimate design.[166] By 1802, Hopkins's popularity among the students at Yale convinced trustees to award him an honorary doctorate of divinity. There was a touch of irony in this because although President Dwight railed against the institution of slavery, he benefited from the labor of a slave named Naomi, whom he had acquired in 1788; Horace and many of his Yale classmates also went on to become pro-slavery advocates in their professional lives. Horace himself later owned slaves.[167]

This was not Horace's first experience with New Divinity. President Ebenezer Fitch and some of the trustees of Williams College were early proponents. Fitch assigned Hopkins's compendium of New Divinity theology, *System of Doctrines* (1793), as required reading.[168] But Horace's experiences as a divinity student were of a different quality, and he approached Hopkins not as a dilettante but as a learned adult. His enjoyment of the scholar's life had led him back to Yale, and his experiences in New York had convinced him of the moral turpitude that awaited the unsuspecting. Dwight prepared students with Calvin's general tenets, but Horace desired something more, and in this search for an abstemious life of Stoic self-sacrifice he found Hopkins.

To Greenfield

Horace completed his divinity studies in September 1804, received his license to preach in December, and wed Mary Austin on the first day of the New Year. Over the next six months, the couple lived in Salisbury as Horace searched for permanent employment.[169] He began a tour of ministerial guest appearances in the Connecticut countryside, hoping his associations with Dwight would result in a permanent appointment. But Dwight's legacy was complicated by Connecticut's shifting political climate. By 1804, federalism was in full retreat throughout much of New England, and Horace, a strict Calvinist and student of the Federalist "Pope Dwight," made an easy target.

Federalist leanings were but one consequence of Horace's education. Throughout his early life, he came under the competing influences of Calvinism and capitalism, the rigid structures of self-expression, and the established habits of mind that defined genteel society. His upbringing emphasized the value of the performative qualities of education; success in business required the appearance and accumulation of knowledge. His father's memorization of facts and ability to recite Milton no doubt influenced this early understanding. At Williams, Horace stumbled and then embraced a more formulaic code of erudition that governed elite communication. Rules of address and standards of poetic beauty instructed by precedent and became honed through practice. Gentility was guaranteed by adherence to categories of behavior—vulgarity was a consequence of ignorance. At Yale, these associations hardened when mixed with Dwight's totalizing concept of civic and religious morality. In the presence of unrestrained freedoms—of action, thought, and habit—society fell into disorder then anarchy. The values of the ancients were the surest guarantees of liberties because they were rigid. The virtues of Greek and Roman rhetoric proved the point. Style and eloquence counted but not as much as one's ability to remain true to ancient convention.

Along with the message of uncompromising structure were the equally stolid but more ethereal requirements of obligatory self-sacrifice. For Dwight, the life of a Christian professional required the abnegation of individual interest—the pursuit of wealth ran contrary to the godly search for legal truths, medical cures, or spiritual enlightenment. Unadulterated by greed, avarice, or the search for fame, professionals could focus on divine gifts and give thanks by fulfilling these obligations. Hopkins extended the significance of these duties, narrowing the boundaries of correct behavior while simultaneously creating a purer and more grandiose Christian asceticism. For Horace, New Divinity connected learned convention with religious cosmology; well-defined rules guaranteed a place among the elite and distinguished the holy from the depraved. Hopkins's vision of human agency provided a more appealing outlet for Horace's oratorical talents and completed Dwight's "Connecticutization" of America. The same evangelism that affected change on Yale's campus could, if properly mediated, affect a restoration of American virtue.

But beneath the luster of stoic benevolence lay pressures of personal interest. Horace's oration in defense of ambition before the Brothers in Unity and his letters in defense of "activity" sent to his family were not simply rhetorical exercises. The desire for success, propelled by an animating goodness, produced influence; virtues, girded by moral rectitude but ensured by public scrutiny, carried godly authority. In this, Dwight and Hopkins acted as guides; their essays, poems, sermons, and personal associations guaranteed their significance and provided them a greater share of temporal and eternal happiness. As ministers, they were the epitome of disinterestedness and, by dint of their convictions, best positioned to affect moral action.

Horace came to see himself as an active participant in America's destiny. Upon the completion of his theological studies, he was equal parts benevolent teacher and political guide, spiritually disinterested but ready to wage war against rampant liberality. But the world surrounding Yale had changed during his education, and his restrictive religious and social outlook now carried different meanings to the uninitiated. His well-intentioned authority met the new social demands of a republican society in open conflict, a conflict soon to be played out among the pastoral surroundings of Greenfield Hill.

2

"Term of Severe Trial"

Moonlight flooded Mary's chamber as she sat morose and heartbroken by the window. Cheerful sounds from her mother's parlor helped but could not compete with the mournful song of a whip-poor-will that reminded her of her husband's absence. Months earlier Horace had received an invitation to preach to the congregation at Greenfield Hill just north of Fairfield, Connecticut. Mary would remain in New Haven until his situation there or at another parish solidified. Their separation was excruciating, and their correspondence effusive. "I have feasted on your letter," she fawned. "You are everything to me." She hoped he would dream of her and that he was as desperate for her affections as she was for his.[1]

Horace remained similarly inconsolable over the summer of 1805, allowing feelings of loss to invade private thoughts and public attentions. Melancholy overwhelmed him and prevented the execution of his duties. Despite a large attendance at the mid-June service, he remained "in low spirits." People looked "strange and alien," and he hoped the church in Branford, just outside New Haven, might call on his services before too much longer, "if for no other purpose, yet for this, that we may be together." His visit to Greenfield was to last five consecutive Sundays, but loneliness and the lack of refined company made even a few weeks apart intolerable. Boarding at the home of Hezekiah Bradley, a wealthy slave-owning member of Greenfield's church,[2] pushed him to the brink. "A loud, course, old blockhead," Bradley was ill-suited for Horace's company.[3]

The couple took to their quills for comfort, exchanging dozens of letters over the course of the summer. "My heart is full when I take up my pen to write to you," Mary opined. "I fear that I love you too much. . . . All my happiness is centered in you." "I am a boy in weakness when separated from you," Horace returned. "This spot, which is the delight of travellers and poets, is to me a gloomy residence. Your absence makes every place a desert." Mary bathed his letters "with tears"; Horace prayed for her "fervently."[4]

But his situation improved markedly over the next few weeks as he took new lodgings with a Dr. Peck and felt a building expectation that the position would last.[5] Mary urged caution; Greenfield, she feared, was rife with factions. Certain families might make their lives there impossible. Mr. Stuart, a family friend, had informed her that Bradley, Horace's former landlord, had certain reservations concerning his ideas of regeneration: "he do'n't believe a word o'ut," she mocked. Brother Milton thought the place too democratic for Horace's liking.[6] Horace was aggravated but steadfast. "I have better information about the feelings of the people here than Mr Stuart can have." The men Mary mentioned were unrepresentative *"black hearts* of the place," Bradley a "violent man and a fool" who took umbrage with anyone outside his "clan." Furthermore, the problems she pointed to were precisely what Horace set out to cure. "If the people are bad in Greenfield, we must make them better."[7]

Unsettled

Horace's guest appearances at Greenfield left church members satisfied or at least satisfied enough to warrant an offer of permanent employment. Horace was lettered and more rigorous than most but also, for the congregation of Greenfield Hill, perhaps the only choice. Tradition recommended the services of a Yale graduate, and since Dwight's departure they had courted but could not convince any other minister of sufficient education to remain for more than a few years. Money might have complicated matters; the eventual offer Horace received included an annual salary of $560, paltry even for a congregation as small as Greenfield. Party feelings in the Connecticut countryside were another problem. The years preceding Horace's arrival saw the slow but inevitable rise of Jefferson's Democratic Republicans and the gradual but vociferous fall of New England Federalists. Jeffersonians entered the 1800s as the younger, egalitarian alternative to the stodgy conservatives, and partisan newspapers carried debates throughout the Connecticut countryside, mobilizing and hardening party lines.[8]

At Greenfield Hill, politics became an important aspect of ministerial selection and ordination. Custom held the local church responsible for the initial approval of applicants, but the final decision was left to a committee made up of officers and pastors from area churches.[9] Conflict rose out of the disjunction between the will of the congregation and that of clergy. In 1801, the parish hired the Reverend Stanley Griswold, a Jeffersonian who, though popular with some, lasted only two years.[10] Griswold's replacement, William McKnight of New York, another Republican, became the majority choice, but the committee later declared him unfit for ordination.[11] Horace's election was equally contentious. *The Bee*, a Republican newspaper published out of Hudson, New York, warned of Federalist machinations. Horace, "*a federalist*, who is now by way of eminence stiled *the* reverend Horace Holley," should "excite the attention of republicans," the author remarked. "We say nothing against Mr. Holley," they continued. "He possesses *one* of those qualities, which the New Testament declares important to a preacher. His readers will readily decide what that quality is." In an ironic turn, Horace was rejected by the majority of the congregation but then ordained by the committee. If *The Bee*'s report is accurate, the committee's decision had dire results: forty-one members "signed off to the baptists [*sic*] . . . 5 to the episcopalians [*sic*]."[12]

The exodus seems not to have affected Horace's enthusiasms. Dwight may have encouraged the appointment through direct correspondence with area pastors but almost certainly promoted Greenfield to his students; it is likely Horace saw it as his best possible start in the profession.[13] The ordination test was a small matter because it merely required Horace to confirm his belief in the central tenets of Calvin's theology: the importance of the Holy Trinity, the doctrine of original sin, that Jesus Christ is the Son of God, and that salvation is "irresistible"—that is, eternal life is guaranteed for those chosen by God.[14] Just weeks later, he assured his wife that Greenfield offered something New Haven and other towns did not: an escape from "failures and scandal." "Here," Horace added, "we shall have more retirement and peace. Nothing can equal conjugal society and confidence."[15] In September 1805, he expressed elation at the thought of a permanent appointment; the promises of a peaceful life in one of the best parts of Connecticut was all he could have asked. He told his father about the machinations of "bad men," but then, five months later, he described the situation in more glowing terms. The few arrayed against him had either left the church or were now compliant. Republican newspapers continued to insult his politics but otherwise had little effect on him.[16]

Mary arrived after his September ordination, giving Horace enough time to acquire more suitable accommodations. The cottage he rented from Walter Bradley, just south of the church parsonage, may have been small, but it was clean and made more livable with the addition of a piano, a gift from Mary's mother.[17] The simple luxury added to their enjoyment of Greenfield but could not absolve their pecuniary concerns. Mary frequently retreated to New Haven, a short day's ride from Greenfield. Horace had a difficult time with the recurring separation and tried his best to reassure her.[18] "Be not alarmed about beig' [sic] poor," he pleaded.[19] Mary did her part to curb expenses but looked nervously toward the future.[20] And despite his enthusiasms, in time Horace came to see life in Greenfield as a "term of severe trial."[21]

Rural Charm

Membership in Greenfield increased but a dark cloud of conspiracy remained. The first of what may have been several emergency meetings held to discuss persistent disaffection with the church's teachings was held at Horace's house on December 3, 1806. Months later three members were considered for expulsion from the church for certain unnamed infractions.[22] But Horace's governance of Greenfield's academy, the same school Dwight had managed decades earlier, gave him a new appreciation for the influence and advantages of teaching. The position was also more lucrative than he imagined. Twenty young scholars at $150 a year in tuition brought in $3,000. After spending $1,500 on books, room, and board, he was left with $1,500 in addition to his regular salary. "Is there a farmer among you that can clear the same sum?" he asked his father after more than two years at Greenfield. "I think not."[23] The experience of teaching also made him more aware of deficiencies in his own education at Salisbury, and he worried about his younger siblings. His sixteen-year-old brother Orville, seven-year-old sister Caroline, and five-year-old niece Maria were developing bad habits from country tutors. Caroline had outgrown them and was developing rustic manners of speech and thought, "extremely rude and masculine." All of this went undetected at home but was sure to bring embarrassment abroad.[24] Orville's situation was even more pressing, and he needed immediate correction if he had any hope of attending college. Horace proposed to take them all in at the rate of ninety cents per week each.[25]

Three years at Greenfield were enough for Horace, and by the spring of 1808 he was ready for more lucrative and perhaps less controversial opportunities. The church and the town of Fairfield were pleasant but isolated and certainly less sophisticated than New Haven. Rural charms diminished with time, and his ambition, frustrated perhaps by a still low salary, might have convinced him to seek other positions. Greenfield Hill church members may have been relieved by the news. Although the official separation occurred that September, they eagerly accepted his petition for a leave of absence that summer in the hopes he could find a pastorate elsewhere. Mary again returned to her mother's home in New Haven and waited.

There seemed to be no shortage of opportunities as the demand for qualified, youthful Calvinists outstripped the supply. Preaching guest sermons to Congregational and Presbyterian churches of New York, Connecticut, Maine, New Hampshire, and Massachusetts was the necessary first step. An extended invitation for a lengthier visit and an offer of permanent employment might then follow. And so Horace went back on the road; in May, he preached at Manhattan's Wall Street Presbyterian, substituting for their eighty-one-year-old head pastor John Rodgers.[26] From here, Horace worked an exhausting, two-hundred-mile route from New Haven to Andover, Haverhill, Exeter, Kennebunk, and Portland before turning south to Boston, where he was to preach before the congregation at the Hollis Street Church. He paused only briefly, returning to Greenfield only to close the school year, oversee the shipment of his and Mary's furniture, complete his dissolution from the church, and, most importantly, collect outstanding tuition from delinquent parents. The latter duty took longer than he anticipated.[27] It is likely that he never received satisfaction on these debts. Months after Horace's departure from Greenfield, brother Orville appeared in Greenfield to collect some of the $500 in tuition Horace was still owed.[28]

Horace wrote to Mary from the road to tell her of natural scenes, local habits, interesting persons, and, more often, churches filled to capacity on word of his arrival. He also tried his best to comfort her; Mary was now pregnant with their first child, and Horace was still without a final offer. "Let your mind not dwell on gloomy prospects, but on those, which are pleasant." And he encouraged her to focus on the happy times soon to come with a permanent settlement. Mary's spirits did improve after a visit from Timothy Dwight, who brought news of Horace's appointment to a church in Albany. Dwight himself had recommended Horace for the position, considering him "the person best qualified for that place, of any he knew," and the congregation anxiously awaited Horace's response. Dwight also confirmed that a church in Middletown, Connecticut, was similarly desirous of her husband's attentions and anxious for his return. "Thus you see my dear Husband," she added, "that you are considerably in demand. I think the great difficulty will be, to make a judicious choice among so many offers."[29]

Dwight was surprised by Horace's invitation to preach at Hollis Street and with good reason. Hollis, or "Old South," had experienced a significant theological transformation at the turn of the nineteenth century, refashioning itself as more inclusive, participatory, and enlightened in its approach to Christianity. Sponsored and reinforced by Boston's rising merchant middle class, this new strain of liberal Congregationalism—later named Unitarianism—based its theology on human ability and divine rationality.[30] In time, Hollis and other churches bound themselves by a unified approach to biblical interpretation and altered understandings of predestination, the Holy Trinity, and God's omnipotence. They abhorred evangelism, reveled in interdenominational similarities, and celebrated their accessibility in both church membership and theology.

Dwight, Jedidiah Morse, and other Congregational heads looked on these developments with increasing consternation, and by the start of the nineteenth century, they began working against the appointments of divergent ministers and professors where they could.[31] In 1805, Morse, then a member of Harvard's Board of Overseers, opposed the election of the liberal Henry Ware to the college's Divinity Professorship on the grounds that he weakened the efficacy of Christianity.[32] Morse was unsuccessful here, but the passing of Samuel West, the liberal pastor of Hollis Street, gave him, Dwight, and the others another opportunity to reassert Calvinism. As a confirmed Hopkinsian with three years of experience in propagating conservative dogma, Horace may have seemed the best prospect for conservative change.

By mid-October 1808, Horace approached the end of his journey in search of a position. In the village of Marblehead, a short, three-and-a-half-mile ride from Salem, he preached before an overflowing crowd who lavished him with their attentions and asked for copies of his sermons. Their devotion was unexpected because Marblehead was a fishing town, a situation he believed was "peculiarly injurious to morals" and particularly suited for a moral leader.[33] But he fixed his attentions on Boston, and he would remain in Marblehead only long enough to ready his preaching schedule. If nothing materialized in Boston, he would accept an offer from the church in Middletown.[34] But Boston did not disappoint. Guest sermons at Hollis Street were better than expected, leaving parishioners and pastors gratified and hoping he could extend his stay as long as possible. "Tell me," he wrote to Mary, "when it will be absolutely necessary for me to be at home" because an "inopportune" visit to Connecticut might cost him the job.[35]

The prospects of the Hollis Street Church, a large, "genteel audience," a "liberal salary," and abundant opportunities to indulge cultural tastes brought sleepless nights. Expectations that the position might lead to fame, perhaps on the scale of Dwight, Hopkins, and Morse, gave full voice to Horace's ambitions. An appointment to Hollis, one of the first and best churches in the country, would help him place his family "above the meanness and malignity of the world," he wrote proudly in a letter to Mary. The current church building was to be torn down and replaced with a more commodious structure. The promised salary of $25 a week, with separate allowances for rent and firewood, was almost four times as much as he had earned in Greenfield.[36] Mary would also benefit from a proper house, and their children would prosper in an environment of refined sensibilities and abundant education. "Care nothing about the world, my love," he closed, "we shall soon be its envy, rather than its pity."[37] There was, of course, the matter of Hollis Street's ecumenical affiliation. How would Horace, a Congregationalist trending toward Hopkins, work out in an avowedly Unitarian church? Decades later, Hollis Street parishioner William B. Fowle remembered Horace was confronted with this question during his initial visit—that is, how he could fit within a theological tradition so different from his own. Horace remembered Fowle and replied only that it "would be an easy matter."[38]

Horace's guest sermons for Hollis Street are no longer extant, but it is difficult to believe he drew in the congregation with hard theological boundaries. A strict Hopkinsian interpretation of Calvin would have cost him the opportunity, but a full liberal conversion would mean an immediate break with Dwight, Morse, and many former associates. Elements of Horace's fully formed theology, evinced only years later, suggest a talent for obfuscation, committing to sound religious principals but confirming or objecting to none in particular. Hollis Street was an opportunity like no other; the size and wealth of its congregation and its proximity to institutions and people of national significance might have moved him to adopt a path between the two extremes. The congregation's motives are equally unclear. Horace's oratorical talents certainly piqued their initial interests, but as a pastor of uncertain conviction he might also have been a less-controversial choice in an increasingly hostile religious and political atmosphere.

Princely Robes

Horace traveled to New Haven for the birth of daughter Harriette but left a month later for Boston with reservations, regretful of leaving and pressed upon by strong emotions. "[I]t is harder parting with you now than ever. My thoughts are traveling back . . . to the little room, that contains our sweet Harriett," he lamented. Departing now might cost him the chance to hear first words or participate in teaching her "father and mother," "Papa and Mama," or simply "Pa and Ma."[39] He mollified these anxieties by making preparations for their settlement—the decision to partake of "house keeping" or "lodging out," the hiring of servants, and arranging travel back to New Haven to collect wife and child. A private residence was preferable to a smaller rented room; seclusion—for both the care of an infant and the quiet of his study—was a premium. The management of household duties required two servants, one for him, another for her. The Hollis Street committee assisted in all of these preparations, finding temporary accommodations and perhaps suggesting qualified domestics.[40]

The committee also worked with Horace on the particulars of his installation ceremony, now set for the second Wednesday in March 1809. It was to be a lavish occasion, replete with specially designed anthems and hymns as well as appearances by Boston's notable pastors. Most impressive of all, however, were the attentions paid to his regalia. Material for a special suit was $12 a yard, his vestments were made of a "princely stuff" costing $150, double the price of silk. The expenses were but a small matter for the congregation, he added, who collected donations in an amount much more than what was required.[41]

Transporting Mary and infant Harriette was not easy. The five-day ride on a sleigh in late February would ill suit a new mother, and Horace wrote to express his concern over the practicalities of such a journey. The conveyance would not be a problem, travel on snowy roads meant carriages passed "as slowly as a cradle." Nursing was another issue altogether, and Horace feared her exposed breast might make her more susceptible to sickness. He also wondered how she would endure the rigors of travel—eating, drinking tea, and traveling long distances without the ability to feed their infant.[42]

Complications of travel aside, Horace's introduction to Boston came with all the pomp and grandeur he may have anticipated. The opening anthem rededicated parishioners to sacred vows, and a closing hymn celebrated ebullient piety. "Behold, God is my salvation!" congregants jointly acclaimed. "I will trust, and not be afraid, for the Lord Jehovah is my salvation. . . . Sing unto the Lord, for he hath done excellent things."[43] Present to lead activities were three of Boston's more notable and most liberal clergy: Joseph Eckley of Boston's Old South, John Lathrop of Old North, and John Kirkland, head pastor of the New South Church and soon thereafter president of Harvard University. Each had led congregations away from the central tenets of Calvinism by defining a new rational Christianity, and so each gave conservatives such as Morse cause for concern.

Eckley's ordination sermon, "They Watch for Your Souls," offered the young pastor-elect advice on how he should discharge his obligations. He encouraged Horace to abide by Christian principles of moral purity, to develop a habit of theological study, and to provide comfort for those close to death. He warned that negligence in these duties would be met by the "scoffs and contempt of the whole class of the wicked among angels and men" and reminded him of the heavenly rewards awaiting the minister who "with fidelity has watched for souls." Eckley asked the congregation to pay heed to Horace's wisdom but to keep him true to his calling, to "animate and encourage" him so that he might "win souls to Christ."[44]

Lathrop reiterated these entreaties in a formal declaration of Horace's ministerial responsibilities. In addition to precepts against the use of classical embellishments, Lathrop referenced the controversies now cleaving Boston's Congregational churches. Disagreements were to be expected among groups of vibrant, educated Christians and a natural consequence of Christian society. Uniformity in religion was impossible. Moreover, spiritual wisdom evolved over time, so it would be foolish to suggest otherwise. To impugn well-intentioned Christians as heterodox was to countermand God's gift of human freedom, and Lathrop enjoined Horace to maintain the same attitude of acceptance, away from "party bigots, and wild enthusiasts."[45]

Kirkland then joined Horace at the rostrum to offer the ceremonial "right hand of friendship" and officially conclude the ceremony. But like Lathrop's, many of Kirkland's sentiments were directed outward toward Calvinist detractors who indulged vengeful appetites by slandering pious Christians. The congregation at Hollis Street, Kirkland proclaimed, came together in unanimity of spirit without regard to narrow points of theology. Attending to such inherently divisive and unnecessary articles removed men from the specific doctrines of the faith celebrated by all. He was confident Horace possessed the character necessary to execute his charge and remain true to the unified vision of religious tolerance without regard to specific doctrinal limits. "Far be it from us to aspire to dominion over your faith," Kirkland added. To enjoy the full blessings of his appointment, Horace need only be a faithful seeker of unbiased truths, a loyal communicant with his best judgments, and a supplicant to godly wisdom.[46]

Horace was well satisfied by the occasion, concluding that all parts added together to a singularly pleasing effect.[47] In the coming weeks, newspapers carried similar thoughts throughout New England; a month later, Eckley bound and published the day's sermons for sale.[48] Conservatives, Jedidiah Morse in particular, remained silent on the matter, perhaps reserving judgment for some later date. The tone of the service might have been unsettling even to those convinced of Horace's predispositions, and the presence of Eckley, Lathrop, and Kirkland seemed to suggest an aggressive spiritual co-opting of the young Hopkinsian stalwart. Their sermons made it clear that Boston's Unitarian leadership would encourage Horace to move beyond narrow, divisive points of theology and toward a celebration of essential doctrines of Christian harmony. Horace's way forward was unclear: Would he remain an island of conservative conviction or become an adaptable, rationally enlightened spiritual leader?

92 Orange Street

Horace's theological transformation might have been suppressed, at least in the short term, by more immediate concerns of settlement and acclimation. The couple resided in temporary quarters for only a few short months before moving to their permanent home at 92 Orange Street, just steps away from the church and amid a thicket of houses owned by members of the congregation.[49] Their neighbors practiced diverse but lucrative occupations. Many were merchants, some were professionals, but tradesmen—shoemakers, upholsterers, printers, and tailors—predominated.[50] They were part of Boston's late-century migratory expansion, a population boom that saw the city nearly triple in size. The same conditions that had earlier sapped the city of its strength—sickness, devastating fires, and war—became the engine of its salvation as a revitalized postwar economy offered new opportunities for a now-depleted labor market.

Jacqueline Carr's intricate study of the Boston tax records from this period show a rapid increase first in construction and shipping trades—joiners, masons, glaziers—and then in commerce—manufacturing, retail, and service jobs.[51] Orange Street became something of an epicenter of the new-moneyed, far enough away from the urban decay of Boston's North End but only a short distance from the central business district and the city's most affluent dwellings.[52] Tradesmen purchased property, educated their children in elite schools, patronized the arts, and assumed the mantle of refined gentility.[53]

It was not long before Horace settled down to the business of ministering to the large but still-growing congregation. In his first year of service, he baptized twenty-two, buried twenty-four, officiated at twenty-five weddings, and admitted twenty-one new members.[54] Mary later recalled his rigorous work habits, wherein he rose early each morning for religious study and contemplation, attended to ministerial duties throughout the day, and returned to his chamber in the evening to review current literature. As Sunday approached, he became more reclusive, working until the early hours of the morning, and when preparing for a subject or occasion, he often forgot meals. Horace dedicated weekdays to visits with ill or infirm congregants. He would arrive, book of poetry in hand, to review the high points of the previous day's sermon and to share comforting verse.[55] In time, he earned a reputation for his oratorical charms, what some later referred to as his "popular eloquence," his ability to fix an audience in their seats and move them wherever he desired.[56] A clear, melodious voice, perfect diction, and lucid illustrations delivered without consulting his Bible gave his sermons a theatrical character.[57]

As his popularity grew, so did his attachments to life in Boston. Letters to Mary, who was on a visit to New Haven in the late summer of 1810, describe invitations to attend commencement at Harvard and the sermons of notable ministers, his preparations for a lecture to the city's ministerial elite, and dinners with interesting Bostonians, including renowned surgeon Joseph Warren and attorney Charles Davis.[58] The cumulative effect of these experiences may have impressed him with a greater sense of purpose or fulfilled an importance stoked by Dwight but held in abeyance during his years of captivity at Greenfield. In Boston, the religious scene was more congenial than expected, and Horace found his fellow pastors even handed in their sentiments and majestic in their oratory.[59] It was a situation very different from New Haven. When Mary fell ill during her visit to New Haven, Horace believed it had more to do with "the narrow, gossiping, spirit of the place" than with anything else.[60]

Accommodation

A theological broadening became more likely because of his appointment. In Boston, strict Hopkinsian beliefs would place Horace apart, whereas a more liberal mind was rewarded with access to interesting people and important positions. It seems he understood this choice from the start, so his first sermons were based on general principles, "Preach the word" (2 Tim. 4:2) and "Receive, with meekness, the ingrafted word" (James 1:21).[61] They were specific on Christian moral principles but unspecific on the finer points of Christian doctrine. Eulogists described Horace's theological evolution only in broad strokes. He avowed truth and sought it with his whole heart, in time gaining a "fuller knowledge, and wider experience" along with the independence of thought that comes with age.[62] According to Caldwell's biography of Horace, Mary objected to the idea that Horace changed his theology to suit ambition and described his shift as a "gradual progress of an inquiring mind." Horace was restricted to Calvinism in his youth, taught by compulsion, and oppressed by dogma. In Boston, internal struggles between unnatural systems and "benevolent sentiment" bubbled forth, allowing him, she claimed, to refocus his energies and divest himself of bigoted dogma.[63] Horace described the conversion in slightly different terms. Any thoughts learned as a young man were, he argued, capricious, ill formed, and based on a misunderstanding of the world. "One event after another . . . in real life, regulates, improves, and matures."[64] In the end, what the world needed was not the high-flown, inaccessible theology of his early adulthood but a practical or more useful approach. His father took exception to the change and only a few years into Horace's appointment at Hollis Street expressed concerns over what he considered an erratic shift. Horace corrected his misgivings, claiming that his "present religious speculations" were unique in their ability to secure a greater share of human happiness and, more importantly, God's favor.[65]

Horace's habit of destroying sermons or, more often, delivering them extemporaneously without reference to notes also suggests a desire to skirt controversy; if nothing were printed, nothing could damage his reputation. Most had difficulty understanding his reticence. One of the family's domestics was so enamored of Horace's sermons that she stole one, placing it under a rug until it could be copied in private.[66] But signs of Horace's wholesale rethinking of Calvinism become clear in the aggregate. In a letter to Miles Day written a little more than a year after assuming the pastorate at Hollis Street, Horace praised his former classmate's idea to compose a parallel translation of the Hebrew Bible. Such a translation could play an important part, Horace concluded, in the remolding of "that portion of our Clergy ... that they should have it in their power to know the ambiguities of the text that exist." In other words, a more realistic reading of the scriptures could lead others away from narrow sectarian lines.[67]

Horace's rational oratory led to increased membership and gave the church reason to support physical expansion; in February 1810, plans were under way to replace the current structure.[68] A temporary merger between Hollis Street and the congregation of First Church, located a short distance from Hollis, gave parishioners a place to worship during construction. This was a natural fit because William Emerson, the pastor of First Church and father of Ralph Waldo Emerson, was an early leader in the liberal Christian tradition. Like Horace, Emerson began his career as pastor to a rural Calvinist congregation but came to Boston in search of more convivial surroundings. And like Horace, he had a broad, liberal interpretation of scriptures and a less-restrictive attitude toward secular high culture, both of which increased his stature in the community.[69]

It took about a year to complete the new, more spacious brick meetinghouse. Horace believed the congregation was now the largest in the city. At 79½ feet long by 76 feet wide, the two-story church could accommodate 130 pews and more than 500 members. The architecture and amenities were impressive; a steeple rose some 205 feet above the center, and Ionic and Corinthian colonnades supported an ornamented ceiling. Arched windows, fitted with venetian blinds, illuminated interior furnishings and focused attention on a decorated pulpit. The entire expense of $65,000 was funded entirely by the sale of pews, each of which brought in an average of $540.[70] Horace's dedicatory sermon on the benefits of "natural religion" in March 1811 was his boldest statement of liberal theology yet. In it, he proclaimed Christian doctrine to be an artificial outgrowth of fundamental truths. The Bible contained facts, whereas men created doctrines.[71]

In time, Horace grew more confident in his role and more vehement in his theological sentiments. His published review of "A Contrast between Calvinism and Hopkinsianism," an essay written by Ezra Ely and published in the April 1813 edition of the Unitarian-friendly journal *General Repository,* moved him from observer to advocate. The review was uncommonly hostile, not to the work itself but to men who published letters in support of Ely. It was an aggressive move sure to place Horace at personal odds with no less than eighteen influential Presbyterian ministers, college presidents, and professors from New England and the Middle Atlantic.[72] Here, prolonged critiques of individual letters led to a more general and particularly aggressive criticism of Calvinist doctrine.

In Horace's view, the division between Hopkinsianism and Calvinism was a meaningless exercise between what he termed "reciprocally jealous bodies." The entire structure of their faith was based on erroneous and harmful assumptions crafted by ambitious men with malevolent designs. Creeds caused an unnecessary restriction of truth "to a few abstract definitions of sectarian partisans." Charges and countercharges created lazy ministers who, instead of enhancing the spiritual lives of their parishioners, were more apt to perpetuate the worst tendencies of creedal logic. Simply put, inconsequential abstractions were forwarding earthly ambitions and setting loving Christians against one another.[73] Through this review, Horace left no ambiguity about his revised associations; though not mentioned by name, Dwight and Morse were clearly implicated. Later that year Horace warned against the damaging influence of "noisy, declamatory, pertinacious, and fanatical" Hopkinsian preachers.[74]

But the scope of Horace's conversion was greater than the sum of specific theological statements, however grandiose or offensive they may have been. Boston of the early 1810s was a world of synchronistic influences, a complicated fugue of politics, class, and culture reinforced by the animating spirit of liberality. The broad and accommodating nature of Unitarianism, divested of conservative strictures and scaffolded by the *energeia* of human will, complemented but did not define these interests. In reality, the force of Horace's convictions may have been secondary to his involvement in elite society or political contexts.

Elite Circles

As a pastor of Hollis Street, Horace enjoyed the natural advantage of authority and proximity. Over the course of his pastorate, he admitted 113 new members to communion in an already large congregation.[75] He had been educated in Federalist principles yet was set apart by obligatory disinterestedness and conditioned to abjure secular desires that were a natural point of reference for an emerging moneyed class. All of this made him an interesting social companion and an obvious choice for gentlemen's clubs and elite societies. Shortly after his arrival in Boston, he was named ex officio member of Harvard's Board of Overseers, a voting member who helped audit university accounts.[76] In 1811, he joined the prestigious Wednesday Evening Club, perhaps as a replacement for Kirkland, who had resigned a year earlier, but almost certainly at the instigation of Unitarian members Reverends William Emerson, Joseph Buckminister, and James Freeman.[77] It was an elite group, limited to sixteen men of high professional attainment who gathered weekly to debate politics, discuss literature, and share genteel conversation. Members benefited from Horace's quick wit and well-studied approach to debate; in return, Horace was rewarded with newfound associations with attorneys Josiah Quincy, John Quincy Adams, and John Davis; physicians John Warren, Nathaniel Appleton, and William Greenleaf; merchants Charles Vaughn and William Wells; and architect Charles Bulfinch.[78]

Moving in elite circles might have compelled him to participate in another of Boston's unique social movements. In the early 1800s, traditional, New England convictions of philanthropic alms to the poor, care for the indigent, and moral instruction for all were organized as an expansive list of institutional humanitarian, mutual benefit, and relief societies.[79] Horace took an early interest in these institutions, traveling to the Massachusetts State Prison to investigate the conditions and visiting Rainsford Island to assist the Board of Health with quarantine laws.[80] The popularity of Boston's humanitarian groups has been described in psychological terms: participation resolved the conflict between lives dedicated to accumulation and a moral compulsion to better society.[81] But membership also solidified community standing, and for Boston's ministers participation in such groups was expected. In time, Horace received invitations to address the Roxbury Charitable Society, the Massachusetts Humane Society, the Washington Benevolent Society, the Ancient and Honorable Artillery

Company, and Boston's Female Asylum.[82] His own charitable organization, the Christian Monitor Society for Promoting Christian Knowledge, Piety, and Christianity, likely elevated his standing. Incorporated in February 1812 with minister John Lathrop, the society attracted the attentions of a few important Bostonians, including Harvard librarian Thaddeus Mason Harris, attorney Samuel Carey, merchant James Morrill, and Reverend Joseph Buckminster, Horace's Wednesday Evening associate.[83]

Other affiliations were just as easily made but more significant. Horace enjoyed active exchange with members of the Boston Athenaeum, the American Academy of Arts and Sciences, and the newly formed American Antiquarian Society.[84] Participation in these societies was similar to participation in charitable groups but more attuned to political interests and far more exclusive, restricted to men of liberal education with the means to subsidize the organization's pursuits. Charter members of the American Academy of Arts and Sciences were some of the country's most revered patriots, and those initiated in the decades after the revolution were thought to represent the best men of letters from diverse fields of practical and academic pursuit.[85] Politicians, medical doctors, college presidents, and theologians dominated the membership roles in the academy at the time of Horace's initiation. Dwight was a member, as was Noah Webster and Jedidiah Morse; but Horace's ties to Unitarian ministers John Lathrop, elected in 1790, and James Freeman, elected in 1793, may have been more important to his nomination. In the Athenaeum, Horace joined the top 3 percent of the city's wealthiest men of business and leisure, the politically inclined, and all manner of learned professionals: owners of textile mills, bank presidents, endowed professors, and fellow overseers of Harvard.[86] The American Antiquarian Society, organized in 1812, brought together those interested in the collection and preservation of artifacts important to American history.

Membership was more than simple intellectual snobbery, although this was part of the appeal.[87] These and similarly directed societies were part of a Federalist impulse that looked to promote American science, literature, and all manner of artistic expression. They appealed to the self-aggrandizing yet civic-minded Bostonian, offered a way to solidify one's place among the city's cultured elite, and created group cohesion.[88] Unified in their concerns for national stability and moral suasion, participants reveled in an atmosphere of mutual support and admiration. Shared learning in adolescence and shared responsibilities in adulthood gave significance to their publications, debates, and recitation exercises.

Just a year before leaving Greenfield, Horace had observed a meteor shower with his neighbor Isaac Bronson, and they had forwarded the results of an investigation to Samuel Mitchill, a professor in Columbia College's Medical Department. It was an amateurish account based largely on interviews with local farmers, but through it they demonstrated a familiarity with scientific inquiry and the larger scholarly community. "We do this," they began, "the more cheerfully, notwithstanding our want of a particular personal acquaintance with you, because we know the ardour and perseverance with which you pursue subjects of this kind." Professors Benjamin Silliman and James Kingsley from Yale College, they added, "have called on us" and exchanged their own findings of the phenomena. Mitchill thought their account worthy of publication and printed their findings in the *Medical Repository* under the title "An Investigation of the Facts Relative to a Descent of Stones from the Atmosphere to the Earth."[89] Horace also reviewed works for the literary quarterly *General Repository* and Boston's *Repertory*, prepared at least one essay for the Athenaeum's journal, the *North American Review*, and composed a biographical sketch of ship captain Amasa Delano.[90]

For Horace, acceptance within elite circles gave him connections with Boston's most influential families. He was liberally educated, professionally recognized, and agreeable in his religious and political outlook. He was also of eclectic interests, a lover not only of religious debate but also of poetry, literature, American culture, natural science, and scientific phenomena—interests that most likely endeared him to the elite.

A Civic Mind

Horace's scientific or literary aspirations amounted to just a few brief exchanges, but the diversity of his learning and associations eventually caught the attentions of the Massachusetts state legislature. In June 1812, he became chaplain of the Massachusetts House of Representatives; four months later he was named to the Boston School Committee.[91] The chaplaincy was an honorific, and Horace was expected only to deliver sermons to mark significant elections and prayers to sanctify regular meetings.[92] The School Committee, however, may have been

Horace's most significant responsibility outside of Hollis Street. Included in the committee's charge were the management and regulation of more than 2,300 students and no less than eight coeducational facilities, including an "African school" and a school located within Boston's Alms House.[93]

Appointment to the School Committee was no passive commitment. Over the years of Horace's service, the committee standardized aspects of instruction, added bells to mark hours of the day, and mandated morning start times. Horace and his fellow committeemen would also make impromptu visits to schools, overseeing and perhaps critiquing methods of instruction. He found forty-five "well taught, and well managed" students on one visit to a school for female orphans. The head mistress had adopted the Lancastrian method of instruction, and the children practiced their letters on tabletops covered with sand, a method employed to save on the costs of ink and paper.[94]

Expectations of secularized moral improvement guided these observations. Comprehensive school reforms of the 1780s had culminated in the adoption of the Education Act, which included regulations governing the structure, composition, support, oversight, and intentions of Massachusetts's public schools. Christian moral precepts and patriotic civic enthusiasm created the basic form; the school day began with prayer and a reading from scripture; and instructors were certified based on their moral qualities. Instructional materials reinforced these principles but also inculcated national pride.[95] The School Committee did its part in moving forward these intentions through its promotion of a uniform system of Sunday schools. The Sunday school, an idea developed of necessity in Great Britain and transported to America in the 1790s, was an interdenominational effort to provide basic instruction to children of limited means and unprepared to enter the public schools. It was an answer to the stigmatized "charity school" and a fulfillment of the committee's charge to influence the moral development of Boston's poor.[96]

The Ebb of Federalism

Life in Boston intensified Horace's political leanings. Commercial interests and durable bonds of English high culture had left many New Englanders in strong opposition to a second war with the British. Federalist sympathies among Boston's elite were especially significant. Embargoes against foreign powers seemed to have a disproportionate effect on the Bay State, and the motivations for war were either overblown, as was the case with impressment, or far too remote, as with Indian hostilities in the western territories. Just before his installation ceremony in the late winter of 1809, Horace complained about the Nonintercourse Act (also known as the Indian Nonintercourse Act), an embargo of foreign goods designed to hurt British and French commerce. "The people here will not be driven from the ocean," he carped. If the Republican government persisted in these measures, the whole of New England was certain to cede, join England, and wage war against the South.[97] In early spring that year, Horace was asked to deliver a prayer at a party for the Federalist minority in the U.S. Congress. There, below portraits of George Washington, Alexander Hamilton, and Fisher Ames, between toasts defaming Jefferson and his "scoundrel democrats," and among throngs of aggravated Federalists, Horace praised the benefits of commerce and offered a prayer that God would return the country to prosperity "after a painful interruption in the course of thy providence."[98]

As the situation worsened and war with England became inevitable, Horace joined fellow Federalists in his condemnation of Republican policies, or what he styled "determined and remorseless Jacobinism."[99] He condemned President James Madison at the start of the war; at least one of his parishioners remembered him as a fervent member of the "old Federal party," never afraid to insert politics into his sermons and on one occasion extending his sermon an additional half-hour to promote the proposed Hartford Convention—a meeting where New England politicians would gather to discuss their secession from the union.[100] Aspects of Unitarian theology connected well with Federalist policy—a rejection of the Trinity was also confirmation of their faith in hierarchical social structure, and an emphasis on moral perfection justified the Federalist principle of leadership by the educated elite.[101] And as war approached, Unitarians took to print and the pulpit to express Federalist sympathies through righteous discontent. Solomon Aiken's "Fast Sermon" of 1811, reproduced in the April 1812 edition of the *Columbian Centinel,* raged against the trampling of Federalists' rights and privileges, the slanderous nature of Republican usurpers, and the illegitimacy of a second war with Great Britain, an action that would serve only the "party purposes" of the malevolent.[102] Horace considered the situation completely untenable. The country, he felt, had abandoned all good sense and sacrificed the blessings of Federalist prosperity on an altar of corrupt southern greed. The best course, however, was not to persist in objection but to let the system collapse in on itself.[103] But he also grew more deliberate in his affections for the English and chuckled at the incompetence of American soldiers. "I am not afraid of being called a tory [sic]," he quipped in a letter to Mary. The couple shared a laugh when Mary reported on the "*brilliant* spectacle of the two ragged regiments" she witnessed in Saratoga.[104] Horace reveled in news of General William Hull's surrender of Fort Detroit, a disgrace that he felt should be placed squarely on the general's shoulders, and he condemned Republicans for their "want of principles . . . in giving him up so quick, untried, and unheard."[105] A friend told Horace about the general's recent appearance in full military dress at a church in Newton, Massachusetts, a display of "characteristic vanity and ostentation" that was said to have "excited no small mirth among the intelligent."[106]

But their mood changed quickly on the arrival of a British fleet in the fall of 1814. Bostonians feared invasion, and panic swept through the city. Mary and Harriette left for New Haven, while Horace, imbued with newfound patriotic zeal, served as army chaplain to the militia regiment at Fort Strong. He now recoiled at British incursions and reveled in American victories. The capture and ransoming of American fishing vessels, attacks on Cape Cod, and capture of its salt works were "too extravagant" even if in retribution for American atrocities in Canada. "British magnanimity," Horace concluded, "is certainly in some danger of becoming a by-word of reproach." He was equally captivated by Captain Thomas Macdonough's victories at Lake Champlain, "the most brilliant achievement in our history . . . not surpassed even in the annals of the British navy." The victory wreathed Macdonough and his men in "hero's glory" and encouraged the desperate hearts of Boston's inhabitants.[107] Horace's duties as chaplain took on greater importance in this atmosphere. Sunday service for the regiment at Fort Strong, located on Noddle Island in Boston Harbor, was a patriotic spectacle attended by local dignitaries and a host of curious onlookers. The sounds of workmen readying the fort's defenses, wielding pick axes, and raising cannon into place mixed with the solemnity of religious worship and "the danger of invasion" to create a lasting impression.[108]

The mood in Boston shifted dramatically in those days. The more Horace's friends became acquainted with the particulars of American victories, the greater their patriotic jubilation; the more certain they were of a British invasion, the more they rallied the war effort. "This town is at present little else than a military school," Horace commented. "We talk of nothing but guns and drums, batteries and forts, breach and cockade. We hardly meet a man or boy but with the ensign of war. The Common is continually filled with troops drilling for service."[109] He, like most Bostonians, was now committed to "bear[ing] the expense of the troops" through increased taxation, a proposal unthinkable just two years earlier. But the threat of war passed quickly, and news of a ninety-day armistice, delivered by way of a merchant vessel from Montreal, brought the city back to normalcy. By early October 1814, fears in Boston were greatly reduced; Mary returned from New Haven, and Horace continued on in his regular pastoral duties.[110]

Entranced

The anxieties of war were a deviation from an otherwise tranquil life of scholarship, society, and cultured retirement. Hollis Street prospered; Horace's professional life flourished; family friendships deepened; and daughter Harriette grew more active and intelligent by the day. After the union with First Church, Horace's annual salary was increased to $2,000, a sum that encouraged the move to a larger, quieter home on nearby Boylston Street. Prosperity also allowed them to host visiting family members. Mary's sister Henrietta and brother Henry stayed for a time, as did Horace's younger brother Orville, who, although now graduated from Harvard, was making "slow progress . . . toward supporting himself."[111] The addition of Horace's younger sister, Caroline, was a more cumbersome commitment. It was Horace's father who first suggested the arrangement; Caroline would take up residence with Horace in the hope that "intercourse with polished society" might improve her manners and that practice in composition would ornament her character.[112] Boston was sure to provide more opportunities than she could hope for in remote Salisbury, a chance not only to practice genteel conversation but to take advantage of various learning opportunities: a dancing school and a riding school, private drawing lessons, tutoring in French, and independent reading with Mary.

Horace's friend Joseph Bigelow, professor of botany and medicine at Harvard, added to Caroline's education by allowing her to attend his lectures free of charge, a fine gift considering the normal price of admission was $10. When their father worried that too long a stay might spoil Caroline for Salisbury, perhaps giving her too much of a good thing, Horace recoiled. "I should be grieved to have her taken away at the very moment when she is doing best," he wrote. It was true that her stay was longer than expected, but it took time to adequately prepare her mind for higher levels of learning. "Nothing," he added, "could be more unfortunate than to have the opportunities closed the moment they are most auspicious."[113]

Of even greater interest was the education of Harriette. At age three, she could carry on complete conversations, and Horace took pleasure transcribing them in Mary's absence.[114] At age seven, her mental faculties unfolded in incredible ways. "The force of reasonable considerations begins to be felt by her," he boasted in a letter to his mother in July 1816, "and the management of her mind and will is every day growing less difficult."[115] She was the object of their affections and the subject of a sentimental poem celebrating "rosy cheek and sparkling eye," the "fairest gifts" of innocence, and fleeting days of "infant mirth." Her uncorrupted purity entranced Horace, her benevolent heart brought comfort to his.

> Young life now bails her rising morn
> And golden hues their radiance lead
> See Hope along the future dance
> Her fairy visions to disclose
> Eager we seize each brilliant trance
> That brighter as we view it grows.[116]

Horace's relationship with Mary blossomed and matured. Their expressions of love became less maudlin as they exchanged opinions about literature, society, and cultured retirements. Correspondence sent during Mary's yearly escapes to the mineral springs of upstate New York and prolonged visits to her mother's home in New Haven allowed them to explore cerebral connections. "We have no need of any sentimental finesses to cultivate our attachment," Horace remarked pragmatically. "I feel a conviction of our growing consent of mind, which fills my best wishes for a permanent complacency in our union."[117] Mary shared her interests in botany and philosophy, her impressions of regional culture, and her literary enthusiasms with her best friend and husband.[118] Horace responded in kind and encouraged her to keep up with her writing in order to improve the expression of her sentiments.[119]

They exchanged newspapers, poetry, and anecdotes and celebrated their love of Frederick Schiller, Lord Byron, Walter Scott, Madame Roland, and Madame Germaine de Staël.[120] Horace transcribed a scene of Schiller's tragic play *Maid of New Orleans* for Mary's benefit, adding his own flourish to make it "more touching and sweet."[121] Madame de Staël's review of German society and habits, *De l'Allemagne,* held a particular fascination. Mary would later recall being "lost in reflection" of the serious character of the German people and of writing crafted with enviable imagination.[122] Horace set their shared passions to poetic verse and dedicated a poem on the subject in the spring of 1816.

> But let HER [Roland] and De Stael all our passions explain,
> And their laws, by analysis clear, bring to view,
> May you the bright secret of happiness gain,
> And live to bless those who would live to bless you.[123]

But no amount of literary exchange could elevate the dreary and uninspired surroundings of life without Horace. Mary was forced to avoid the theater and pined for a resumption of shared interests. While vacationing in New York in October 1812, she found not an interesting or intelligent person in the place. "All the people seem to me stupid," she groused.[124] They were best when together, either living in Boston or traveling. Horace's obligations kept him in town for much of the year, but trips to Salisbury, Ballston Springs, and Niagara Falls offered much needed revitalization. Mary memorialized their travels in poetic verse. On the road from Hudson to Albany, they traveled with a group of friends and enjoyed lively, intelligent conversations. After parting, they exchanged private carriage for stagecoach and were forced to interact with common travelers. The contrast of emotions inspired Mary to compose a poem recalling the beauty of earlier conversations, where "friendship, and science, and taste were combind, / And philosophy gave to the whole its fine tone." The elegant beauty of intelligent minds added pain to their parting.[125] On first sight of Niagara Falls, she channeled Homer, contemplating "Far-famed Niagara, thy twin sister streams," waters that rushed furiously "e'er since the world began," and the "soaring eagle" dipped in "feathery foam."[126]

But they were most comfortable in Boston, a city that grew larger and more cultivated each year; in the 1810s, it was almost unrivaled among American cities in the number of museums, theaters, concert and exhibition halls, and publishing houses it had. The almost daily public festivals, concerts, exhibitions, and dances added to entertainments, creating an environment hard to match. The Holleys lived within a block of Boylston Hall, a commodious three-story structure with a market, galleries, and a one-hundred-foot-long exhibition space.[127] The Linnaean Society and Edward Savage's New York Museum, both housed there, provided views of exotic animal specimens, wax figures, paintings, and artifacts from the natural sciences and other fields. Savage's museum featured a re-created panorama of Rome touted to be "as large as nature."[128] Theatrical and musical performances at Boylston, Columbian Hall, and Federal Street Theater offered patrons similarly exotic spectacles. Proprietors announced the arrival of comic operas, dramatic readings, and circuses under gas lights to enthusiastic audiences.[129] The city itself was fast becoming an artistic landscape. The architecture of Charles Bulfinch, an associate of Horace's in the Wednesday Evening Club, enriched Boston with public buildings and private dwellings built in the so-called Federal style. As a selectman, part of Boston's governing body, Bulfinch oversaw the renovation of parks, streets, and entire neighborhoods, transforming a colonial town into a city of the new republic.[130]

Horace and Mary became popular figures both within their church and without, indispensable to the lives of their parishioners and a necessary complement to Boston's fashionable society. Horace's engagements took him to all parts of the city; Mary joined when she could but settled her attentions on Hollis Street, where she provided emotional comfort to members of their increasingly large congregation. The frenetic pace of urban life, the pleasures of cultured society, and the ponderous professional obligations of Hollis Street made life in Boston exciting.

Discontent and Approval

Proximity to and association with persons of national importance aggrandized Horace's sense of significance, not without justification. Sometime before November 1814, he received and ignored an offer to become the president of Transylvania University in Lexington, Kentucky, the first institution of its kind west of the Allegheny Mountains. The board's decision to pursue Horace was almost certainly guided by their own perceptions of eastern colleges. Increasing numbers of Kentucky's legislative leaders saw formal education as the necessary prerequisite to public office, and in the 1800s and 1810s those with means looked east to fulfill these expectations.[131]

There was also the question of Transylvania's current president James Blythe. Copastor of Lexington's Presbyterian church and the school's former professor of natural sciences, Blythe had experienced his own spiritual transformation following the death of a son in the opening months of the recent war. Blythe's sermons now railed against "calumniators," "false testifiers," "liars," and others he deemed deleterious to the public weal. Sermons titled "A Portrait of the Times" and "Our Sins Acknowledged" concentrated on Kentucky's most immoral associations, secret societies, the state legislature, and, most of all, slave owners.[132] His attack against the latter was a problem for a few reasons. In Kentucky, the number of slaves increased 225 percent from 1792 to 1800.[133] The rights of ownership, guaranteed by the state constitution of 1792, were broadly based and geographically distributed to all but the newest counties; close to 25 percent of all householders owned slaves—Fayette, Scott, Woodford, and Jessamine Counties had averages much higher than that. Of the fifty-eight delegates to Kentucky's Constitutional Convention of 1799, only one did not own slaves, and twenty-eight of them owned ten or more.[134] Kentucky's population boom of the early 1800s only increased the desire to own slaves, and the ratio of slaves to the total population rose from 16.1 percent to 22.4 percent between 1790 and 1820.[135]

Blythe's abolitionist agenda may have prompted the initial offer to Horace but almost certainly drove what followed. Critics insisted that Blythe's scandalous, hate-filled sermons undermined the school, the town, and the state. To retain Blythe, one editorialist exclaimed, "would be to set up a scare crow at their door, forever banishing the hope of that patronage which they invite and desire."[136] Until Transylvania appointed a new president, citizens of the state would show it little regard and continue to send their sons off to the institutions of the East.[137]

In November 1814, Transylvania University board member and native Bostonian James Prentiss reached out to Thomas Baldwin, minister of Boston's Second Baptist Church and one of Horace's close friends.[138] Prentiss likely knew Horace by reputation, if not by personal contact, and believed him of "eminent talents & respectability." In his offer, Prentiss promised a situation replete with funding and the most "promising advantages" in all of the western states. The proposed salary of $2,500 per year would, he added, go much further in Lexington than in Boston, sufficient enough for Horace to raise his family in a fine style. If, however, Horace should decline, Prentiss asked for another name, "a man of the world, easy and agreeable in his manners, religious & moral in his habits, not too fond of exposing his particular principles . . . in religion or politics." That man should be "a general scholar" and a popular orator with "dignity of character."[139] Horace's refusal was no doubt the product of Transylvania's very public troubles.

Public Trust

In Lexington, criticism of Transylvania increased with news of a planned relocation in the early summer of 1815. By moving the school to a lot a mile outside of town, trustees hoped to alleviate the prohibitive cost of student boarding— the price of a room in Lexington ranged between $140 and $230 a year.[140] The move, they argued, would benefit the moral health of students, who suffered temptations because of the town's many taverns, billiard rooms, and theaters.[141] Many disagreed. Anonymous editorials published under the names "Peter Porcupine," "Philo-Honestus," "A Spectator," and "Native Kentuckian" protested the action and moved beyond calls to replace just Blythe. "Peter Porcupine" asked, "Gentlemen, pray what right have you to give your votes in the management of this college? who gave you the right?"[142] "Philo-Honestus" called the planned move one of the "most flagrant outrages against moral honesty—that ever disgracesed [sic] a public body."[143] "A Spectator" and "A Native Kentuckian" deemed the planned relocation an intolerable violation of the "public trust."[144] Most suggested that Transylvania's reputation could benefit from reorganization of the board of trustees.

"Citizens of Kentucky" pressed for direct legislative action and hinted at religious intolerance. They hoped to attract the attention of lawmakers and force a reorganization "to exclude the influence of local and partial views [and] . . . religious intolerance."[145] Subsequent calls for legislative oversight disparaged the board's resolve, attention to public duty, and basic aptitude. A work entitled "Public Schools and Colleges" asked why schools, like every other civil institution connected with the public interests, were not regulated by the state. In the case of Transylvania, the author argued that "Permanent Self-Created Aristocracies" flouted the public will, created "sinecures for idle and useless favorites," and otherwise ignored the state's original commandments. These actions were all the more outrageous considering that the legislature endowed Transylvania with "public funds." Such an endowment, the author continued, entitled the legislature full power over board appointments.[146] "Censor" was more histrionic, calling the recent controversy a subject deserving of the legislature's most "profound attention." Transylvania, "the oldest foundation in the western country of a literary description," should be not only protected but also elevated to a position worthy of its legacy. The board, he declared, failed to discharge its duties and should be removed. Kentucky should follow the lead of other states and govern the schools with political appointees.[147]

Trust Expired

And so what began as an assault on the leadership of Transylvania had by the end of 1815 become an issue charged with legislative implications. A confluence of public opinion, private anger, and internal desire now moved Transylvania to the forefront of legislative concern. Perhaps sensing the enlargement of public scrutiny, the board renewed its efforts to locate and hire a permanent university president, offering the position once more to Horace in 1815 but rescinding the offer a short time later.[148] By December 1815, the state demanded answers, and the legislature announced the formation of a committee to investigate the causes of Transylvania's damaged reputation.[149]

Transylvania's board responded a month later with a concession. Enrollments were low, they agreed, but the same could be said of most colleges. The school had languished during the war for lack of matriculates and suffered now because of the exorbitant cost of boarding. If the university's standing were diminished, it was because calumniators convinced thousands that the university lay in a languid and mismanaged state.[150] The legislative committee was unmoved by these arguments. Most of Transylvania's students, they concluded, were children, and even their numbers were rapidly diminishing. Rival institutions, some with tuitions nearly three times as high, fared much better. Through their lack of attention, their division, and the confused and disorganized attempts to appoint a president, it was charged, the trustees had negated and willfully dismissed the public trust.

Legislators also concluded that President Blythe did not hold the public's confidence and should have been replaced years earlier. The recent offer to Horace Holley, they concluded, was rescinded "not because the capacity or talents of Doctor Holly were doubted, his moral conduct reproachable, or his christian [sic] deportment called in to question" but because he did not agree with certain tenets of Calvinistic orthodoxy. Degeneracy went beyond the board of trustees, and legislators now believed that Transylvania's professors inculcated students with pro-British sentiments, praising the monarchy over the U.S. Constitution. The committee recommended the dissolution of the board and replacement of long-standing trustees with members of the House and Senate.[151]

The ensuing months witnessed a flurry of activity from the board. Efforts to remove the shroud of indolence prompted the resignation of James Blythe and a renewed search for a new, more popular president.[152] The board now offered the presidency to Dr. Thomas Cooper, a former Pennsylvania judge and current professor at Dickinson College. But the annual salary of $1,200 was too low; Cooper believed he could make at least $3,000 in Philadelphia and even more in South Carolina.[153] The position was then offered to the Reverend Luther Rice, Baptist minister from North Carolina, and then, after Rice's rejection, to the Reverend Philip Lindsley, vice president of the College of New Jersey, who also declined.[154]

In the fall of 1817, a renewed effort to dislodge Transylvania's trustees began with politically and religiously charged rhetoric. The editor of the *Kentucky Gazette* insisted that the school could achieve more under a "President of popular character." Kentuckians, the *Gazette* continued, had the duty to promote a renovation so their school might invite "surrounding youth of the west to flock to it." Here, the author continued, could those "ambitious of literary distinction . . . reach the heights where 'fame's proud temple stands.'"[155] Change required the complete banishment of "bigoted sectarianism and intolerant federalism" from the board. The university would continue in a state of languor unless "radical change" was effected. Charges of Federalist influences continued into the winter. "Will a proud, independent, republican legislature, look on and tamely submit to this?" one author asked.[156]

On November 15, 1817, trustees again met with the intention of nominating a president, and once again their attention turned to Horace Holley. Reports reflect the trustees' desire to restore public confidence and the need to act quickly lest the state remove them from their positions. Charles Humphries begged for expediency, arguing that "public sentiment required the Board to make an appointment." If the board were to fail to elect a president, it would be the last time they would meet, he warned. Others believed that inaction might be understood as negligence, leaving the trustees open to charges of party politics. John Pope argued that if members were to neglect an appointment, it would be said that "they were bigots, and had introduced a religious test into the board." And at least one trustee was reportedly "hurt" at the idea that he operated under "bigoted feelings."[157]

But an attempted third nomination could not halt a rising tide of ill will. In the December session, members of Kentucky's state Senate established a committee to "reduce the number and alter the mode of electing the trustees of the university." They proposed measures that would expel the current board, name a new body limited to thirteen members, and then require those positions to be filled by biennial elections.[158] The new body would comprise six current board members—John Brown, Charles Humphries, Henry Clay, Edmund Bullock, John Pope, and Lewis Sanders—and six newcomers—John Mason, Robert Trimble, Robert Wickliffe, Samuel Woodson, Thomas Bodley, and James Prentiss, all of whom were chosen for their national reputations.[159] The bill passed through the Senate without a dissenting vote and through the House by a vote of fifty-six to nineteen.[160] Clay, Pope, Brown, and the other state-appointed trustees went to work immediately; their first action was to offer the presidency once more to the thirty-six-year-old Horace Holley, who now consented to a visit.

Ambitions

Horace passed into the prime years of his life with little doubt of success. In Boston, he reaped the rewards of a nimble, educated mind. Professional credentials and a willingness to adapt theology to circumstance embedded him within elite society; a vigorous appetite for genteel company established him as one of the city's most important characters. As a Unitarian minister in one of the country's fastest-growing cities, Horace enjoyed a privileged position. He was a religious leader yet also distanced from the contagion of controversy that dominated rural areas; he was political but removed from base material pursuits and therefore naturally disinterested. He sat between competing visions, enjoying the benefits of all, subject to none. The ambiguous, undefined nature of his popularity explains his appeal among members of Transylvania's trustees, who, when sent reeling by public criticism, determined to elect a champion of the middle way. Disputation was a quality they hoped to avoid in the university's next president. Horace's literary talents were important but not as significant as his ability to remain above controversy.

Horace's own motivations are unclear. The advantages of Boston were uncommon, but so too perhaps were those of Lexington, according to reports. Ambition was another matter entirely. The passing of Yale's longtime president Timothy Dwight in January 1817 and the subsequent election of Jeremiah Day might also have pushed Horace to rethink the trajectory of his career. The prestige of Hollis Street was not insignificant, but the position at Transylvania was something different. As a student, Horace had witnessed Dwight's influence firsthand; his sermons, essays, and even poems took on unique national significance. Like Dwight, Horace had begun his career in the pastoral surroundings of Greenfield Hill, and, like Dwight, he enjoyed the benefits of a growing national esteem. If Prentiss's descriptions were reliable, Kentucky offered the best opportunity to match and perhaps surpass the deeds of his former mentor.

Reports coming out of Lexington in 1817 might have confirmed his best hopes. Education was to be the centerpiece of Governor-elect Gabriel Slaughter's plan to build a unifying social and material infrastructure in Kentucky. Transylvania figured large in this new identity and was to become both a figurative and a literal center of Kentucky's literary reputation.[161] If this assessment was correct, Horace's opportunities would be boundless. Fresh infusions of money from the state could set Transylvania apart from all other institutions. The mantle of leadership would give Horace control over these funds and the ability to remake the school according to his own design. The matter required further investigation, and so, in the winter of 1818, Horace set his sights west.

3

"The State of Society"

Horace set out for Lexington in early February 1818 intent on investigating the offer from Transylvania. There was little doubt he would accept as long as the university was free from sectarian division and the community agreed to support his plans. And so he mapped a circuitous western route through eastern colleges. A "tour of inquiry," as he called it, would inform him of the character of—or, more accurately, the expectations for—higher learning in the western frontier. He understood Harvard well enough—his position on its Board of Overseers made that possible; he knew Yale and President Jeremiah Day better than most, but a broader view of education, something gained only through direct observations, could guide his own understanding in a way other experiences could not.[1] Horace also understood that Kentuckians expected other qualities from their newly appointed president, a man perhaps who could lead the school toward something more refined, more elegant, and who had a recognizably higher and definitively eastern style. As a Bostonian of not insignificant literary accomplishments, Horace would have some effect in Lexington. Yet his success would depend on his ability to translate the character of an eastern education to the situation of the western citizen.

A scrupulously maintained travel diary, something he hoped one day to present to members of Boston's Wednesday Evening Club, allowed him to catalog the most significant events of his trip. He did this, of course, in spite of objections from friends. It was foolish, some argued, to presume he could make the trip sound interesting. "Everything along this road is known too well to need, or permit an account to be written," James Freeman suggested.[2] "Books of this class are usually filled with little else than commonplace and egotism," another friend argued. Unmoved, Horace promised to restrict his accounts of "stages, taverns, beds, food, distances, and information derived from drivers and inn-keepers" typical to such works.[3] He had something far more sophisticated in mind: not only a catalog of industry, science, the arts, and natural scenes but also a narrative of "distinguished men and their public works" and "the state of society at large," the manners, character, and "modes of fashionable entertainment" encountered over months of travel. His "business," Horace wrote, was "not only to get information about schools, colleges, hospitals, and various public institutions . . . but about the state of society at large in all the particulars . . . whatever may illustrate character or increase my own or others' happiness."[4] Timothy Dwight's earlier work *Travels in the Northeastern States of America*, a book compiled over his years at Yale but published posthumously, may have been a guide for Horace, but there were hundreds of other contemporary models.

Individual letters complemented the narrative and allowed a more personal reflection of American society. Horace kept a strenuous pace and wrote scores of them; few recipients were able to keep up. "It is a mystery to me," wrote wife Mary, "that you find time to write so much and attend to everything beside. I am concerned that your health should suffer with so much exertion." She could only apologize for those who failed to reciprocate. Friends from Boston and parishioners from Hollis Street had little to contribute or could not write a "letter of frendship [*sic*] or taste" because they could not write as easily or as interestingly. "Therefore," she added, "you must depend entirely upon *les dames* for all you get in this way."[5] As well as he could, Mary wrote close to seventy letters of her own, responding to her husband's observations and anecdotes with gossip and news from Boston.

Whereas the journal was intended for public viewing, letters to Mary were almost certainly not. Time and again he cautioned against sharing or allowing others to copy his private thoughts. "I scribble without care and without restraint," he wrote from a Virginia tavern.[6] "You see," he cautioned in a letter from Washington, "how free they [my letters] are, and how unfit to be circulated. Be very careful on this subject."[7] His thoughts on Lexington "ought not be repeated," he later wrote, because he gossiped unabashedly and informed her of everything from the awkward to the untoward.[8] His opinions of women and clergy were meant to be especially sacrosanct. Before relating an untoward anecdote from Washington, Horace cautioned, "I may tell you a little slander here, but you will not repeat it."[9] Before discussing the touchy religious situation of Kentucky, he warned, "I do not want my remarks about clergymen in this vicinity to become common talk."[10] A "bad use" of his words was a constant fear. When stagecoach robbers absconded with mail headed north from Baltimore, he worried that a letter containing unflattering remarks about the women of Philadelphia might fall into the wrong hands. Though the criminals stole only the parcels containing money, there might still be letters lying around the scene of the crime. He shuddered at the thought that a few interested passersby might somehow decipher his meanings and publish his private thoughts.[11] Mary promised to keep quiet. "You know," she wrote on one occasion, "I am sufficiently scrupulous."[12]

Taken together, Horace's reflections give voice to lesser-known and somewhat misunderstood features of higher education in the early republic. Leadership of these institutions was his particular concern, and, as he soon discovered, the significance of denominational influence was an amorphous challenge that no university or president could escape. In Boston, the strength of Horace's avant-garde Christian rationalism was its ambiguity, yet those interested in higher education often expected confession-driven, theologically neutral moral leadership. His experiences here are important; the ability to negotiate contradictory religious expectations was a skill that no successful university president could do without.

There was also the question of intellectual prestige. The form and function of "useful knowledge," a phrase used to describe the gentlemanly pursuit of education, shifted in this period. Scientific learning, the hallmark of useful knowledge, was once accessible to laymen through unsophisticated observations but now required a complicated vocabulary, access to expensive scientific equipment, and elite education.[13] Schools of medicine benefited from the trend and all along the cities of the East Coast were becoming the most identifiable signs of collegiate prestige. Horace's reflections on scientific education underscore the mechanics of this educational shift and help explain the rise of medical training in early America. His journey of 1818 was thus an intellectual as well as a physical passage. The dual forces of popular demand and personal ambition were unfamiliar but became increasingly common to this new generation of college leaders.

Introductions

Letters of introduction were an essential part of Horace's preparations and something Bostonians could not do without.[14] A visitor to the city once described the exceptional joy and enthusiasm "the better sort" of Boston had for presenting and receiving introductions. "In their investigation of a man's respectability," they wrote, "the place at which he lodges, and the persons to whom he may accidentally bring letters of introduction, are infinitely more [useful] than his learning, abilities, or general manners."[15] "Letters here are almost indispensable," another visitor to Boston in 1816 opined. "I could not in this city as in Morocco draw around me [friends] . . . by the splendor of my equipage or the length of my retinue; nor is it conformable to the customs of the place to send presents to the chief men as a prelude to acquaintance."[16] It was not uncommon for those bound for the city to carry twenty or more introductions simply to conduct routine business.[17]

Horace may have collected just as many. Former president John Adams's letter of introduction to Thomas Jefferson was perfunctory but useful. Horace, Adams stated blandly, was "frank enough, candid enough, social enough, learned enough and eloquent enough." The task was nearly impossible, and only with the help of Jefferson's Kentucky allies could he succeed.[18] Massachusetts senator Jonathan Mason and Virginia governor James Preston were more lavish in their estimation of Horace's abilities. Mason placed him at the very top of Boston's elite literary society; Preston considered him a particularly interesting social companion.[19] Other Bostonians introduced him to John Vaughan, a member of the American Philosophical Society in Philadelphia; to former secretary of state Robert Smith of Baltimore; and to the faculty of the College of New Jersey, Columbia College, the University of Pennsylvania, and William and Mary. With each new friendship came the possibility of a new letter, another encounter, and more opportunities for sociable visiting. And so by the end of his trip a string of letters connected Horace from Boston to Kentucky with few gaps.

Fashionable Visiting

The Providence Express set out on an early February morning from Earle and Company at 33 Court Square, just blocks from the Boston city courthouse. Horace sat in silence as he waited for his carriage's departure, listening to voices outside while contemplating the months he would be removed from friendly and familiar scenes. Sadness, he wrote, overtook him as he reflected on his last sermon at Hollis Street Church, thought of wife Mary and daughter Harriette, and was momentarily distracted in thoughts of home and of Lord Spencer's hymn *Wife, Children, and Friends*.[20] The first night of his journey intensified his loneliness. A blizzard pushed the carriage off the road two or three times, pitching the cabin forward and jolting passengers out of their seats. Horses and stage then became stuck in a thick wintery slush, and only with the combined efforts of driver, passengers, and the occasional borrowed mule did they continue.[21] In Hartford, the group exchanged a carriage badly in need of repairs for one recently painted; the still-wet "Spanish brown" paint inconveniently came off on clothing and left an odious smell. Cold weather forced travelers to leave the canvas drawn, a necessity that made the interior air stultifying. The smell of paint mixed with the body odor of unwashed travelers was repulsive in the extreme, no less than "criminal thoughtlessness, or selfishness, on the part of the stage proprietors," Horace recollected.[22]

New York may have been just as Horace remembered it, bustling and boorish. Feral pigs ate their way down refuse-strewn city streets and presented coach drivers with an almost constant hazard.[23] But the city had changed in ways Horace did not expect. It was somewhat more religious, or superstitious, and certainly less cultured among society's elite. The well-appointed home of friend Isaac Bronson gave at least some relief from this vulgarity.[24] Horace objected to what he termed "fashionable visiting," the practice of mixing in polite company simply for the sake of vanity, and so endeavored to make these visits meaningful encounters.[25] Religious habits were of particular interest to him, and, as a well-known Boston minister, Horace made an interesting companion for others. New Yorkers, by his estimation, displayed a unique mixture of ignorance, greed, and piety. The city's gentry were less "intellectual and literary" than the people he was accustomed to and infinitely more "fanatical" in their convictions.[26] Social engagements hosted by Bronson introduced Horace to the city's most notable artists, wealthiest merchants, and, most importantly, its most respected intellects. Through Bronson, Horace was able to arrange meetings with faculty of Columbia College and members of the New-York Historical Society.

Most found his theology and social temperament amusing if not entirely appropriate. At the home of attorney Archibald McVickar, he was introduced to Elizabeth Codwise, a devout Presbyterian by reputation who he believed had "conceived great prejudices" against him even before his arrival. Horace's frank discussion of the female form, now one of his favorite topics, no doubt justified suspicions of heterodoxy. His observations of New York's women entertained the crowd but left the pious Mrs. Codwise perplexed. It was a habit, Horace felt, that required no apologies. His journal entry detailing the encounter begins, "I have no disposition to be such a sort of philosopher as shall silence my sympathies for good and elegant society, or render me incapable of admiration for accomplished women."[27] He described a New York socialite known only as "Miss F" as "pretty but not beautiful," having neither the "height nor muscle enough for dignity of the first order." Another partygoer, "Miss Henderson," was tall with a "fullness of muscle" that left her buxom but not corpulent. Mrs. Codwise admitted that the conversation had made her forget she was speaking to a clergyman. Horace found this observation more a "complement [sic] . . . than a censure," adding, "a clergyman should be courteous & natural like other men, and not always carrying the tones and doctrines of the pulpit into common conversation."[28]

He was equally candid about his flirtations with members of the opposite sex. At a party hosted by artist James Trumbull, Horace observed the young Miss Delancey. He had become acquainted with the Delancey family through her cousin William, a recent Yale graduate. When Miss Delancey informed him that William now pursued a degree in divinity and would be "the first Divine Delancey in the family," Horace flirtatiously replied, "He is not the only one." Later, at the home of Nathaniel Prime, he was introduced to the daughter of New York merchant John R. Livingston. The beauty of Miss Livingston so overwhelmed him that he asked for her "bow and quiver," for "many seemed to be wounded and [wondered] from whence the arrows came."[29]

Characters of a University

New York's various social distractions could not, however, make up for a lackluster educational scene, and Horace thought Columbia College, the city's chief institution of higher learning, nothing more than a shabby and unremarkable preparatory school.[30] Columbia's students paid $80 a year in tuition, a sum higher than the fee at any other college of the day, but were educated with inferior methods and provided only paltry resources—the library held but three thousand books. Most egregious of all was the complete absence of scientific instruction. Horace concluded that the entire enterprise was a ruse to support bloated faculty salaries. Columbia's president William Harris, a tired and stodgy old man, was the worst offender; at $3,500 a year, his salary was more than double that of many of his contemporaries.[31]

Horace's experiences at Columbia's medical college were better, though only slightly less disappointing. He found lectures here erudite, practical, and eminently accessible. Dr. Wright Post described the properties of human teeth through a comparison with those of sharks, rattlesnakes, lobsters, and mastodons, all being composed of similar material and comparable in how they react to trauma.[32] Courses on the medicinal uses of mercury, diseases, and the functions of various organs were of equal quality. But Columbia's medical students were less impressive, and the instructors were in part to blame. One spoke too rapidly; others were boring, boastful, or bland, and so only a few students took notes or seemed to care about the material.[33]

Good Christians

A short stop at the College of New Jersey punctuated an otherwise uninteresting trip south from New York to Philadelphia. Horace thought the recent appointment of Ashbel Green, who had replaced Samuel Smith as the college's president six years earlier, to be an unqualified mistake. Green, a staunch Presbyterian of unbending disposition, was ill suited for either pulpit or classroom and perhaps least appropriate as a college president.[34] His expectations were uncomplicated: students were to conform to Calvinist principles without question. It was, Horace concluded, a restriction Green carried "too far" because it inhibited moral development.[35] But the school was not without hope. Professor of ancient languages Phillip Lindsley shared Green's religious convictions but disagreed about the inculcation of dogma.

Like Horace, Lindsley had also been offered the presidency of Transylvania. Twice the preceding year the Transylvania Board of Trustees had made offers to him and both times been flatly rejected. Although no informal explanation of his decision exists, it is likely that Lindsley's attachments to the College of New Jersey and to the town of Princeton in particular were enough reason to stay. He had completed his education there and had become an assistant teacher after graduation and a senior tutor a few years later. In 1813, he was appointed professor of languages and by 1817 was established as the school's fifth vice president.

When President Green neared retirement, Lindsley, as vice president, was his most obvious replacement. Lindsley's wife, a charming and "well informed" woman, also appeared pleased with her surroundings. In a conversation with Horace, she made it clear that the people of Princeton satisfied all the wants of "social spirit" she had had in her native New York.[36]

Horace's tour of the campus, provided courtesy of Lindsley, left him convinced that this was indeed an institution on the rise. Brick, stone, and other architectural features created a feeling of gravitas, and a well-stocked college library, exquisitely designed scientific equipment, and genteel furnishings left him deeply impressed.[37] Enrollment reflected quality, and of the school's 150 students 113 were from states outside New Jersey.[38] More impressive still was the college's annual printed circular, an "excellent regulation" that, as Horace understood it, gave accounts of student scholarship, manners, and "whatever it may be of importance" to parents and guardians.[39] The real reason behind the publication was somewhat less magnanimous. Students, it seems, were increasingly reckless with their money, running up bills at local businesses and engaging in "numerous evils which necessarily arise among young persons from excessive expenditures of money." Issuing a circular that contained an accurate reckoning of student expenses would, school officials hoped, curb improper behavior by limiting the amount of money parents would provide.[40]

Top Hats

In Philadelphia, dogmatism was just as prominent. Through conversation with an Episcopal minister, Horace learned of a young couple that were in each other's company past nine o'clock on a Saturday evening. To members of the church, this offense was censurable because Sabbath began at sundown on Saturday. Speaking with other Episcopalians of the city was often difficult and absent "flow & freedom." It was here also that Horace first came into contact with Swedenborgian Christians. He was introduced to Jonathan Condy, president of Philadelphia's Swedenborgian congregation, and William Schlatter, a prosperous Philadelphia merchant newly converted to the faith. Both were, as Horace discovered, zealous supporters of "the sublime doctrine of the illuminated baron" Emanuel Swedenborg. Condy attempted to unravel the complex mysteries of the faith, and Schlatter bragged of his donations to the Philadelphia temple.

The Christian Church was failing and, according to Condy, would soon be replaced by "New Jerusalem," a church where exclusive worship of Jesus Christ would prevail. Horace found their ideas nothing more than a "curious mixture of sense, truth, and extravagance."[41]

John Vaughan, one of the city's most prominent Unitarians, connected Horace with members of the American Philosophical Association and then to trustees and faculty of the University of Pennsylvania. Members took an interest in the "fine and the useful arts" of Boston, but Horace's educational mission also seemed compelling or at least worthy of their attentions.[42] They also delighted in his social charms. At the home of wealthy Philadelphia banker Thomas Biddle, members asked for his opinions on history, the social manners of their city, Quakers, and recent political controversies. At attorney William Meredith's home, the company delighted in pointing out Horace's odd-sounding "Bostonisms." Mrs. Meredith said he pronounced "have" as "hev" and "absorb" as "abzorb." Not to be outdone, Horace pointed out Meredith's "Philadelphianisms," her pronunciation of "disconary" for "dictionary," "agin" for "again," "lezure" for "leisure," and "reci-ta-tive" for "recitative." Others probed Horace on his northern perspective and observations of Philadelphia's society, local mannerisms, and, of course, seemingly endless supply of beautiful young women.[43]

But Horace reserved his most effusive praise for the University of Pennsylvania Medical College. There he attended lectures, interviewed faculty, and gathered what he could through his observations of medical students. Nathaniel Chapman's lecture on venereal diseases differed from the theories Horace had heard at Columbia: Chapman argued that unnamed irritants, not sexual intercourse, often encouraged gonorrhea. More generally, though, the disease occurred when males encountered females with leukorrhea, a whitish vaginal discharge. He found proof of this theory among Philadelphia patients, males "in the married state [who] suffered long from this cause in the wife." Because these men had obviously not strayed from fidelity, their wives were to blame.[44]

The atmosphere at this medical college was different from any he had previously encountered. Here students donned top hats, stomped their feet to signal appreciation during lectures, and applauded at the conclusion of each class. For Horace, the medical college was the sine qua non or the true university ideal, a place where the "éclat of lecturing" reached its fullest expression and academics became more than a profession. Professorial pay added even greater luster. Each session, close to five hundred students purchased $20 tickets from each of the college's professors, who averaged roughly $8,000 a year in annual salary, more than double that paid to Harris at Columbia.[45]

Investigations into the Medical College were interrupted by something Horace identified as an "obstruction" in his vision. A foreign body, which he took to be a hair caught in his right eye, appeared with no warning. His proximity to the best medical minds in the country, as he described them, was a fortunate coincidence. In search of a remedy, Horace called first on Dr. John Dorsey, the university's newly elected professor of anatomy. Dorsey deduced the obstruction to be a "co-agulated lymph" and recommended immediate treatment with a rinse of brandy and water.[46] When the eye became inflamed, Horace switched to a mixture of milk and water; when this failed, he sent for Dr. Phillip Physick, a professor of surgery and, according to Horace, "famous for curing diseases of the eye." Physick recommended an immediate bleeding to reduce the inflammation, a "dose of salts," and an eye wash regimen of rose water and soft bread to prevent further damage. He was instructed to eat only oatmeal gruel and to remain in complete darkness for three full days and nights to dissolve the offending particle.[47]

While recuperating, Horace busied himself with well-wishers and visits from Kentuckians who happened to be in the city. William Morton and Drs. Walter Brashear of Bardstown and Elisha Warfield of Lexington shared ties with Transylvania and came to reaffirm his faith in the position and, more importantly, to communicate the good will that Kentuckians shared concerning his appointment.[48] The timing of their visit was fortuitous. Since his departure, Mary had become increasingly concerned that her husband would actually take the position in Kentucky; she would be forced to leave family and friends behind and suffer the great unknowns of the western wilds. At first, she thought the issue would resolve itself in her favor. A few weeks after his departure, Boston newspapers reported that the Kentucky legislature had upended the Transylvania Board of Trustees. In a letter to her husband written the following day, Mary noted: "I should be sorry that bigotry should have such a triumph, & that you should be deprived of the opportunity of showing yourself disinterested, & independent, & not governed by mercenary motives. I feel easy now that you will not accept, but I am coquette enough to wish that you may have the power of refusing."[49] His response, written immediately upon the receipt of her letter, was likely received with disappointment. He confirmed that a change in the board had been made but corrected her misgivings about the implications of that change: "The meaning of this alteration is precisely the opposite of what is reported. It is designed to put down clerical bigotry, and to introduce a more catholic influence into the government of the institution." Opposition was now "turned out"; members of the new board were all "friends, and all laymen." Furthermore, the Kentuckians he met in Philadelphia assured him that he had the full backing of the people and that opposition would be "small and transient." He concluded, "There is no danger, my dear."[50] Importunate medical advice aside, Horace's visit to Philadelphia affirmed the support of the citizens of Kentucky and, in his observations of the state and the prestige of Philadelphia medicine, reaffirmed the place of collegiate medical training.

"The Baltimoreaus"

The road south took him first to Lancaster and then to York, Pennsylvania, by way of the mile-and-a-half-long covered bridge over the Susquehanna River—an impressive structure that he heard cost some $200,000.[51] The conditions of the roads improved the farther south he traveled, and he arrived in Baltimore after only a few days. The streets of the city were "delightful," and the scene, when viewed from atop a local church, interesting but not remarkable.[52] Though he would only stay in the city a few days, or as long as it would take to get a steamboat to Washington, his visit was productive. At Mrs. West's boardinghouse on South Gay Street, Horace was reunited with fellow Bostonian Thomas H. Perkins, a well-connected Massachusetts businessman who also happened to be passing through. Perkins did his best to keep Horace occupied, providing introductions to William Eaton, former U.S. ambassador to Tripoli; Robert Smith, former secretary of the navy and secretary of state under James Madison; Baltimore merchant Robert Oliver; and many others. Perkins was, in Horace's estimation, a "perfect gentleman," and he remained indebted to him for "an early acquaintance with many delightful people."[53]

"The Baltimoreaus," he remarked in this same letter to Mary on March 12, were "very polite to me, and prompt in their attentions."[54] Dinners and social gatherings at the homes of Baltimore's elite helped him evaluate the city's social characteristics and educational offerings. He met Charles Carroll, the former

Maryland state representative and one of the last surviving signers of the Declaration of Independence. More interesting was the composition of Baltimore
society. It had an unsettled nature; people were not yet grouped into classes, "as
in the older cities," the consequence perhaps of Baltimore's "rapid growth."[55] His
estimation of Baltimore's intellectual climate was based almost entirely on his
interactions with professors from the city's medical college. At William Eaton's
home, Horace was introduced to Drs. William Gibson and Elisha DeButts, both
on the medical faculty at the recently chartered University of Maryland. His
"considerable conversation" with Gibson about the state of the medical school
was no doubt revealing.[56]

Representatives from Baltimore's Unitarian church soon followed with "attentions" of their own. Their formal written note of introduction amused him
because it was made "quite in the style of a public character," an impersonal
touch from a young congregation. They invited him to preach the following
Sunday, but Horace thought better of it; the group did not have a meeting
space of their own and he did not like the idea of preaching in the Baltimore
city courthouse.[57]

Gadabouts and visits were welcome but taxing, and just three days after
his arrival in Baltimore Horace began to complain about a hectic social calendar. "I cannot do everything, be at home with my pen and paper, go out
to all public institutions, go to dinners and suppers, make calls, receive calls,
attend to acquaintances . . . eat, drink, sleep . . . and get to write to everybody
every day, or every week."[58] His mood was lifted somewhat by the thought of
meeting Elizabeth Patterson, the celebrated former wife of Napoleon's brother,
Jerome Bonaparte. Elizabeth, the daughter of a wealthy Baltimore merchant,
had established herself as one of Baltimore's most beautiful women by the time
of her marriage, attracting attention for her cosmopolitan elegance and intelligence as well as her penchant for low-cut, tight-fitting French clothing.[59] Yet
her marriage to Jerome on Christmas Eve in 1803 was doomed from the start.
Napoleon saw no political benefit in a marriage alliance with a Maryland family, considered it to be illegitimate, and refused to allow a now pregnant "Madame Bonaparte" to step foot on French soil. Jerome, despite his assurances to
Elizabeth to the contrary, eventually consented to his brother's wishes and was
granted a divorce by the French court.[60] The entire affair made for high drama
in American newspapers and caught Horace's attention. Now at age thirty-three

in 1818, Elizabeth lived alone with her twelve-year-old son, wealthy but mostly removed from the public eye.

The morning after Horace arrived, he recruited Perkins for some innocent sightseeing, and the two paced "up and down" Elizabeth's street in the hopes of catching a glimpse of the beautiful recluse. When they did, Horace examined "her figure and her walk" from a distance but made no attempt to introduce himself. The experience left him all the more desirous of a personal encounter; he would, as he noted in a letter to Mary, "take some pains" to win an introduction.[61] Most of Perkins's friends knew of Madame Bonaparte, but few knew her well enough to furnish him with a proper introduction. The problem was soon remedied by a chance meeting with Mrs. Groves, Patterson's former teacher, who agreed to make the introduction despite reservations that the relationship would not be remembered. The scheme worked, and Horace successfully arranged for a meeting the following day.

Patterson, as Horace recollected in a letter to Mary, was far from the "beau ideal" but possessed her own unique charms. She was "not tall [and was] inclined to corpulancy" but had "dark hair and eyes, a fine complexion and color, a small mouth, pretty lips, teeth not perfect, a finely formed chest, and an admirable play of face and features." She was both self-possessed and entertaining, reserved yet without the "stiffness" seen in other women of her status. Her anecdotes were delivered with "ease and eloquence." Horace was smitten.[62]

Patterson was also a Francophile without equal, correcting Horace on the "picture of French society" and French customs. The French, she boasted, were vastly superior to the English and their American descendants in every way. Where the English were "a dull, fat, heavy, and prejudiced race," prone to overeating and drinking, the French had "more vivacity, a better literature, more the art of conversation and society, [were] less prejudiced, and more temperate, and are happier and make others happier." They were also less inhibited sexually and more honest in their opinions of others, and they married not for political or economic gain, but for love. She repined her American birth and the lack of "finished society" found here. "Baltimore," she concluded, "is excessively dull and I am more than half the time oppressed with ennui and prey [sic] to go to sleep."[63]

Horace dismissed Elizabeth's maudlin temperament in the letter he wrote to Mary shortly after his visit. "She says that no one can be happy in America who has lived in Paris." But, according to Elizabeth, to be happy was to be beautiful, charming, and rich, to live in Paris, and, above all, to travel in the best circles.[64] It was an unrealistic opinion. He repeated these words in a letter he sent to Elizabeth herself only a few days after his departure from Baltimore. "Your definition of 'happiness' has made me laugh a thousand times," Horace chided. "Take out Paris, & you have all the other conditions of felicity. If you would not accuse me of too great freedom, I should say, there is something like ingratitude in a lady so much the favorite of beauty, wit, and fortune, so much admired and beloved, not being happy."[65]

But the letter was also scandalously flirtatious, even by Horace's standards. He began with a prolonged debate over how to properly address her, wondering if he should begin "My dear Madam," "Ma chere Madame," or the "beautiful Mrs Patterson." "I am quite at a loss," Horace surmised, "to know how you would receive any one of the forms, and therefore I have rejected them all, and written none, and mean to have the discussion of this question confined to my own breast." His words were meant not as criticism but as palliative for ennui: "even a dull employment is occasionally found to be, in a degree, a remedy for this evil." He reflected on his impressions of Gilbert Stuart's portrait, how much the "beauty and poetry" of Stuart's copy paled in comparison with the original. And he closed with a poem, "changing the name in the chorus" from hers to "Jeannette" for the sake of the rhyme. It began,

> Where shall we go to find a face,
> In which a faultless beauty shines,
> Where every charm has lent a grace,
> And every grace a love entwines?
> For such a portrait who shall set
> But beauty's self the fair Jeannette?[66]

Horace exchanged letters with other women he met on the trip, but none that was so overtly coquettish as this one. He included none of this communication with Elizabeth in his letter to Mary and wrote only to tell her she "had a new rival."[67]

Holy of Holies

In Washington, Horace came closer to realizing just how influential and politically important his presidency in Kentucky could become. Elite strangers,
congressmen, senators, foreign ambassadors, and even the president embraced
his designs. They had seen university presidents in the past, but Horace was
something different. As a leader of a progressive and inclusive stream of Christian thought, he represented a refreshing, perhaps revolutionary, alternative to
sectarian dogmatists who had limited the reach of education in the East and
frustrated Jefferson's ambitions for secular education in Virginia. Some hoped
his success could mean the end of sectarian inculcation and the start of a new,
more enlightened national trend.

Horace timed his arrival in Washington perfectly. With Congress in session,
he could visit the homes of political associates from Massachusetts and his new
political allies from Kentucky. Harrison Gray Otis, the longtime Massachusetts
senator, and Nathaniel Ruggles, a congressman from Massachusetts, opened
their Washington homes to Horace. Stephen Austin, Mary's cousin and longtime
friend, provided introductions to Josiah Meigs, the federal Land Office commissioner, and to Meigs's son-in-law, John Forsyth, a congressman from Georgia.
In the letter that accompanied these introductions, Austin correctly surmised
Horace would "no doubt have friends enough of [his] own"; he only wished for
him "to know some of mine & that they should know you."[68]

Otis and his wife, Sally, were especially helpful. "I am truly much indebted,"
Horace wrote to Mary only days after his arrival in Washington, "for their attentions and kindness, for the pleasure of being at their table, for the use of their
carriage to all the parties, for the offer of their horses at any other time, and for
various courtesies."[69] Otis seemed intent on introducing Horace to as many of
his Washington allies as possible. Morning calls to President James Monroe,
Henry Clay, John Quincy Adams, and Otis's friends in the House were some of
the first Horace made there.

The House and Senate chambers had been destroyed by fire in the recent
war and were still under construction at the time of Horace's visit. He found
their temporary accommodations "low, dark, dirty and unpleasant" but was
awed by the spectacle of congressional oratory.[70] Horace found Henry Clay's
three-hour argument for the creation of a U.S. ambassadorship in Argentina

"quite eloquent" but Georgia congressman George Forsythe's two-hour rebut-
tal "slow, self possessed, and cold." The visit also affirmed the fact that not all
elected officials were men of literary or oratorical skills. More than a few of the
representatives he met were there for no discernible reason. They sat "drawing
pictures . . . as a mode of killing time," never engaged in debate, never made use
of the congressional library to "extend their information," and became clouded
by prolonged periods of ennui broken only by nightly high-stakes card games.
Horace saw no great shame in this behavior, however, for "in a body so elected,
a few only can be men of distinguished talents."[71]

Henry Clay was curious but reserved. It was his first meeting with Horace,
and, as the newly elected head of the Transylvania Board of Trustees, he was
unsure how the Bostonian would fit. Clay asked Horace to preach before the
House of Representatives, perhaps as a test; if he could convince a room filled
with argumentative intellectuals from across the country, he would likely have
success in Kentucky. Horace agreed, and the sermon would take place a week
from his arrival. It was not long before his time was "well filled up" with social
calls. Thanks to Otis, he was "continually brought into contact with persons
whom [he] long wished to know."[72]

Dinners at the Otis house brought him the bipartisan attention of Federal-
ists and Democratic Republicans alike. Here, Vice President Daniel Tompkins;
Governor James Barour of Virginia; Senators Alexander Hanson (Maryland),
Eligius Fromentin (Louisiana), Rufus King (New York), and William Hunter
(Rhode Island); Representatives Nathaniel Terry (Connecticut), James Porter
(New York), and John Parrot (New Hampshire); as well as many other members of Washington's political elite engaged in polite conversation with Horace,
played chess, exchanged anecdotes, and discussed his plans for Kentucky. He was
thrown somewhat by the manner in which the politicians, judges, and military
officers addressed themselves at these events—referring to one another as "Mr.
Speaker," as in "Mr. Speaker, will you push the wine about?" or "Mr. Vice President, shall I have the honor of a glass of wine with you?"—and for the most part
the politicians made terrible dinner companions. They were on the whole too
reserved or too guarded to discuss anything of interest—only when the toasts
began and the wine flowed did the group lose its solemnity.[73]

Anecdotes, told in the intoxicated afterglow of dinner, could be amusing
and instructive. One story in particular, shared by Otis, interested Horace so

much that he recorded it in a letter to Mary. Some years earlier Richard Derby, the son of a wealthy Massachusetts shipping family, had desired an appointment to the foreign embassy in England. He traveled to Washington to seek out Otis, Hanson, King, and others he believed could influence the appointment. Yet his manner of pursuing the position "was almost incredible" as he defied every convention of taste and etiquette. In his quest to make their acquaintance, Derby would invite himself to their private dinners, "crowd" himself into their tables at local taverns, and "smuggle" himself home in their carriages. At first, his presence was only a passing nuisance. "At Crawford's at Georgetown," Horace related, "where Mr King, Mr Otis, Mr Hanson, and others were, [Mr. Derby] was turned out not forcibly but by orders given to the innkeeper to tell Mr Derby the table was private and no gentleman admitted but by invitation." When this restriction failed, they made sharper reproofs. "[Mr. Derby] put his head into Mr King's carriages one evening at a party and said, 'Ah well, you have three spare seats here; you will be glad to have me take one, won't you?' Mr King immediately said to the coachman, 'George, drive on, drive on.'" And when Derby wheedled his way into a party held by Colonel Benjamin Hawkins, the longtime agent for Indian Affairs, the company was more than slightly annoyed. Michigan's territorial governor Lewis Cass "roasted him sadly," and Derby went away disgraced. The story was cautionary, "showing the extent of idiocy, ambition, and avarice in his mind."[74]

Other engagements were slightly more convivial. Foreign dignitaries, a usual sight at the homes of Otis and his friends, left an impression. The scenes were sometimes exotic, often confusing, but almost always memorable. The wife of French ambassador Jean-Guillaume, Baron Hyde de Neuville, amused him with her French accent. "She said to a lady, 'You must put on de close, or you will be frozed.' At another time . . . 'In Vashington in de summer, de hot be very strong.'"[75] Spanish ambassador Luis de Onís y González-Vara made a colorful spectacle, wearing "all his stars and crosses on his breast at the party." British ambassador Charles Bagot was an "Englishman in his taste for angling and shooting." J. S. ten Cate, the Dutch chargé d'affaires, sang "extremely well" in his duet with the Spanish ambassador's daughter. The same, however, could not be said of Chinese ambassador Punqua Winchong, who, "with his Chinese costume and his queer hat," attempted an authentic rendition of a Chinese song. The company burst into laughter so boisterous Horace was certain the man took offense.[76]

Acceptance of Horace in polite society was guaranteed by Otis, yet only after Horace's sermon did the "distinguished" gentleman of Washington take notice of him. Most newspapers of Massachusetts proudly carried news of the event; a short essay printed in the *Essex Register* made the request to speak seem almost an afterthought. Horace's "elegant manners and distinguished talents" were certainly worthy of notice, for "the eloquence and elocution of this worthy man excite attention in every place he visits."[77] The service was crowded, and Horace's experience was exhilarating. It was the "most intelligent audience" he had addressed, and he gave them the best of what he had. He preached that day, as he normally did, "extemporaneously" or "off the top of heads," using only an outline to guide himself in the finer points. The purpose was, as he later explained in a letter to James Freedman, to "illustrate the reality, truth and importance of religion independently of authority of a written revelation."

His sermon was "calculated to ... remove prejudices, to illustrate the great principles of morality and religion ... and to promote a useful Catholicism."[78] He had delivered this sermon perhaps a dozen times before his trip to Washington; he would deliver it at least a half-dozen times more before he returned to Boston. It began with a comparative summary of the Trinity, how Christian sects interpreted the doctrine and how these differences masked essential truths. Sectarian division, Horace maintained, was based on misinterpretation and misguided bigotry. He then transitioned to other imagined points of friction, concluding that abstract metaphysical quandaries, the root cause of division, were immaterial to the first principals of Christian morality—the love of God, love of neighbors, charity, and good works. It was an uncomplicated point delivered with an eloquence, lucidity, and verve that left many convinced, or at least satisfied, that he was orthodox, or orthodox enough.

As he left the rostrum, he was met by a crowd of impressed well-wishers to share some "agreeable chat." Three former classmates—Secretary of War John C. Calhoun, Congressmen Thomas Hubbard of New York and William Lowndes of South Carolina—seemed especially thrilled at Horace's performance and called on him that night to reminisce "over college scenes." Days later he must have beamed as he wrote of the "considerable impression" his sermon left on the assembled audience. "Some of the members of Congress have applied to me to have it printed," he boasted to Mary—this would be impossible of course, but the compliment was appreciated nonetheless.[79] He struck a more modest tone with friend James Freeman, writing to him, "I hope and am led to believe, that a good impression was made."[80] The following day Otis appeared at Horace's door and confirmed his success when he announced, "Sir, I give you joy." Earlier that day Virginia governor James Barbour had passed Otis a letter of introduction for Horace's visit to President Monroe. It seemed all of Washington was opening before him.

But the sermon also caught the attention of Protestant leaders throughout the city. Episcopal minister William Wilmer, pastor of St. John's Church, denounced Horace as a "false prophet in sheep's clothing."[81] And Horace was aware of others preaching against him—for instance, an unnamed "narrow minded man" who warned his parishioners about Horace's novel philosophies and untoward behavior. Horace expressed concern not that so many now found him objectionable but that so many "small minded men" had entered his profession. "The community," he wrote in a letter to Mary, "could be more benefited . . . by an enlightened and truly liberal clergy. . . . [W]e have too many fools among us, and those who, if they are not fools, if they have a knowledge of books, still have no just knowledge of human nature and of the powers and wants of the human mind."[82]

But criticisms seemed only to enhance his standing with his new political allies. Henry Clay and his Kentucky contingent were pleased by his sentiments. Wealthy Lexington merchant Richard Higgins was so impressed that he promised him "one of the best saddle horses in the world to go to any part of the state" and other extravagant hospitalities upon his arrival. Kentucky congressman Joseph Desha told Horace that his religious feelings were his own, that they would "suit the great majority of Kentuckians perfectly."[83] Most of the other representatives of Kentucky agreed that he was certain to meet some resistance but that this opposition would be "feeble and transient."[84] The only Kentuckian to voice caution was Margaret Talbot, wife of Kentucky senator Isham Talbot. Margaret, a Roman Catholic from the West Indies, had experienced religious bigotry in Kentucky and claimed Horace would find the same, that he "should not be contented there" if he settled. Horace dismissed her warnings as importunate Catholic grousing. Catholics, he wrote, were not contented in any part of the country where their "own mode of worship" was not found.[85]

His new Kentucky friends became even more availing of their time and attentions after his sermons; Horace dined with Henry Clay no less than half a dozen times in the weeks that followed. At these dinners, he met a motley crew of the war hawk's favorite military heroes: famed Indian fighter General William Henry Harrison; Commodore Stephen Decatur, the youngest captain in the U.S. Navy; and Colonel Luke E. Lawless, a pioneering member of Legion Irlandaise, the Irish liberation army that had fought under the direction of Napoleon.

Dinners at Clay's house were decadent, eleven-course meals featuring roasted mutton, oyster pies, duck, macaroni, jellies, and pudding. Clay no doubt made a fascinating host, regaling visitors with his recent trip to Europe. He told the group about a dinner with Horace's favorite literary icons—a laconic Lord Byron, a loquacious Walter Scott, and the celebrated Madame Germaine de Staël. De Staël, Clay blithely observed, was "certainly not a Bourbonite, if she were not a Buonapartist."[86] Though she benefitted from the wealth of the court of Louis XVI and was nearly a victim of the September massacres, she became an ardent defender of the American-style democracy in her later years.

Others frequented Clay's table, but it was Horace, Luke Lawless, Stephen Decatur, and Clay who did "the principal part of the talking." Decatur shared information concerning Commodore Matthew Perry's impending duel with John Heath. Perry had slapped Heath on a recent expedition to Italy and demanded satisfaction. "Perry," Decatur noted, "will fight Heath, not so much on account of the man himself, but out of regard to the navy and to finish the atonement for an outrage which neither he nor his friends ever thought of justifying."[87] Luke Lawless, now a resident of St. Louis, was no stranger to dueling. A dispute over personal honor in France had left him with a limp that noticeably impaired his walk.[88] Despite his propensities to violence, Lawless was, Horace surmised, "an accomplished man and talks with taste and elegance."[89] William Henry Harrison, however, was "a dark looking man" with "straight hair like an Indian." Harrison seemed determined to introduce a proposal for a federally funded system of military schools that would combine an emphasis on physical health with a rigorous education in science. The late war showed that military training was nearly impossible unless begun at a young age. Horace applauded the idea, not for the martial character it might give to schools but for the discipline that it was certain to inspire.

Excitement about Horace continued to build over the remaining weeks of his visit. The "cheerful and accessible" Rufus King, whom Horace considered "the great man of this place [Washington]," tried his best to convince him to take the appointment.[90] The East, King concluded, was too fixed and offered no opportunities for change; the atmosphere in Kentucky was "plastick" because "the mind is kept on the alert."[91] Nathaniel Pope, a congressional delegate from the Illinois territory, wooed Horace with stories of the frontier West's growth and industry. Longtime friend Charles Bulfinch, one of the principal architects of the Capitol building, excitedly told Horace of favorable reports published about him in a Baltimore newspaper. Mississippi congressman George Poindexter promised to send his son to Lexington, seven hundred miles from the family home in Natchez, if Horace took the presidency.[92] And Secretary of the Treasury William H. Crawford, currently in the midst of fighting his own "dirty sectarian spirit" in Georgia, hoped that Horace could recommend a like-minded man for the presidency of their state university.[93] "All the accounts and advice, which I have received concerning my appointment in Lexington, are to induce me to accept of it," Horace noted in a letter to James Freeman. "Every man I meet, excepting those from Boston and its vicinity, say, 'accept.'"[94]

President Monroe was now also convinced of Horace's abilities, and during a planned meeting, both agreed that the best way to ensure harmony in education was to stabilize the influence of competing religious positions. In this way, denominations would "check and balance each other, that no one should get power enough to absorb or crush the others." "Authority," Horace added, "should be kept in the hands of a civil government"; theological "expostulation & remonstrance" should be left to the pulpit. Only in a climate of religious toleration and acceptance could the nation guarantee civil liberties. Monroe was, according to Horace, in perfect agreement with him, although Horace did add, "These are my own sentiments, and I have long been convinced of their soundness and importance. Leave the sects free and let them correct each other."[95]

A slew of invitations to dinner, parties, and other social gatherings now came daily. "Tomorrow evening is Mrs Adams's; saturday evening Mrs de Neuville's; monday evening Mrs Bagot's; tuesday evening Mrs Taylor's; and wednesday evening Mrs Munroe's; and then," Horace added in exhaustion, "I go away."[96] The Adams's dinner was "handsomely spread"; plaster busts of Greek gods and goddesses surrounded solid silver wine carafes, dessert knives, and forks.[97] One evening at the home of William Crawford, Horace was treated to French delicacies courtesy of Crawford's personal French cook.[98] At the home of British ambassador Charles Bagot, guests were announced as they entered the room.

Servants dressed "in livery" embroidered with blue and white cords, and they served an assortment of exotic appetizers.[99]

It was the toniest affair of the journey. Gentlemen were in "full dress" and well tailored. "I do not remember seeing a single pair of loose pantaloons," Horace noted. The women that evening were equally stunning. Mary Charlotte Bagot, the ambassador's wife, wore a gown of white silk "interwoven with flowers," satin shoes, and a gold turban. She had a "faultless" shape, and her bust was, Horace recalled, "the beau ideal for the artist to study." The same, however, could not be said of some of her guests. Mary Hunter, wife of Vermont congressman William Hunter, was "a faded belle, without that kind of cultivation, sentiment, or manners which ought to supply interest when youth and beauty are gone." Susanna Crawford, wife of Secretary of the Treasury William Crawford, was "a very plain woman, without accomplishment." Mrs. Calhoun was "very small and very ugly," an "uneducated country girl" with "no conversation." And a certain "Miss Forrest" had a skull "shaped like some of those heads in the transition from the monkey to the human in the plate that you have seen . . . in medical books."[100]

The mood of these dinners was more convivial than he expected. Wine flowed a little longer, guests stayed later, and the stories were more risqué. On one occasion, he learned of a tawdry affair involving New Hampshire senator Clement Storer. "There are committee rooms near to the hall of the senate [sic] and the House of Representatives," the story began. Outside the committee rooms were young women, some very attractive, selling fruit and liquors to members of Congress. When representatives found that one of the committee rooms had been locked from the inside, they knocked "importunately" and waited to see who might appear. When the door opened, Storer and a young girl came out, "having been there to make some bargain about fruit, as the story goes," Horace added wryly.[101]

Philadelphia was evidence of what medical education could bring to the dignity of a college, and Washington impressed him with an even greater significance. In one of his last letters before departing the capital, he presented a concise summary of his successes to Mary. He enjoyed easy access to the most distinguished houses in America, mixed easily with "republican and temporary royalty," and left assured that his prospects in Kentucky could only bring more esteem and respectability on a national stage. "The table which was uncomfortably high for me when I was a boy," Horace concluded, "I sit at now with ease & eat from . . . without anxiety."[102]

Theological dissimilarities in New York, New Jersey, and Philadelphia made a compelling case for a more interdenominational religious training, yet these same conditions also made his theology a target for his enemies. Protestant churches along his path gave him a mixed reception, treating him with either suspicion or outright contempt—Baltimore's churches refused even to acknowledge his presence. Trouble was also brewing at home. Shortly after his departure from Washington, Mary warned him of machinations by "the great E Ely," Calvinist Philadelphian minister Ezra Stiles Ely, who had recently published invectives against her husband in the *Quarterly Theological Review*. The first essay, a review of an oration delivered by the Reverenced Joshua Bates, president of Middlebury College, raged against the "Socinian of Massachusetts." "Mr. Holley is a bag of wind," Ely wrote. He "emits his poisonous breath, like the serpent which charms its victim, to benumb those faculties of the youthful mind."[103] He is also "fierce for moderation" yet "outrageously mad for liberality" and particularly dangerous in any position that brings him into contact with youths. The West Lexington Presbytery of Kentucky had thus grievously erred in their passive acceptance of Horace as president of Transylvania; Kentucky Presbyterians and laity were now certain to fall under his Socinian spell. Ely appealed for Kentuckians to send Calvinist pastors to fill this position lest the "fountain of science in Kentucky to be poisoned with rampant Socinianism." Another essay-length review inserted Horace into a discussion of Kentucky's confused religious atmosphere. Several unnamed "Bostonians" of his persuasion had, according to Ely, removed to Kentucky and prepared the way for "a religion like that of Mr. Holley." "We cannot wish success," he concluded, "[and] we think it the curse of God, sent to Kentucky."[104]

For now, Horace thought of such comments as hurtful but limited reactions from an unenlightened few. A complete resolution of the disagreement was impossible, but a tenuous balance might be found. "A few clergymen of each denomination," he wrote to Mary, "and especially those who are most jealous of me, should be introduced into a connection with the college" to set them at odds with one another.[105] In other words, conflict could be avoided by creating a logjam of disagreeing sectarian theologies—pitting Presbyterians against Methodists against Baptists. The road ahead would not sway him from his course.

Genuine Virginian

Horace's trip south proceeded by way of Mt. Vernon, Virginia, in mid-April. The estate, now owned by Washington's nephew, Supreme Court Justice Bushrod Washington, was unused, and the main house was empty for much of the year.[106] The road up to the house badly needed repairs, and buildings were neglected for most of the year and falling into shambles; the gardener, a "paralytic" named "Old Ellis," one of the president's former slaves, remained on the property but was not of much use. The house itself was "cheap and perishable and awkward"; oddly arranged rooms and slipshod construction took something out of the enjoyment of the visit. Nevertheless, the "sacredness of [Washington's] character and memory" forced itself on his mind as he walked the grounds or was led through the house by its resident servants.[107]

Woodlawn, a thousand-acre tract of the Mt. Vernon estate, was considerably more genteel. After his death in 1799, George Washington had willed the property to his nephew Lawrence Lewis and Lewis's wife, Nelly, granddaughter of Martha Washington. Lewis lived on the proceeds from his estate and was, as his wife described him, a "genuine Virginian," a man disinclined for business who wanted only "to have plenty of servants for every purpose." Horace found him a "plain, amiable, mild, sensible, and respectable looking man" and considered the property gorgeous, filled with "jonquils, daffodils, hyacinth, and other flowers now in full bloom." The home was well appointed, comfortable, and, more importantly, full of items once dear to the president: furniture, candlesticks, china, pictures, and the shoe buckles Washington had saved for special occasions. That night Horace slept under a quilt that had remained on the president's bed for years.[108]

A long, dreary coach ride to Charlottesville ended in disappointment. Jefferson was no longer at Monticello; he had left only days earlier for a visit to Poplar Forest, his summer home eighty miles south of town. Undeterred, Horace remained committed to seeing the plantation and to visit the home of James Madison along the way. His visit to Monticello was satisfactory enough. But after dining with members of Jefferson's family, he chose not to travel south and see the former president in person. Jefferson later mentioned his disappointment at missing him. His family, Jefferson noted in a letter to John Adams, was quite impressed with Horace. He was pleased that Horace had chosen to take up the cause of "rational Christianity" in Kentucky, for there it would "thrive more rapidly" than in Virginia. Kentuckians were "freer from prejudices than we are, and bolder in grasping all Truth." "The time is not distant," he concluded, "when we shall be but a secondary people to them." The greediness and excessive taste for luxury in the East was eroding the character and poisoning the "minds" of "our maritime citizens."[109] Adams's response was complimentary of Horace but slightly less so to the West: if Horace were to succeed in the cause of rational Christianity in the West, he would indeed be a "light shining in a dark place."[110]

From Monticello, Horace decided on a northern route by way of the Ohio River rather than continuing south through the Cumberland Gap. This route would of course add hundreds of miles to his trip but allow him to investigate Pittsburgh, Cincinnati, and other prosperous river cities.[111] Added to the frustrations of missed opportunities, the slow pace of travel, and the costs of a new route were troubling letters from Mary. Relocating to Lexington would, she claimed, bring irreconcilable woe.[112] When in late February, word had come that the Transylvania Board of Trustees was in the throes of another sectarian struggle, her fears had subsided. Horace had written to allay her concerns, but this response had only brought new worries for his safety. "I fear you will suffer from the badness of the roads as you advance," she wrote as he made his way to Philadelphia.[113] "It would be dreadful if you were to get sick so far off," she cautioned as he continued on to Baltimore.[114] The gravity of her suffering seemed to be matched by that of Horace's devoted Hollis Street parishioners. Members Nathan Davis and newlyweds Josiah and Eunice Gould thought the world might descend into permanent darkness should Horace leave them for Kentucky.[115]

Mary's mood had improved in the intervening weeks, and she even joked that her recent bouts with depression were likely the result of her pregnancy. Twins, she reasoned, must be the cause of her suffering. This joking was mitigated somewhat by an abrupt and oddly placed closing: "They say the Kentuckians, tho they offer a great salary, will never pay. That it is not their fashion to pay their debts."[116] Some seventy days into his trip, she experienced a depression so severe that she feared for her life. Their family physician, Dr. Jackson, attributed it to the sudden onset of warm weather, recommended against bleeding, and said only that she should keep calm and silent.[117] But the illness worsened, grown stronger now by Horace's successes in Washington and the certainty that he would take her from Boston. "Perhaps," she wondered, "it is a consciousness amounting almost to conviction . . . that the approaching event is to be the period of my existence. I prepare for it as I should prepare for my funeral!"[118] To make matters worse, their daughter, Harriette, was now home with what her doctor believed to be the chicken pox. Her sickness required all of Mary's attentions and exhausted what little strength she had left.[119] Horace's responses were conciliatory but resolute. He would refrain from judgment about the position until he reached Lexington, was sorry for her illness, and promised a speedy return as soon as he accomplished his business.

The muddy roads and icy cold of the Shenandoah trail, the constant fording of streams, and the absence of bridges were difficult but did not detract from Virginia's rolling landscape, fecund fields, strange animals, and remarkable geology.[120] What most interested Horace were the people of the South and acts of "attention" that he had never seen in the Northeast. Jacob Reamer, innkeeper of a tavern in Woodstock, Virginia, offered Horace a free map of "roads, distances, and public houses." In the town of Strasburg, a slave from the home of "an old Dutchman named Stover" came down to the carriage with a plate of crackers and "a decanter of cherry bounce," a tradition that evidently went back twenty-five years. Southerners were always amiable, always ready with a joke or an anecdote, and had a more refined, genteel sensibility than he found in the East.[121] "Gentlemen," Horace wrote, "speak of each other with more mildness and respect in this part of the country than among us."[122]

Horace's spirits recovered somewhat after reaching Pittsburgh. "All the world" seemed to be there when Horace arrived in mid-May 1818. The town resembled New York from atop a nearby hill. Streets bustled with activity despite a cold, wet rain that brought down coal soot from the air. The effect was immediate. "Everything," Horace commented, was "blackened by the smoke & soot of coal." Pittsburgh was indeed a "dirty looking place." But where the scenery disappointed, the company almost certainly did not; Kentuckians were everywhere. "Every time I go down from my chamber or come in from the street, I am introduced to some Kentuckian newly arrived." The Kentuckians were cordial and treated him as though he were already a native. They also shared his distaste for dirty Pittsburgh and promised that, in comparison, Lexington was "as neat as a bandbox."[123]

From Pittsburgh, the trip continued along the Ohio on a flat-bottom boat. Here he joined nearly a dozen other passengers and six horses on a journey that was, by his accounts, tedious and unremarkable save for the occasional "sawyer" or felled tree that would nick the bottom of the boat.[124] Accommodations were poor, to say the least. Sleep was infrequent and short in duration when it came. The temperature on board was either too hot or too cold and compelled him to remain in the same clothes and boots for the entire trip. His straw mattress did "tolerably well" in accommodating his sleep, though it provided no lack of aches. Worst yet, at the estimated four- or five-mile pace of the current, the five-hundred-mile trip would take at least seven days—that is, if the weather did not cause the boat to run aground. River passage down the Ohio would "be very uncomfortable for a lady," he cautioned.[125]

He entertained himself with observations of the "manners and character" of the people he met. Kentuckians seemed a particularly resourceful people. When the sun began to tan him, his "Kentucky companions" suggested he fashion a wearable parasol by cutting and attaching a sheet of heavy cardboard to his hat.[126] With this contrivance, he was "as well defended as a Chinese mandarin." When the boat stopped for supplies on the shore near one Kentucky village, Horace experienced his first taste of Kentucky hospitality. After purchasing milk from the "fine large matron" of a local tavern, he noticed bread baking on a nearby fire. When he asked for some, the woman replied, "Stranger, take as much as you wish, for thank God we have corn enough. Will you have butter and white bread?"[127]

"The Field Is Wider"

After disembarking at Maysville, Kentucky, on May 24, Horace turned south and, now on horseback, headed down the well-traveled Maysville Road. In the town of Paris, he was accompanied by an assortment of genteel company, all sharing their excitement in the university's prospects.[128] The next day, Henry Clay, Senator John Crittenden, and a crowd of Lexingtonians greeted his arrival at Sanford Keene's boardinghouse. Promises of good will and support continued, as did assurances that opposition was insignificant.[129] Even the town was better than he imagined. In his first letter home from Lexington, Horace described Transylvania's campus as the best he had ever seen and the surrounding homes as equally tasteful and beautiful. There were also more New England transplants than he expected, evidenced in the town's music, fashions, and gentility.[130]

The next morning he awoke to find thirteen letters from Mary, Harriette, Thomas Freedman, and others that had been delivered to the Lexington post office. He had, of course, precious little time to respond. Too many people demanded his attentions, and there was too much to see. A tour of the town's Athenaeum gave evidence of culture, but the university was in a depressed state, despite a record number of matriculates. Transylvania's library reminded him of the one at Columbia College: there were few books and fewer students who took notice of them. There was a scientific apparatus for experimentation, but it was similarly inadequate. It was not long before he uncovered other challenges. Students, he discovered, were not arranged by class, and there was an almost complete lack of student regulations. But these problems only bolstered his spirits and convinced him that the university was an empty vessel waiting to be filled. "Almost the whole is proposed to be left to me to arrange," he bragged to Mary.[131]

Transylvania's trustees promised a liberal annual salary of $3,000 and agreed to bring the school's library and laboratory up to his standards and to place most everything else, including laws and curriculum, under his direct authority. It is worth noting that Horace's salary brought him in line with or ahead of his contemporaries at Harvard, Yale, and the College of New Jersey. It was also significantly more than the sum paid to Kentucky governor Gabriel Slaughter.[132] But perhaps the greatest influence on his decision was the Kentuckians' hopefulness. Even long-standing and bitter rivals in politics and religion joined in unanimous support of him.[133] Horace gave sermons to divided congregations and impressed even the harshest and most bigoted men.[134] Presbyterian minister Adam Rankin was the first of a series of ministers to give their blessings. Yet when James McCord, minister of Lexington's Second Presbyterian Church, asked Horace to give a sermon at the church, it was not without some consternation. He was determined to have Horace preach but was frightened that the Presbyterian General Assembly might condemn him for it. It was a regrettable situation, Horace lamented, for "the fear of that Assembly is a great check upon the independence and inquiry of the clergymen belonging to its jurisdiction."[135]

His extemporaneous manner of speaking and nonthreatening, somewhat ambiguous appeals to common Christian orthodoxy seemed to pacify his opponents.[136] A published report of his sermon in Lexington's Episcopal church was favorable. Horace Holley, the author began, "gave us a very learned, luminous, and interesting exposition of . . . those views, which are entertained by the orthodox christians [*sic*] of all sects, and which are embraced by himself. . . . [H]e differs in no material respect from the great body of christians in the U. States." Lexington's Protestant clergymen "declared themselves entirely satisfied . . . and are willing to give him the right hand of fellowship as a brother Christian."[137]

Kentucky's Baptist congregations seemed just as pleased. There was a division in their church, Horace noted, one side headed by Jeremiah Vardeman, the other by Ambrose Dudley. They disagreed over matters of their own faith but reached common ground on their appreciation of his appointment; both agreed to send their sons to Transylvania should he accept the position. Governor Slaughter, a member of Vardeman's congregation, gave Horace his unqualified approval and held out a compelling offer. If Horace agreed to assume the presidency, Slaughter would recommend that the state legislature increase the state's level of "patronage" to the school. Stories of sectarian division and opposition appeared to have been exaggerated. None opposed him, and everything appeared to be in harmony.[138]

By this point, Mary may have opened each letter expecting confirmation of his acceptance. And when the news came in a letter penned on June 15, it came with a flourish as Horace attached personal ambition to moral responsibility. "I believe," he began, "it is in my power to do more good in this region than in any other, at this moment. My life has not been half as useful in Boston, though it has been of great value there, as I am persuaded it will be in Lexington." Parishioners at Hollis Street would surely concur, for the "field is wider, the harvest more abundant, and the grain of a most excellent quality."[139] To reject his call was to give in to cowardice. Mary responded with an uncommon degree of forbearance, if not acceptance. "My mind," she confirmed, "has become somewhat accustomed to the idea & I am ready to bear the challenge." Yet members of the congregation would not be easily pacified, she stated. When he returned to Boston, he should expect to find profound suffering and despair among those most loyal to him.[140]

The Academic

Horace's tour of eastern cities and eventual visit to Lexington confirmed his expectations. Each stop assured him that sectarian differences, however prevalent nationally, could be managed and in most cases smoothed over in

Lexington. Regional manners of speech, dress, and appetite varied, but religious fanaticism—that blind devotion to unexamined dogma—was everywhere. It therefore was his duty and obligation to bring light to the dark places of the world. Lexington was an inchoate mass of opportunity and untapped potential that could be easily directed with just the right combination of leadership and moral authority. As the president of Transylvania, Horace could also groom a generation of rational Christians, young men loyal not to denominational creed but to a more logical approach to religion. Equally compelling were the ways society related to this new position. A college presidency opened new worlds of social opportunity in New York and Philadelphia and offered greater national relevance in Washington. He was part of a shared national impulse but also set apart by an uncommon intellectual gravitas. Senators, congressmen, and even President Monroe recognized and admired him in ways ministers could not understand.

Horace's journey also framed his perception of higher education. He found, for example, that language, theology, and other hallmarks of a liberal arts education were now somewhat muted by an emphasis on scientific inquiry and experimentation. Furthermore, he recognized that the energy, sophistication, and indeed dignity of a university were merely an extension of its resources and curriculum. The medical college at the University of Pennsylvania gave elegant testimony to this fact, just as the regular classes at Columbia showed the deleterious effects of inertia and apathy. Harvard and Yale recognized the trend and opened medical schools in response—both were almost immediately successful. Medical training was therefore the most authentic expression of an eastern-style higher education and would be the easiest way for Horace to build Transylvania into an institution of national esteem. Kentuckians, it seems, either significantly underplayed or simply ignored brewing discontent in their rosy predictions of unanimity. In time, complications and confrontations would undermine Horace's efforts, but not before he carried out at least some of his ideals.

4

"A New Era of Literature"

Horace returned to Boston in mid-August and prepared for the awkward task of disillusionment or the formal resignation and release from Hollis Street. Seated before church leadership, he begged leave to take a position already accepted, insisting that this new appointment possessed a deeper, more magnanimous significance. It was, Horace repeated, out of an obligation of duty, a belief in the potential usefulness of the cause, that he move forward. The wider field of opportunity in an emerging part of the country, the necessity of encouraging right religion among newly settled, uncultured inhabitants, gave the mission an air of benevolence.[1] His congregation was probably unsurprised by the request; Lexington's *Kentucky Gazette* had already published word of his decision on June 26, and New England newspapers had repeated the information weeks later.[2] Boston's *Invisible Rambler* hailed his election as "the commencement of an era of Philosophy, Reason and Free Inquiry in the West"; for the *Boston Commercial Gazette,* Horace's presidency represented "a new era of literature" in America's remote wilderness.[3] Some congregants of Hollis Street agreed, responding with reluctant but firm acquiescence. His attachments, they declared, were long-standing, their affections deep and resolved.

In his official letter of release, members of the laity expressed their "pain and reluctance" of acceding to the request. Horace, they opined, was both teacher and pastor, praised for the peace and tranquility that he carried into the parish, a message rooted in spiritual equanimity and strident moralism. Some considered him one of Boston's strongest intellects, but they also reveled in the importance of his plans and vowed best wishes for his good fortune.[4] Over the course of his nine years at Hollis Street Church, Horace had presided at more than 280 funerals, 359 marriages, and more than 500 baptisms of infants, youths, and adults.[5] Even years later friends in Boston would turn to him for assistance in family disputes or for advice.[6] One parishioner was so moved he commissioned a portrait of Horace by Gilbert Stuart and refused to part with it.[7]

Equally dismayed but similarly impressed were the members of Horace's cherished Wednesday Evening Club, the American Academy of Arts, the Athenaeum, and the Boston School Committee, the latter reluctantly ending Horace's term after only two years. Friends could continue associations and vicariously experience his sacrifice through the exchange of letters and, more importantly, scholarship. Attorney John Davis and Dr. J. C. Warren, Horace's associates in the Wednesday Evening Club, sent along a supply of favorite works: Winthrop and Oliver's *Lectures on Comets*, George Adams's *Essay on Electricity*, Pierre Bulliard's *Dictionnaire élémentaire de botanique*, and other tomes for his edification or to be placed in the school library.[8] Judge Joseph Story participated in a similar exchange in the hopes that distance would not "break up the very pleasant and friendly intercourse of years."[9]

Civilizing the West

The whole of Boston, it seemed, followed their example, giving up their beloved minister for the more pressing concerns of the western wilds.[10] It was a sacrifice they were perhaps compelled to make. By 1818, the established Northeast contrasted sharply with the heavily peopled but newly settled West, a place where cultures, customs, and politics conflated in an enigmatic mix. To some, Kentucky was America personified. Thomas Jefferson believed the state preserved the emergent republic, a territory at once independent and interconnected, built of the same lofty idealism that stoked the "Spirit of '98" and precipitated the fall of Adams's Federalists. Jefferson's Kentucky Resolutions, the constitutional challenge to the Alien and Sedition Acts of 1798, used the state's celebrated autonomy as a basis for definitive action. In Kentucky, Jefferson also found a defense against European pretention. When the celebrated French naturalist Comte de Buffon promoted the idea that the America West was deleterious to mental and physical development, Jefferson commissioned an expedition to Kentucky to document prehistoric evidence of giant mammoths and mastodons.

Others were less laudatory in their assessments of the area. Even now, some fifteen years after the Louisiana Purchase of 1803, Kentucky remained a wild, untamed, "dark and bloody ground," the land of Indian traders, tax dodgers, religious bigots, and savage white hunters as ready to scalp as be scalped.[11] The "full-blooded Kentuckian" was, according to popular lore, aggressive by nature, given to excess across a range of self-satisfying behaviors.[12] Here, individual autonomy was so pervasive it threatened the very stability of American union. In the late 1780s, secessionist agents in the Spanish conspiracy worked to remove the territory from federal control. In 1794, U.S. military officers suppressed tax rebellions in western Pennsylvania but hesitated to press the issue in Kentucky for fear of inciting an uncontrollable reaction.[13] Aaron Burr's visit to the state aroused no small amount of suspicion, and in 1805 he was accused of agitating unpredictable Kentuckians into preemptive war with Spain.[14] The state's rough-and-ready, mythically aggressive nature reached its height during the War of 1812, when enthusiasms for war swept Kentucky youths into military service. The state's militia experienced a disproportionate share of total American casualities and became known for bellicosity.[15] British soldiers believed Kentuckians to be "wretches suborned by the Government and capable of the greatest villainies." They were, one British officer argued, "the most barbarous, illiterate beings in America."[16]

Recent news out of Lexington might have confirmed the worst impressions. In 1817, faculty in Transylvania's Medical Department began a quarrel that degenerated to a pamphlet war and ultimately a duel. Professors Daniel Drake and Benjamin Dudley clashed repeatedly over breaches of professional etiquette. Drake criticized Dudley for teaching outside his field.[17] Dudley accused Drake of the criminal mishandling of an autopsy and of attempting to bring ruin to the department.[18] The argument grew out of control, and Drake eventually engaged not Dudley but Dudley's friend, Professor of Obstetrics William Richardson, in a pistol duel—Drake shot Richardson in the leg but then saved him through the prompt application of a tourniquet.[19] A truncated version of the affair enjoyed wide circulation in newspapers of the Northeast;[20] readers might not have any familiarity with Kentucky or Transylvania but knew that two of its *scholars* had engaged in a violent, nearly lethal confrontation.

There were also the more recent problems involving Robert Bishop and Ebenezer Sharpe. Bishop, Transylvania's testy, cantankerous, sometimes abusive professor of natural philosophy and history, objected to Horace's appointment because of professional disappointment, which he clothed in orthodox opposition.[21] He had long desired to be the head of the institution and was angry at the state's takeover of the school, an unsurprising position, perhaps, as he was also a member of Kentucky's Presbyterian Synod. Soon after Horace's election in 1817, Bishop began casting about for new opportunities.[22] When it was clear that none existed, he wrote to the university's trustees to protest his subordinate position to Horace: "I am a plain Republican, and therefore speak plainly. Whatever may be the talents and acquirements of our new president, it is a most degrading thought—a thought under which no mind which has any sense of independence can act with vigor—that his services to the institution as compared to mine should be considered by the Board as three to one. . . . If the Board wish me to act with spirit and feel as a man when attempting to discharge my duty as a professor, I must be placed immediately, as to salary, on an equality with the president."[23]

Ebenezer Sharpe, Transylvania's professor of dead languages,[24] resigned shortly after Horace's appointment, claiming his decision had everything to do with the mysterious and unknown intentions of Transylvania's new president. His letter to the trustees, later printed in the pages of the *Weekly Recorder,* attacked Horace's theology as "Socinian" and claimed the Unitarian faith was "under every form hostile to the best interests of the human race." Because it was reasonable to assume Horace would preach and inculcate religious principles, Sharpe felt it was impossible for him to remain at the university.[25] The resignation was an ominous but for the time being isolated indication of discontent. In a letter to fellow Boston pastor James Freeman, Horace took exception to the term "Socinian" but dismissed Sharp as an absurd outlier isolated in an "ultra orthodox" newspaper, and he remained optimistic about his ability to settle Lexington's religious tumult. "I hope," he maintained, "to be in a situation to assist in putting to shame the spirit of party, and to build up the cause of catholic christianity [*sic*] and of sound philosophy."[26]

Transylvania's board moved quickly to locate Sharpe's replacement, hiring T. Chariton Henry, a Presbyterian minister from South Carolina, as professor of languages and John Roche, a respected Episcopalian and graduate of Trinity College, as tutor. They also recruited Horace to procure a second tutor in languages, someone who, trustee Henry Clay hoped, could be promoted to professor when circumstances permitted. "Get a Baptist if you can," Clay cautioned, "one well qualified." If denominations were equally represented, there would be less chance of sectarian infighting—or at least the appearance of such. Yet Clay remained certain that any opposition, particularly by Presbyterians, was remote. "We have done nothing, nor shall we do any thing justly to provoke them."[27] And so amid tearful farewells and preparations for yet another journey west, this time complicated by travel accommodations for a wife, daughter, and infant son, Horace began his reconstitution of the school's faculty. The past year had conditioned his understanding of collegiate character and built an expectation for the relevance of his position. Success in the eastern schools, when he found it, had almost nothing to do with theological balance; it was built on distinguished men of literary talents, scientific abilities, and, more importantly but less frequently, elite connectedness. University professors of Boston, New York, and Philadelphia shared their affinity for arts and sciences with respected elites. Transylvania's academic prestige, Horace believed, would be magnified by the recruitment and retention of similar characters.

Important Characters

Horace's acquisition of fellow Bostonian John Everett set an important precedent. John was young but promising, his siblings all fully matriculated and accomplished: Alexander was the newly appointed chargé d'affaires to Holland; William was professor of Greek and Latin at Harvard; and Edward was a minister at Boston's Brattle Street Church. John was equally gifted, "the first scholar" among his graduating class at Harvard, Horace praised, just as advanced as brother Edward, and, though only eighteen years old, he was "double that amount" in intellectual and moral maturity. The choice might not have concerned Transylvania's board, but Horace's offer of $600 a year, the same rate one could expect at Harvard, almost certainly did. In the letter to Clay explaining his offer to Everett, Horace defended his decision, claiming that the salary, although high, was immaterial to the benefits of his "connexion with the college." Everett was well versed in the ancient routines of Harvard and, as such, a perfect complement to Horace's sentiments and eastern-style reforms.[28] Horace may have overextended his mandate, however, with the additional selection of P. D. Mariano, the thirty-four-year-old Italian émigré hired to join Everett as tutor of modern languages.

The circumstances that brought Mariano to Horace's attention are, like most details of Mariano's life, unknown. Eulogists remembered him as a disaffected colonel in Napoleon's Grande Armée, an elegant gentleman, and an accomplished scholar who hoped for political appointment but settled for a teaching position and the adventure of western travel. It may have been Mariano's attachments to Everett that secured the appointment; together they established the *Journal of Belles Lettres* a year after their arrival in Kentucky. But Mariano also may have fit Horace's expectations for learned deportment. He was expert in ancient and modern languages, said to be of delicate, refined tastes, and possessed a cosmopolitan sophistication that could help set new faculty apart from old.[29]

Horace, Mary, Harriette, Horace Jr., and the two newest members of Transylvania's faculty set out for Lexington in early October. The journey was familiar to Horace but progressively unsettling for Mary; the farther west they proceeded, the worse the roads and more dilapidated the towns. Mary found all parts of the scenery disagreeable, far from the "informed towns of New England." She was both unaccustomed to and unprepared for what she described as the "slovenly" state of western society. She found the town of Wheeling, Virginia, irrecusably common, with all the "vices of Virginian society" but none of its genteel character.[30] The party arrived in Lexington in late November, a short forty-six days after setting out from Boston. Students placed candles in the windows of the new college building as a crowd of locals cheered Horace's advance. The family took lodging at Clay's Ashland estate before renting from Clay's in-laws on Mulberry Street, just a stone's throw from campus.

It was just two weeks into the start of the new school year, but the effects of Horace's presidency had already taken shape.[31] Advertisements touted the enhanced prospects of the college, previously little more than a grammar school but now an institution worthy of "dignified style," a reputation acquired from its newly elected president.[32] Transylvania was, according to the *Niles' Weekly Register*, now "in a condition to afford as good education as is given at other colleges in the U. States,"[33] just substantially more affordable and unquestionably closer to the homes and troubled hearts of Kentucky parents.

The construction of a new college building added luster to these prospects and gave advertisements a natural focal point. A more commodious three-story structure built by local architect Matthew Kennedy replaced the original two-story seminary and may have been more impressive than anything the town had seen. Kennedy's basic design mimicked that of eastern colleges but added several unique touches, including arched doorways, elaborate balustrades, windows that changed size and shape depending on placement, and a cupola standing high above the center. Within lay thirty rooms, including a chapel, dining facility, lecture halls, and enough space for one hundred boarders.[34] Students' long-standing criticisms of the high price and inconvenience of in-town room and board now diminished, and at least some of the many promises Horace received while on his initial visit now came to fruition, even if they did not yet know how to spell his last name. In a letter to President James Monroe, Kentucky plantation owner James Taylor boasted of sending his son James to Transylvania, home of the "Celibrated Doct Holly [sic]."[35]

The Unorthodox

Criticisms from religious leaders were less easily diffused, however, and within a month of Horace's arrival Clay began to fear the worst. He begged Horace to remain cautious, for the Presbyterians, it seemed, were now set to undermine his reputation. In December 1818, a contributor to the Weekly Recorder found irony in Horace's appointment: "There is something mysterious or paradoxical in the whole of the business respecting Mr. Holly's [sic] being called to Lexington. He is from Boston, the famous, and with Kentuckians, the despised seat of tories [sic]."[36] To others, Horace's election was part of a sinister cabal determined to quiet Presbyterian opposition and to win eastern allies.[37]

The durability of religious anxieties forced Clay to revise his earlier predictions; now, in December 1818, he claimed that he had "never doubted" the severity or permanence of their hostilities. Horace would have been perplexed by the admission because over the course of the year and as recently as September he had been promised that sectarian infighting had died down and that dispute-ready theologians were now agreeable to his coming, placated and enlightened by the logic of his message, united behind the university's common cause. Clay's advice now was simple but frustrating: Horace was to refrain from all religious discussion and stay away from the Sunday pulpit. "[I]t should never be lost sight of by you, that you have come among us not in the character of a Reformer, but to place yourself at the head of an institution of learning," Clay cautioned. The only time he should appear before a congregation, any congregation, should be to exhibit his oratorical abilities. A reasonable request, as Clay saw it, because Horace's mission was not to convert Lexington to the Unitarian faith but to lead as chief patron of its university, "to prepare the minds of millions & millions of youths born and unborn"—a mission, he reminded him, which was far more grandiose.[38] To Horace, the news was likely disappointing but not disastrous. After all, Unitarianism was a faith born in contention and had encouraged no small amount of debate during his time at Hollis Street. He was well aware of the dangers of bigoted adversaries in newly settled areas but remained convinced of the faction-healing powers of his logical, self-evident message. A few of Kentucky's more vociferous religious leaders publicly agreed to reserve judgment until evidence of Horace's theology came to light, but some were ready to declare him heretical, if not in fact then by association. Individual citizens expressed their apprehensions; whether he might show himself to be a heretic or a hero remained to be seen. It was clear to one editorialist at least, though, that the university was entirely lost.[39]

For the leaders of Kentucky's Presbyterian Synod, Horace's attachments to Socinianism, Arianism, or Deism were largely immaterial; of greater concern was his eastern-minded approach to education. Professors of eastern universities, they argued, often compared Christ to Socrates, Confucius, and the heathen mystics. Too often had Kentucky parents welcomed home sons with infidelity in their hearts and corrupting self-interest in their minds. The danger was what Horace's presidency could mean for the state's moral health; any change to the university's established habits could have disastrous implications.[40]

Undeterred by brewing acrimony, Horace spent the weeks leading up to his inaugural working at a frenetic pace, preparing his first courses in rhetoric, logic, and moral philosophy, reorganizing the curriculum, reforming entry and disciplinary requirements, and readying his opening address. His installation ceremony on December 19 was a celebration of Lexington's intellectual promise, a self-congratulation for efforts to wash the school clean of narrow-minded religious enthusiasms and partisan jealousies. Many wished to attend as participants, distinguished observers, or curious spectators—so many that the crowd outgrew the small schoolhouse chapel, and the entire affair had to be relocated to the Episcopal church, a short walk south of the main building.

The Public Scholar

The procession from the chapel to the church itself became an impromptu spectacle of conspicuous erudition. Students arranged themselves according to class and led members of Transylvania's Philosophical Society, who in turn led Horace, members of the faculty, the school's trustees, and smaller groups of judges, senators and congressmen, clergy, town trustees, physicians, bankers, and townspeople. The service was similar to a clerical installation, with organ music, prayers, and hymnals adding a solemn, meditative structure to the events. Horace's opening prayer deepened the significance; his oath of office, administered by principle trustee Robert Wycliffe, celebrated the ties that bound Horace to the interests of the commonwealth. He was presented with articles of symbolic importance: a Bible as a reminder of the moral force that guided the interests of the school, a set of keys conferring upon him the ownership of Transylvania, and a "volume of science" to remind him that instruction remained his central obligation.[41]

The centerpiece of the occasion was his address, a distillation of his thoughts on education in the western country drawn from a lifetime of direct experiences and recent travels. He began with an appeal to the genius of the West in a clever, if undisguised, attempt to distance himself from wrongheaded eastern associations, those aged Federalists who sneered at yeoman farmers and reviled the thought of backwoods science. The West, Horace began, was in fact perfectly situated and uncommonly prepared to lead the country to its full destiny. There a wave of enterprising young Americans carried hopes unbound; rising generations considered not the Atlantic but Lexington as a cultural polestar. "We are," he pressed confidently, "ceasing to feel like colonists who have left the mother country . . . and who always look back for the inventions and improvements which society is expected to introduce." Citizens of the West, of which he now counted himself, were not only self-reliant but also self-possessed, grown confident by circumstance and resolved to inveigh against Federalist intrigues. The cause of education, correctly instituted, would project and protect republican ideals across unimaginable distances—sentiments that would have made durable impressions on even the most recalcitrant objectors.

But to grow the West, Horace continued, Lexington must first establish itself on solid pedagogical ground and, ironically, rethink education on an eastern model. All educated members of society throughout time agreed on one indisputable fact: languages, ancient and modern, were the crux of all learning. Daily drill begun in earliest youth was essential to building strong minds and stronger character. A thorough and accurate knowledge of dead languages gave mastery of English, a quality that was required of all "respectable and useful citizens" fitted for public life or private pursuits and that lent scholars a distinguished air. Those who had studied ancient languages could tell who had not.

The balance of Horace's address concerned the most damaging misconception of higher education: early matriculation. Youths of Kentucky, Horace observed, entered at ages considered inappropriate in most settled parts of the world. When a boy completes a course of study at the age of fourteen, fifteen, or sixteen, he leaves with superficial and incomplete ideas, learning last what he should have learned first. A longer period of education was required; too frequently did Kentuckians take but a brief season of "scrap learning," as Horace termed it, before returning home or being pressed into a profession. The focus should be on training children correctly and patiently, grooming them from the nursery to grammar school to academy to college. The culminating product would be precision: "fewer declaimers and more thinkers; fewer volunteers for six months, or a year, and more regular troops." The young men nurtured by Kentucky's education would advance the learned professions—law, religion, and medicine—and elevate the farmer, merchant, and mechanic above their normal station.[42]

Only by educating its citizens could Kentucky remain free in mind and spirit; only by establishing a school of lasting significance could it undermine foreign insults and condemnations of America's literary character. It was only logical that Transylvania should direct these efforts; the force of tradition, location, and newly directed state support compelled it. As the fountainhead of scientific and literary knowledge, the school could control the distribution of learning as well as the tone and tenor of its delivery. Efforts to inculcate particular doctrine or establish one party over the other would be frustrated, and the school, carefully managed, could extend the values of liberal learning into dark and darkened places of the emergent West. Far too often had jealousies and intertown rivalries disrupted unified efforts to build up such an institution. Such a prolific distribution of academies, seminaries, and colleges among a people so widely disbursed destroyed academic potential.[43]

The publisher of the *Kentucky Gazette* later described the address as a masterful display of elocution. In connecting the interests of the university with those of the community and the interests of the community with those of the American West, Horace gave flight to visionary fantasies of national importance. If Lexington were the shining example of erudition it purported to be, Transylvania must be its lodestar.[44] Horace's comments also evoked recent developments in Danville, a village some forty miles south of Lexington. Danville was the original home of Transylvania Seminary and the potential residence of a new institution of higher learning. Ousted Presbyterian members of Transylvania's board were particularly enthusiastic about the prospects of reestablishing a place for orthodox Christian teaching and pushed hard for state sanction. A more pious school built on the "ROCK OF CHRISTIANITY," as one advocate boasted, was needed now more than ever.[45]

Transylvania's recent decision to elect Horace and Horace's proud display of classical learning added substance to these fears. Latin and Greek authors of "heathen lore" would, critics charged, overwhelm young minds, polluting and corrupting personal virtues by providing ungodly examples. Other arguments intended to make Horace's position untenable. If he ignored biblical precepts and removed himself from theological discussion, youths would suffer an ignoble fate. If he exposed Unitarian beliefs to public scrutiny, the results would be even worse. Silence indicated complicity and malevolent intentions.[46] If there was to be a single fountain of education, it should be a fountain of moral purity, not of heretical poison.

And so Horace was launched into conflict only a few weeks into his administration, not in open debate but through a campaign of vigorous institutional promotion. He countered opponents by courting legislators, which drew a critical eye. His message was simple but elegant: higher learning was not a bastion of religious inculcation but a showpiece of public intellect and a symbolic tool to extend scientific liberality to unsettled parts. Months later, in a speech before Kentucky's House of Representatives, Horace asserted the necessity of taste and "enlightened moral settlement" through education. With a concerted effort and more extravagant financial support, Kentucky could outshine sneering Europeans and haughty easterners by pressing forward ideals that were both advanced and atavistic, liberal sentiments built on ancient traditions. It was a grand vision, more than many expected, but to which none objected. An anonymous contributor to the *Western Monitor* noted the "power and energy" of his message. He projected vehemence "perhaps never surpassed" in discussions of this sort.[47] Supportive essays in Kentucky newspapers incorporated elements of Horace's message. The friendly *Western Monitor* gave a laudatory rendition of the speech, reporting that Horace "plead[ed] the cause of education with a power and energy seldom equaled, perhaps never surpassed."[48] "Public assistance . . . is a matter of state interest and policy," declared the author of one essay published in the *Louisville Public Advertiser*. An infusion of state assistance would place Transylvania "upon a footing of high respectability and prosperity" as it would gather into itself youths from the American West. All Kentuckians would share the greater esteem, enlarged national influence, and new sources of income. The necessity of educating the West was made all the more compelling by the potentially damning influence of certain states that would either rule or dissolve the American union. Only Transylvania could stand as the countervailing protagonist to insidious plots.[49]

The state's response was bittersweet; Transylvania received an annual appropriation but also more competition for public assistance.[50] Danville's newly formed Centre College now had formal sanction, title to the former assets of a defunct academy, and a share of state funding when and if it proved solvent.[51] A month later, charters for three more colleges were added: Southern College in Bowling Green, Urania College in Glasgow, and Western College in Hopkinsville, all under the same legislative stipulations as Centre.[52] But even these measures seemed to support Horace's vision for a tiered system of education; grammar schools would feed regional colleges, and only the best of these students would attend Transylvania, Kentucky's lone university. Shortly after word of the decision came down, Horace wrote to friend Joseph Story to boast of the resplendent prospects that accompanied his position. It seemed as though momentum carried the mission forward, tamping down sectarian angst to influence the "fortunes of millions."[53] With financial scaffolding now in place, Horace could explore improvements to the Medical and Law Departments.

Practitioners

Despite this boast to Story, long-standing tradition made Horace's efforts more difficult than he had most likely anticipated. In early Kentucky, as in most of early America, health care was the part-time occupation of amateur dilettantes, well-intentioned dabblers, and outright charlatans. Treatment guided by family tradition and passed down orally or through reference guides supplemented apothecaries, who dispensed practical knowledge along with exotic herbal remedies.[54] Medical doctors remained in short supply; Lexington's population doubled between 1806 and 1818, yet only two physicians were added to the city directory in that same period.[55] The homegrown nature of Kentucky medicine might have affected Transylvania's earliest attempts at formal medical instruction; the trustees had announced their intention to establish a medical program as early as 1799, but the plan suffered repeated setbacks. Inadequate equipment, few books, and a limited supply of matriculates hindered growth and gave others little encouragement.[56] Only one of the school's medical professors could claim proper educational credentials, and most doctors had entered the profession through the natural sciences, as battlefield surgeons or, as in the case of Reverend James Fishback, as doctors of divinity.[57] Benjamin Dudley, the instigator of the nearly fatal duel with William Richardson, considered himself certified after only a short apprenticeship under a local physician.[58]

Attempts to regulate or otherwise advance the medical profession came and went with little notice. In 1803, the Lexington Medical Society, a creation of the Transylvania Board of Trustees, called for laws regulating medical practitioners and railed against "the various fatal consequences which result from the indiscriminate admission of men into the practice of physic." Without a means of academic credentialing, "the most ignorant pretender" was placed on the same level as the rigorously trained scientifically minded physician. Medical exams, members of the society argued, could limit the "swarms of Quacks in medicine" that degraded the profession.[59]

Horace approached the challenge unencumbered by past failures. His first and most pressing concern became recruitment, not to supplement but to reconstitute Transylvania's faculty after eastern models, and for this task he turned to former tutor and friend Benjamin Silliman. It was now close to twenty years since the two had first met, and in that time Silliman had established himself as one of the country's leading scientific minds. As Yale's first professor of chemistry and editor of the *American Journal of Science,* Silliman was a superior reference. Horace reached out, first to procure the entire run of Silliman's journal, then to solicit nominations for academic posts.[60]

The board also assisted, rehiring Dr. Samuel Brown, one of the school's earliest and best-trained medical faculty. Brown had graduated from Carlisle College and had attended two years' worth of medical lectures at the University of Edinburgh, but it was his former connections to the school and the Presbyterian community in particular that made his appointment so valuable. In the board's letter of offer, trustee William Humphries noted the present "misunderstanding" with a "certain class of people" but left the matter there.[61] Horace was not unfamiliar with Brown; the two had met years ago in Boston, and it is clear he supported the decision.

Horace was probably more excited by the appointments of exotic traveler Constantine Rafinesque; the cantankerous Dr. Granville Pattison, lately of the University of Glasgow; and esteemed Philadelphia doctor Charles Caldwell. Rafinesque, the school's new professor of botany, natural history, and modern languages, had seen more of the world before the age of twelve than most Americans of the day could imagine. Born in Constantinople and relocated to France as a child and to Italy as a young adult, Rafinesque had embarked on a career in shipping while nurturing interests in botany, mineralogy, and most other branches of natural science. His initial visit to Kentucky in 1818 came by way of a botanical tour of the western states sponsored by Transylvania trustee, wealthy shipping magnate, and amateur botanist John Clifford. The two had shared an active scientific correspondence since their initial meeting—some sixteen years earlier while Clifford was on business in Livorno, Italy—and the friendship intensified after Clifford's move to Kentucky, a land of abundant yet undocumented plants, animals, and fossils. In Rafinesque, Clifford found an energetic peer, a friend of science who could share his enthusiasms for what others saw as commonplace and uninteresting.[62]

Clifford encouraged Rafinesque to seek more permanent accommodations in Kentucky with the hope of employing him in his fossil museum, but he also saw him as a potential standout in Transylvania's new Medical Department. By the late 1810s, Rafinesque was a notable member of America's expanding scientific community, publishing books, pamphlets, and scores of articles, short essays, and letters in respected periodicals. Though of eclectic tastes, Rafinesque was interested primarily in the discovery and taxonomy of native species and is credited with naming 6,700 plant species over the course of his career. His contributions to the *American Journal of Science* in particular may have caught

Horace's attention and probably warranted a personal recommendation from Silliman, though the appointment was almost assuredly a product of Rafinesque's friendship with Clifford.[63] Excited, perhaps overjoyed, by the prospects of a lengthier stay among Kentucky's exotic wilderness, Rafinesque let it be known that he would take a position without remuneration, asking only for free housing and an allowance for candles and firewood. The board's offer came almost as fast as his acceptance.

Science of the West

Money saved on Rafinesque was spent on Charles Caldwell, Horace's first and, to his mind, most appropriate choice to lead the burgeoning Medical Department. Caldwell, the son of humble North Carolina planters, had studied for the Presbyterian ministry before committing to a career in medicine. He entered the University of Pennsylvania's medical college in the age of Benjamin Rush, the redoubtable social and scientific mind of the American Revolution. But Caldwell's relationship with Rush was less than ideal, a difficulty, Caldwell later recalled, born of uncredited scientific findings and a contentious thesis defense. Their mutual enmity had lasting consequences for Caldwell, who had desired a professorship after graduation but had to become a private instructor instead, a position that held neither the dignity nor the esteem he desired.

Caldwell had fair claim to his frustrations. He was one of the first graduates of an American institution to publish his medical thesis and the first to promote others to do the same. His edited collection of theses, all written by graduates of the University of Pennsylvania, appeared in 1805 to glowing reviews. "A work like this," one author concluded, "has been long called for, from the increasing number and value of productions of graduates in medicine in the United States." The only complaint was that the work had not been completed sooner.[64] Caldwell's introduction to the collection expanded its importance a bit further. Medicine in the United States, he began, differed substantially from the rest of the world. Climatological oddities, regional customs, and unique occupations made treatments from the Old World inappropriate for the New—a fact attested to since the first days of settlement. "Ask a native of the United States," Caldwell continued, "who has visited foreign places, and he will tell you, that the diseases of his own and of other countries differ from each other no less strikingly."

Furthermore, American illnesses were by their very nature "gigantic," born of extreme environments and rugged living. European cures were developed to combat less-virulent sickness, their approach to healthy living fitting the soft comforts of European life. America also possessed plants and minerals unseen in other parts of the world; new medicinal possibilities therefore added another unique quality to the practice and another reason to share American theses. Most importantly, these works spoke to a growing national intelligence. Caldwell believed Americans could take ironic pride in the diseases, ailments, infections, and outbreaks that plagued its cities and countryside. Works of foreign science injured the esteem and genius of the republic because they undervalued native talent. "As it is in British works that we must search for accurate accounts of British diseases, British remedies, and British practice," Caldwell proudly declared, "so it is in American publications alone, that a system of medicine truly American must be ultimately found. To continue in a state of medical pupilage to our parent country, long after the expiration of our national minority, is unmanly and humiliating."[65] A reliance on British medicine was tantamount to dependence on the British Parliament.

The theses included in Caldwell's collection somewhat justified his boasts. Thomas Horsfield's study on "poison-ash, poison-vine, and common sumach" promoted the medicinal value of the elixirs derived from native plants.[66] John Walker studied the properties of the dogwood trees, convinced that "every country possessed an antidote to its diseases."[67] Alexander May's research on nosology, the classification of diseases, ignored the work of ancient and modern Europeans and presented the testimony of Philadelphia physicians and contributors to the *Medical Repository,* America's first medical journal. Peter Miller concluded that pains of childbirth would be assuaged if women ignored precedent and followed the diet of Native Americans.[68]

As editor of *Port-Folio,* a Philadelphia-based literary magazine, Caldwell pressed home these beliefs. Scattered among poems, book reviews, and political essays were lectures on chemistry and human anatomy from American medical professors, essays concerning recent American medical advances, objections to quackery in American cities, and attempts to tie the fate of the American union with science and literature.[69] The War of 1812 gave special impetus to his endeavors. The war, he reasoned, presented "a period . . . pregnant with consequences of high concern to the literary and scientific reputation of our country." War might undermine the economy and give rise to want and destruction but could never extinguish the "springs of intellect," interrupt the "operations of the mind," or "obstruct the walks of science."[70] In a sense, war with Britain completed the process of scientific separation, a process that began with the emergence of a unique American medical tradition.

For Caldwell, as for most university-trained physicians, the local and regional trumped all other concerns. Ancient authorities might be implicated, but the veracity of one's methodology depended more on geographical proximity than on the age and success of older treatments. Consultation with local doctors, the observations of American medical professors, or, failing these approaches, the palliative maxims of Native American traditions were simply more relevant in cases of well-known afflictions. In rewriting the rules of medicine, students at the University of Pennsylvania could claim a distinction as unique as their surroundings; their expertise was unmatched among even the great scientific minds of Europe. By codifying these studies, Caldwell placed himself as titular head of an emerging medical tradition.

A mixture of chance and opportunity brought Caldwell and Horace together. The death of Caspar Winstar, Pennsylvania's chair of medicine, coincided with Horace's visit to Philadelphia in February 1818. Caldwell, then age forty-eight and long embittered by failed attempts to secure a professorship, approached Horace at the eulogy for Winstar and followed with a letter proclaiming his appreciation for the ambition of building a medical school in Kentucky.[71] The eventual offer of $1,000 per year was a bit underwhelming, much less than he felt entitled to, but a position as chair of the Institutes of Medicine and Clinical Practice, the same title held by Rush, was impossible to resist.[72] According to Caldwell, his interest in the West had long predated the encounter. His reputation among western physicians meant that aspiring medical students from Missouri and Kentucky had sought him out regularly. They had attended his private lessons in abundant numbers and had suggested he establish a school in their territory.[73] This may have been true, but Caldwell's enthusiasms were also no doubt equally prompted by frustrated hopes, a predicament that Horace and many recently arrived Kentuckians could appreciate. The West offered a fresh start, a way for Caldwell to defeat the obstructive influence of Benjamin Rush and to right the wrongs of ignoble circumstance while promoting the interests of mature, patriotic, and nationally relevant American medicine.

Granville Pattison, the twenty-eight-year-old former lecturer in anatomy at Glasgow's College Street Medical School, might have brought even greater attention to Horace's efforts had he accepted the appointment. Pattison had gained early repute for his teaching, surgical skill, and regrettable but perhaps unavoidable illegal exhumation of cadavers for demonstration. His arrest and trial, which left him acquitted but still vilified by the citizens of Glasgow, as well as a widely publicized affair with the wife of a colleague convinced him to seek other, more healthful climes. The death of Caspar Winstar offered just such an opportunity.[74] But shortly after his arrival in Philadelphia in the autumn of 1819, Pattison learned that the position at Pennsylvania was filled, leaving him more than a little disconcerted about his next steps.

Caldwell, perhaps aware of Pattison through mutual associations, precipitated Horace's eventual offer of employment, and, by all indications, Pattison accepted; Caldwell wrote to confirm that he and Pattison would arrive in Lexington just before the start of the fall semester. By October, Horace considered Pattison a full-fledged member of the medical faculty, advertised him as the school's professor of anatomy, and published letters of introduction furnished by Pattison to build the young professor's reputation in America. Dr. Ashley Cooper of London and Drs. King, Barclay, Thompson, and Brown of Scotland described Pattison, as Horace recalled, in "language of uncommon force." Pattison's promise of carrying along his collection of anatomical specimens was almost too good to be true. "No lecture in the United States," Horace beamed, "is believed to have such abundant means for anatomical demonstration."[75]

For Horace, the recent appointments to Transylvania linked eastern éclat with western education; Brown, Caldwell, Rafinesque, and now Pattison were men of science, not religion, who could impart legitimacy to Transylvania's larger efforts through their education, accomplishments, and academic reputation. "With such men," Horace beamed, "it is not extravagant to say that this Medical School offers as many inducements to our young gentlemen as the Schools of the Atlantic." All that remained was to fill the school with sufficient numbers of qualified matriculates, young men who could by their presence "prevent despondency on the part of the professors" while adding "character and reputation" to the university.[76] Reports made clear that Horace's hopes were indeed achieved—Transylvania now flourished under its distinguished faculty and new president, and by the summer of 1819 the number of students in the regular classes reached 140.[77]

The importance of the Medical Department warranted special attention in Transylvania's frequent advertisements. Promotional essays published in the *Western Monitor* and other periodicals complimented the prestige Lexington now enjoyed but invested their native institution with even greater significance. The medical school was, in the words of one report, "essential . . . to the lives and health of the people." A respectable medical school in the West created more and more affordable opportunities for aspiring doctors. A greater supply of well-trained physicians would frustrate the baleful influences of long-standing superstition and amateur quackery.[78] Transylvania was without competition, rapidly enlarged with young men from Mississippi, Missouri, Alabama, Arkansas, and all parts of the western country. All of this, of course, was made possible by the addition of men well known throughout the scientific world. "With professors like these," the ad continued, "what may not our University accomplish!"[79] The students themselves rejoiced at the improved situation of their school. In the *Kentucky Gazette* in mid-March, students published a public declaration of gratitude for their "universally beloved" president, a man "highly esteemed by the students . . . [who] never attempted to instill into the minds of the students, any sentiments that are not purely orthodox."[80]

The university's reputation earned it a place of honor during President James Monroe's visit to Lexington in the summer of 1819. Horace, along with assembled trustees, faculty, and students, received the president, General Andrew Jackson, and Kentucky's governor, Isaac Shelby, with all the pomp and grandeur one might expect from Lexington's putative seat of science and literature.[81] Horace provided the official welcome after a well-crafted address from tutor John Everett. The substance of Horace's speech was not unlike what he presented on his inaugural: Transylvania was a newborn but held the promise of reforming the western mind, building "cultivated taste," and developing "practical wisdom."[82] Monroe followed with his own salutary oration, praising Kentucky's unmatched growth and the like-minded cultural temperament of its citizens. "We are one people," he beamed, "and as you brought with you an equal portion of intelligence, according to the respective numbers, with what you left behind, it is not surprising that your cultivation and improvement should bear the test of any fair comparison." He took special notice of Transylvania and believed the university to be a testament to the state's intellectual foresight.[83] Henry Clay found himself swept up by these enthusiasms. Writing from New Orleans on May 6, he applauded Horace for the great praise that now circulated in the East; sons from every part of the country, he reported, were arriving at Transylvania with high expectations. "This is," he continued, "what we hoped."[84] Carrying out these expectations, however, would require more than just a few appointments and more significant alterations.

The "Perfectibility" of Religion

Horace's first academic year drew to a close with few changes but a rapidly growing base of support; marginalizing the so-called orthodox appeared a simple matter, certainly less of a difficulty than Henry Clay had imagined. Horace felt secure in his position, so secure that he ignored Clay's warnings and returned to the pulpit, delivering seven sermons over the spring and summer months of 1819. A five-by-four-inch notebook recorded outlines and talking points arranged in logical progression: notes reduced ideas to lists of statements, verses, three-word phrases, or sentence fragments. The advantage of his system was flexibility; Horace could dwell on or drift through individual thoughts but remain within a well-reasoned, prestructured argument. Outlines also gave the appearance of extemporaneous thought; by glancing across a page, he could access significant points of discussion but remain unencumbered by specifics.

Horace's first sermon, delivered during Transylvania's spring commencement, began with an expression of remorse. He apologized for remaining silent, claiming his reticence to preach was from a need to maintain balance between religious and moral instruction; any semblance of sectarian impropriety would harm the institution. Religion did have a place in the university but should be tempered by reason. Christian morality, for example, had both spiritual and intellectual meanings. Avarice, meanness, intrigue, cunning, "excessive ambition," and other immoral dangers were held in the same regard as intellectual failings, the love of "bad books," "misguided studies," and a "contempt of practical wisdom." Christian duty meant self-control and purity, but it also meant a commitment to learning. Other sects' preaching was useful, he contended, but most sermons were "too mystical," focused only on the speaker's authority. Of greater import were connections between spirit and intellect or between classical mythology and Christianity.[85]

Horace linked education with Christian morality throughout his summer sermons, arguing that intelligence, advanced by improved modes of instruction, helped unfold God's eternal plan. Just as discoveries in astronomy, geography, and chemistry enhanced scientific understanding, so too could Christianity benefit from intellectual progress. In reality, Christianity was a complement to science. "Reason and common sense" gave fresh life to theology, updating it for the modern world; without rationality, religion remained superstition. "New thoughts and illustrations" deepened faith and brought Christianity to the learned and unlearned.[86] Horace considered the rejection of the Trinity, his most controversial point, an example of religious progress. A belief in separate divine persons was both unnecessary and antiquated.[87]

The perfectibility of religion claimed greater significance when yoked to the destiny of the republic.

The finer points of Horace's theology crystallized over the summer, reaching a peak during President Monroe's tour. The sermon Horace delivered on July 4 in honor of the president's visit to Transylvania directly attacked the bigotry that pervaded the state. He condemned the technical language of artful demagogues who employed rarified terminology that confused the faithful. But his attempts at theological simplicity might have been as equally mystifying. In answering the question "What must I do to be saved?" he proceeded down a twisting metaphysical path where human potential became both the equivalent and the product of divine revelation. Religion and nature, he argued, must unite as one to achieve God's favor. Attending to a moral life and obeying divine law would satisfy the mind. The importance of mind extended beyond temporal satisfactions and became the eternal imprint of existence. If mind was truly eternal, God was its perfected form.[88]

Reactions to Horace's semiopaque cosmology came quickly. Critics described his sermons as being of "a very peculiar character," too philosophical, inscrutable, difficult to define, and unquestionably heterodox. Horace's refusal to publish these sermons, save his address to President Monroe, also caused concern; without print, his words became "as shapeless and yielding as the air on which they were impressed," evaporating into the ether before the full weight of ignominy could be comprehended, one critic complained. He refused to com-mit his thoughts to paper while attacking the veracity of others, so that same nameless author concluded, he "is in the pulpit a mere braggadocio."[89] Without quotable passages, opponents were left to wonder at the implications of potentially irreligious sentiments and to base their arguments on pure speculation and hyperbole. Convinced that Horace devalued the Bible as a source of divine wisdom, a contributor to the *Weekly Recorder* attempted to expose the subterfuge. "Let any candid man answer, [Is this] sentiment marked deism? Is it not the very plan of Rousseau and of Paine? The whole tribe of the worshippers of nature are just alike."[90] The absence of published theology gave Horace's address to President Madison special attention. The pseudonymous author "Common Sense" scrutinized every line, parsed and critiqued most phrases, and found fault with everything—vocabulary, style, and the arrangement of Horace's prose and ideas. Short, "ill sounding words" weakened the opening lines; repetitious ideas added nothing of consequence; and improper, ill-defined phrases robbed the speech of vitality.[91] Others attacked Horace's personal habits and private affairs. His Sabbath-evening parties attracted a motley collection of irreligious characters. "All kinds of tunes and songs" contributed an unwholesome quality and gave some reason to leave early.[92]

Questions regarding Horace's theology were relatively insignificant in light of these other critiques of his literary and moral reputation. Theological arguments could be dismissed as perturbed sectarian ramblings, but, as the university's president, Horace personified academic credibility, the epitome of sound judgment, incorruptible morals, and revered intelligence; he represented the institution's best hopes and greatest potential. So although supporters remained silent on matters of doctrine and Unitarianism, their defenses of Horace's scholarly aptitude were immediate and robust. "Uncommon Sense," "Fair Play," and other essayists answered Horace's detractors with countercritiques of their own, questioning the merits of the assaults and formulating reasoned apologies when possible. In an essay titled "The Reviewer Reviewed," Fair Play turned the table on literary critics by pointing out defects found in the work of one assailant—the use of parentheses, word choice, and awkward phrasings. The attack against Horace was, Fair Play argued, "ridiculous as well as base," having neither the intelligence nor the capacity to comprehend subtle points.[93] "Uncommon Sense" mirrored these sentiments and took pains to describe instances in which Common Sense displayed the same characteristics he condemned in Horace.[94]

An unnamed essayist claimed all accusations regarding Horace's personal associations with "irreligious men" were absolutely and utterly false, arguing "that Sabbath evening parties are not frequent at Mr. Holley's, but that sometimes friends call there on that evening unasked." Furthermore, only "solemn tunes" were played on these occasions.[95] The entire exchange must have perplexed Horace. Never before had his academic credentials or basic literary abilities been questioned. If anything, his position as one of Boston's most esteemed clerics had opened doors to Boston's intellectual society. He might have been aware that any college presidency would bring scrutiny, but he was almost certainly unprepared for the sectarian enmity regarding his prose style.

Perhaps it was anxiety over his reputation that stoked his scholarly ambitions and convinced him to join newspaper editor William Hunt's new endeavor. Hunt, a transplanted Bostonian and Harvard graduate, had come to Lexington in 1815 with the hopes of entering the growing but fiercely competitive newspaper trade. Soon after his arrival, he became coeditor and then owner of the *Western Monitor*, a paper in direct competition with and largely indistinguishable from other regional offerings.[96] Hunt, perhaps elevated by his success, approached Horace in early 1819 with an idea for a periodical of "intelligence, and taste, and literary acquirements" to be aimed at an increasingly urbane western readership.[97] The *Western Review and Miscellaneous Magazine* would be, they hoped, the western corollary to cultured periodicals of New England, a storehouse of learned grace, and an outlet for the region's best literary and scientific minds.[98]

The *Western Review*

High-minded aspirations aside, neither Hunt nor Horace had any proof that the scheme would work—in fact, all evidence pointed to the contrary. In 1803, newspaper editor Daniel Branford had published the *Medley*, a periodical replete with "Prose and Verse from the most respected authors," but the venture lasted all of one year.[99] The *Review*, like the failed *Medley*, was altogether different from the semiweekly reports of international news, billingsgate editorials, and exchanges of theological insults that filled most of the region's newspapers. As a work of scholarly refinement, the *Review* would replace controversial content with an eclectic assortment of poetry, literary reviews, anecdotes from elite society, scientific essays on "natural curiosities" of the West, and other works intended for educated westerners. The function was to be complimentary as well as didactic, a showpiece of western ability as well as a tool for the propagation of western erudition. "It will," Hunt boasted in an early advertisement, "be among the main objects of the work . . . to develop the natural history of the western states, to cultivate and improve our literary taste, to communicate the most interesting literary intelligence, and to vindicate, while it endeavors to advance, the literary character of our country." Hunt's expressed prohibitions against sectarian or party dissent left readers free to enjoy "liberal, enlarged, and philanthropic views." "All controversy on religious and political topics," he announced, "will be carefully excluded."[100]

Hunt assumed editorial duties and printing costs, while Horace, Constantine Rafinesque, Charles Caldwell, Edward Everett, and other literary Lexingtonians supplied genteel content. But early volumes owed more to Horace than to others; the first six issues, published from August 1819 to January 1820, featured more than a dozen of his contributions, including essays on law and education, translations of French poetry, excerpts from travel journals, anecdotes, and critiques of recently published books. Some of this material was drawn from his private collections; the translations of Madame de Staël's work, poems, and excerpts from his travel journals had been composed years earlier; his essay "On Education in the Western Country" was likely a reprint of his inaugural address. But Horace also contributed a healthy array of original titles written specifically for this publication. And these more recent productions became a powerful means of scholarly self-promotion, a way to demonstrate well-rounded erudition while communicating a mastery of specific fields of study. The types of works Horace published—or perhaps felt compelled to publish—may suggest the public's estimation of his scholarly ability or at least the expectation of what a scholar from New England should be capable. More directly, his contributions were a means to establish his authority on subjects with which he might have been familiar but for which he had no other credentials.

A graceful facility with classical Latin and a fluid mastery of French were some of the more obvious signs of academic prowess, abilities any true scholar and certainly any scholar of New England should demonstrate. Horace himself touted the benefits of language training and repeated that message on behalf of Transylvania. Most Kentuckians would have therefore assumed he could render English into Latin and translate French and German into the common tongue with ease and aplomb. Yet the number and quality of Horace's publications in these languages suggests at least a measure of self-possessed anxiety. Reprinting his English translation of Madame de Staël's *De l'Allemagne*, for example, was a relatively simple matter but became complicated by public expectations. He had completed it years earlier and for Mary's private use but delivered a revised draft for publication, correcting words and phrases from his earlier version perhaps out of fear of criticism.[101] His Latin ode to the American republic was short and awkwardly phrased. Horace was aware of his shortcomings; the work was the last of the volume and prefaced with the sentence "Hosce versiculos, non admodum limatos": "These verses are not very polished."[102] But the attempt was significant nonetheless and proof that he could compose at least a few lines of classical prose. He may, however, have stretched the bounds of credulity with "Free Translation of an IDYL," by eighteenth-century Swiss poet Solomon Gessner. Horace's translation appears to be little more than an edited version of an earlier translation published in 1802.[103]

Reprinting his inaugural address was intended to solidify his position as the state's chief educator. Curious bystanders, concerned supporters, and caustic rivals alike had begged Horace to distribute the address ever since its delivery; his resistance probably had more to do with the *Review*'s publication schedule than with a hidden agenda. The speech—including a defense of dead languages, an attack on immature scholars, and an argument for the dissemination of republican values—was arranged according to one specific goal, state support of Transylvania's educational mission. The eloquence of his argument—his command of the subject and the rarified but accessible language he used to convey ideas—gave readers confidence in a greater knowledge of higher education and Kentucky's place in a larger academic world.

Another work titled simply "Libraries" carried these points and this notoriety further. Nothing, Horace argued, was more central to learning than books—a good library was a "nurse of the scholar . . . [and the] nourishment indispensable to his life." A prodigious supply of books allowed professionals to avoid reduplication of effort and helped liberate society from the "slow and painful progress" of rediscovery. American libraries, he continued, were woefully inadequate when compared to the vast repositories of Copenhagen (270,000 volumes), the Imperial Library of Petersburg (300,000 volumes), the Royal at Paris (370,000 volumes), and the unmatched collections at the Vatican, which counted an amazing 500,000 books. Harvard remained America's largest library with a paltry 30,000 volumes. The desire and need for books were especially strong in the West, a place removed from historical precedent and the advantages of tradition. He concluded that each college and university should be provided a "nuculus [*sic*]" of no less than 10,000 books, a seedbed that in time could grow to European proportions.[104]

Horace also extended his academic credibility to works on the legal practice; a desire to certify himself as an instructor in Transylvania's law program might have spurred such essays as "Bail" and "Trial by Jury" and reviews of certain publications. Each was purposely didactic, intended to educate and thereby to confirm his status as legal expert. "Trial by Jury" started with a lengthy history of jurisprudence buffeted by reference to "Blackstone, Bacon, Reeves, and a long list of other respectable English lawyers." "Bail" shared a similar tone, moving the history of prison debts from medieval England to recent decisions by the Kentucky state legislature. Both essays displayed competent awareness of criminal procedure by questioning basic premises and lobbying for rational improvement. Horace faulted Kentucky's approach to criminal bail, which, per statute law of 1796, allowed prisoners the right to exit their cells but forced them to remain within ten acres of the jail—a measure intended to promote "the preservation of his or her health."[105] This, Horace argued, was contradictory to the assumption of innocence and exempted the "truly wretched . . . [from the] common rights of humanity."[106] Certain long-standing traditions regarding jurors were also in need of Horace's legal disposition. Kentucky law compelled jurors to remain in confinement until they reached unanimous agreement, the assumption being that the absence of food or rest would promote quick justice. Horace found this law outlandish, productive only of "disagreeable effects." "What would the judges of the court of appeals say if they were required to be locked up without nourishment, until they unanimously agreed on questions which should come before them?" he quipped. The benefits of jury trial would be just as vouchsafed with a verdict decided by a simple majority.[107]

Horace's most prolific legal offering appeared in his review of Robert Walsh Jr.'s essay "An Appeal from the Judgments of Great Britain Respecting the United States." Walsh, a Pennsylvania attorney, was responding to criticisms of American slavery by English authors with pointed attacks on contradictory British policies and practices. As a slave owner himself, Horace could appreciate the logic of Walsh's defense. The American colonies had been compelled to accept slavery by British merchants, landowners, and Crown-appointed officials. The fact that British authors now faulted Americans for an institution the British themselves had created was the height of imperious egotism. Horace agreed that slavery was evil, but an "evil entailed upon us by our British ancestors" that could be rectified only after a "long time" and by "very slow degrees." Plans for colonization, he argued, were the best and most efficacious route.[108]

Readers might have been impressed with the scope of Horace's abilities, and that was the point; his intellectual aptitude needed reinforcement and, in the case of law, establishment. His authorship, however, remained semianonymous, with the pen names "T," "U," and "P. P." affixed to most contributions.[109] But the disguise was less cryptic than it seemed; pseudonyms were common for works of this nature—lending detached objectivity and personal distance from public opinion. Disassociating the author from authorship also imparted an uncommon, somewhat rarified quality in certain contexts; the vast majority of works printed in the *North American Review* in this period, for example, displayed no reference to authorship whatsoever.[110] The desire for credit, especially for shorter pieces, may in fact have appeared vulgar to educated readers; after all, Timothy Dwight, Jedidiah Morse, and other American ministers of the early nineteenth century rarely made overt connections between themselves and their works.[111] But the content of individual essays would have made attribution a relatively simple affair for locals familiar with Horace's already published opinions.

Editors from around the country lauded these initial attempts to produce a cultured, learned journal in Kentucky. A contributor to the *Carlisle Republican* saw the *Western Review* as a corollary to western expansion; few had sought to comprehend the West's abundant curiosities, literary establishments, or commercial productions.[112] A notice published in the *New-England Galaxy* judged the first edition of the *Western Review* a "work of merit," and newspapers from all parts of the country reprinted that first edition's content.[113] The *Western Review* was also considered worthy of emulation: two months after the September edition was published, former Transylvania professor Joseph Buchanan, now of Cincinnati, began publication of the *Literary Cadet and Cheap Advertiser*, a literary digest that charged patrons 20 percent less to publish advertisements.[114]

Publication

Horace's literary contributions may have validated public confidence, but it was science and medicine that brought new life and new identity to the school. Scientific publications by faculty were some of the more significant indications of academic change, and a new approach to certification placed Transylvania at the center of a particular and particularly unique western medical tradition. As the directing influence of this change, Horace deserves more than a little credit for its success; faculty appointments and administration of resources created the inertia that propelled his vision.

The first and, for Horace, most meaningful way to build academic reputation was through publication, a talent his newly appointed professor of natural science came ready to exercise. Over the course of the fall and winter of 1819, Constantine Rafinesque was second only to Horace in the number of contributions to the *Western Review*, but unlike his president, Rafinesque asked that his full name and academic title appear at the head of each work.[115] His essays were short, few stretching beyond two pages of typescript, most of which was in the form of lists; the essays' significance came not from their size but from their subjects. In his investigations of "different Lighturge" and "peculiarities" of botany in the West, the discovery of new shrubs in Kentucky, and a description of an ancient Indian village just outside Lexington, Rafinesque hoped to recenter America's scientific interests and to add luster to his own professional standing. Just as "multifarious lightnings" occurred more abundantly and in a greater variety in the West than anywhere else in the world, so too was Kentucky situated among four sui generis "natural sections," habitable zones dissimilar from each other in both character and vegetation.[116] Observations and discoveries of Kentucky's abundantly exotic plant and animal life clarified the special qualities of the West. Within a few months of his arrival in Kentucky, Rafinesque identified two new species of fox, nearly a hundred new species of fish, and scores of plants, shrubs, and trees.[117] Opportunities for discovery seemed limitless along Kentucky's untouched streams, barren plains, and dense forests, and Rafinesque hoped that his readers might "value the exertions" by which he had been able to "accomplish so much in so short a period of time."[118]

As the head of Transylvania's Medical Department, Charles Caldwell may have felt a disproportionate responsibility for scholarly publication. Caldwell, like

Rafinesque, arrived at the university with an already impressive record, replete with essays on individual medical issues and punctuated by his collection of medical theses. His most recent work, a multivolume biography of Nathaniel Green, lay outside the scope of scientific interests but was no less impressive. Absent from his collected works, however, was a grand or specific vision for medical education, a statement that both defended Transylvania's medical tradition and established Caldwell's place at its head. His inaugural address as head of the Medical Department, reprinted for sale in November 1819, therefore offered Caldwell the chance to demonstrate leadership by describing how abstract expectations might translate into material benefits.

Horace's influence is unmistakable throughout Caldwell's address. For Caldwell, medical training was vital to the advancement of western ambitions and a natural corollary of the West's "unprecedented march . . . from wilderness and destitution, towards maturity, opulence, and glory." And, like Horace, Caldwell argued that a proper medical school provided a path to intellectual equality with eastern authorities, could assist Kentucky in the dissemination of republican virtues, and safeguarded the morals—and pocketbooks—of western families. Three young men could be educated at Transylvania for the price of one educated at an eastern school. Education in populous eastern cities, laden with "idleness, the attractions of amusement, the allurements of pleasure, and the seductions of vice," would bring irreparable damage to impressionable young men.[119]

Caldwell also claimed a significance suggested in his earlier works but carried to fruition in his adopted home. Citizens of the West, he argued, surrendered themselves to the erroneous authority of well-intentioned but ill-equipped "influences." "On the atlantic [sic] states," he proclaimed, "or on Europe, you are dependent for the higher and more important part of the education of those, who are to be your chief depositories of natural science, whose province it ought to be to disclose to you many of the native resources of your country, and who are entrusted with the care of the health and lives of yourselves and your families." In other words, a reliance on eastern authorities stripped westerners of self-esteem, placed them in a humiliating state of perpetual tutelage, and extinguished the spark of gentility that engendered "higher prerogatives of cultivated life."[120] Put simply, legitimate medicine legitimated society.

Of equal importance were the medical improvements attained from a western-centered education. Caldwell repeated advice from earlier publications, warning that medicine of the Old World was inadequate for the New; different afflictions in different parts of the world required different approaches. The "strong and peculiar character" of the West made inauthentic learning, theories abstracted from centuries-old principles or precedent, inadequate. "Peculiarities," Caldwell warned, "can be learnt only from actual observation, and a knowledge of the most successful method of treating them must be the result of experience."[121] Research was helpful only when united with direct examination; weather and environment were just as important as general properties for the cure of illness. The challenges of medicine were greater here in the West because of anomalous climate.

Caldwell capped his address with a promise and prediction. By establishing the Medical Department on firm ground, Transylvania would act like a "seat of civil government," a central storehouse of medical knowledge for the western states, not an autonomous relationship—ignorant of or at odds with eastern universities—but a corollary to already established practices. "Were I addressing myself exclusively to physicians," Caldwell continued, "I might say, that it is like an additional ganglion, which, by its local action, sustains and reinvigorates the languishing influence of the system to which it belongs." Doctors of Lexington, like those of Edinburgh, London, Paris, Göttingen, Pisa, and other European cities, could enjoy a "kindred atmosphere" of learning, the school itself being a "lamp of science" burning throughout the West.[122]

The strength of these publications was in their sincerity. Rafinesque's passion for exotic species was matched only by Caldwell's vigorous defense of medical education. Both argued for an independent-minded, scientifically literate West, and both depended on the triumph of these ideals for future personal success. Rafinesque's reputation was now intimately attached to local environs, just as Caldwell depended on western particularities for original medical doctrines. Horace supported both men with equal enthusiasm, granting Rafinesque long absences to pursue botanical observations and allowing Caldwell free reign in the restructuring of the Medical Department. Caldwell's reputation began slowly to outshine even Horace's. A friend of Dr. Samuel Brown wrote to Brown in December 1819, "I think Caldwell has hit the Kentucky taste exactly. . . . I wish to God that he may have eulogized them into the humor of placing your institution on a footing of permanent respectability and usefulness."[123]

There now seemed to be no shortage of eastern scholars willing to make the journey west. In September 1819, Horace made inquiries about Edmund Clark, a recent graduate of the University of Pennsylvania.[124] In October 1819, famed French linguist Peter Stephen DuPonceau recommended friend W. Francis Norris, a Catholic priest from Philadelphia, for a position as language instructor.[125] A month later Harvard president John Kirkland asked Horace to consider recent graduate George Salmon Borne of Kennebunk, Maine.[126] But Horace determined to make more strategic use of his appointments, for although offers to unknown easterners might curry favor with longtime associates, local friendships were becoming more valuable. It was perhaps out of a strategic concern for state funding that Horace tried to recruit John Rowan, the longtime Kentucky legislator and recently appointed appellate judge, for a position in Transylvania's law program. Rowan first considered but then rejected a professorship; though he was favorable to Lexington, financial considerations kept him from giving the matter greater thought.[127] Rowan's service in the Kentucky House of Representatives from 1813 to 1817, his recognized leadership in fugitive-slave legislation, and his popular opposition to the Second Bank of the United States would have made him a powerful ally.

Panic

Horace had every reason to seek out political friendships. Kentucky's economy reeled in the wake of America's first large-scale recession—the so-called Panic of 1819—and calls to reprioritize the state budget put Transylvania's yearly stipend in jeopardy. High-minded educational hopes now seemed less practical in light of bank failures, mortgage forfeitures, and depressed crop prices. State legislators split into opposing factions that year: those favoring a policy of debt relief, who argued for a suspension or forgiveness of certain debts, and those pressing the interests of creditors. Champions of relief won a majority in the Kentucky House and Senate that fall and set out to balance a teetering state economy. All prior legislative actions were now questioned; those of the outgoing governor, Gabriel Slaughter, came under special scrutiny. In this atmosphere, Slaughter's past and present support of Transylvania probably worked against the university. His November address to the Kentucky House, pleading for greater not reduced sums of financial assistance for the school brought the issue to a head. "By aiding in the extension to the Transylvania University that fostering care of government," Slaughter argued, Kentuckians would continue to secure the benefits of "elevated character," remain free from expenses incurred by eastern colleges, and be confident in the knowledge that their youths were under the influence of proper, moral ideals.[128]

Horace lacked a direct legislative voice but remained determined to sway the public and public policy to Transylvania's advantage. In January 1820, he published a lengthy summary of the school's current condition—the number of students, division of classes, curriculum, tuition, and other matters—in the hope of inspiring continued support. The school boasted high enrollments, possessed a rigorous academic schedule, and was, he argued, within reach of every citizen regardless of income; tuition remained "small [so] as to bring an education within the reach of the sons of the poor."[129] The effort may have drawn the attentions of legislators but certainly made an impression on the editors of the *Literary Cadet* and *Pittsburgh Gazette*. Transylvania had a "formidable and imposing appearance," a "phalanx of talent" that gave westerners a point of pride but left Ohioans with a sense of "mortification and regret." The school was necessary to the future prosperity of the West—a guarantor of independent minds and a means to create intellectual balance with eastern gentlemen.[130]

Despite a laudatory and hopeful inaugural address by Governor-elect John Adair, the legislature's session in the winter of 1820 made one modification to Transylvania's share of state funding: an act granting Kentucky colleges "fines and forfeitures" incurred by individual counties.[131] No one came out in direct opposition to Transylvania, but at least one representative implied that Horace, like all New Englanders, was nothing more than a pretender. At issue were salesmen from eastern cities who undercut Kentucky merchants. Mr. Hayes from Nelson County rose to defend a $50 tax by attacking "Yankee Pedlars [*sic*]," calling out Horace by name, and referring to him as a "spiritual pedlar" who, like all New England clergy, "dealt out diabolical and unscriptural doctrines."[132] The assault on Horace and Transylvania was no doubt mixed in with current debates over relief legislation and the Missouri Compromise. Henry Clay wrote Horace a short time later to urge patience. Word of the recent unpleasantness in the House chamber had reached Washington, but no one thought Horace worse off because of it. "The times are unfavorable to success," Clay advised, "and we must not therefore be discouraged. . . . [W]e should, on the contrary, redouble our efforts to deserve it, and it must come at last."[133]

By 1820, Horace had a better understanding of his assailants. The Breckinridges, a clan of "malevolent Presbyterians," seemed to draw themselves up in opposition to the university's designs and to Horace personally, but to little lasting effect.[134] The *Weekly Recorder*, published in Chillicothe, Ohio, continued to stoke the fires of religious angst, but as Horace argued in a letter to a friend, its efforts had small effect. Vitriol and prejudice by certain westerners against Yankees remained in the aftermath of the Missouri Compromise but now was ebbing, and so Horace wrote to Boston friend Willard Phillips in March 1820 that he remained confident that these foes would do no permanent damage. "Our University is prosperous," he continued. "We have many students, and gain upon the public mind. We are without any rival yet in the West, and probably shall be for some years. We are hated by a sect, but are out of its power. Presbyterianism is as bitter as gall, but dares not bite, although it growls in its den."[135]

And so it was with a renewed confidence that Horace launched out in search of state financial support. Anonymous editorials by others repeated well-worn arguments and Horace's sentiments—that public assistance of the university was a matter of grave concern for the state's moral and political future. Legislative apathy, one author argued, was not only misguided but also destructive. The amount of time spent passing unjust acts could have been better spent on the university.[136] As summer exams neared, the *Western Monitor* recognized Transylvania's esteemed young minds, thoroughly trained and ready to answer esoteric questions with speed and precision.[137]

In April 1820, Horace returned to the pulpit for another series of public sermons—and his critics spoke out just as quickly.[138] "Zolius and Co." found fault with everything. And in a ten-part series titled "Peritimatist, to the Reporter," the author criticized most of the *Western Review*'s content: the literary reviews, essays, and poems lacked genius; Rafinesque's works were pseudoscientific; Caldwell's address only "so so." The author questioned Horace's essays in particular, though not by name: "this Mr. U. or T. or T. U. or whatever else he may call himself" was nothing short of a charlatan—corrupt, misguided, and ill tempered. The author warned readers to be wary of fake displays of education and not to mistake "solemn foppery for profound erudition!"[139]

In November of that year, the legislature, perhaps moved by these impassioned pleas, set out to investigate their claims, sending a committee of twenty legislators to the school to examine the state and condition of learning as well as areas of deficiency. The result, as Mary Austin remembered, was beyond ridiculous. The men appeared on campus perfectly astonished; "scarcely one," Mary recalled in a letter to Horace's brother Orville, "had ever drawn a literary breath before." Horace welcomed the group with an impassioned speech outlining the institution's mission and needs, as he had done before, appealing, as Mary wrote, "to their generous & their selfish feelings so as not to be resisted." And for two days, the men sat through classes in every department—languages, poetry, medicine, "all of which were as new to them as if they had lived in the world before the Flood"—astonished, she concluded, by a higher education. Some went away claiming they "had learned more in a day than in their whole lives."[140]

A Medicine for the West

Undismayed by legislative apathy, personal affronts, or even the ebb and flow of sectarian angst, Horace spent the first years of his presidency dedicated to the improvement of the Medical Department. The first step, apart from recruiting adequate faculty, was to resurrect the Lexington Medical Society, an organization founded alongside Transylvania University in 1799 but reduced to infrequent meetings and of little substance in the intervening years. Much of the society's activity, when there was activity, focused on advocating for more rigorous standards of licensure.[141] But for Horace and Charles Caldwell, the advantages of such a society far surpassed these limited goals. Caldwell may have touted his own experience with the Philadelphia Medical Society, which by the time of his departure from that city held weekly meetings, enjoyed a large and growing endowment, and acted as a forum for the distribution of advanced medical knowledge.[142] The Philadelphia Medical Society was also, in the words of member Benjamin Smith Barton, a body that mingled "science with pleasure," an intellectual home to medical students, practicing physicians, and medical professors from the University of Pennsylvania; Benjamin Rush served as the group's first president.[143] By reestablishing Lexington's medical society, Horace hoped to inspire the same level of discourse and scholarly aplomb. Written into the society's now state-approved constitution in 1821 were explicit instructions governing membership and academic responsibility. Junior members, consisting mostly of Transylvania medical students, publicly declared their acceptance of societal law; their one and only requirement was to produce a medical thesis and argue it before the membership.[144]

The Medical Department's student exams were given greater emphasis and were considerably more stressful for prospective students. In a letter to his sister, student James Sterrett described in December 1820 his fears of the coming spring exams and the day he would be seated before the president, professors, and trustees. "They tell us that they will be incommonly tight and rigid in these examinations of us and they say we shall not pass if we eve[n] miss one question . . . for they tell us the whole future prosperity of the University depends upon those they let pass in the Spring." If they made poor doctors, it would reflect poorly on the university; the "whole Western Country," Sterrett added, "will have their eyes upon them." Passing was by no means guaranteed; others had failed, and failure meant the student had to repeat the entire course and stand again for his exam the following year. "The professors," he continued, "want to rival every other school in the world."[145]

The second and more significant change was the addition of a medical thesis to the graduation requirements. The thesis, popular at eastern colleges since the late eighteenth century but initiated at Transylvania with the incoming medical class of 1819, brought the éclat of Philadelphia medicine to Lexington and added the rigor Caldwell and Horace had hoped for. Theses also allowed Horace a share of academic credit; each began with the honorific inscription "Submitted to the examination of the Rev.d Horace Holley." More than one hundred theses are archived from the years of Horace's presidency, eight- to thirty-page essays on a range of medical issues: abortion, fractured teeth, mania, cholera, dysentery, melancholy, and the less deadly but equally uncanny "dyspepsia." Each begins with a short history of the topic, moves to a symptomatic description, and closes with recommended treatment options. The similarities between Transylvania's theses and the collection published by Caldwell in 1804 are unmistakable; subjects either were of local concern or made Transylvania the locus of medical knowledge. In their descriptions of both well-known and lesser-known diseases, infections, injuries, and procedures, students paid homage to their school by citing anecdotes from Transylvania's professors. By requiring the production of theses and then storing the originals, Transylvania became a repository for medicine, the "ganglion" that could both enlighten and enliven currents of scientific thought in the West.

Three theses were presented to the trustees in 1820, eleven in 1821, and all showed marks of Caldwell's influence. "On Influenza as It Appeared in Lexington and Its Environs" and medical topographies of certain Kentucky counties tied diagnosis and treatment to natural circumstances, fluctuations in temperature, the flow of streams, prevalence of caves, elevation, and other matters related to local situation or "atmosphere."[146] Student James Sterrett argued that the diseases of Bowling Green, a county situated in the southwestern portion of the state, were more "bilious," a condition he attributed to slightly warmer temperatures and low-lying country. People south of Kentucky's Green River were more susceptible to "Pleurisies and Catarrhal afflictions—that is, respiratory illness—because of dramatic climate shifts in late spring and early summer.[147] A study of Bath County in eastern Kentucky found humidity and "sudden vicissitudes of weather" responsible for congestive diseases. Kentucky's unpredictable climate also became the basis for studies of dysentery, hepatitis, and a variety of nervous disorders, hypochondria, apoplexy, and hysteria. Diseases themselves were connected to circumstances of southern states. Infant cholera was more abundant in the United States and particularly lethal in Lexington, where it claimed the lives of 173 children in 1818.[148]

Other theses made no claim to originality whatsoever; students considering typhus fever, the "Proximate Cause of Inflammation," "Phthisis Plumonali," "Hydrocephalus Internus," and the benefits of injections included lengthy self-effacing prefaces. Thomas Elliott's study of typhus proclaimed "there is literally nothing new under the sun," and John Lancaster Jr. began his essay on tuberculosis with the disclaimer, "It would be presumptuous for me to suppose I had any thing materially new to offer. All that I hope for is that there may be a spirit of investigation."[149] John O. Hodges surrendered his study to the "laudable purpose of collecting into a small space the scattered ideas which it has taken centuries to produce."[150] But like their locally defined counterparts, these more general surveys drew primarily from observations made by local experts. Professor Rafinesque revealed the effects of the atmosphere on human health, while lectures by Caldwell and Brown created the context and expertise necessary for diagnosis. Caldwell was "foremost . . . [in the] reformation and improvement" of knowledge concerning typhus fever. Another student began his study of dyspepsia with the obsequious homage "To the Professor of the institutes of Medicine in this University we are principally indebted, for our arguments . . . in regard to the process of digestion, with whom we believe, the facts originated, or under whose guidance, they have become efficient."[151] Doctor Brown's lectures and observations also found their way into the footnotes. Some students, however, believed the theories of Caldwell's former colleagues were more compelling. James Guild's study of cholera made extensive use of University of Pennsylvania professor Charles Meigs; others gave lavish attention to the discoveries of Benjamin Rush. Student Reuben Berry went so far as to directly contradict Caldwell's teaching on dysentery: the illness, Berry argued, was not contagious, as Caldwell argued, but spread by atmospheric anomalies.[152]

Attending to the sui generis nature of American illness gave students an equally unique calling; they were, according to Caldwell, the first to root out and identify the causes of local ailments. Studies on well-known topics were less original but of equal importance. By collecting medical knowledge—uncovered sometimes from centuries of tradition and practice, sometimes from the collected wisdom of their professors—students built the rudiments of an advanced medical library. Moreover, in formalizing the process of medical discovery and treatment and then claiming authority based on the teachings of highly educated medical experts, the thesis requirement promoted professionalized medicine, removing care from the hands of uninitiated apothecaries, midwives, and amateur physics. The thesis was also part of a larger, more systematic academic process, creating a unified network of intellectuals that acted as a corollary to the Lexington Medical Society. Caldwell might have imagined dignified alumni someday scouring the society's library for information, meeting to engage in sophisticated debate, or, like the members of its Philadelphia counterpart, publishing the society's own medical journal. It was perhaps with the intention of legitimizing itself that Transylvania now also began offering honorary medical degrees to already established doctors. In 1820, Burr Harrison of Bardstown, Joseph Knight of Shelbyville, and Bernard Farrar of St. Louis were honored within the first years of Horace's arrival in Lexington.[153]

Restoration

The Medical Department's unquestioned success renewed faith in Horace's vision and gave strength to other long-suffering programs. Student enrollment grew at unprecedented rates, spreading Transylvania's fame while adding repute to its faculty and credibility to its president. Science made all of this possible. Rafinesque's exotic talents and Caldwell's respected but previously unrecognized abilities created an intoxicating, if somewhat enigmatic, mixture of culture and erudition. The mass of Kentuckians might not understand the cataloging of roadside weeds, dissection of corpses, or collections of colorful rocks, but most of them recognized these activities as the habits of refined, cultured intellectuals that populated eastern cities. Knowledge begat culture, which itself was evidence of prosperity, or so Horace claimed. Transylvania was the "lamp in the forest," a budding resource of state pride that could, if provided the right fertilization, reap economic windfalls and place Kentucky at the center of a burgeoning, rapidly expanding continent.

The appearance of scholarly aplomb, bolstered by a thoroughgoing attention to publication, made all of this possible. Essays and poems found in the *Western Review* demonstrated Horace's eclectic yet sophisticated mind; Rafinesque's productions made rarified scientific knowledge seem less abstract but retained the same elite qualities. Caldwell claimed even greater repute through the collection and preservation of medical theses. His students researched local afflictions and gathered information related to common ailments in order to create the first repository of medical knowledge in the West. Transylvania seemed almost predestined for success, limited only by a few remaining vestiges of darkness and distraction. These vestiges were considered but aberrations, and by the spring of 1821 the possibilities of expansion seemed limitless.

The earliest portrait of Horace, commissioned by an unnamed Hollis Street parishioner. Gilbert Stuart painted the original in 1821, and artist Rembrandt Peale converted it to a lithograph for use in Charles Caldwell's book *A Discourse on the Genius and Character of the Rev. Horace Holley,* published in 1828. Courtesy Transylvania University Special Collections and Archives, Lexington.

Transylvania trustees commissioned this first of two portraits of Horace by Kentucky artist Matthew Harris Jouett in 1820. Here, preaching cords found in Stuart's portrait were replaced by the more fashionable and religiously neutral high collar. Courtesy Transylvania University Special Collections and Archives, Lexington.

Horace's visit to Andrew Jackson's home, the Hermitage, in 1823 was commemo-
rated by Tennessee portrait artist Ralph E. W. Earl. The work was added to Earl's
private gallery of distinguished southern gentlemen. Courtesy Tennessee State
Museum, Nashville.

This second portrait of Horace by Kentucky-born artist Matthew Harris Jouett was commissioned and completed a short time before Horace left Kentucky in 1827. The addition of a quill and parchment is elegant testimony to Horace's more scholarly deportment. Courtesy Transylvania University Special Collections and Archives, Lexington.

John Milton Holley (1777–1836), portrait by Edwin White, 1844. Horace and brother Milton passed hundreds, perhaps thousands, of letters to each other over the course of their short lives. Courtesy Salisbury Association Inc., Salisbury, Conn.

Papyrotamia images of Horace and Mary Austin, completed just prior to their leaving Kentucky in 1827. Silhouettes were captured with the assistance of candlelight, a "profile machine," and white paper and then

were recast in papyrotamia, a once popular but mostly forgotten decorative art. Cut paper was fashioned into the image, glazed, and mounted in a frame. Courtesy Transylvania University Special Collections and Archives, Lexington.

Luther Holley (1755–1826), center. Woodcut impression made during his time in the New York state legislature. This rather bland imprint captures almost none of the features later described by Mary Austin Holley in *Discourse on the Genius and Character of the Rev. Horace Holley*. From E. B. O'Callaghan, *Documentary History of New York*, vol. 4 (Albany: Charles Van Benthuysen, 1851), 1024.

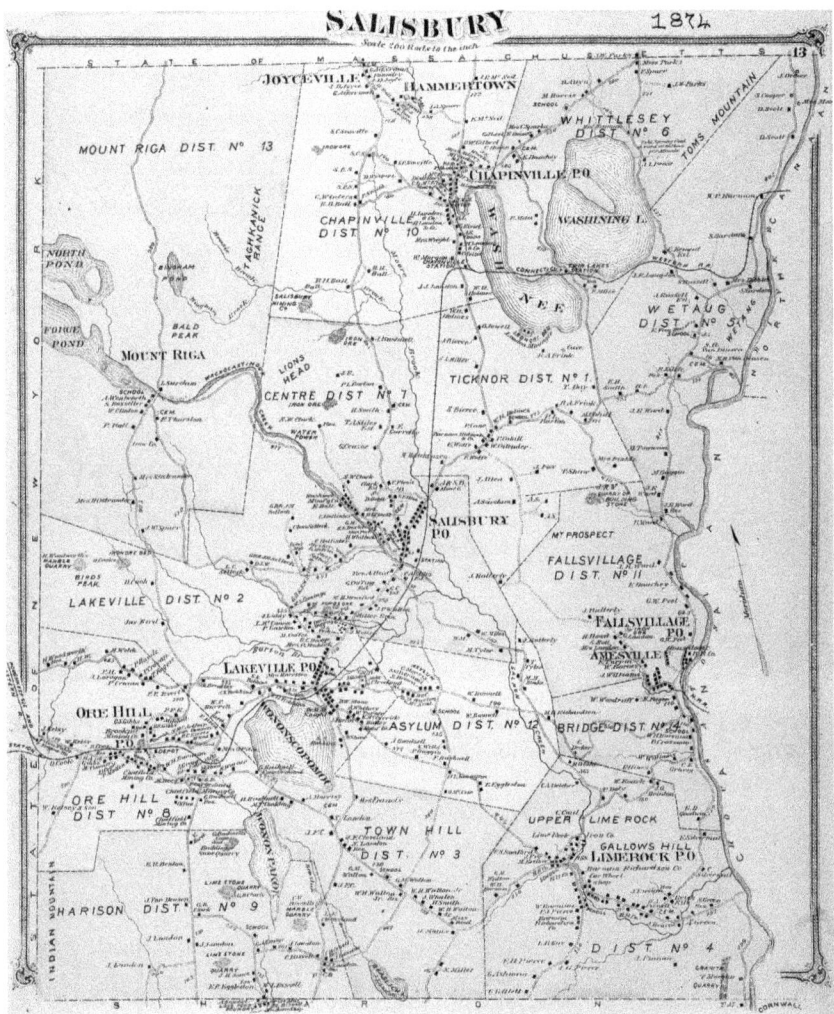

Map of Salisbury, 1874. Courtesy Salisbury Association Inc., Salisbury, Conn.

Lakeview home of Luther and Sally Holley (*right*), 1899. A hotel (*left*) was added to the original home sometime after Luther's death. Courtesy Salisbury Association Inc., Salisbury, Conn.

West College, the first and most versatile building on the Williams College campus. At the time Horace was a student at Williams, the building housed a chapel and dining hall and was the institution's main boardinghouse. Lithograph by C. Currier and E. Valois, 1790. Courtesy Williams College Archives and Special Collections, Williamstown, Mass.

A Front View of Yale-College and the College Chapel in New Haven by Daniel Bowen, 1786. Courtesy Yale University Art Gallery, New Haven, Conn.

Timothy Dwight (1752–1817), portrait by Jonathan Trumbull, 1817. Dwight's impression on Horace was immediate and long lasting. Horace patterned his career and gauged his success after Dwight's example, following a path to Greenfield Hill and a career in academia. Courtesy Yale University Art Gallery, New Haven, Conn.

Greenfield Hill, drawing by John Warner Barber, c. 1830. The First Presbyterian Church is on the right, Horace's school on the left. Courtesy Connecticut Historical Society, Hartford.

Hollis Street Church in the first years of Horace's pastorate. This building was replaced in 1811 by a more commodious structure. From James H. Stark, *Antique Views of ye Towne of Boston* (Boston: Photo-Electrotype Engraving, 1882), 323.

Transylvania University, drawing by Matthew Harris Jouett, 1818. Completed shortly before Horace's arrival, the main building was considered to be the most impressive structure in Lexington. Adjacent, but not shown, were a dining hall and separate living quarters. Courtesy Transylvania University Special Collections and Archives, Lexington.

Constantine Rafinesque (1783–1840), artist unknown. Horace struggled to understand Rafinesque's value as an instructor and scholar, despite his numerous contributions to the natural sciences. Courtesy Transylvania University Special Collections and Archives, Lexington.

Henry Clay (1777–1852), portrait by Matthew Harris Jouett, 1818. Clay was Horace's original and most significant supporter in Kentucky. Their affiliation also speeded Horace's departure when Kentucky politics drifted toward Jacksonian populism. Courtesy Transylvania University Special Collections and Archives, Lexington.

Joseph Desha (1768–1842), portrait by Katherine Helm, c. 1909. Desha's address to the Kentucky legislature, delivered shortly after his gubernatorial inauguration in 1824, asserted a more restrictive policy of state support of higher education and signaled the end of Transylvania's golden age under Horace. Courtesy Transylvania University Special Collections and Archives, Lexington.

5

"TRACES OF VAST DESIGN"

The toll road from Georgetown to Lexington was easily the best part of John James's trip. For twenty-five cents, the young Cincinnatian could travel most of the twelve-mile carriage ride without fear of bumping over tree roots, rumbling over holes, or getting stuck in muddy water. The road, crushed smooth under the weight of passing wheels, introduced him to the bucolic scenes of an aristocratic countryside. He was impressed with stately homes and found their adjoining gardens and carefully arranged trees picturesque. But when James arrived in Lexington on the afternoon of July 7, 1823, he was immediately taken by the contrast. Verdant landscapes of well-maintained estates gave way to a rundown, nearly dilapidated town where everything looked in need of fixing or demolition. Lexington's roads were paved, but with large, roughly hewn stones. Uneven sidewalks made foot traffic even less inviting. Shabby homes, neglected businesses, and a completely unremarkable courthouse, without a clock, contributed to the appearance of decline: "no where the newness and freshness of Cincinnati," James observed. James, a twenty-three-year-old law student, had come to Lexington to visit a friend but was most interested in the town's chief attraction, Transylvania University. It was the only thing keeping Lexington afloat; without it, James believed, the town would not exist. More than two hundred vacant homes deepened his impression of decline; Lexington's aspirations to become the seat of western commerce and a city as large and as dignified as Philadelphia now seemed impossible. "The traces of vast design," he concluded, "are perceptible throughout the place."[1]

James's criticisms were apt. Wartime embargoes, the recent bank panic, and persistent inflation worked against Lexington's ambitions in a big way. Migration to Kentucky had given rise to fast fortunes but had slowed in recent years. The state's population soared to 220,000 by 1800, grew to more than 400,000 by 1810, but slowed in the following decade. The town of Lexington suffered a similar fate, adding only 953 residents in the 1810s and less than 750 in the 1820s.[2] Traffic along the Ohio compounded the problem. When the steam engine made one-way traffic down the Mississippi obsolete, the river towns Pittsburgh, Cincinnati, and Louisville reaped the rewards. Cincinnati took advantage of its position as a hub of eastern and western commerce and flourished; in 1820, its population was 9,642, nearly that of Lexington and Louisville combined.[3] Louisville's population grew from 1,795 in 1800 to 4,012 in 1820 and was greater than 11,000 by 1830. In Lexington, however, local traders foundered, fields went fallow, all of the ropewalks closed, and hundreds became jobless.[4]

An unexpected transition occurred in the years after Horace's arrival in Lexington. Rather than just an ornament of learning or symbolic evidence of the town's maturing potential, Transylvania became the focus of the economy. James estimated that more than half of Lexington's population was either directly or indirectly affiliated with the university, and he was probably not far off. Transylvania was the natural focus of all public discussion. "Every thing that transpires in it is known and talked of," he remarked.[5] But attention to it was deserved. Transylvania's main building was the largest he had ever seen. Its medical library was more impressive still, filled with three thousand volumes of accumulated medical knowledge from Europe and America. His arrival coincided with commencement ceremonies, and James saw the mass of students, parents, interested observers, and dignitaries as a testament to the estimable opinions westerners had of the university.[6]

James was especially interested in meeting Horace Holley, the man most credited for Transylvania's meteoric rise. He thought Horace had a dignified appearance, with a finely shaped head, active expressions, and a rather stocky frame, but he also judged him a poor excuse for an intellectual and certainly not the man others described. Every part of him seemed artificial and affected, "the result of great study, and of an incessant effort to be elegant, and not from that innate warmth of heart," James scoffed. Parties at the Holley house were well-attended spectacles. Mary stood by the door and greeted everyone. Horace seemed to be everywhere at once. James thought Horace an obsequious flatterer who tried to make a spectacle of his learning through trite observations. He spoke Latin in labored tones and pronounced English with unnatural precision. James thought even less of Charles Caldwell, the head of the Medical Department and Horace's star professor. When Caldwell entered a room, it was always with

hat in hand, a trick, James observed, to show the "fine craniological developments of his head." Caldwell, "the most solemn fox" he had ever seen, was apt
to use "big words" not out of habit but for effect and spoke almost without end,
at one time for nearly a half an hour nonstop and without anyone else entering
the conversation. When Horace suggested that James take a master's degree
at Transylvania, James abjured. Cincinnati, James concluded in his diary, was
less erudite but more settled and less apt to be taken in by a charlatan scholar.[7]

Some of James's fellow Cincinnatians would have disagreed. In 1820, a
contributor to the city's periodical the *Literary Cadet* lauded Horace's brilliant
intellect; the colleges in Cincinnati had everything they needed except a man
of "splendid talents" like Horace. Every published notification of his success,
every instance where this success drew national attention, became a source of
shame for Ohio's colleges. Attempts to match Transylvania's medical school were
doomed from the start, and so the contributor concluded that "it would be idle
in us to attempt to gain the ascendency over them."[8] In Kentucky, boastful essays
in local and regional papers congratulated their president and celebrated the
brilliance and grandeur of his faculty and the "manliness" of his students. The
editor of Frankfort's *Western Monitor* made it clear that Horace's reforms had
carried the school beyond all expectations.[9] The editor of the *Kentucky Reporter*
"heartily congratulated" the public for the perfected state of the institution. The
commencement of 1821 was almost beyond description: "we have never heard
from students of the same age and standing, a series of exercises delivered."[10]

Competition

Promotions were vital in this age of college building. State-chartered schools,
long dormant because of apathy or want of funding, sprang to life in the economic boom years of the republic. By the time of James's visit, the number of
American colleges and universities stood at forty-three, roughly double the
number in existence at the time of Transylvania's founding in 1780.[11] The growth
of higher education was most conspicuous in Kentucky, Tennessee, Ohio, and
the western half of Pennsylvania, where founders laid ambitious plans for
growth and looked on regional rivals with undisguised envy. The economic and
political benefits of college building created a context for intense competition;
colleges offered a way for towns to attract business but were also a source of

local pride and anxiety.[12] When Transylvania's trustees attempted to relocate the school in 1815, citizens of Lexington rebelled. The honor of hosting a college also carried national significance; periodicals published annual reports of the number of matriculates and graduates from each college; size was considered evidence of quality.

Printed catalogs, started at Transylvania in 1820 but a long-standing practice at eastern universities, became the most effective means of institutional promotion. They were, Horace bragged in a letter to his father, a "mark of an uncommon advancement in literary and scientific enterprise."[13] Publication was meant to announce one thing: the total number of students. Rival cities received copies—the publisher of the *Pittsburgh Gazette* thanked Horace for sharing the first edition of the Transylvania catalog in 1820 and declared himself "much indebted" for the favor of "witnessing the rising greatness of the western country."[14] Cincinnati's *Literary Cadet* gave a similar though somewhat muted appreciation, noting the school's "very fine formidable and imposing appearance."[15] In addition to the catalog, Horace added regular notices of commencement ceremonies and "Academical Exhibitions." Printed notices of commencement listed the governor, judges, members of the legislature, and various other prominent public men who were in attendance.[16] Notices of commencement exercises, performed at different times throughout the year, gave the titles of student addresses, dialogues, and forensic arguments.[17]

Horace kept constant check on Transylvania's place among American colleges, enrollment, and the production of bachelor and master of arts degrees as well as medical degrees.[18] He was also aware of his position locally. An article in the May 1819 edition of the *National Register,* clipped and pasted into his scrapbook, made plain the relationship between the city of Edinburgh, Scotland, and its famous institution of higher learning. Edinburgh possessed no major commercial market and was not a center of politics or ancient religion, yet it prospered, the article contended, because of the fame and reputation of its university.[19] To Horace, the parallels were obvious. In the spring of 1819, he counted a little more than 100 matriculates at Transylvania; that number increased to 280 in 1820 and then to 375 in 1821, and by 1822 the school enrolled some 400 students.[20] Horace estimated that residents of the state of Kentucky as a whole saved between $14,000 and $60,000 a year by educating their sons at home; this amount, of course, was in addition to the tens of thousands paid to Kentucky merchants by students from other states.[21] He envisioned Transylvania as the savior of Lexington and himself as the cause of that prosperity. He also saw himself in a larger context and gave constant attention to Transylvania's rank among American universities, with success measured in the number of matriculates. "We are about the third in the US for numbers," Horace proudly announced to Orville in the winter of 1821.[22] Only Harvard and Yale presented a challenge.[23]

Questions

Support from the Kentucky legislature had improved since the inquiries of 1820 but was still short of Horace's expectations. In October 1821, allies in the House of Representatives looked to place Transylvania atop a larger system of public education, making Transylvania the state's sole university and primary beneficiary of state assistance. Centre College in Danville and Southern College in Bowling Green would take direction and funding from the Transylvania Board of Trustees.[24] Robert McAfee, a Transylvania alumnus, argued that a Transylvania-led system was necessary for the state's moral health and political influence. Without it, Kentucky was doomed to fall into obscurity and a "state of barbarism!" He pleaded with fellow congressmen to appreciate the value of their native institution and lend assistance through a "permanent donation," the full proceeds of the Bank of Kentucky, which he estimated at $120,000.[25] Thomas Moore of Mercer County argued that Transylvania was "emphatically a state institution," appropriated for the public interest. When the state had taken control of the school, legislative support was an implicit and expected condition.[26] Richard Anderson of Jefferson County called the state's paltry attempts to fund its chief literary institution nothing less than an "act of literary suicide."[27]

Horace joined these Transylvania supporters by delivering an address to both houses of the legislature on the subject of education, perhaps outlining a plan for a tiered system of public instruction. A short time later he wrote to Professor Samuel Brown to claim success. "I have the pleasure to inform you," he began, "that I am not stoned out of Frankfort."[28] To friend Benjamin Bussey he announced, "The impressions, I believe, were strong, and promise good fruit. . . . We have broken the ice on the score of patronage."[29] Before the end of 1821, the legislature made good on its promises, granting Transylvania half of the net profits from the Bank of the Commonwealth of Kentucky in a pool of money named the "Literary Fund." In practical terms, the bill appears to have added $20,000 to the school's account, a full $5,000 of which seems to have gone into the Medical Department.[30]

Good will was not unanimous, however. Some saw no reason for legislative aid. In early 1822, Representative Joseph Hardin likened Transylvania to his hogs. Neither, he argued, benefited from free handouts. "But when I see [my hogs] have been doing their best and have run their noses pretty deep into the snow, to encourage them, I throw them an ear of corn, and they run away contented. Just so it is with the University," he continued, "it has got along very well and supported itself, and I have no idea now to undertake to feed it from the public treasury." The argument fell flat. The problem, the editor of the *New Hampshire Sentinel* concluded, was that Hardin could not see the "distinction between a college and a pig-sty."[31] Horace thought Hardin's speech a poor reflection of the state and believed the press reports of it would damage the reputation of all Kentuckians.[32]

Political advantages mirrored an equally advantageous religious climate. Presbyterian opponents seemed to drift further into obscurity with each passing week. Horace thought his opposition "nearly silent" in November 1819.[33] A year later, Mary declared them mostly irrelevant.[34] And by March 1821, Horace considered the influence of his enemies "waning day by day."[35] Early editorial attacks and retorts slowed to a trickle before eventually halting altogether—the result, it seems, of almost universal satisfaction with enrollments and Horace's management of the university.

Prosperity

Increasing enrollment was one thing, but devising strategies to improve education quite another, and in a short time it became clear that Transylvania's curriculum needed reform. The regular classes of 1819 and 1820 struggled to meet Horace's expectations, performing poorly in their examinations and embarrassingly in commencement orations. The problems, he believed, were inadequate instruction and improper focus.[36] Attempts to correct the former began in the summer of 1820, when Horace poached the best instructors from the preparatory school and realigned the faculty. His newly instituted hierarchy of academic posts gave preference to the subjects and professors he knew best:

philosophy and ancient languages.[37] He reassigned faculty at will and with little justification, changing Robert Bishop's assignment from natural science to mathematics and then to history before adding philosophy, theology, and geography to his responsibilities.[38] Some of the changes made were out of Horace's hands. Both of his favorite tutors, P. D. Mariano and John Everett, returned to Boston in 1821; Everett took up the study of law, and Mariano intended to open a French school but died shortly after his return.[39] Constantine Rafinesque stayed at Transylvania but became an annoyance. Rafinesque's services to the university had always been free, save the expense of room and board, but problems started when he began to disappear from the campus for weeks and sometimes months at a time on various biological excursions.[40] Added to this problem were claims that Rafinesque's scientific findings were falsified. Horace excused most of Rafinesque's quirks so long as he was publishing, but his eccentricities became almost too much to bear, and by the winter of 1821 Horace complained to brother Orville, "I am sorry that we have the Constantinopolitan in our corps." Rafinesque was allowed to remain only through the pleading of others, who claimed he was one of the most respected naturalists in Europe.[41]

Horace showed equal determination in his own classroom. By the spring of 1821, he was teaching courses in law and philosophy. Teaching law was a helpful but unwelcome addition to his workload. His ambitions to start a law school suffered for want of qualified instructors but had no trouble attracting students. This imbalance left Horace, who had roughly one month's worth of experience in teaching law some fifteen years before his arrival in Lexington, as the school's primary professor.[42] His instruction in common law, using Roman emperor Justinian's *Corpus iuris civilis* and Emmerich de Vattel's *Law of Nations,* was well intentioned but probably rudimentary. Horace never appreciated or felt invigorated by the subject. Despite his love of argument, he found the law a dry and unoriginal use of one's talents; poetry, philosophy, and "works of taste" were better suited to his temperament. "I do not in the least regret that I was not a lawyer," he confided in a letter to Mary. Law never suited his talents or the "elegant engagement of the mind" so necessary for success in the world.[43]

Horace was better equipped for the study of moral philosophy, a mixture of metaphysics and ethics, and took to its instruction with almost manic enthusiasm. Thomas Brown's four-volume work *Lectures on the Philosophy of the Human Mind* became the basis of this instruction. Horace was entranced by the series and recommended it to Milton as "one of the best and most interesting works in the world . . . rich and glorious beyond comparison."[44] Brown, a professor of philosophy at the University of Edinburgh from 1810 until his death in 1820, was a rationalist of the Scottish Enlightenment who, like David Hume, Adam Smith, and Thomas Reid, argued for the primacy of human reason in the search for truth. But where Hume and others concluded that a supreme being was imperceptible and therefore unknowable, Brown considered the sensory operations of the human mind to be confirmation of God's existence. The study of the mind was facilitated by the observation of mental states, both those produced by the nervous system—pain, hunger, muscle ache—and those produced by emotions. The power of ethical judgment sprang from these conditions and gave one a greater sense of individual happiness and moral obligation to the community. The decision to do good or evil was thus a consequence of natural, not artificial, conditions.

Horace asked students to read excerpts and debate the merits of Brown's postulates; digesting the material in this way gave students a "severe test" of their abilities, he reasoned, and a better appreciation of true religion.[45] Brown's lectures also gave Horace an elevated appreciation of education. The "science of education" was, for Brown, the "noblest of all arts of man" and the "animating spirit of every other art."[46] Horace's challenge was to instill the virtues of a system through appeals to natural principles.

The study of Greek and Latin took a more central place in the curriculum. Future Confederate president Jefferson Davis, a fourteen-year-old freshman at Transylvania in 1821, later recalled the demanding but proficient language instruction.[47] Davis's classmate William Henry Harrison Jr., the son of the then current general and future U.S. president, complained that too much attention was placed on language, that "days and nights" in the study of Xenophon, Virgil, and Gibbon made young men ill prepared to make their "figure in the World." Study of laws, politics, and the Constitution were more appropriate.[48] Graduation requirements were soon changed to include English translations of Latin authors Virgil and Cicero along with several Greek texts.[49]

The pedagogy of handwriting and mathematics received similar attention. Instruction in the former was improved through the incorporation of copper tracing plates.[50] In the summer of 1821, Horace sent Professor John Jenkins to Harvard to learn the latest methods of teaching mathematics.[51] Other improvements encouraged physical health and mental discipline. A newly formed student militia added physical training to the daily routine, and a revised examination system pushed underclassmen to their limits.[52] Under Horace, year-end exams, completed ahead of fall commencement, became grueling, three-day exercises. Students began the tests with mathematics, history, and geography before transitioning to English and rhetoric. Horace stepped into the process later with the goal of making the exams as trying and difficult as possible, grilling students with uncommon tenacity. He questioned them on everything but fixed his attentions on pronunciation, rhetoric, and oratorical eloquence.[53] Those who succeeded demonstrated a command of a range of subjects and the ability to turn disparate facts into practical wisdom. Jefferson Davis struggled with his mathematics exam and was humiliated by having to repeat the same course the following year.[54] The entire mood of the campus changed in these early years of Horace's presidency. Gone, it seemed, were the days of raucous youths playing illicit games and participating in destructive behavior. Students now maintained a fastidious attention to their appearance. Swallowtail coats, brass buttons, crepe trousers, buckskin boots, and rigid, highly starched collars mimicked eastern style and gave the students what Horace would describe as an "orderly" appearance.[55]

Horace's zealous commitment to academics was less popular with the medical class. In the winter of 1821, building anger erupted into full-out rebellion when medical students complained about his overinvolvement in their program. They assembled in the university chapel and, according to Horace, confronted him en masse with a great ruckus. Only through his "firmness and perseverance" was the group pacified.[56] Caldwell, the titular head of the medical program, took charge of matters and sought to permanently correct the problem by reforming the examination process, suggesting not one but two separate medical exams. Under the current system, students were obliged to answer questions before a large body of professors, trustees, spectators, and, of course, their president. With two exams, a plan already adopted by the University of Pennsylvania, students could focus first on medical subjects asked by medical professors before moving on to a more general test of literary and scientific knowledge.[57] The transition was important for reasons beyond the preservation of student sanity. By marking one part of the examination process as the exclusive privilege of medical professors, Caldwell instituted a measure of professional separation. The school's success, he argued, required Horace to distance himself from medical affairs and to trust in the medical faculty's professional judgment. To see the matter done, Caldwell pledged his professors' reputation, interests, and honor. "Their report," he stated in a letter to trustee James Buchanan, "shall always be impartial and just."[58] It was an acceptable solution, and a trustee soon wrote to Henry Clay to say that the situation between Horace and the medical students had been "amicably and satisfactorily adjusted."[59]

Horace understood the challenge as an artifact of something more sinister, a "cabal" of disappointed politicians and religionists out to harass him at every turn.[60] But there was little he could do. The Medical Department drove enrollment, and its students represented half—and at times more than half—the total number of matriculates. When freshmen James Sterrett arrived in Lexington in 1820, he found it difficult to secure boarding because of the massive influx of would-be physicians. He was similarly astonished by the geographical distribution of his classmates, many of whom came from southern and eastern states. "Never," Sterrett wrote in a letter to his sister, "did Philadelphia in all her array show to the world such a class of students."[61] The program matured quickly. Students could now choose from among six separate specialties: general practice, medical theory, obstetrics and "diseases of Women and Children," botany, chemistry, and pharmacology. At a medical museum, replete with mineral and anatomical specimens preserved in wax, students observed severed human limbs, decomposing cadavers, and a vast assortment of bones. An affiliated Lexington hospital offered them the opportunity of practicing on the mentally ill.[62]

The gradual separation of medical from regular faculty was a source of tension, and Horace's initial enthusiasm for Caldwell waned quickly. By 1820, he thought Caldwell a fair professor but also a "great poser," without learning or taste, "made up and artificial[,] . . . a great talker, and a good deal of a bore, very vain, & without tact."[63] He now also faulted Caldwell's nationalistic approach to medicine. Holding American doctors above their Old World counterparts was dangerous and opened the door to an "abundance of rash conclusions."[64] But it was a price Horace had to pay in order to continue receiving state funding and public attention, which continued to flow to Transylvania because of its medical school's éclat. In February 1821, Horace, perhaps seeking a respite from aggravation, sent Caldwell to Europe with $16,000 and orders to procure all the books and scientific apparatus he found appropriate.[65] A year later Horace took pride in offering the school's first honorary doctorate of medicine.

Housekeeping

Horace's salary seemed appropriate to his efforts, at least for the first two years of his appointment. His initial $500 yearly housing allowance was enough to rent a large two-story brick home and its adjoining twelve-acre lot "in the pleasentest part of Lexington." Included on the grounds were a milk house, smoke house, ice house, chapel, slave quarters, and a stable. Pasture land gave just enough room for three horses and two cows. The job of maintaining the estate fell on four hired black servants: John, their waiter and gardener; Amy, their clothes washer and cook; Cooper, their coachman; another female housekeeper from Boston; and a young girl, hired simply to "wait upon the door." The servants' combined salaries were at least $338 a year.[66] The weather took some getting used to, but fresh milk and butter from his cows and a good supply of produce made them all grow fat. Frequent parties were expensive but necessary because they gave Horace and Mary a touch of their former lives.[67] Accommodations and prospects were so good that Horace hoped brother Orville might relocate to Lexington. His own influence, Horace bragged in a letter to their father, was such that he could easily procure Orville a position.[68]

Horace's expenses soon matched and then exceeded his income, however, as the burdens of keeping a large estate and a full complement of servants were outdone only by his desire to maintain the lifestyle of a sociable eastern gentleman. But his situation became nearly untenable in the wake of a postwar depression that left the state with an excess of currency. The value of paper currency in Kentucky dropped precipitously against the value of gold and silver, and Horace saw the real value of his salary diminished month after month. In July 1821, he estimated paper currency at roughly 50 percent the value of specie, and by October he believed his salary of $2,500 was actually worth less than $1,700 in silver.[69] Depreciation led him to rethink his situation. The family released all but two of their servants and moved from their commodious fifteen-acre estate to the "Old Seminary," a 130-by-40-foot brick house just south of the main building that housed the student refectory.[70] It did not have the dignity of their former home, but, as Mary explained, it was "comfortable, cheap, & convenient."[71] The value of Kentucky notes recovered somewhat in 1822, reaching as high as 80 percent of specie, but Horace continued to curb his expenses, selling his carriage to pay outstanding debts and taking over the duties of food shopping.[72]

Transylvania felt the effects of inflation more acutely. A young William Henry Harrison Jr. tied the dearth of matriculates in 1819 to the "scarcity of money."[73] When a near doubling of prices in Lexington hurt enrollment, trustees responded first by appointing special bill collectors and publishing threats to sue for back payment and then by dropping the price of tuition from $50 in 1821 to $40 in 1822.[74] The "horrible" financial predicament, as Horace termed it, convinced him of the need for the state to return to a "specie medium," calling in all excess paper currency and issuing new notes backed in precious metals.[75]

The issue of specie-backed currency was tied to a larger controversy that pitted Jeffersonian Republicans against Henry Clay's nationalist agenda. Jeffersonians, such as Kentucky appellate judge John Rowan, rooted themselves in theories of majoritarianism, state sovereignty, and restricted government. Protecting small, landowning yeoman farmers against rapacious institutional creditors was vital to principles of freedom, and so Rowan and others argued for a policy of "relief" and helped pass laws favorable to debtors. An "antirelief" party, backed by Henry Clay, posited a different vision in which a strong national government secured mercantile prosperity and held fast to the laws and powers delimited by the state constitution.[76] Clay's insistence on sound, specie-backed currency and his implicit message of elite governance resonated with Horace, who by 1821 gave up his reticence to make overt political declarations in favor of a determined advocacy of Henry Clay and the antirelief agenda.[77] Clay's opponents, Horace now declared openly, were "uneducated and half educated." Their "political quackery" brought low the condition of their state.[78]

When members of the so-called relief ticket won the midterm elections of 1822, Horace considered their success a sign of permanent instability as well as a "great inducement to leave [Kentucky]."[79] The problem, as he understood it, was a destructive excess of democracy; stability and prosperity were impossible in a system where public opinion carried so much weight.[80] He lectured members of his senior class on the virtues of federalism and discussed his opinions on the relief debate in public lectures.[81] But he also attempted to use the issue to garner more support for Transylvania. After all, true "RELIEF," Horace argued in the March 1821 edition of the *Western Review,* could come only through a liberal endowment to the university.[82]

Removal

However poor the situation in Lexington appeared to Horace, Mary thought it worse. Despite the attentions of and invitations from well-meaning Lexingtonians, she spent most of her time in the house.[83] She retreated from society and escaped into her correspondence, keeping an active exchange with John Everett, who, only a few months after his departure from Lexington, decided against law and was now on his way to the Netherlands to take a position with the American ambassador.[84] Sharing puns with family members was a special treat uncommon in a town where "the most direct meaning of the most common words is barely understood," she sniped in a letter to brother-in-law Orville. She thought Lexington crude and entirely without taste or elegance. The only antidotes to her misery were an active mind and the shared education of their children. At home, Mary took charge of instruction in languages, music, drawing, and English. Horace Jr. was too young to begin his studies, but this did not stop Mary from plotting a course for his improvement. "Children," she boasted in a letter to Orville, "cannot be taught languages too soon nor too many of them."[85]

When Mary's health declined, as it usually did in the summer months, she and Horace took refuge in local mineral springs or traveled the countryside in search of exotic scenes. She found the sulfur-rich waters of the Blue Licks, a resort just forty miles northeast of Lexington, restorative.[86] A visit to the Shaker village at Mount Pleasant introduced her to utterly "ridiculous and absurd" religious spectacles.[87] The family's trip to St. Louis was an opportunity to witness the beauty of the endless prairies, exotic flowers, and ancient wonders of the western countryside. The city itself, however, was somewhat disappointing— Horace described it as "dirty and fetid" but its citizens as accommodating and complimentary.[88]

Horace enjoyed the trips and relished the chance to examine Kentucky's fertile, gardenlike pastureland, ancient Indian mounds, and dense woods. He also found that traveling improved their children's health.[89] Mary remained implacable, and in June 1821 she and the children left Lexington on a planned four-month vacation in New England. She was so excited by the prospect of returning home that she forgave the inconvenience of traveling with four-year-old Horace, the drudgery of overland carriage rides, and the cramped, dangerous conditions and rude "low order" passengers of steam-powered riverboats.[90]

When she returned to more familiar New England environs, friends and family were welcoming, though they had difficulty recognizing her because of her new ruddy appearance; some considered her and the children strange, like "Country Cousins."[91] Adding satisfaction to the comforts of "home" was the prospect of a permanent return there. In New Haven, she learned that Horace's former parishioners had never abandoned the hope that he would someday retake the pulpit at Hollis Street or somewhere else. Mary found many who would gladly raise funds for a new church and pay anything if he would only consider it. She repeated all of this, including her thoughts on the matter, in a series of letters to Horace. The climate of New England was more healthful, the people more genteel, and if Horace could only "breathe this air," she mused, he would not hesitate to accept her proposition.[92] In Boston, others mourned Horace's absence and swore that "they had had no pleasure" and "never went to Church" since he left. They begged "over and over" for Mary to pass their love to him and prayed he would rethink his circumstances. Mary thought of a dozen reasons why he should accept and a dozen more why she needed to extend the original four-month trip through the winter.[93]

Other family members agreed and found no reason for Horace to continue in his present position. For Orville, recent events in the Kentucky legislature were reason enough to leave the state. The "half-horse–half-alligator committee of the Kentuckian Legislature to the University," he quipped to Mary, "must have neighed most delectably as they witnessed the marvels of science and wheeled their scaly bodies around among the monuments of learning."[94] Luther, as Mary reported on her trip east in 1821, begged Horace to abandon "that confused state of things as soon as possible."[95] Mary pressed forward, prompting friends to collect the funds necessary and, when they reached $20,000, to make Horace an official offer. By November 1821, promises of a new church made it appear there was "little doubt that all things will work together for good."[96] John Everett wrote to inform Mary of rumors that certain Bostonians were ready to make the appointment.[97]

Mary's absence weighed on Horace, so he busied himself with work, taking on extra duties at school and delivering sermons and lectures to local groups.[98] At home, he lived "a monk's life," as he described it to Milton, which brought everything into perspective. His improvements to the school enlarged his fame, but the lack of legislative assistance, the diminishing value of his salary, and religious rivalries undercut his once-glowing optimism. If problems in Kentucky did not abate, he would gladly abandon the school.[99] He spent the Christmas of 1821 in solitary confinement and described himself as "extremely melancholy," having no one to talk to, "no society" and no "soul with which to sympathize," save a few members of his senior class. [100] Part of his loneliness stemmed from his fear of sectarian spying, a persistent concern that scheming ne'er-do-wells would make private words public.[101] It is possible that Horace was referring to rumors of marital infidelity; a story that he had a bastard child, according to one source, became "a feast for the scandal,"[102] but nothing more of the allegation exists.

His misery was also caused in part by the failure of the *Western Review* and, with it, by the end of his ambition to bring eastern cultivation to the heart of Kentucky. The project faded only two years after its inception when it became too difficult to procure subscribers and willing contributors. There was never a shortage of contributions from Rafinesque, of course, but Horace quickly tired of his work. "Rafinesque writes so much nonsense," he confided in a letter to Orville in October 1820, "that I have told [William] Hunt he ought not to publish any more of his communications if the work is intended to be kept alive."[103] Three months later Horace complained that the latest volume was filled almost entirely by Hunt, save one contribution by himself.[104] The June 1821 issue was the last of the series. An essay titled "Valedictory," penned no doubt by Hunt, complained and chastised Kentuckians out of frustration. The once-sparkling hopes he and Horace had to bring culture, taste, intelligence, and significance to the far reaches of the American West had ended because of public apathy. In retrospect, Hunt added, the entire project amounted to little more than the "disconnected efforts of a few friends of learning." He hoped the series might continue one day, but the prospects looked grim.[105]

Periods of loneliness and depression were tempered by fits of dedicated enthusiasm, and at times Horace seemed energized by his challenges. In early 1822, he scolded Mary for her disagreeable predisposition and reminded her of the value of their present sacrifice. There were many, he reminded her, who loved her in Lexington; her irascible disposition was of her own making.[106] She had also forgotten, he reminded her, that the poor of Kentucky lived better than the poor in New England; everyone, "even the middle classes," could improve his or her situation. The state's climate and comforts were also superior, and in Kentucky people had more but worked less.[107] He agreed that the prospects in Boston were flattering and that a position there would be as honorable as any in the country, but he also made it clear that if he did quit Transylvania, it would be for Mary and nothing else. "My family," he wrote Milton, "would no doubt be more happily situated in Boston, and would have a better chance for support." Horace could manage the strange and uncultivated people of Kentucky, but it was "more difficult for a woman to be contented in a new society than it is for a man."[108] At one point, it seemed as though his return to Boston were imminent. When Henry Clay asked him to speak before the January 1822 session of the Kentucky legislature, Horace declined, saying that he would not return to the capitol until he decided his "future course."[109] In order to keep him there, certain trustees proposed adding a house to his salary.[110]

Horace contemplated a visit to Boston to investigate opportunities and promised to accept any reasonable offer from a church in New York or Boston.[111] But his letters to Mary now mixed declarations of action with an equal amount of indecision and objection. He agreed that a return to more settled parts of the country would give them more happiness but was never their main object. The purpose of uprooting the family had been to accomplish something more meaningful. The western country possessed native talent, but without a directive agent its people would be forever isolated, backward, and behind the rest of the country. Horace looked on their current privations as the consequence of performing a public service; Transylvania would become an object of supreme attention, he assured her, "if I persevere."[112] Mary responded with greater insistence, and, in turn, Horace promised to take any "good offer in Boston, or any Atlantic city." He meant a position that matched his current salary or offered $2,500 and a housing allowance. But even if this condition were met, he felt the decision to leave would be regrettable. Even if he had to live as a bachelor, he would "hold on till my grey hairs and the law of mortality should finish my course in the grave."[113]

As the winter of 1822 turned to spring, two things became clear. The first was that an appointment at a Boston-area church was just a matter of time; Mary's efforts mixed with the news of Horace's potential acceptance made it seem as if an official offer were forthcoming. The second was that Mary would not return to Lexington of her own accord. Her original four-month trip stretched into a year and promised to go well beyond that unless Horace collected her. So he set out from Lexington in the summer of 1822, aggrieved by Mary's delays but hopeful about the prospects of a new position.[114] Returning to Boston did something to rejuvenate him as people there seemed starved for his attentions and even more desperate for his return than he anticipated. In a letter to his father, Horace wrote of informal proposals that made a permanent offer for an "advantageous position" seem not just likely but inevitable. He delivered guest sermons to immense crowds and was pleased by the enthusiasm of their response. The contrast between the cool sea breezes and liberal attitudes of Boston and the humid air and bigoted, hateful personalities of Kentucky might have seemed never more apparent.

A final decision, however, would have to wait for an official offer. Mary reluctantly agreed to return to Lexington, perhaps comforted by the idea that it would be a short stay but satisfied by the addition of Horace's twenty-two-year-old sister, Caroline, who joined them in Salisbury. The decision to include Caroline was for health concerns; her persistent cough, perhaps the threat of tuberculosis, convinced father Luther to allow the trip. Luther's reservations were abated by Horace's frequent letters from the road confirming improvements to Caroline's health; her cough seemed to diminish with each mile.[115] Leaving so late in the season and so near to the start of the school session meant that the trip would have to be made at a rapid pace. The first part of the journey took a fairly well-defined route and then relied on the recently completed National Road to carry them over the Appalachian Mountains and into Wheeling, West Virginia, where they could catch a steamship down to Maysville.[116]

Colonel Morrison

News of Horace's leaving Kentucky reached Thomas Jefferson through friend Benjamin Waterhouse.[117] Jefferson seemed convinced the deal was done and was saddened by the news. "I had hoped," he complained, "he would have dropped a spark of reformation there, where I thought, from their freedom of mind, it would have kindled and spread rapidly."[118] But there was no offer, at least for now, and Horace returned to his duties at Transylvania that fall. His deflated salary was still an issue—he reported the value of Kentucky currency at 70 percent of specie in January 1823—and so he wrote the board of trustees to complain of the many "inconveniences" occasioned by personal finances. The board responded by claiming poverty, that a salary increase or one paid entirely in specie would be difficult because university revenues—tuition and state donations—were received in the same depreciated currency. They did, however, offer to allow him to live in his house rent free, granted him the right to collect fees for signing diplomas, and sanctioned a course of public lectures on philosophy, allowing him to charge $10 per student for a twenty-four-lecture series.[119]

Horace's situation was greatly improved in April when the value of Kentucky currency returned to 80 percent of specie. Fresh sources of improved money meant that Horace could return to an active social life; his appearance at the theater became almost as frequent as his and Mary's parties. Although thrown "in the eastern style," without dinner and only light refreshments, these parties were no doubt expensive in the aggregate.[120] But Horace's prospects looked even better after a $70,000 donation to Transylvania from James Morrison, the recently deceased member of the Transylvania Board of Trustees. In late April 1823, Horace admitted that plans to return to the East were doubtful or at least "not fully digested."[121]

Colonel James Morrison had enjoyed a long and dignified career before ever reaching Kentucky. A veteran of the Revolutionary War and former sheriff of Allegheny County, Pennsylvania, Morrison became one of Kentucky's leading merchants and statesmen shortly after his arrival there in 1792. He grew rich from the state's expanding hemp industry, and as a land commissioner, legislator, tax officer, navy quartermaster, and bank president he leveraged the state's commercial interests for his own benefit. He became a member of the Transylvania Board of Trustees in 1810 and was elected board chairman in 1819, serving in this role until his death in the early spring of 1823. Henry Clay visited him in the weeks leading up to his death and told Horace of the stoic fortitude with which Morrison bore his illness.[122] When news of Morrison's passing reached campus, the trustees ordered all faculty and students to wear a band of crepe on their left arms in recognition of his service.[123] Morrison's decision to bequeath some $70,000 to the university came as a surprise to no one, except perhaps his son, who later tried and failed to contest the will. Clay was named executor of the estate and was instructed to carry out Morrison's wishes on the following terms: the university would receive $20,000 for an endowed "Morrison professorship" in natural philosophy or mathematics—a 6 percent yearly return on this sum would support a $1,200 salary—and the balance of his estate, valued at between $40,000 and $50,000, was to fund the construction of a building to be named "Morrison College."[124]

Horace agreed to deliver a funeral oration as part of a commemoration ceremony. The speech, later published in twenty-six typescript pages, included encomiums to Morrison's character and, of course, praise for the endowment, "unquestionably one of the most useful and honorable acts of this highly useful and honorable life." But what began as a panegyric transitioned into an outright defense of rational religion and became a way for Horace to announce his unique blend of rational theology and education. The real purpose of schooling, he now declared, was not in books, definitions, or experiments but was to "unfold . . . [to] minds the laws of the visible universe"—that is, to comprehend the works of God and, in so doing, to cultivate a student's intellectual powers and moral sensibilities. An education freed from creedal statements and superstition, open to possibilities of human potential and grounded in logic, taught them "how to be useful, honorable, and happy for time and eternity." Morrison was offered as a representation of this ideal, a Christian in morals and actions but without the tincture of sectarian bigotry. His religious principles were formed from diverse sources but fundamentally sound.[125] The oration was eloquent and direct, containing only a touch of Horace's usually stilted prose. Clarity ensured a wide readership and, on at least one occasion, plagiarism; New York governor DeWitt Clinton admitted stealing a few phrases from it for one of his own speeches.[126] Horace, however, anticipated the worst. "My oration," he confessed in a letter to Milton, "will probably be assailed on several accounts, because of its heresy in religion, because Morrison had enemies, because the university has enemies, because I have enemies, because all compositions find faults, and because attacks must be made whether there is reason for them or not."[127]

He guessed correctly. Shortly after the speech became public, an anonymously published series of pamphlets titled *Literary Pamphleteer* made all other criticisms of him appear weak by comparison. Each of the *Pamphleteer's* four volumes was dedicated to attacks on Horace's character and leadership; Horace alone, the authors complained, was responsible for the rampant yet heretofore unknown graft, corruption, deceit, vice, and immorality that infected the university. Publication of a dedicated exposé, the authors claimed, was necessary because Lexington's newspapers lacked the courage or intelligence to lay open the school's real circumstances; too much smoke, they argued, was thrown up to disguise their president's malevolent intentions.[128]

The author of the first volume, known only as "Citizen," was almost certainly Presbyterian minister John McFarland, head pastor of a small Lexington-area Presbyterian church.[129] Denominational scheming, Citizen argued, was an illusionary distraction from more significant issues. The case against Horace was occasioned by nothing more than the "cause of sound, practical literature in this state." At issue were recent donations and suspicious expenditures, and it was clear to the writer that Horace had "misapplied, and prodigally wasted" vast sums of public money, funds that could have otherwise gone toward the construction of seminaries, grammar schools, academies, and colleges throughout the state. Horace oversaw the distribution of close to $50,000 in donations from the legislature but raised the price of tuition to $60 per year, an "unprecedented sum . . . unaccessible to nine-tenths of the citizens of Kentucky," Citizen groused. Despite the massive outpouring of state assistance and amounts made from extravagant tuition, however, the school was nearly bankrupt. Horace, Citizen continued, maintained legislative support by misrepresenting the number of students in the printed catalog. By including everyone, from the "little boys in the Grammar School" to those who matriculated only part of the year, Horace gave a false accounting; the true number was far less than the four hundred reported and instead something closer to ninety.[130]

To these charges were added more personal ones. Horace enjoyed a lavish salary yet never contributed to charitable causes. He was a fixture in "the theatre, the ball room, the Card table, and all those places to which the vain and dissipated resort," and he encouraged others to do the same. On campus, Horace was little more than a thinly disguised Unitarian cleric, there to inculcate his beliefs through courses on philosophy, references to "Socinian pamphlets," and bald intimidation. Is it right, Citizen asked, to pay him to "laugh and brow-beat your sons out of the little religion which they may possess?"[131] Volumes 2, 3, and 4 followed in rapid succession, each claiming religious neutrality; those suggesting that the pamphlets were driven by Presbyterian enmity, they argued, sought only to confuse the issue. By making it "entirely a Presbyterian cause,"

Horace and his supporters meant to bring other denominations to their side.[132] The author of volume 2, "A Christian Republican," mostly ignored religion and focused instead on Horace's curriculum. He found hardly a redeeming feature in the school, a place where instructors taught "many fooleries and jarring theories."[133] The author of volume 3, "A Friend to Truth," found it unreasonable to accept that a few "learned men from Boston" should have such a dominant voice in education. Their influence was by its very nature corrupting and against the "republican spirit" of their fathers.[134] And the author of volume 4, "Voltaire," described Horace's "chameleon like" behavior, arguing that he changed his theology to match his congregations. When Horace had first appeared in Kentucky, he had refrained from preaching out of a concern for keeping his infidelity hidden from view, but he grew bolder over time and now preached heresy without fear of reprisal.[135]

Students leaped to Horace's defense by addressing the pseudonymous authors of the *Pamphleteer* by name. Charges that Horace sought to inculcate heterodox religious principles were, in their words, "FALSE and ENTIRELY WITHOUT FOUNDATION."[136] Another group of recent graduates mirrored these frustrations. Horace, they argued, had done nothing but add to the graduates' cherished and cultivated religious sentiments. It was true that he attended the theater and numerous social events, but he never sat at the card table. He was "entirely harmless and inoffensive," they added. All of the accusations against him were either misrepresentations or outright lies.[137] But counterclaims did nothing to pacify Horace's detractors; in fact, the students probably only exacerbated the situation by drawing themselves into the debate. The same students that defended him, one author claimed, were party to Horace's immoral behaviors.[138]

Eastern Nabob

Aggravation over these attacks might have convinced Horace to embark on yet another lengthy job-seeking excursion, this time to Tennessee's Cumberland College. The school, located in the town of Nashville, was preparing for expansion and its leading trustee, Senator Andrew Jackson, was in search of a new president. Jackson was certainly no stranger to Horace's work, having visited Transylvania on at least two occasions and, more recently, sending adopted son A. J. Donaldson there to study law under Horace's personal direction.[139] It is doubtful, however, that Horace seriously considered the offer, but the trip provided an escape from Lexington, and that was perhaps enough.

The 560-mile journey, narrated in letters to Horace's father, offered its share of exotic spectacles. Horace remarked on the wonders of Mammoth Cave, where the family spent the better part of a day walking below ground, and was mystified by the Chameleon Spring, whose waters mysteriously changed from blue to red to black to white.[140] The Catholics at Bardstown were an even better attraction. The cathedral architecture, paintings, and stained glass all gave a good if slightly excessive impression. Horace found the "mummery" a bit too grandiose for his liking, and the family nearly burst into laughter at the site of the "superstitious" artifacts, stoles, miters, chalices, and other vestments.[141] But the citizens of Bardstown and other places welcomed him with great fanfare, asked him to speak on any matter he pleased, and always gave a positive reaction.[142] Horace found the people of Nashville particularly welcoming. He received invitations to preach there before a "large number of respectable citizens" and was asked to make public appearances throughout his visit.[143] Ralph Earl, one of Nashville's more distinguished artists, was so taken by Horace that he asked him to sit for a portrait. Horace, never shy of these attentions, was flattered by the prospect of adding his "bald pole" to Earl's "gallery of heads," which included portraits of President Monroe, Kentucky governor Isaac Shelby, Tennessee governor William Carroll, and others.[144]

At Jackson's home, the Hermitage, located just east of the town, Mary, Harriette, and Caroline attended balls while Horace observed their surroundings and calculated the value of the position at Cumberland College. He found Jackson, though gaunt from a recent illness, a "prompt practical man" and gracious host who kept a hectic schedule but managed an equally active social calendar. Jackson's wife, Sarah, though short, "quite fat," and without cultivation, was a fine and benevolent woman.[145] Horace's visit to Cumberland College was less satisfactory. It was, he concluded, "prostrated for the want of funds," lacking both students and teachers. The problems he had in Kentucky, securing legislative assistance and convincing citizens of the value of education, seemed to be repeating themselves here. Tennessee's currency was better than Kentucky's—valued at 73 percent of specie at a time when Kentucky paper was trading at a little less than 50 percent—but this was small consolation.

Pleasant memories of the excursion evaporated soon after the family's return to Lexington. Instead of responding with praise for Horace's recent summary, Luther wrote in September 1823 only to express his desire to have Caroline home. Her "dashing about the Country," attending balls, and meeting interesting people would no doubt spoil her for an eventual return to rural and unexciting Salisbury.[146] More discouraging news was found in the pages of the *Pamphleteer*, which used firsthand reports of the trip to highlight Horace's irascible, haughty, and immoral nature. The author had it on good authority that Horace had arrived in Nashville with "all the pomp of an eastern Nabob," but that his grandiloquence was lost on the "plain republicans" of the town. His appeals to wicked behavior, dancing, and card playing had in particular brought great offense.[147] Horace also returned to Lexington to find that intense scrutiny now extended to his students. Before he had left for Tennessee, he had authorized the publication of all twenty-five senior commencement addresses. Nine were on subjects related to theology, and every one of them was denounced as "rank deism" or an obvious attempt to insult the Bible. Horace's students, one essay argued, made it seem as though the "path to heaven was paved by the study of the sciences." This was the result parents might expect from a university so full of "contagion" and with an avowed deist as president.[148]

Horace had long resisted the urge to take part in the attacks and counterattacks, but this recent assault was too much. Publishing a four-part series of essays in the *Kentucky Reporter* under the name "Ultor," he defended each student thesis in turn, claiming the negative description of the theses as a "monstrous body of infidelity" and nothing more than "sectarian slander against the University" and the rhetoric of an "intolerant alarmist."[149] Other defenses of the theses followed; nearly all agreed that the assaults were the result of a larger Presbyterian cabal, an attempt to seize the College of New Jersey in Princeton and consolidate gains with control of Transylvania.[150]

Honors

But before the situation could degenerate further, something intervened to offset Horace's disappointment: an honorary doctorate of law from Cincinnati College. The practice of conferring honorary doctorates had been common since the first days of colonial colleges. In early America, a master's degree was the highest academic honor students could achieve, usually granted to postgraduate instructors or professors in recognition for years of service. Until the 1860s, doctorates in divinity, literature, philosophy, and law were available only at European institutions; American universities awarded them as ceremonial honors as part of year-end commencement. Many of America's most celebrated characters received honorary degrees; however, only ministers attached the prefix "Dr." to their names and made it part of their official title. The distinctions should not be conflated: wherein politicians, merchants, and other public figures considered these titles relatively meaningless honorifics, ministers and scholars thought them much more significant.

The tradition of ministerial certification provided a rationale for these endorsements. Much like the title *reverend*, granted by a body of respected peers at the time of licensure, the designation "DD," for "doctorate of divinity," became a way to recognize and publicly confirm the value of one's intellectual standing. Horace's current and former theological influences—Samuel Hopkins, Joseph Eckley, John Lathrop, and Samuel West, his predecessor at Hollis Street—had received the distinction. And because most college presidents were also ministers of high standing, the title *doctor* became ubiquitous among them; Yale president Timothy Dwight received the DD in 1787; Harvard president John Kirkland took his in 1802. An honorary doctorate of laws was similar, but it did have one important difference in that it signified respect among a scholarly, not ministerial, audience. Both Dwight and Kirkland added the abbreviation LLD, for doctorate of laws, to their names in 1810; Dwight's successor Jeremiah Day received his LLD shortly after his inauguration in 1817.[151]

At Transylvania, Horace used master of arts degrees to recognize professors Robert Bishop, John Roche, and John Jenkins but reserved doctorates for special circumstances.[152] In 1823, he offered the MA to friend Samuel Wilson along with an apology. "You deserve this and more," he began, "but we have no degree in this country that is so appropriate. LLD and DD are not suitable to non-professional scholars, and PD, a title in Germany, Philosophia Doctor, is not yet established either in England or the United States." Horace hoped Americans might one day adopt the distinction, but doing so would require an emancipation from "Anglican precedents."[153]

Horace's decision to award Henry Clay and appellate judge John Boyle doctorates of law in 1822 was out of flattery, but the honorary doctorate of divinity given to college president Martin Ruter that year was symbolic of scholarly repute.[154] Ruter, a former professor of Oriental languages at Cincin-nati College, had recently accepted the presidency at the newly created Augusta College in Bracken County, Kentucky. The timing of Ruter's degree, or rather its proximity to Horace's, hints at collaboration and the trading of professional favors.[155] Granting the honor to Ruter might have confirmed Augusta's status as a legitimate college; Cincinnati, perhaps acting in repayment of the debt, con-tributed a similar stature to Horace. The decision to award Horace a doctorate of law rather than a doctorate of divinity might have been significant, indicating Horace's desire to extract himself from religious distinctions. Nevertheless, the degree was ironic given his antipathy for the practice and teaching of law.[156]

The distinction of receiving the honorary degree might have changed his opinion, though, and in the fall Horace seems to have embraced his role as profes-sor of law. In November 1823, he gave an introductory law lecture titled "Rank, Duties, and Rewards of American Lawyers and Statesmen," in which he praised the goals and central objects of legal training. "Law," he began, "forces a man to study human nature, government, the relations of society." Divines possess unique emotional qualities of sympathy and feeling; physicians have a natural attention to detail; and lawyers see the whole picture and reason in logical terms. But lawyers are also separate because they surrender themselves to the common good and, in so doing, embrace hardship. Truly, he reasoned, only the "greatest and best and most useful men in the world" can join the practice of law.[157]

But Horace reserved the bulk of his time for the study of moral philosophy, and for this he remained fixated on the work of Thomas Brown, still considering Brown's *Philosophy of the Mind* "the most valuable book in the world." The writ-ing was prolix but offered students an understanding of even the most abstract metaphysical principles.[158] When he returned to the pulpit, he put aside ideas of conversion or rational religion and spoke only about the applicability of Brown's philosophy to more basic discussions of teaching and learning. A sermon titled "On the Interests of Learning and Humanity" was his most refined understand-ing of higher education to date. The purpose of a university, he declared, was to tame brutish human instincts by developing within students' comprehensive self-knowledge, a complete understanding of the senses or "bodily and mental powers." The study of nature was important because nature contained all the laws and principles of the world, but books helped students digest revealed truths. The failure of Rousseau and Pestalozzi was in their disregard of books. Transylvania, he concluded, was the natural head of a statewide system of education because it had the most books, the most instructors, and the best discipline.[159]

Reputation

Philosophy and law were also significant to Transylvania's status among other institutions of higher learning. The school, Horace argued, enjoyed a higher place than Princeton, which focused too much on theology; had more respectability than Harvard or Yale, which possessed programs in law and medicine but produced perfunctory scholars; and was simply better than the military school at West Point, an institution that would be forever "subservient to civil and military engineering." At Transylvania, medicine was important, but "intellectual and moral philosophy—eloquence, the efforts of genius"—reigned supreme. Theology was taught according to these precepts, as a dispassionate science that could be quantified, categorized, and dispassionately discussed.[160] There was little wonder, he concluded, why the school remained at or near the top of numerical rankings.

Horace repeated many of these boasts in a report to the Kentucky legislature in December 1823. Recent accusations of mismanagement and malfeasance had brought unwanted attention to the university, and the state asked for yet another accounting of finances, instruction, and student behavior. Horace answered questions of exorbitant tuition costs in simple language: the price was high but "proportioned to the excellency of the instruction." Allegations of heretical teaching were equally false; instructors, himself included, simply encouraged "freedom of expression." Rumors of student misbehavior—youths sneaking away to play cards or billiards—were laughable. Demands on a student's time were too numerous to permit such activity. His students were the moral and intellectual equals of those in the "principle institutions" of the East.[161]

It was hard to ignore Horace's success. His opponents, though bolder now than in the past, were marginalized. And legislative support, although not completely satisfying, was on the upswing. Enrollment was at a near record high and could only improve. By 1823, states west of the Allegheny Mountains had more than two million inhabitants, but only one in five thousand attended college.[162] Most important of all and most determinative in Horace's decision to remain was his standing among others in his profession. Earlier that year

Joel Collins, one of the early founders of Miami University of Ohio in Oxford, had asked Horace to forward a copy of Transylvania's by-laws so they could be imitated.[163] A few months later President Jeremiah Day of Yale asked Horace for advice on how he might improve the office of the president.[164]

The comparative advantages of his position added an inducement to stay. Bigotry, legislative apathy, and financial exigency existed everywhere, but Transylvania's situation offered the brightest hope of success. Other colleges were struggling to maintain basic decorum. Sylvanus Thayer was appointed superintendent of West Point in 1817 and fought student disorder for much of his tenure.[165] In 1818, the College of William and Mary in Virginia and Middlebury College in Vermont suspended students for "disrespectful conduct" or full-scale rioting.[166] In the spring of 1823, Harvard and Yale were nearly undone by devastating student rebellions. At Harvard, two opposing student groups fought openly and caused endless mischief and copious damage—President Kirkland ended the dispute by expelling forty-five members of the senior class.[167] At Yale in early 1823, nearly the entire student body fought against citizens of New Haven and ended up suffering, according to one report, "bruised limbs and bloody faces."[168] In December of that year, the College of New Jersey suspended a large contingent of rebellious students for general disobedience.[169] The same climate simply did not exist at Transylvania, and it was difficult to argue that Horace was anything less than advertised or that rebellious behavior could be held back by overt religious instruction.

The balance of Horace's presidency would depend on his ability to marshal support for a reimagined university, one divorced from religious implications and unburdened by charges of orthodox or heterodox teaching. His reimagined curriculum and examination system were both important steps in this direction. However, claiming distinction based on the merits of his secular qualifications—the teaching of philosophy and doctoral honors in law—was a more significant declaration of his intellectual independence. It was a difficult idea for many to grasp. The actual substance of higher education still mystified the uninitiated, but the assumption of excellence often rested on the perceived quality of moral instruction—a college was nothing if not a place to groom pious Christians. Without an overtly Christian message, youths would fall victim to their passions and degenerate into brutish philistines. Charles Caldwell ran a similar risk in his attempts to wrest the medical program from Horace's control, separating the process of certification, and thus authority, from the hands of nonspecialists. Ironically, Horace hoped for a similar revolution of thought in which academics would be irrevocably separated from clerical attachments.

Horace was not alone in these efforts. A national trend toward the compartmentalization of religious instruction, occasioned by the fracturing, multiplication, and popularity of Protestant denominations, convinced many schools to build separate programs dedicated to theology. These programs, denominated "seminaries" to distinguish them from colleges or schools, began in 1808 at Andover; nine others followed, including at Princeton (1812), Yale (1822), and Harvard (1824). For denominational leaders, the recent growth of theological seminaries was a profound blessing.[170] Lessons, grounded on biblical principles and taught by respectable ministers of the gospel, would safeguard the morality of children. "It will be an awful matter," one author claimed, "if Christians shall suffer their own children to degenerate into heathens."[171]

For established colleges, separate schools of theology allowed presidents to preserve the appeal of moral instruction while simultaneously expanding the breadth and autonomy of secular academics. But the separation did little to quell dissent, and some institutions promoted themselves as standard-bearers of religious virtue, the proud beneficiaries of pious students who uplifted the entire student body. Leaders of Bowdoin College could only wonder at the grim "state of things" at colleges where the "voice of religion was hushed."[172] The proprietors of Dartmouth College claimed an even greater share of student piety: 65 of 146 students were religious. "I am well persuaded," a statement read, that "the pious students give in no small degree, a tone to the general deportment and habits of the others."[173] Christian periodicals now altered their annual assessments of student enrollment to reflect the number of professing Christians, "those with the appearance of religion." In April 1823, the *Evangelical Witness* found only 12 religious persons out of 302 students at Harvard, 39 out of 156 at Brown, 50 out of 234 at Union College, 16 out of 221 at Transylvania, and 115 out of 373 at Yale. Harvard, Transylvania, and the College of South Carolina were especially heinous in that they had no Bible groups, prayer circles, or religious societies whatsoever.[174]

Horace gave up on the idea of a seminary at Transylvania a few years after his arrival, hoping instead to force theological separation through internal improvements alone. Optimism in his educational expertise was warranted:

the student commencement exercises of 1823 were the best yet, Transylvania's name enjoyed a national reputation, and in December that year he counted 377 students—44 in law, 191 in medicine, 118 undergraduates, and 24 in the preparatory program, the second-largest student body in the country.[175] Challenges remained, but friends multiplied. "Good," he reminded brother Milton, "rather than evil, is the result."

But maintaining legislative support was no mean trick; Horace considered Kentucky governor John Adair a "poor creature, lazy and inefficient."[176] He understood the fickle nature of politics and saw his position as especially precarious in the wake of the relief controversy. Henry Clay, Horace's first and most consistent champion, was simultaneously popular and infamous for antirelief legislation, and criticisms of Clay were sure to extend to others. If Transylvania were to grow beyond the theological boundaries of its competitors, Horace would have to assume the burdens of leadership, skirt controversy when possible, and develop a science of education that others could accept.

6

"A Time of Fruits and Flowers"

Louisiana was hotter and more uncomfortable than Horace expected. The weather was stultifying, made worse by heavy air that sat thick in his chest and by taunting, all-too-infrequent breezes wafting in from the nearby window of his boardinghouse. The temperature had already reached a sultry ninety-two degrees by June 1. Just how much it would rise that summer was anyone's guess. Mary was too bothered by the heat to write; Horace was too excited by his prospects to remain silent. And so in a letter to his daughter he described the college, the presidency, and the fine 240-acre plantation that could all be his for the asking. There were two available options for his university, both within sight of New Orleans, both with easy access to the Mississippi. Neither was inexpensive, costing between $25,000 and $30,000, but most of the money had already been committed by enthusiastic supporters. "I consider myself," he closed, "as almost at work already improving my plantation, and preparing it, for a college."[1]

A reversal of public sentiment, something he had grown to expect in Lexington, seemed unlikely in the fresh, liberal atmosphere of Louisiana, a place rife with former Bostonians, where the market stayed open on Sundays, children ran around nearly naked, and theatergoing was considered a respectable pastime. Horace Jr. loved New Orleans, declaring his intention to live there for the rest of his life; Mary never knew a place more friendly or accommodating.[2] Horace, grandiose as always in his expectations, was certain the town would become nothing less than "an immense city, the emporium of the West" destined to rival and then surpass New York.[3] A month earlier friends from Lexington had shared news of Horace's enjoyment of the place. Louisiana in the "time of fruits & flowers," one friend concluded, would appeal to anyone. April and May were fine months for a visit, but the season, friend Benjamin Dudley promised, would grow less hospitable in the coming weeks.[4]

The circumstances that had brought Horace to Louisiana—Kentucky's vulgar politics, malevolent cabals, depreciated money, and lackluster public support—now made sense in the aggregate and confirmed the trajectory of his career. As president of a university in New Orleans, Horace could improve the best intentions for Transylvania while reaching his full potential as educator and scholar. Louisiana's governor and the state's leading and wealthiest citizens pledged their support for a university but left Horace with the freedom to decide its fate; there was already talk of an all-expense-paid trip to Europe and $10,000 for the purchase of books and scientific equipment.[5] All of this was possible if Horace could just survive the oppressive Louisiana climate.

But July was even worse, and the unrelenting heat started to do damage to his system. By the middle of that month, fever had given way to vomiting and then to something else entirely when a strange "prickly heat" and rash gave him the sensation of being "stuck with pins and needles all over the body." Eating became difficult, sleep all but impossible. These were the first stages of yellow fever and the last days of his life, though Horace, endlessly optimistic, thought them nothing more than "a good symptom of a successful acclimation," something common to all good and hearty migrants to the Deep South. When the fever and rash and vomiting and sleepless nights became too much, he and Mary booked passage on the first "packet ship," or small schooner, bound for New York.[6] Horace was convinced he could live in Louisiana but thought it unreasonable to attempt to do so in his condition; a season of rest and recuperation in Salisbury, he concluded, would restore him and add vigor to the plans. On the day of their departure, however, he expressed reservations about leaving. He planned to host boarders that summer in an impromptu, privately run summer program to make money before the start of the regular school year and was now also confident that the worst part of his illness was over; a mixture of sulfur, molasses, and hot baths had cured the ague. The prickly rash was abated by the generous application of a stiff clothing brush to his skin.[7]

His reluctance to postpone the start of his latest academic enterprise was understandable in light of his somewhat unexpected departure from Lexington earlier that year. It was an ending that seemed almost impossible just years earlier when public sentiment and national opinion had combined to lift him and his school to unprecedented heights. Between 1824 and 1827, the final years of Horace's presidency, national conversations about the potential of the American West were framed by his achievements, and in discussions concerning college building Transylvania was either the sine qua non of western success or the cause of its inevitable decline. Businessmen saw the school as a model for economic recovery; denominational leaders promoted their own schools as a safeguard against the secularism promoted there; town fathers throughout the Midwest and South hoped a local college would garner the same respect enjoyed in Lexington. The editor of the *Boston Patriot* reported that students from other states brought upward of $100,000 into Kentucky each year,[8] which was more than enough reason for others to gamble on a similar academic enterprise.

Transylvania offered a guide to these ambitions. When a body of concerned citizens came together to build a college in Oxford, Ohio, they looked to Lexington and recruited professor Robert Bishop as their first president. Farther south, Princeton professor Philip Lindsley accepted the presidency of Cumberland College at Nashville because of what Horace had accomplished in Kentucky. In his inaugural address, he posited a relatable goal to his audience: "the example of Transylvania University," he claimed, was attainable and "prominently within your view."[9] When the short-lived College of New Orleans closed, former president Theodore Clapp recommended students attend Transylvania rather than any other school.[10] Thomas Jefferson's plans for the University of Virginia were born of many things, not the least of which were Horace's experiences.[11] Their correspondence reflected common concerns, and Jefferson hoped he and Horace might continue their open dialogue in the spirit of equal improvement.[12]

Easterners had come to see Horace as a peerless intellect, singularly able to translate the condition of the restless West to the settled condition of the East. In April 1825, Massachusetts congressman Edward Everett recognized Horace's accomplishments with local honors.[13] A month later Harvard professor George Fickner wrote to Horace for advice on how his troubled university might handle students who did not want to pursue a degree: "how they behaved & whether any jealousies grow up between the two kinds of pupils—in short," he added, "how long you have pursued this plan, how it operates, & how it can be best carried into effect."[14] In December that year, Jared Sparks, editor of the *North American Review,* asked Horace to review Henry Marshall's two-volume work

The History of Kentucky and in so doing provide a "full account ... of the condition, rising greatness, & respects of the west."[15] New Englanders were the most verbose in their acclamations; in his description of Transylvania, the editor of the *New Hampshire Sentinel* described Horace as the "polished gentleman, erudite scholar ... who presides over that school of science, and who has raised it from a mere inconsiderable academy."[16] Even Jedidiah Morse, long antagonistic to Horace's religious affiliations, was forced to recognize Transylvania's "flourishing condition" in his book *A New System of Geography* in 1824.[17] William Woodbridge and Emma Willard's textbook *Universal Geography, Ancient and Modern,* made implicit the connection between the advanced cultural conditions found in Lexington and its famed institution of higher education.[18] This sentiment was repeated time and again in almanacs, periodicals, and anything intended to introduce or promote the American West.

Horace's notoriety made his home the first stop for foreign dignitaries and American statesmen visiting Lexington. Russian minister Pyotr Ivanovich Poletika, a certain "Mr. Palmer" from Rome who claimed he knew Napoleon, and many others made it a point to seek him out.[19] Count Charles Vaudois of Piedmont, "an Italian gentleman" and nobleman visiting Lexington from the island of Sardinia, was unaware of Horace but was told of his brilliance by the most learned men of the East.[20] General Andrew Jackson, the Marquis de Lafayette, and presidents Madison and Monroe sought out Horace's attentions. They came to Lexington for no other reason than to witness the splendor of Horace's university, which by the start of 1824 had become the centerpiece of expansionist ambitions and a sparkling jewel of national acclaim. Horace's professors were published with great alacrity. Jesse Bledsoe, professor of common and statute law, published his introductory series of lectures that year; Robert Bishop added a survey of world history; and Constantine Rafinesque continued to churn out books and articles. All of this publication, of course, was seen as the product of good leadership. The student body stabilized at four hundred that year, with medical and law students now dominating enrollments. Horace's law class reached forty-eight in 1824—only one-quarter the number of the Medical Department but an encouraging total nonetheless.[21] The Medical Department's prosperity was also now unquestioned. The editor of the *Cincinnati Literary Gazette* praised its success and its professors' notoriety, declaring it "the only one of which the extended Backwoods can at present boast."[22]

Pressure

None of these accomplishments helped Horace's reputation among the small but vociferous body of disaffected malcontents in Kentucky, however, and their attacks resumed at the start of 1824 with new vigor. Hopes to appease his religious objectors were laudable but ultimately fruitless. In the spring of that year, the Transylvania trustees invited leaders from each of Lexington's churches to deliver sermons in the university chapel on alternating Sundays as a means of promoting denominational equality and equal representation in the affairs of the school. But Presbyterian ministers John Breckinridge and Nathan Hall looked on the request with suspicion and asked the board, through an essay published in the *Western Monitor,* to clarify several points: if they had freedom to preach doctrine, if the reason for this request was to give Horace a rest from his duties, and if their participation was meant to signify a compromise with Horace.[23] The board responded with cool detachment; if Breckinridge and Hall were to participate, they would not be permitted to use the pulpit as a means to spark "religious controversy or personal abuse."[24] Hall and Breckinridge took umbrage at this restriction and dismissed the scheme as a means of misleading the public. They would not, they returned, aid any scheme that produced an impression "that what was wrong is rectified, and what was wanting, is now supplied."[25]

Just as word of Presbyterian disaffection reached Horace, another more personal attack was launched. A twenty-eight-page pamphlet titled *A Plain Statement,* published in January 1824, told the story of former student John Trotter, who had suffered expulsion just a year earlier. Sometime in late 1823 Horace had reprimanded Trotter for a variety of misbehaviors, including absences from public declamations. Trotter approached Horace on the street to argue over the matter, and their conversation degenerated to insults and accusations. Transylvania's trustees called Trotter in for questioning and, finding that he had acted improperly, expelled him.[26]

Trotter, the pamphlet continued, claimed that the original offense, argument, and expulsion were all the results of theological differences. He said that he had been immediately affronted by the president's gross misconduct shortly after Holley's arrival at the school. President Holley was consistently and obsessively abusive, ridiculing and deriding students "by the lowest species of ridicule, and sophistry." He degraded Christian doctrine and took pride in the knowledge that his remarks would offend anyone of common religious sensibility. Trotter believed that he was not alone in his feelings and that a large body of students found Horace abusive but were too afraid to "endure his abuse . . . [or] draw his fury." Trotter would not be cowed and refused to take part in certain heretical readings, and for this he was reprimanded. He had objected for the sake of his classmates, and when he encountered Horace on the street, his emotions got the better of him. The whole affair, the pamphlet's author concluded, was "illegal, unjust and oppressive."[27] But the matter did not end there. A short while later Trotter was granted admission to Centre College on the strength of a recommendation from Transylvania professor Robert Bishop. The contents of that letter of recommendation were rumored to defame Horace's character; Bishop agreed with Trotter and, in so doing, condemned Horace. Bishop's participation in the matter exposed long-running hostilities that had begun when Horace first assumed the presidency and intensified when Horace had altered Bishop's teaching assignment. The letter to Centre aggravated an already tense relationship between Horace and Bishop, and by September 1824 Bishop announced his plans to leave Transylvania.[28]

To these volleys were added repetitions of previous charges, counterattacks, and more of the same. Those critical of Horace claimed he possessed cheap and superficial intellectual skills that impressed only the most dimwitted. He was a philanderer who spent more time in the billiard hall, ballrooms, theaters, and racetracks of Lexington than the classroom. Worst of all, Horace was an apostate, an impious Judas, an odious character so totally undeserving of fame or respect and so completely inappropriate to lead youths.[29] Pseudonymous authors responded to the attackers, attackers retorted, and the cycle continued throughout the year. Following the dialogues between Horace's assailants and his advocates demanded a great deal from readers. In one line of debate, an author known only as "Fenlon" regretted his inability to return the charges made by "Calvin" and so engaged other objectors instead: "I am happy that he [Calvin] has expressed his sentiments about natural religion which are in strict accordance with those of President Holley; for the defense of which 'A Senior' has charged him. . . . 'Austin' in the Advertiser has been misinformed, if his question was designed to communicate what he believed to be fact."[30]

Essays critical of Horace were punctuated by a series of pamphlets written in similar tones. A nine-page pamphlet titled *President Holley and Infidel-*

ity appeared in April 1824, followed shortly thereafter by *Plan of Reform in Transylvania University* and *Remarks to the Public Respecting President Holley.* Horace's critics now also called out William G. Hunt, editor of the *Western Monitor,* for his biased but thoughtless defense of Horace. Hunt, "the friend and apologist of Mr. Holley," one essay began, took the responsibility of answering for Horace but was just an "echo" of him, a defender without any sense.[31] Hunt himself responded to the "unparalleled audacity," arguing that it was an editor's privilege to choose what material made publication, "whether an article offered was 'designed to point out real abuses in the management of a public institution,' and whether the limits of the paper, having regard of course to other paramount claims, could admit it."[32]

Another editor found the consequences of publishing critical essays even less appealing. When John McCalla purchased controlling interest in Lexington's *Kentucky Gazette,* he joined what he thought to be the popular side by publishing essays unflattering to Horace and the university. The public thought differently. A town meeting held in early spring nearly erupted into violence as Horace's supporters threatened to cancel their subscriptions unless McCalla promised never to publish works of this sort again. Mary Ann Corlis described the chaotic scene to husband John. Public sentiment in the meeting was universal. Those assembled said "they felt the importance of the University to the town & that they not only would defend Mr. Holley with their voice but they would fight for him." Fearing for the future of his paper and perhaps for his health, McCalla relented.[33]

All of the claims and counterclaims seemed only to inflame the situation while simultaneously casting doubt on Horace's leadership. If enough charges existed, the thinking went, at least some must be true. In late March, the editor of the *Boston Recorder* found the situation deplorable but concluded, "If we may judge from what appears in the papers merely, the affairs of the College cannot have been very well conducted."[34] Supporters of Nashville's Cumberland College read the endless debates and saw opportunity. Lundsford Yandell, a medical student at Transylvania but loyal to his home state of Tennessee, described the advantages of the debacle to his father, Wilson, in December 1824. Horace was a "man of transcendent genius" and "splendid learning," but because of his "imprudence he has reduced the University to a bankruptcy of reputation which can never be returned." "Now," he concluded, "is the time for Cumberland College to put a stand with the proper kind of management it might now prosper." Students from other states were, Yandell continued, anxious to leave Transylvania and would, with the right encouragement, take their medical education in Nashville. If Cumberland could just attract a few notable men from the East, it would rival Transylvania in just a few years.[35]

Perseverance

Horace responded with stoic reserve, convinced that Presbyterians were behind the rancor but he was reluctant to take part in the debate. Letters to Milton in 1824 were absent any major description of the trouble, simply stating, "I . . . leave it to my students and other friends to defend me."[36] He found comfort in ancient wisdom and clipped quotes on slander for his scrapbook: "The worthiest people are most injured by slanderers," "To be slandered ranks us with men of the greatest merit," "Slander is the revenge of a coward, and dissimulation his defense," and "Slanderers like flies that leap over all a man's good parts to light only upon his sores" were pasted around articles either praising or condemning him.[37] At times, he seemed unperturbed by the trouble. As the July commencement ceremonies of 1824 neared, he boasted to his father about the "fame and influence" his school had achieved and the great crowds of curious citizens who would flock to witness the commencement spectacle. On the subject of debate or divide, he added simply, "Our enemies are foiled."[38]

In times of stressful anxiety, Horace's best refuge was his work, and he returned to it that year with relentless energy. His schedule, described in detail to brother Milton, gave little opportunity for external complaints. His day began at nine o'clock with a visit to the chapel for courses in oratory and ethics. He reserved ten to eleven o'clock for administrative work—dealing with delinquent students, providing written comments to student work, and observing his professors. At eleven, he prepared for a twelve o'clock lecture to his seniors on the subject of mental philosophy. At one, he lectured members of the law class. Dinner was at two, followed by a series of afternoon meetings with faculty and members of the board. To these responsibilities he added private lectures and meetings with local societies, correspondence, reception of visitors, walks, and visits to the Athenaeum. Saturdays and Sundays were filled with more of the same, plus worship and student oratory exercises.[39]

His involvement in the law school now also intensified. The catalog for 1824 lists Horace as professor of civil and national law and political economy, an impressive title to be sure, but one he was forced to take. Repeated attempts to recruit additional faculty in the law program had failed. Lexington attorney William Barry had at first accepted a position as professor of natural and physical law, but he withdrew despite attractive offers of salary paid in specie. A similar offer was then made to and declined by Judge John Boyle, chief justice of the Kentucky Court of Appeals.[40] Much of the work in the law school seems to have been under the charge of Jesse Bledsoe, professor of common and statute law.[41] Privately, Horace had from very early on doubted Kentucky was the right place to begin a law practice, going so far as to dissuade brother Orville from a planned relocation in 1819. "The work of a lawyer here is hard and irregular, and the fees are not great," he had warned. Part of the problem were the Kentuckians themselves, who as clients would challenge Orville with boorish behavior. Politics, the next natural use of his law degree, was equally inopportune, with low fees and questionable colleagues. If Orville truly desired either the law or politics, he should try New York.[42]

Horace used his introductory law lecture in 1824 to make sense of his position and, perhaps, add legitimacy to his honorary doctorate of laws. The profession, he admitted, was not his by training but came with his role as caretaker or "affectionate, intelligent, and effectual nurse" of Transylvania. His declining influence in the Medical Department eased the transition and may have increased the significance of these responsibilities. The Medical Department was important, he admitted, but only because it contributed to the efforts of the law program. Celebrated men of medicine brought prestige to other professors, drew students to the school, and created more opportunities to hire more faculty. The larger the institution, the better the quality and more significant its accomplishments, for, as Horace reminded his students, "great institutions make great men."[43]

Enthusiasm for the powers of legal oratory plus a growing dissatisfaction with the political climate inspired Horace's participation in social clubs, specifically the Kentucky Institute and the African Colonization Society. He helped establish the former in January 1823 and as the group's first president ensured the active participation of Transylvania's professors—one report claimed that upward of half the members were his faculty. The institute was an imitation of the Wednesday Evening Club of Boston, a place where leading merchants, politicians, ministers, and intellectuals could gather to read and discuss each other's scholarship. Horace, remembering the failure of the ill-fated *Western Review*, made sure to include the following proviso in the initial charter: to retain membership, each participant would have to produce at least one essay. The society appears to have been a success; by the time of its first anniversary, celebrated on January 29, 1824, Horace was able to announce the increased esteem shared by the membership and to express a more refined understanding of their mission. They were, he concluded, the promoters and preservers of the American West, its "history, antiques, manners, and character," with special attention to the natural world.[44] The editor of the *Cincinnati Literary Gazette* called the Kentucky Institute a "germ of a learned Society," a young but promising seat of science and literature. Constantine Rafinesque, the group's secretary, shared his recent discoveries with characteristic zeal; Drs. Caldwell, James Blythe, and Daniel Drake contributed medical and climatological essays; and Horace commented on the morals and "peculiar manners" of Western people.[45]

The extent of Horace's involvement in the African Colonization Society is less clear. In Kentucky, the "peculiar institution" of slavery grew, but with mixed support. The certainty of gradual emancipation, a position championed by both Thomas Jefferson and Henry Clay, induced a combination of fear and benevolence among many slave-owning Kentuckians. The end of slavery was assured; the destiny of former slaves was not. Proponents of "colonization," or the relocation of enslaved Africans to the West African nation of Liberia or elsewhere, posited a future where freed slaves undercut wages, encouraged rebellion, or worse. Those of a more benevolent disposition argued that colonization would allow blacks to develop without interference from whites.[46] Most members of the African Colonization Society were slave owners themselves; Clay owned twenty or more.

Horace's participation in the group becomes understandable in the context of his past experiences. Samuel Hopkins, his early theological influence, considered slavery an evil without qualification, though Timothy Dwight was less committal. Horace had cast aspersions on slave owner Hezekiah Bradley of Greenfield Village in 1805, but his first visit to the South in 1818 convinced him of the humane nature of slavery; its brutality, he believed, was exaggerated by "small minded and zealous men" with little direct experience. In the company of wealthy plantation-owning Virginians, Horace concluded that slavery was evil but only because it retarded agricultural production, encouraging sloth among otherwise industrious farmers.[47] A trip to Cincinnati in the summer of 1824 confirmed these ideas. On seeing the town's bustling industry and commercial vigor, he remarked, "It is a great advantage to Cincinnati unquestionably to be without slaves."[48] In Kentucky, outright objections to slavery all but guaranteed the objector's political defeat or, as in the case of Transylvania's former president James Blythe, a quick exit from public life. Sensing perhaps that the issue was relatively safe, Horace offered his opinions on the matter in the *Western Review*, arguing that the situation could only be rectified by time; sudden emancipation was impossible, and the end of slavery would require incremental steps. Plans for colonization, he argued, were the best and most efficacious route to this end.[49] In a letter to Orville in 1820, Horace declared the island of Haiti to be best suited for the project, not because it was more settled but because it was closer. Horace's position was hardly benevolent, however, and he admitted a great fear "that we shall never get rid of this monstrous evil, a black population." His only consolation was that whites were destined to increase in population faster than blacks.[50] On a visit to Baltimore in July 1824, Horace was interested to meet Jonathan Granville, a Haitian official sent to America to encourage settlement. The plan was impressive, but Granville was more interesting, and Horace admitted his surprise to find someone of Granville's color so intelligent.[51]

His objective detachment to the issue should have made owning a slave easier for him, but when the family first arrived in Lexington, he chose to employ and not own his servants. His position changed in the summer of 1825 when in a letter to Milton he declared proudly, "I have bought a negro to day, and have thus become a slave owner." His purchase of a thirty-three-year-old female housekeeper for $250 and negotiations for a male servant at $400 now made sense, Horace argued, because slaves were better workers and became "attached to their masters." "I intend to own all my servants," he concluded.[52]

Caroline

Mary backed away from her earlier attempt to leave Kentucky permanently or at least resigned herself to a life in Kentucky. It is unclear if she still hoped for a return to Boston, but it is likely that disappointments of the previous years conditioned her against such a hope. Money was still an issue, and it became increasingly obvious that no Boston church could match Horace's salary. The social life of Lexington was still shallow, but reading, composing poetry, educating Horace Jr., and enjoying the company of Horace's sister, Caroline, did much to relieve her ennui. Caroline had been with the family since the fall of 1822, much to Mary's delight, but her extended stay was a constant source of worry for father Luther, who in the spring of 1824 insisted on her return—both he and her mother were advanced in years and might have needed her for basic assistance. Horace delayed the trip as long as he could for Mary's sake but ultimately agreed to return Caroline after the close of the current school year in July. Mary's disappointment over the matter would remain but would be ameliorated by the budding romance and eventual marriage of daughter Harriette to William Brand, son of prosperous Lexington merchant John Brand. Inasmuch as his opinion mattered, Horace considered Brand an "honorable young man" and fully and enthusiastically approved of the union.[53]

Horace offered to escort Caroline to Salisbury to escape the summer heat, but he also used the trip as an excuse to see the Erie Canal and revisit scenes he had first encountered on his trip from Boston to Lexington in 1818. Leaving Mary, Harriette, and Horace Jr. at home would make for an easier and less-expensive trip. Mary, also bothered by the excessive heat, was left to take short excursions on her own.[54] Horace's letters to Mary in the summer of 1824 provide a detailed account of the trip, from his arrival in Cincinnati to his visit to Canada and ultimately his stay at Monticello. He was, as usual, interested mainly in the character of these places, how their people were educated and to what effect.

He found Cincinnati more beautiful than Lexington, with well-paved streets and well-built homes but without the charm he expected. Public buildings were ugly or "in bad taste"; the College of Cincinnati was simply "wretched," with broken glass and decaying woodwork.[55] College president Elijah Slack was even less impressive. Though a pleasant and agreeable sort, Slack lacked the appearance and intellect Horace expected of someone in this position. Cincinnati, he concluded, was better than Lexington in many respects "but behind us far in literature, science, society, and union of feeling."[56] Buffalo and Upper Canada (Ontario) offered their share of interesting sites and people; stops at Rochester and Schenectady allowed visits to brothers Myron and Orville.[57] At New York,

Horace tried unsuccessfully to fill the newly endowed Morrison professorship with someone he hoped could fill holes not only in the intended subjects—mathematics and natural philosophy—but also in French, German, Spanish, and Italian. His best prospect in the city was Henry James Anderson, a graduate of the medical school at Columbia College. Horace described him as young but accomplished and, as such, probably unwilling to "go to the backwoods" for a position he could get in New York.[58]

In Philadelphia, Horace observed the strange dietary practices of a Jewish community. In Baltimore, he hoped to reunite with Elizabeth Patterson but was disappointed to find her absent.[59] At no time during the trip did he seek a return to the pulpit. Unitarians in Baltimore desired his presence and suggested that an offer of permanent settlement was forthcoming, but Horace was less than enthusiastic; although he might consider a position in New York, the thoughts of accepting the pastorate anywhere else, "even with the promise of a competent salary," were now unattractive in light of his more refined academic interests.[60]

The highlight of the trip was a long-awaited visit with Thomas Jefferson, something Horace had attempted on his trip in 1818 but, arriving too late in the season, found only a vacant house. This time Jefferson was waiting, and the eighty-two-year-old former president looked exactly as Horace expected—a tall, finely dressed older gentleman with broad shoulders and a clear voice. Jefferson was somewhat physically diminished by his age—his hair was completely gray, his hands trembled, and he moved only with great effort—but his mind was still strong and full of ideas for his university. The two had exchanged only a few letters on the subject in the years preceding the visit, a product, Horace discovered, of the excessive demands on Jefferson's time. Jefferson complained that he received and responded to more than twelve hundred letters a year. It was an endless annoyance that frustrated times of quiet study.[61]

Horace marveled at Jefferson's plans for the University of Virginia. Expenses related to the buildings and grounds of the university totaled around $300,000, a full $70,000 more than the cost of the White House. Jefferson's plans for his professoriate were equally impressive. He recruited the bulk of his faculty from England and offered each $3,000 a year, the same salary paid to Horace. They would enjoy equal status, without hierarchy or rank. Governance would be limited, as would rules. A board made up of students would perform the lion's share of these responsibilities. More shocking were the limitations and freedoms. Professors would lecture no more than two hours a day, no morning prayers would be held, and students would be allowed to choose from a selection of courses.[62]

Opportunity

The trip to Monticello buoyed Horace's spirits and prepared him for his "university campaign" that fall. "We open under favorable auspices," he reported in a letter to brother Milton in October, shortly after his return to Lexington. The number of students, although decreased, was still healthy; Thomas Matthews, a young but distinguished Cincinnatian, took the Morrison Professorship; and Transylvania's rank among American universities was as high as ever. Best of all, Horace concluded, the Presbyterians were all but defeated.[63] The mood in the Kentucky legislature regarding the university remained positive despite allegations of financial mismanagement and moral turpitude. The state submitted to Horace and the trustees yet another list of questions, this time regarding Transylvania's financial health, the amount of public funding received, debts paid, and bills outstanding. In addition to these questions were those related to student behavior, curriculum, and enrollment, specifically why the number of law students had dropped from forty-eight in 1823 to thirty in 1824.[64]

The response to these questions, prepared by Horace, certain trustees, and several members of the faculty, urged patience. The school continued to draw enrollment from western states, continued to profit Lexington's economy, and remained a source of incalculable pride to the state. The number of students in the regular classes was not as low as estimates suggested; a true accounting was complicated by the attendance of students for only part of the school year.[65] Problems in the law school were real but fixable, having everything to do with the inability to attract qualified professors. As soon as this problem was rectified and two or three more law professors hired, the law school would not only grow but also "become one of the most distinguished schools in the Union." The Medical Department needed little defense; enrollment was still high, and expectations for continued growth remained. There was, however, the issue of space; medical classes took place either in a rented building or in a professor's home. If the department were to continue, it would need a sizable donation for the construction of a dedicated medical hall.[66]

The six-member legislative committee tasked to review these answers responded with unqualified praise. Horace's explanation of student enrollment was sufficient; the curriculum was deemed conducive to morality and taste; and the school's finances were judged to be adequately managed. "The public patronage," the committee's report continued, "has resulted in manifold profit to the state." Other financial benefits arising from the school, the money saved by Kentucky parents, and the money brought into the state by out-of-state students were not included in the report but were no less significant. Moreover, Transylvania was the surest safeguard against "foreign manners," the habits of mind learned at eastern schools that alienated children from the "simple republicanism of the father." For these and other reasons, the committee concluded, Transylvania was of "infinite importance" to both the present and distant future of the state.[67]

Plaudits were short-lived. The gubernatorial election of 1824 pitted relief-minded Kentucky House member Joseph Desha against Christopher Tompkins, an antirelief judge from Bourbon County. Tompkins rehearsed standard antirelief postulates, arguing for financial stability through specie-backed currency and a return to abstemious living.[68] Desha countered with emotional pleas, claiming to be "a friend of the people" and a determined advocate of small farmers. His supporters described him as a "practical farmer" and painted Tompkins as a "champion of the 'rich and well born'" and completely ignorant of public suffering.[69] In the end, appeals to public sentiment were too much, and Desha won in a commanding fashion, garnering 60 percent of the vote and dominating everywhere outside central Kentucky.[70] As a sign of things to come, Desha went right to work, supplanting antirelief judges on the Kentucky Court of Appeals with those friendly to relief measures. The "New Court, Old Court" controversy may have tipped the balance of power in Desha's favor, but it took the state to the brink of civil war.[71]

Beginning of the End

The year 1825 began with a familiar blend of optimism and agitation; Horace's friends circled around him, his enemies probed for weakness. "We are still in confusion in our politics," Horace reported to brother Milton in mid-February,[72] but signs of prosperity were everywhere. Enrollment rebounded in a big way; some estimated the total number of matriculates at four hundred, others put it closer to five hundred, but more significant was their distribution. More than half the students were from outside the state, a significant total considering how hard westerners had worked to establish local colleges.[73] That year the *Charlestown Courier* believed Transylvania's prospects were "never as flattering."[74] The editor of the *Richmond Enquirer* compared Lexington's university to Richmond's own and asked, "How is it possible . . . that the University of Virginia should not succeed?"[75] The *Pensacola Gazette* declared Horace a man of "vast acquirements," uniquely qualified to advance the interests of learning in the western states.[76] And an unnamed visitor to Lexington that year believed Transylvania to be the "light upon the shades of ignorance and obscurity."[77] But news of success was usually couched in news of local opposition. A contributor to the *American Mercury* of Hartford, Connecticut, found current aggravations illogical, concluding, "There never was a people so bent upon the destruction of a real blessing as some Kentuckians are."[78]

Horace's opponents, perhaps emboldened by the success of relief-minded Kentuckians, grew more hostile over the early months of 1825, fabricating and revising charges to gain a larger appeal and calling for his immediate resignation. A series titled "Dr. Fishback, and Transylvania University," published in the *Western Luminary,* revisited the circumstances of Horace's appointment and early attempts to limit his preaching and manage his infidelity.[79] Another report claimed Methodist and Baptist students had abandoned the school. Horace ignored the first and dismissed the second as "entirely a lie" and the product of "a few Presbyterian priests." He was inured to religious bickering but grew concerned with potential problems from the Relief Party. "Desha could alienate more persons from me than all the Presbyterian priests in the state," he declared apprehensively in a letter to Milton. The problem, as Horace saw it, was the union of four groups: Jacksonians, who conflated Horace's interests with Henry Clay's; members of the Relief Party; "obstructionists"; and Presbyterian troublemakers. It was a formidable union, but one Horace believed "too heterogeneous" to last.[80]

Articles in the *Western Luminary* in the early spring of 1825 attempted to cement the connections. One author likened Transylvania to the prodigal son in the Gospel of Luke, who needed constant attention and money from his father to remain solvent.[81] Critics also referenced the exorbitant costs of tuition and board at Transylvania and claimed the institution was accessible only to the wealthiest citizens.[82] But rather than dissolve the school, a move that most were now unwilling to take, they suggested restricting it to preserve the "real and lasting advantages . . . gained to our town."[83] "Other colleges," another contributor to the *Western Monitor* suggested, "are rising and are rising too, it is believed, in a great measure, from what is wrong and wanting in Transylvania University. Their gain in this case will be loss to Transylvania."[84]

Horace addressed some of these allegations in his January address before the Kentucky Institute. He described the university as an island of freedom in a state beset by the grossest intolerance in religion and politics. Political and religious enemies gathered in an unholy alliance against intellectual freedom and the right of "unrestricted investigation" in matters of religion, politics, and philosophy. "Protestant Popery" cast a malevolent pall over the state and threatened to retard cultural development and economic progress. In the East and in the most famous cities of Europe, commerce benefited from the liberal thought, literary and scientific publications, and inventions derived from educational institutions. But great ambitions required great outlays of public assistance; with such assistance, Lexington could rival London and Paris.[85]

Strangers

There was much to divert Horace's attentions from petty rivalries. The addition of Creole boarders to his home, the first of whom arrived in the summer of 1824, helped restore and then exceed his former salary. Wealthy Louisiana planting families took an early interest in Transylvania but hesitated to send more than a few children there because most of them spoke only French. Personal recommendations by Henry S. Thibodaux, president of the Louisiana Senate; Theodore Clapp, former president of the failed Orleans College; and New Orleans attorney Martin Duralde changed the families' opinions.[86] The Louisianans agreed to attend Transylvania, but only on the condition that they live with Horace, paying him a substantial sum for room and board, of course. In the summer of 1825, Horace added twelve young Louisianans at $200 a piece per school year, or $2,400 total, and all of it paid "in good money." "It is a good deal of trouble," he complained to Milton, "but the income is considerable." Horace now estimated his combined income to be close to $5,000 silver, and this amount did not include monies received from private lectures.[87]

The impending visit from the General Marquis de Lafayette that spring provided even more distractions. Transylvania's glory was on full display the day of his arrival, but the grandiloquence of the occasion—the ceremonial dress, student performances, exhibitions, and parties—was all part of a larger attempt to impress Governor Desha and the members of the state legislature who accompanied Lafayette. Horace's opening address evoked his accomplishments and lobbied for continued public funding. Transylvania, the "principal institution of letters and sciences" in Kentucky, Horace began, was the fulfillment of the grand republican experiment of 1776 and an example of the "blessings of liberty." He bragged about the school's appeal among western states, the prestige of its faculty, and the rigor of its coursework but reserved the bulk of the speech for more dramatic statements about the school's larger mission in relation to current controversies. The purpose of Transylvania, Horace declared, was to lead "Republican Scholars" on a path to the "victory of truth over error, of liberality over intolerance." These goals were all the more important given the expansive potential of American education. The "multiplying schools and colleges of the west" would need guidance, something Transylvania was uniquely positioned to offer.[88]

Horace's boasts papered over real concerns regarding both the future of the school's finances and his faculty. Troubles with Constantine Rafinesque, the eccentric professor of botany and natural history, continued to annoy. He had always been in the habit of disappearing without notice for days and sometimes weeks at a time in search of biological specimens, but in 1825 he simply vanished. When he did finally emerge, perhaps three or four months after his initial departure, he found his rooms in the university emptied and his belongings, including vast stores of accumulated scientific collections, in a jumbled heap. His position as university librarian was revoked, and he was told to leave. Constantine did so but only after pronouncing curses on Horace and his university.[89]

Transylvania's law school posed an even greater challenge in spite of Horace's best hopes for its success. "We shall make a great department of this," he assured brother Milton just before the start of the fall semester of 1825, "and bring numbers, fame, influence and money to the university by it." He proudly estimated a fivefold increase in the number of law students over the next few years.[90] But problems began when attorney Jesse Bledsoe, the school's only law professor, abruptly resigned, presumably to focus on private practice.[91] When hurried attempts to replace him failed, first with local attorneys then with attorneys from surrounding states, the trustees were forced to suspend the program.[92]

The timing of this suspension could not have been worse. Governor Desha's opinions on Transylvania and on education in general remained unclear, and the university was again in the throes of financial difficulties. In October 1824, hoping to stave off attack, Horace had written to Desha a few weeks after his election and before the start of the next legislative session to ask for a private meeting so he could explain Transylvania's significance. Desha's endorsement, he added, was vital to the school's success. "It is," Horace had concluded, "in your power to render us essential service, and to promote, in an eminent degree, the interests of learning and science your attachment to the cause of civil and religious liberty you have long provided."[93]

Desha's response is either no longer extant or never existed—the latter is far more likely given what lay ahead—but Horace did receive an indirect response. Desha, in his opening address to the combined houses of the state legislature in November, removed any doubts about where he stood. He began with a review of recent court decisions and described his involvement in the new court controversy as a battle between the powers of popular freedom and the powers of aristocratic control: he represented the former, whereas eastern creditors, federal justices, and highly paid state employees represented the latter. As governor, Desha was compelled to identify then rectify affronts to public liberty. Abolishing the appellate courts was a step in this direction. It was unconscionable, Desha added, that any noble republican should be subjected to foreclosure or jail. Furthermore, by criminalizing debt and abnegating relief measures, Kentucky courts created an environment of fear that resulted in "extensive emigration" and a depleted economy. Reversing this trend required a complete revaluation of state priorities, and he recommended the reduction of salaries and a "curtailment of . . . other public expenditures." Lowering the pay of appellate judges from $2,000 to $1,500 and the "dismissal" of Bank of Kentucky employees were necessary first steps.[94]

Desha was especially critical of Transylvania, the longtime "favorite of the state" and beneficiary of "the funds of the people." The legislature donated liberally with the idea of improving the school, but these ambitions were frustrated by mismanagement and wanton extravagance. For Desha, salaries at Transylvania were the most egregious example of misuse; the president, he argued, made

nearly twice as much as the best-paid state officials, a sum "wholly dispropor-
tioned . . . to the services rendered." Tuition rates had become unnecessarily
high—an artifact of the president's lavish pay—and they ensured the attendance
of only the very rich. On balance, Transylvania was the sole preserve of an
"aristocracy of wealth," wholly incapable of assisting the poor and completely
against the principles of republican governance. Another audit of the school's
finances was necessary, and the legislature should now demand answers to
questions regarding salaries, income, state assistance, and outstanding debts.

Desha also extinguished lingering hopes that Transylvania would be placed
atop a system of public education. Extending the benefits of learning to all levels of
society and all parts of the state required more than could be provided by just one
institution, and Desha envisioned a more practical and local approach wherein
district schools would provide instruction on practical matters. Classes would
take place in the "leisure months" so children could work the family farm. "On
this plan and this only," Desha declared, "can the patronage of the government be
extended equally to all, and the benefits of literature be diffused throughout the
whole body politic." Under the current system, he concluded, wealthy dullards
had a better chance of emerging than poor but brilliant intellects.

Transylvania's answers to state queries were presented to the state on November 29, nearly a month after Desha's address. In their now anticlimactic
response, the trustees suggested that all recent problems stemmed not from
bungled finances but from a lack of state support. For the school to be successful, the legislature would need to dedicate more, not less, money to it.
Transylvania professors were paid well below rates received at other colleges,
so it was difficult to retain or simply attract new faculty. This was a fundamental error, but one they believed was born of fundamental misunderstandings.
The success of any institution of higher learning was in direct proportion to
its professors' abilities and notoriety—the higher their fame, the higher the
cost. Such was the case with the Medical Department, which enjoyed national
renown but required high rates of professorial remuneration. The problem, as
trustees imagined it, was that few in the state legislature had any experience
with the academic marketplace; the pay rate of a professor simply could not be
expressed in terms equal to that of a merchant or farmer. Horace's salary was
the most pressing concern. Presidents of Harvard, Union, Columbia, Virginia,
and Princeton made between $3,000 and $4,000 a year, were provided homes,

and had no teaching obligations. How, they asked, "can Kentucky expect to command the services of literary men, at a less price than her sister States?"[95] Desha's influence combined with already significant opposition made a warm reception unlikely. And when trustees misguidedly followed the report with a petition for $4,000, the legislature erupted into abject chaos.[96]

Resignation

The implications of Desha's speech and the legislature's rejection of future support left Horace with few options. He was no doubt insulted by the prospects of diminished salary, particularly at a time when commonwealth paper was already so devalued, but Desha's plans for education were grave. Horace was used to criticisms from faceless enemies, but this was different. Without the benefits of state assistance or absent such assistance, the sanction of state leaders, further progress would be impossible. As he reflected on the past seven years, he might have considered the trajectory of events—successes mixed with failures and the persistent attempts by both Mary and his adversaries to speed his departure. Recent events suggested that even more trouble lay ahead: depreciated currency, the overthrow of Kentucky courts, and the rise of vulgar politics were troubling signs. Moreover, however often or however loudly he proclaimed the end of a Presbyterian threat, it was clear religious adversaries would remain. Recent troubles within Transylvania itself were probably more of a concern. He might have grown to accept his diminished role in the Medical Department, but the suspension of the law school was harder to justify. All of these events foreshadowed eventual collapse, either of the state government or of Transylvania. Either way, Horace's best option seemed clear, and so on December 23, 1825, he signed a letter of resignation. His plan was to finish the academic year and formally end his duties immediately after the September 1826 commencement ceremony. Horace thanked the trustees and begged their forgiveness in light of their support. Their university enjoyed a "solid and extensive" reputation despite the worst men's best efforts against it. And in spite of his personal reservations, he gave assurances that the school would "continue to flourish."[97]

News of the resignation was repeated in most major periodicals, usually with regrets. Friends, trustees, and supporters of the school insisted he remain, promising that well-placed allies in the legislature would set matters right. Horace was unconvinced. Things were too far gone, "Jacobins" too lively and "too numerous" now, to allow recovery. It would take years, generations perhaps, before the state would make adequate recompense; until then, the prospects of education in Kentucky looked bleak. In truth, he found it hard to imagine the state could ever emerge from the chaos. In Kentucky, the tail wagged the dog. "I am more of a federalist than at any former period of my life," Horace insisted to Milton, "and have a more deliberate detestation of an excessively popular government." "I can do better elsewhere," he proclaimed in a letter to his father.[98]

Horace's relentless optimism brought new and unprecedented opportunities. A return to the pulpit may have been attractive years earlier, but he was too invested in education and too distinguished by it to consider a change. After all, whatever esteem he held and whatever prestige he enjoyed at the national level were based on the strength of his intellectual, not spiritual, leadership. Rumors that he had accepted the pastorate at a church in Boston were reported and repeated, but without a basis in truth.[99] Other rumors surfaced that Horace would leave for a trip to Europe and then assume the presidency of "a university in Louisiana."[100] The origins of these reports are equally unclear, and at the time such a position was out of the question. Continuing along this path, perhaps investigating other college presidencies, was fraught with undeniable challenges. Horace confided his worst fears to Milton, concluding in a letter in early 1826 that the entire country embraced the same detestable "Jacobinican" spirit. Kentucky senator Charles Rowan was "as vile a demagogue abroad as he was at home" but not unrepresentative of a chaotic populist sentiment. The possibilities of growing a college, any college, in the United States seemed unlikely in this climate.[101] The only answer was to leave the country.

A career as a European university president was impossible; even teaching there would have been highly unlikely given prevailing opinions of education in America; some Europeans considered it immature, most thought it farcical.[102] Horace's best chance was to duplicate the success he had with Creole boarders—that is, to convince Louisiana planting families to consider a similar arrangement on a larger scale. A parent-sponsored "traveling academy" through Europe had clear advantages over all other forms of education. Boys could learn art, history, philosophy, politics, and languages through unfiltered lenses, experience culture firsthand, and gain unprecedented knowledge of world politics. Plans were undeveloped in late 1825 but carried forward on the strength of his enthusiasm. Success required commitments from families, a carefully planned itinerary of cities, and enough letters of introduction to carry it through.

But events intervened to complicate Horace's withdrawal from Transylvania. Luther passed away in mid-March. It is hard to judge how deeply his death affected Horace. Their relationship was sometimes rocky, but hard feelings never lasted for more than a few months, and the tone of their correspondence had grown more familiar in recent years. There were signs of growing debility as Luther approached his mid-seventies, such as a shaky hand that made it difficult to write, but Horace admitted he was "not prepared for the blow," having had no other information about his father's health. He remembered Luther fondly and wrote to Milton to express his admiration for the "triumphant example of the power of industry, integrity, good sense, and benevolent affections" their father provided. The thought of never seeing him again made his "heart sink." But Horace, never one to allow sentimentality to interrupt logic, also expressed to Milton his interest in his share of the family estate.[103]

This somewhat callous insistence was driven by necessity. Horace had never watched his spending and had always considered professional appearances and the hosting of interesting parties of greater value than sticking to a budget. Debts had followed him from Boston and had multiplied in Lexington, making a trip to Europe, even one funded by the wealthy parents of his students, difficult to manage. A life of abstemious living allowed him to repay creditors sometime in late 1825, but he had little in reserve. However, fate intervened that summer when the Transylvania trustees, unable to locate a replacement and desperate for a hire, now begged Horace for another year. He accepted but claimed the decision was about concerns for Transylvania's present circumstances. His real reason was much less magnanimous.[104] By October 1826, Horace was, by his own reckoning, worth around $4,000 in household goods, books, and slaves. The eventual auction of the family's possessions along with the sale of his share of his father's estate brought in a good sum.[105] It was enough to help with some debts but well short of the $50,000 he thought he should have been worth if not for the "prodigious drain" of his former habits of hospitality.[106]

The delay in effecting his move to Europe offered more than just a pecuniary advantage. He and Mary were also thus able to be present at the birth of their grandchild, a "fine hearty boy" named William Holley Brand.[107] Horace's ambitions for Transylvania's law school also returned and in a big way. Part of him now wanted to see the school reestablished, with him as professor of natural and national law. He also hoped to recruit Louisianans Edward Livingston and Pierre Derbigny, coauthors of the civil code of Louisiana, as faculty. He planned to operate the school as a summer program. If he could manage these changes, he would abandon his plans for international travel and remain in Lexington for good.[108]

But any lingering doubts Horace had about his decision to leave were corrected after the legislative session of 1826–1827. Governor Desha, in his annual message read before the combined houses on December 3, reiterated his commitment to common schools and his disregard of Transylvania, a place for "the children of the rich." Graduates of the school, he argued, formed an "aristocracy in society" at the expense of the poor or "democracy of the country."[109] Horace took these statements as a sign that Transylvania's situation was beyond repair and admitted as much to friends. The school needed assistance that the state was unwilling to give; there were "some active friends of learning" in Kentucky but a great deal more apathy.[110]

Traveling

Horace increased the pace of his preparations for the traveling academy, readying a public auction of the family's possessions, including their slaves, and completing a travel itinerary that was becoming more elaborate by the day. The trip was to begin in March; he and his family would make their way to Louisiana, collect the students, and book passage from the port of New Orleans to Le Havre in northern France.[111] Horace reckoned he could take no more than twelve boys and none older that fifteen years of age; to assume responsibility for older students was folly. Paris would be their home, though London, Rome, Madrid, and St. Petersburg would be the focus of several and repeated excursions. Each student would be charged $300 a year in addition to all other expenses.[112] The curriculum was to be intensively classical, with Greek and Latin used as the basis for instruction in mythology, geography, and history. The greatest benefit of studying ancient subjects in dead tongues in the Old World would be the removal of "some of the prejudice against ancient languages" in America.[113] The entire course, Horace reckoned, could take around six years to complete, a fact he relished because it would permit his family to take in "the most interesting points of the old world."[114] His salary was to come from the profit from the low individual tuition fees, which would be very little, with proceeds from speaking engagements and the sale of a travel diary, to be completed en route, making up the difference.[115]

The more elaborate the plans, the more European friends and allies he would need for comfort, entertainment, and access to important people. For these connections, he needed letters of introduction and so began with preparations similar to those he had made for his first cross-country trip in 1818, just on a much larger scale. Horace wrote scores of letters, perhaps a hundred or more, to past colleagues, associates, and acquaintances, who in turn passed his name on to others. By February 1827, he had an admirable list of friends and an even more impressive collection of foreign contacts, including Lafayette, Swiss author Benjamin Constant, Professor William Buckland of Oxford, French philosopher Peter DuPonceau, and Albert Gallatin, the current American ambassador to England.[116] Some of his friends, such as Henry Clay, Charles Caldwell, William Lee, and Edward Everett, wrote half a dozen or more letters apiece. Horace, a "literary and philosophical inquirer" and a "citizen of great merit," they said, had increased learning in the United States and required polite attentions for his study of the "older world."[117]

Kentuckians feared they might be left out of the plan. U. Bouligny of Georgetown wrote to Horace about the expedition in February 1827 and wrote again when he failed to receive a reply. He asked first for reassurance that the trip was still proceeding as planned and second for help convincing his father that the venture was worth the money. "I am almost certain that if he was sensible of the benefit that I should receive by going with you that he would agree to it," Bouligny assured.[118] Henry Clay Jr., then a student at West Point, asked his father for permission to attend the traveling academy. Proceeding with an education "under so learned a man," he pleaded, would be a worthy endeavor.[119] His father was not as sure, responding, "I think Mr. Holley's project most quixotic. You will find it will so turn out. It is a scheme to enable Mr. Holley, at other people's expense, to gratify his inclination to pass a few years in Europe." Furthermore, even if the trip had merit, Horace was not the man to lead such an expedition.[120]

Things came together much faster than expected, and by January 1827 it was necessary for Horace to request early withdrawal from his duties at the university, leaving at the "half yearly session" on the first Monday of March.

"Circumstances," he reported in his letter to the Transylvania trustees, "which have become known to me within a few days, put it in my power to carry into execution a design, which I have long cherished, of going to Europe."[121] News of Horace's departure opened old wounds. Publishers of Cincinnati's *Literary Cadet* and the *Rhode-Island Statesmen* called the resignation nothing short of a coup by a cabal of jealous and scurrilous professors who in their need to wrest control sought retribution for some "unprincipled and unprovoked hostility." Others, they claimed, had joined in an unholy cause and for nearly a decade had worked to disparage the reputation of the "virtuous President." The "cause of Literature in the West" was permanently damaged.[122] Transylvania students responded with equal consternation, and the trustees were forced to grant dismissal to many who desired to leave on account of Horace's resignation.[123] But family friends showed solemn acceptance as they honored Horace with a series of balls and ceremonies. Trustees commissioned a second portrait by Matthew Jouett to hang in commemoration of his presidency. Horace returned thanks and distributed portraits of the family made in the style of "papyrotamia," paper mounted on black paper.[124]

Horace bid farewell to Lexington and Transylvania on the evening of March 25 in an address before students, faculty, trustees, and friends. He gave a heroic retrospective of his years there, with only brief mentions of current financial difficulties and the "war" fought over his appointment, reminding them of the school's decrepit state in 1818 and how in just nine years he had brought the number of graduates to 550.[125] But dulcet memories mixed with a bitterness that was not so easily put away. When his thoughts turned to bigoted enemies, his excitement could not be contained. After commenting on the nagging wound that sometimes healed but usually persisted throughout his tenure, Horace threw his handkerchief to the ground and stomped on it. The gesture was enough to bring the crowd to their feet.[126]

The editor of the *Kentucky Reporter* summarized the "strain of unaffected eloquence and feeling" and the heartfelt sentiments that left the audience overwrought with emotions. "President Holley has gone from among us," the essay continued; "we who knew him well, shall cherish the recollection of his social virtues—the polite urbanity and open-hearted hospitality of the gentleman, and the frankness and liberal spirit . . . which characterized the man."[127] Friends thanked Horace for his years of attentions and for the affections and support he had given them over the years. They wished him health and prosperity in an environment less stifled by sectarian enmity.[128] Trustees gave thanks for his "distinguished services" and celebrated his accomplishments. Mary, inspired not so much by the loss of dear friends or the removal from cultivated company but by the absence of a daughter, penned a lengthy poetic farewell she titled "On Leaving Kentucky." "In sorrow I met thee with eyes half averted," it began. "In sorrow I quit thee, thou bright spot of earth."[129] It was a maudlin, romantic vision of a place she had come to in heartache and quit in haste.

Horace, Mary, Horace Jr., and a dozen young Louisiana students departed Lexington as scheduled, amid a crowd of mournful friends and in sight of Harriette's tears. A train of well-wishers walked alongside them for miles.[130] After a two-day carriage ride to Louisville, the family boarded a steamship for passage down the Mississippi.[131] Mary remained grief-stricken through the early part of the journey, unable even to read or play her guitar.[132] The scenery improved her mood, and as they floated past Tennessee and into Mississippi, she took note of the variety of foliage and the strange cottonlike substance that hung from the trees, "like the long grey beard of an old man." Louisiana was even better, full of the most beautiful scenery she had ever seen, with "luxuriant" soil and more like paradise.[133]

Their arrival in New Orleans was greeted with a mixture of confusion and disappointment. What happened next is somewhat unclear, but it appears the planters had second thoughts about sending their offspring on a trip to Europe. Horace's hopes for a traveling academy were either ignored or subverted in favor of a more affordable local scheme to reopen the defunct College of New Orleans. The *New-England Galaxy* reported that plans came to an abrupt halt when parents failed to "fulfill their part of the contract." A close friend claimed that Horace's hopes "were blasted."[134] Mary later described his acceptance of the change in plan as a realization of material benefits and a bending to the "beauty of utility."[135] His true feelings lay probably somewhere in between. Horace's intentions could have been obscured by language barriers or simply misinterpreted. The plan he had unveiled before them, which he had given the rather haughty title "A Plan for Education for the Few Who Can Afford It," had all the markings of a traditional education, save excursions to foreign cities and the astronomical price.[136] The plan ended abruptly but was replaced just as quickly by another.

The College of New Orleans, chartered in 1811 with an initial endowment of $15,000, had struggled to find students, faculty, and administrators, closing and reopening several times but never enrolling more than a hundred students. State assistance was not the problem. In 1819, the initial grant was supplemented by a $4,000 annual stipend. Two years later the state added another $1,000 to this amount and then another $7,000 in 1823.[137] Part of the problem was a bias against local teachers; the trustees believed only northerners could educate southern youth. The school's first president, Yale graduate Theodore Clapp, resigned only a year after his appointment, for unknown reasons.[138] Horace would have made a fine replacement. His years at Transylvania gave him a strong reputation among the city's wealthiest families and notoriety among the state's political leadership. The fact that he was a New Englander may have been an added bonus.

But Horace was averse to repeating the same mistakes and so would need to be convinced that his efforts would be well supported, both by parents and by the state. A visit by Louisiana governor Henry Johnson no doubt convinced him. The two had a great deal in common. Both were friends of Henry Clay and shared a vision for internal improvements and antipathy for the chaotic populism personified by Andrew Jackson.[139] But where Desha gave free reign to divisive politics, Johnson sought accord, and in his inaugural address in 1824 he equated "party spirit" with treason.[140] His feelings on public support for higher education were equally encouraging, and he suggested that higher education could raise Louisiana to the "eminent rank" enjoyed by the settled parts of America.[141]

Horace shared news of the offer with Milton less than a month after arriving in New Orleans. In early May 1827, he remained determined to visit Europe but would now return to New Orleans in November 1828 to carry forward plans for another university.[142] He would, of course, need faculty, and for this he turned to friends in Lexington. He promised William Barry, the Lexington attorney who had turned down a position at Transylvania, a long and prosperous life in Louisiana. The climate was perfectly sublime, and his ability to make money would be abundant. "The practice of law is much more agreeable in New Orleans than in any of the Anglo-American States," Horace added. Its legal system was based on common sense, not on abstractions.[143] Other offers to former colleagues and associations were no doubt written in similar tones.

By June 1827, Horace was settled on the idea of remaining in Louisiana to open his college and spent days looking at possible locations. An advertisement advancing the school in familiar ways was circulated in French and English. The promise of home instruction and its attendant benefits of local character were mixed with appeals for the consolidation of wealth. Educated elsewhere, Louisiana's sons were removed from the bosom of their homes and returned as foreigners, unadapted to the state's unique qualities. Their absence also deprived the state of much needed revenue, which could be put to better use at home. Horace Holley, the ad continued, was well known, having "already had the care of many of our sons for years."[144]

A pledge of $30,000 by the college's supporters was a tremendous sum and certainly enough to find a suitable location, most likely a plantation house. Another $10,000 had been set aside for books and scientific equipment to be purchased during Horace's trip to Europe.[145] The plans changed again, however, and Horace now intended to remain in Louisiana for the foreseeable future. Before classes could begin, he and Mary would draw support from student boarders. "Your father is so bent on making money," Mary bragged in a letter to Harriette; the "little boys" were to arrive soon after the new college home had been prepared.[146] But July brought excessive heat and humidity and caused what Horace thought was a weather-related illness. Headaches turned to a fever and then a rash. The fact that the sickness persisted gave reason for concern. The usual remedies—warm baths and generous doses of various elixirs—provided some relief, but Horace became convinced that a return to cooler climates was necessary. The fresh sea breezes were sure to be helpful; time among old friends in Boston could restore him to full health.

The ship carrying Horace, Mary, and young Horace Jr. left the harbor of New Orleans at five o'clock on the evening of July 22, carried by auspicious winds and a general cheerfulness among the passengers. Passage to New York aboard the mail-carrying "packet ship" *Louisiana* was expensive, costing $112.50 for all three members of the family, but necessary. Mary was the only woman on board, which gave the family the exclusive use of the "whole aftercabin," an enclosed area at the stern of the ship.[147] Horace continued to write letters, but only sporadically, suffering from the onset of mysterious headaches that seemed to increase with frequency.[148] He fell victim to yellow fever on July 31, 1827, after only a week at sea and a little more than four months since leaving Lexington.[149] He never reached his destination, and his body was unceremoniously deposited somewhere off the coast of Florida.

Memories and Memorials

Mary and Horace Jr. disembarked at New York and then grimly proceeded north to Boston by way of New Haven.[150] Reports of Horace's death were carried in newspapers around the country; the longest and most complete of which were published in New England. The *New-England Galaxy* dedicated a poem memorializing "the man of wondrous mind" who came and left the earth too quickly. Horace, the "favorite pupil of the late President Dwight," was a "valuable man" and a forward-thinking "eminent scholar" who enjoyed distinction "beyond any of his contemporaries."[151] Members of Boston's Hollis Street Church celebrated Horace's life and mourned his passing in a memorial service that September. His successor at the church, John Pierpont, delivered a eulogy that stretched more than thirty pages when it was later published. Memories of the man had been obscured by his absence; few had seen him since he had left Boston nine years earlier, and those few had seen him only for a moment when he returned to Boston in the summer of 1822. But the length of the eulogy was testimony to the diligence with which he had given himself to the task of bringing higher education to the West, "eight years of honorable toil, attended by too little honorable support, and followed by too little honorable reward." Pierpont's personal recollections were limited by only a handful of encounters, but he recalled Horace's powerful intellect and acquisitive mind in florid terms. Horace was distinguished from his contemporaries by the strength of his oratory. His "extemporaneous, popular eloquence" rendered obscure subjects useful and made abstractions appear concrete. All of this was attended by Horace's charismatic charm; his ability to enter an assembly and "chain" listeners to their seats was unparalleled. Whatever faults he possessed came not from a defect in character but from an overzealous commitment to virtue. Horace was too open with his feelings, which exposed him to unnecessary hostility. This was especially true in his theology, which unfortunately had exposed him to the most wild and unfounded accusations. But even the harshest critics could not tear down or distract from his indomitable will.[152]

Kentuckians processed news of Horace's death with their characteristic mix of remorse and reproach. A eulogy presented before a large assembly in Lexington not only remembered his accomplishments but also chastised those who had worked against him.[153] Henry Clay sent along his condolences, but not until months after Horace's death had passed and only after Mary reached out to him. Colleagues contributed remembrances of Horace for Pierpont's oration but said little more. Most of their attention turned to finding his replacement and putting the last of the Morrison endowment to its intended use. Transylvania's students became some of Horace's most vigilant memorialists and asked Professor Charles Caldwell to publish a memoir of their late president.[154] Caldwell responded with something less biographical and based more on his impressions of Horace's character. The project would continue a short time later but with new assistance.

Mary returned to New Haven and was faced with the difficult task of settling family affairs. She had some money, but their three-month stay in Louisiana, with Horace unemployed, had depleted her savings. The education of nine-year-old Horace Jr. became a growing concern, and Mary seemed less certain that a collection would ever be taken up on his behalf, though she would see the matter done regardless of the difficulty. "I am too proud to beg, though I am not ashamed to dig," she wrote Orville. Though conciliatory, Henry Clay was unwilling to recommend Horace Jr. for entry into West Point because he was "entirely too young."[155] Horace Jr. was eventually placed in the care of William Wells, who operated a school in Cambridge.[156]

There seemed to be a market for a published memoir of Horace, but doing this herself could be a problem for Mary. She first considered Jonathan Everett but then turned to Orville, who she thought might be more able to engage the project and less afraid "to hazard any thing on religious points."[157] Caldwell forwarded a copy of his remarks before the medical class, and in February 1828 Mary responded with a request to incorporate them in "some memorial of the Genius and character of him we have lost," an encomium to Horace's talents and his "almost heroic" exertions spent in the accomplishment of these feats. Friends would lend assistance and provide liberal subscriptions. Caldwell's acceptance in this endeavor, she closed, would be returned by the "grateful sentiments of her who is left in darkness."[158] His agreement came with a pledge to allow Mary a full share of any proceeds.[159]

The collaboration took only a few months to assemble, a remarkable achievement given the scope of content. Caldwell expanded his discourse before the medical students to nearly one hundred pages, and Mary contributed biographical information, including previously published essays and scores of excerpted correspondence in a two-hundred-page appendix. Caldwell's impressions of Horace were meant to be laudatory but accurate reflections of Horace's temperament and abilities. Mary was much less measured in her description and gave attention to the early years of Horace's life, his tutelage under Timothy Dwight, and years as a minister in Connecticut and Massachusetts, but she directed the majority of her effort to Horace's years at Transylvania. And here she remembered only the highest peaks of his achievements and the lowest deprecations expressed by his enemies. She hoped that the compilation of sermon notes would serve as "complete vindication" of the charges of apostasy and that a full recounting of Transylvania's finances, graduation statistics, and many letters of support would cure accusations of mismanagement and restore Horace's reputation.[160]

The book *A Discourse on the Genius and Character of the Rev. Horace Holley* appeared to mixed reviews, a testament perhaps to unsettled feelings about Horace's time at Transylvania. Some considered it a lively and particularly well-written account; others found it too panegyrical and unnecessarily verbose, with "high sounding words and impertinent expletives."[161] There was truth to both claims. Mary's recollections of her husband were sincere though not objective. Religiously inspired attacks dominate her account of his years at Transylvania, but these events were much less significant to Horace and much less determinative to the ultimate shape of Transylvania. Presbyterian enmity worked well as a foil to Horace's heroic liberalism, but it also obscured his contributions to higher education.

But Horace's final years at Transylvania were also the most fruitful of his life. It was a time of plenty, and swelling enrollments had a palliative effect. For many, numerical gains were enough to bring Transylvania into larger national discussions and more than enough to legitimize Kentucky's claims of political significance. Horace was at the vanguard of these moves and played his part well. But this was also a time when educational ideals were conflated with political ideology, and colleges and universities became the most obvious targets in an era of populist politics. Horace had a talent for reinvention but found it impossible to reconcile the basis of his profession with the foundations of the new republic. When Kentucky's economy devolved into chaos, many in the state looked for salvation from within and blamed those from without. American universities, the oft-misunderstood, obscure, and abstract creations of high-minded idealists, crumbled under the weight of public scrutiny. The people demanded transparency from an inherently opaque process, and Transylvania's president paid the price. Horace's plans for Europe and then New Orleans remain final testaments to his enterprising spirit and a pattern others would emulate but never duplicate.

CONCLUSION

For Mary, Horace's death was the start of a more independent life. She returned to New Orleans as governess to a wealthy family but visited Lexington often to see her daughter and grandchildren. Later, Mary became convinced of the opportunities that abounded in Texas and followed cousin Stephen F. Austin in his efforts to colonize the territory, contributing mightily to these efforts by publishing the first English-language history of Texas and promoting settlement, independence, and then annexation. She carried the memory of her late husband throughout her remaining years, but *A Discourse on the Genius and Character of the Rev. Horace Holley* was the last time she would ever write about him specifically.

Tributes to her husband emerged decades after her death in 1846 and always bore resemblance to her earlier work. In 1896, Robert Peter and his wife, Johanna, authors of the first histories of Transylvania, looked back to *Discourse* and placed Horace in a larger "decline and fall" narrative.[1] Horace stood as the best and last attempt to create a distinguished western university but failed because he could not hold at bay the forces of religious jealousy. In the years of attacks and insults, the Peters found the cause of the school's waning national influence. In the end, they concluded in a second book on Transylvania published in 1905, Horace's "adversaries had triumphed . . . by the use of unholy weapons. Defamation followed him even to the narrow confines of his ocean death-bed."[2]

The school experienced a brief historic revival in the wake of these publications, and Horace was once again returned to prominence, this time as a reminder of institutional glory. Matthew Harris Jouett's portrait of Horace, found in a refuse pile and later purchased from a secondhand store, was returned to the university and hung proudly in the chapel.[3] *The Transylvanian*, a periodical subsidized by the school, devoted article-length works on the years of Horace's presidency.[4] Promotional pieces recalled Horace and claimed Transylvania's place of distinction among regional competitors.[5] And on February 14, 1911, Transylvania held a special ceremony in honor of Horace's birth.[6]

Turn-of-the-century advocates for southern education also read the Peters' histories of Transylvania with remorse but in them also saw opportunity. For Kentuckians, Horace represented "the golden days of Kentucky life," a time when Lexington stood on equal ground with eastern cities and even surpassed them in the promotion of free-thinking liberalism. Some wished Horace had been born later, "in an age when his community could have appreciated the largeness of his views."[7] Others placed him among a constellation of heroic Kentuckians but singled him out as the state's foremost intellect and father of higher education. Southerners frustrated by the annual exodus of their sons to eastern colleges looked to Horace as a model for what was and could be.[8]

Horace became permanently linked to the fate of southern education, but without much reflection and almost no attempt to place him in broader contexts. In many ways, however, he represented a regressive rather than progressive influence. Federalism had effectively died out in the wake of the War of 1812, but the ideals of elite, autocratic governance remained fixed in Horace's mind throughout his life. Transylvania was attractive because it gave him the chance to re-create the West in an atavistic image of the East. He had many opportunities but made no effort to modify his rhetoric to match the emerging populist agenda of Kentucky because this agenda was antithetical to his educational beliefs. To him, higher learning was just that, higher and better because it was less accessible to the hoi polloi. True democracy would always be reserved for society's elite.

Everything Horace created or attempted to create in Kentucky was an extension of this one overriding concern. A constant ratcheting up of entry requirements ensured that only the sons of wealthy parents could attend—only the rich could afford to become so well versed in classical languages before matriculating. Medical and legal programs gave flight to his highest ambitions for education because they were further removed from rudimentary "academical" instruction. They also happened to increase his prestige on a national level, and for this Horace was grateful, if sometimes a bit overzealous. When conflict with medical students effectively removed him from the program, he focused his efforts on law. The *Western Review* and the Kentucky Institute promoted these same interests but to less acclaim and much less effect. In the end, building a scholarly network in Kentucky on the same terms as those of Boston proved impossible.

Horace's theological ambitions faded during his presidency because they had to; he was dogged by a recalcitrant few who continued to disagree with him and became increasingly reluctant to share his beliefs. But the focus of these beliefs and the content of these arguments have always been obscured by a concern with the so-called Presbyterian menace. Horace's objection to the hard rules and divisive creeds of Christian denominations is considered evidence of a progressive intellectual agenda. Historians and amateur historians fixate on the religious dispute because an abundance of preserved evidence focuses on that dispute. However, when the dispute is read within the context of Horace's life and with an eye to the political climate and social setting, there is little to support this reductionist approach and much that argues for the contrary. Unitarians of Horace's ilk replaced divine law with a natural one, delimiting even God to basic principles of redemption and salvation. Moreover, there was nothing in Horace's cosmology or personal life that suggested a progressive belief, spiritual or otherwise. Religious adversaries objected to his preaching because it was inscrutable or too philosophical. But, read carefully, criticisms show either an ignorance or an unfamiliarity with Horace's spiritual bent. His morality was always more of an issue—visits to the theater and raucous parties became more devastating to his reputation than any of his theological claims. These attacks were not his undoing, but they did contribute to the narrative of arrogant eastern elitism tendered by his political opponents.

Forgotten in this story of progressive zeal and regressive antipathy, however, is a greater historical significance, and the lessons from Horace's life extend well beyond these boundaries. There is more than a temporal connection between his life and the decades of the early American republic. The same events and values that pushed the country toward social maturity, nationalism, and cultural sophistication also compelled Horace to take up a lifetime of learning and defined his approach to his chosen profession. In this way, Horace is an indirect reflection of larger social change, and he is unique in his ability to shape our understanding of that change. His educational leadership is the central point of this connection. Education—best conceived of in both formal and informal contexts—is fundamental to our understanding of this period, because within it lies the roots of American identity—an identity both inherited and created, born of unique circumstances, lofty ideals, and even loftier ambitions. Historian Bernard Bailyn once defined education as the "entire process by which a culture transmits itself across the generations."[9] If this is true, then Horace's significance is greater and more impactful than that of most of his contemporaries. When considered in this way, he can be seen as a directive force, able to distill, generate, and carry forward the intellectual culture that became one of many reference points in American life throughout the nineteenth century.

Father Luther stood at an important historical cross-current and because of this was able to introduce Horace to a wider world of possibilities. Liberal capitalism, the guiding power behind the republican spirit of the 1790s, disrupted established bonds that linked farmers to local communities—mutually dependent labor was replaced with more compelling economic ties wherein merchants sold local products to faraway markets. In these new financial realities, the individual won out over the community, and personal self-interest challenged long-standing relationships.[10] Luther was prohibited from farming but adapted well to the life of a merchant. He succeeded because he adjusted to an individualized definition of prosperity. His commitment to self-directed advancement was common among men of his station, and it became the catalyst for a period of increased college matriculation. Luther and other prosperous merchants of the late eighteenth and early nineteenth centuries also hoped to leverage their financial successes into more permanent social gains. Enrolling their sons in elite educational programs did not guarantee a place among the well-heeled, and well-connected, but it did offer a more promising start. There were only five hundred collegians in North America at the time of the Constitutional Convention in 1787, but twenty-two of the fifty-five delegates were college graduates.[11] It was a trend that would continue for some time, and American colleges remained the preserve of ambitious would-be politicians, enterprising young professionals, and determined social climbers.

Horace's own collegiate experiences, first at Williams and then Yale, evince other and equally compelling historical themes. Classical learning, for example, figured prominently in the curriculum because it helped transmit republican principles. Social responsibility, disinterestedness, and other high-minded ideals of Enlightenment-era philosophers undergirded republican thought but were not easily explained or comprehended by youth. Educators of the early American republic believed classical principles were best communicated through classical illustrations and that the survival of the republic depended on a rigorous inculcation of Greek and Roman examples.[12] In this way, political ideals and the definitions self-governance, liberty, citizenship, and even freedom became rooted in the indefatigable progress of human history. In time, individual lessons coalesced around a central theme, federalism, and this became an internalized driving force throughout Horace's adult life.

Federalism experienced a precipitous decline in the wake of Thomas Jefferson's election in 1800 but remained a significant cultural undercurrent for decades to come. In the case of Horace Holley, Federalist leanings were deeply held and more durable than any specific theological position; at Hollis Street, he dropped John Calvin but remained loyal to John Adams. His convictions were shared by cultural and intellectual leaders of the early 1800s; artists, physicians, university professors, publishers, benevolent groups, and elite societies all displayed Federalist sympathies long after the party's dissolution.[13] They did so because federalism represented more than just a political philosophy and was better understood as a complete body of material and ethereal principles, beliefs, and assumptions. Horace's ministerial and educational careers were demonstrative of this new postpolitical Federalist cultural influence; its legacy is one of the durable tensions in the history of American education: access versus privilege. For Horace, education was both tool and function of social separation. The republic was a fragile thing, summoned to existence by men of high standing and even higher convictions who claimed distinction through disinterestedness. Egalitarian rule was defined in the negative as the absence of personal self-interest and the separation from material concerns. Although Horace spent the balance of his career trying to increase enrollment, a university education was nevertheless reserved for the wealthy, and medicine, law, and the ministry for the select few.

Horace's education also brings into focus the synergistic connections between American religion, politics, and the economic realities of the early republic. In the late 1790s and early 1800s, federalism offered a compelling alternative to the chaos of the French Revolution, and Calvinism reinforced political stability while offering guidance for the nation's moral destiny. At Yale, Horace learned both philosophies and was taught that the world outside New England was a dark and untamed place. Through a life of ministerial service, he, like any other student of Timothy Dwight, could facilitate cosmologic and terrestrial order. He took this charge seriously, even going so far as to mimic the first steps of Dwight's ministerial and teaching career at Greenfield Village. But implicit within Dwight's message was a call to intellectual leadership, and Horace, perhaps recognizing the limitations of Greenfield, traded a life of serene but peripheral significance for a grand vision of social purpose. His near decade-long ministerial career at Boston's Hollis Street Church gave him the vehicle to enlarge the scope and durability of that vision. The fact that he reversed his theological positions was beside the point and perfectly in keeping with the new traditions of liberal capitalism.[14] Horace, like his father before him, unencumbered himself of prior obligations in order to achieve personal success. His Unitarian pulpit became a means to an end rather than an end in itself.

Horace's journey to Lexington in the summer of 1818 offers another glimpse into the evolving qualities, expectations, and characteristics of early-nineteenth-century American education. Science, medical science in particular, was recognized as important by important people. It was by its very nature advanced. It was complicated and esoteric but also useful and, as Horace came to realize, respected as the height of erudition, providing the essence of what he termed the "character of a university." Reviving the medical school at Transylvania was a calculated risk but one that paid off. Under Horace, Charles Caldwell, and affiliated medical faculty, the Medical Department flourished, as did the regular school and then the law school. Horace grew enrollment because he was able to tap into a rich vein of cultural capital; in the end, a medical degree had the same cultural resonance in Kentucky as it had in other parts of the country.

In this way, Horace Holley is also well positioned to inform us about the era of college building in early America. Lexington looked at the school and saw a symbol of intellectual esteem and an engine of economic recovery. Nearby towns and villages hoped to duplicate Lexington's success, but with less animosity. Success, however, required college leaders to do what Horace could not: strike a balance between populism and elitism. In the 1820s, Jacksonians opened the door to increased educational opportunities by requiring institutions to become more economically and socially accessible. The shift was more dramatic than most historians believe. The Morrell Land Grant Act of 1862, that singular event that gave rise to an era of state-funded higher education, was a continuation, not the beginning, of a process started by Horace's defeat to the Relief Party. The same populist spirit that carried him out of office in the mid-1820s pressed forward new assumptions and new definitions of learning that persist to the present day. Horace might have succeeded under a series of Whig governors in Louisiana, but his gains would have been temporary.

On balance, the value of Horace's life and career is best explained in the context of an emerging profession. And in this Horace represents a transitional figure who, along with his contemporaries—Philip Lindsley at the University of Nashville, Frederick Beasley at the University of Pennsylvania, Josiah Quincy at Harvard, Sylvanus Thayer at West Point, Jasper Adams at the College of Charleston, and other university presidents—began the slow but inevitable pull away from denominationally minded academic leadership. As the most identifiable members of this emergent group of professional men, college presidents of the early republic provide the best views of this trend. They were reflections and promulgators of societal aspirations whose livelihoods depended on their acceptance by a wider body of students, parents, and community leaders. They considered themselves a part of the traditional professions of law, medicine, and theology but remained detached from regular practice. Self-proclaimed authority allowed detachment and gave the American professoriate a unique independence from other occupations; expert knowledge was their privilege and the most attractive part of an otherwise humble station.

Influence was based on provenance but was communicated through the strength of intellectual productions. For some, a New England education was qualification enough; many could and did claim distinction based on this one fact alone. But to prove their genius, scholars generated works that spanned academic and literary genres. Poetry communicated artistic depth, science proved the quality of their logic, philosophy gave the appearance of a graceful yet substantial intellect. These scholars wrote for the benefit of a small audience but enjoyed wider acclaim among those who recognized the value of their productions.

Most significantly, American academics of the early republic were distinguished by their secular orientation; an increasing number of them were unwilling to participate in theological squabbles or make any public religious declarations whatsoever, even when this stance exposed them to charges of immoral behavior or improper teaching. The most reasonable position was the one Horace adopted late in his career: spiritual ambiguity. By remaining above the fray, or at least outside of it, academics could focus their attention and discourse on other, less-controversial fields of study. The expanding reach and growing list of highbrow literary and scientific journals provided new outlets for this scholarship; honorary doctorates confirmed associations with like-minded peers.

Accumulated productions, like those of Horace and his faculty and students, also forever changed the perception of higher learning in America. Medical theses, essays, poems, speeches, and other works of erudition allowed universities to transform themselves from repositories of existing knowledge to creators of new ideas. In time, publications by academics overshadowed the works of amateur dilettantes, and by the late nineteenth century scholarship became the almost exclusive purview of university-employed practitioners. Early American academics shaped and controlled this change, first as a means of self-preservation and then as a way of regulating the legitimacy and production of knowledge. The legitimizing function of the early American academic has not, however, been explored to any great effect; doing so could offer valuable insight into the rise of the modern American research university.

ACKNOWLEDGMENTS

This project, like most of its kind, benefited from support provided by a small army of archivists, mentors, colleagues, friends, research assistants, and family members. I acknowledge their contributions here, but in the end it seems rather shallow to simply count names because it does no real credit to those who spent countless hours discussing the central subject with me, searching through archives, answering emails, counseling, and editing (and then reediting) multiple drafts. I do my best to recognize them, but a true acknowledgment of their sacrifice is impossible in this space.

Horace Holley's letters, sermons, poems, and essays as well as the equally abundant supply of primary and secondary sources needed to bring these materials into a meaningful context are preserved but widely scattered. Locating them was the best but also the most challenging part of this project. Horace sometimes gets his own archival folder, but more often his materials are found mixed with papers of the important and significant or bundled with the papers of the important but not quite known. You will find him in unindexed boxes marked "Miscellaneous" or files labeled "Other Correspondence." Crumbs of evidence led me to large caches or down blind alleys and, by the end, took me from Massachusetts to Texas, from major university archives to small, semi-personal collections and everywhere in between. And so none of what appears in this book would have been possible if not for generous financial support, first and most importantly, by Transylvania University, and second, by the Burnham-McMillan Research Award, funded by Western Michigan University's Department of History. As Transylvania's scholar-in-residence, I was able to spend a month on campus and in close proximity to the central hub of evidence. Supplementary assistance by way of the Burnham-McMillan Award allowed me to travel to many other state and local historical societies, special collections, archives, and libraries. Western's Department of History also sponsored research assistants—Adam Horos and Erik Freye—who made invaluable contributions to several arduous but essential components of the research effort.

An exceptional team of archivists, curators, and librarians directed these endeavors and made my visits worthwhile. At Transylvania, I had the honor of working with Special Collections Librarian Ms. B. J. Gooch. Many of the best works of Kentucky history over the past twenty years share a deep and abiding appreciation for B. J.'s archival support. Spend an hour in Transylvania's archives, and you will understand why. Her knowledge of the collections is matched only by her energy and enthusiasm for research. She is a student, teacher, and scholar, endlessly fascinated by Transylvania's history and exceptional in her commitment to her craft. I owe her a large share of my appreciation and will be forever grateful for her work on my behalf. Reading the finished draft will always remind me of my time working with her and afternoon coffee breaks spent discussing Horace Holley, debating politics, and celebrating our mutual appreciation of Kentucky basketball.

Katherine Chilcoat and Laura Carlson of the Salisbury Association were also instrumental during the research phase. Katherine's stewardship of archival collections allowed this work to take its final shape—she turned photocopying into an art. She is herself a rare find. Her passion for historic preservation and commitment to education set an enviable example. Laura is equally gifted, and I thank her for her warm and accommodating assistance during my visit. I would also like to extend a special note of appreciation to Jim Bricker, senior library technician in the Special Collections and Archives at Miami University of Ohio; Barbara Austen, Florence S. Marcy Crofut Archivist at the Connecticut Historical Society; Linda Hall, archive assistant, and Katie Nash, college archivist and special collections librarian, at Williams College; James Holmberg, collections curator for the Filson Historical Society; Delinda Stephens Buie, rare books curator for the Rare Books Library at the University of Louisville; and the librarians and archivists of the Houghton Library at Harvard University, the Clements Library at the University of Michigan, the Dolph Briscoe Center for American History at the University of Texas at Austin, the Fairfield Museum and History Center, the Kentucky Historical Society, the Margaret L. King Library at the University of Kentucky, the Kentucky Digital Libraries Association, the Maryland Historical Society, the Massachusetts Historical Society, the New-York Historical Society Manuscript Department, the David M. Rubenstein Rare Book and Manuscript Library at Duke University, and the Manuscripts and Archives division at Yale University.

Many contributed to the heavy lifting of this project, and I am equally indebted to my colleagues in the Department of History at Western Michigan University for organizational, conceptual, and editorial assistance. Professor Wilson Warren gave consistent encouragement and thoughtful contributions throughout each phase of the project. Professors Marion Gray, Edwin Martini, David Benac, and Sally Hadden also gave generously of their time, and I hope the finished product does justice to their labors. Substantial assistance also came from the anonymous readers assigned to review the original manuscript at the University Press of Kentucky, and I thank them for their feedback.

Last in order, but an order of magnitude greater than the rest, are the friends and family who listened to me more than they should have, gave more time than I expected, and offered more encouragement than I deserved. Special thanks go to Professor Thomas H. Appleton Jr. of Eastern Kentucky University, who refined my appreciation of and approach to Kentucky history; to Dr. Walter H. Bower III for his astute theoretical perspective, which gave the work both form and substance; to Phil Gold for his longtime friendship and undying belief in this work; to Lynn Aulick for advice only a philosopher-poet could provide; and to my sister, Jackie McNaughton, for her help as a special research assistant. But the most significant contributions were, of course, from my wife, Carrie Anne, who traveled to every archive, read every word, re-read every chapter, and did her level best to support me through the highs, lows, and self-sequestered isolation of historical research and writing. This book is a small part of what I owe to her.

NOTES

Abbreviations

CHS   Connecticut Historical Society
CL   Clements Library
DBC   Dolph Briscoe Center
MHS   Massachusetts Historical Society
SA   Salisbury Association
TU   Transylvania University Special Collections and Archives
WC   Williams College Archives and Special Collections
UL   University of Louisville Rare Books Library

Introduction

1. The precise dimensions and architecture of the main building of Transylvania University at this time is found in Clay Lancaster, *Antebellum Architecture of Kentucky* (Lexington: University Press of Kentucky, 1991), 129, and *Kentucky Reporter* (Lexington), May 23, 1825. Ceremonial "badges" were created by local artists from Lexington, Louisville, and Cincinnati (Horace Holley to Milton Holley, March 20, 1825, Holley Family Papers, Connecticut Historical Society [CHS], Hartford).

2. Horace Holley, "Address to Lafayette," May 25, 1825, Horace Holley Papers, Transylvania University Special Collections and Archives (TU), Lexington, Ky.; *Kentucky Gazette* (Lexington), May 26, 1825.

3. *Catalogue of the Officers and Students of Transylvania University* (Lexington, Ky.: T. Smith, 1825); George W. Pierson, *A Yale Book of Numbers: Historical Statistics of the College and University 1701–1976* (New Haven, Conn.: Yale University Press, 1983), at http://oir.yale.edu/1701–1976-yale-book-numbers#A; *Catalogue of the Officers and Students of Dartmouth College* (Concord, N.H.: Jacob B. Moore, 1825); *Portsmouth Journal of Literature and Politics,* November 11, 1825; *Commercial Advertiser* (New York), October 5, 1825.

4. *Argus of the Western World* (Frankfort, Ky.), November 16, 1825.

5. See Frederick Rudolph and John R. Thelin, *The American College and University: A History* (Athens: University of Georgia Press, 1990); George M. Marsden, *The Soul of the American University: From Protestant Establishment to Established Nonbelief* (New

York: Oxford University Press, 1994), 72; John S. Brubacher and Willis Rudy, *Higher Education in Transition: A History of American Colleges and Universities, 1636–1968* (New York: Harper and Row, 1958), 153; Charles Caldwell, *A Discourse on the Genius and Character of the Rev. Horace Holley* (Boston: Hilliard, Gray, Little, and Wilkins, 1828); Mattie Austin Hatcher, *Letters of an Early American Traveller, Mary Austin Holley, 1784–1846* (Dallas: Southwest Press, 1933); Romie D. Judd, *The Educational Contributions of Horace Holley* (Nashville, Tenn.: Cullom and Ghertner, 1936); Niles Sonne, *Liberal Kentucky: 1780–1828* (New York: Columbia University Press, 1938); Rebecca Smith Lee, *Mary Austin Holley: A Biography* (Austin: University of Texas Press, 1962). One notable exception to this general adulation of Holley is James Rodabaugh, the biographer of Robert Bishop, the first president of Miami University (Ohio) and long-time professor at Transylvania. According to Rodabaugh, Bishop, not Holley, deserves credit for Transylvania's later success (*Robert Hamilton Bishop* [Columbus: Ohio State Archeological and Historical Society, 1935], 40).

6. Caldwell, *Discourse*, 97, 70–71.

7. Sonne, *Liberal Kentucky*, 17–19, 173.

8. Holley is referenced in more than one hundred books, edited chapters, articles, and biographical entries. The more notable works of American history in which he is mentioned include Richard Wade, "Urban Life in Western America, 1790–1830," *American Historical Review* 64 (October 1958): 14–30, and Alice Felt Tyler, *Freedom's Ferment: Phases of American Social History to 1860* (Duluth: University of Minnesota Press, 1944). Holley figures prominently in a large number of state and regional studies, including Arthur K. Moore, *The Frontier Mind* (Lexington: University Press of Kentucky, 1957); Clement Eaton, *The Growth of Southern Civilization, 1790–1860* (New York: Harper, 1961); Thomas Clark, *Kentucky, Land of Contrast* (New York: Harper & Row, 1968); Fletcher M. Green, *The Role of the Yankee in the Old South* (Athens: University of Georgia Press, 1972); Steven A. Channing, *Kentucky: A Bicentennial History* (New York: Norton, 1977); John Dean Wright, *Lexington, Heart of the Bluegrass* (Lexington: University Press of Kentucky, 1982); Michael A. Flannery, "The Significance of the Frontier Thesis in Kentucky Culture: A Study in Historical Practice and Perception," *Register of the Kentucky Historical Society* 92 (Summer 1994): 239–66; Craig Thompson Friend, *Along the Maysville Road: The Early American Republic in the Trans-Appalachian West* (Knoxville: University of Tennessee Press, 2005); James A. Ramage and Andrea S. Watkins, *Kentucky Rising: Democracy, Slavery, and Culture from the Early Republic to the Civil War* (Lexington: University Press of Kentucky, 2011). Holley's influence in the history of education is best represented in Donald R. Come, "The Influence of Princeton on Higher Education in the South before 1825," *William and Mary Quarterly* 2 (October 1945): 359–95; Frank L. McVey, *The Gates Open Slowly: A History of Education in Kentucky* (Lexington: University Press of Kentucky, 1949); Henry G. Baker, "Transylvania: A History of the Pioneer University of the West, 1780–1865," Ph.D. diss., University of Cincinnati, 1949; James F. Hopkins, *The University of Kentucky: Origins*

and Early Years (Lexington: University Press of Kentucky, 1951); James L. Miller, "Transylvania University as the Nation Saw It: 1818–1828," Filson Club History Quarterly 34 (October 1960): 305–81; Merle Borrowman, "The False Dawn of the State University," History of Education Quarterly 1 (June 1961): 6–22; Charles William Hackensmith, "Ohio Valley Higher Education in the Nineteenth Century," Bureau of School Service Bulletin 45 (March 1973): 1–135; John Dean Wright, Transylvania: Tutor to the West (Lexington: University Press of Kentucky, 1975); William J. McGlothlin, "Rev. Horace Holley: Transylvania's Unitarian President, 1818–1827," Filson Club History Quarterly 51 (July 1977): 234–48; Eric H. Christianson, "The Conditions for Science in the Academic Department of Transylvania University, 1799–1857," Register of the Kentucky Historical Society 79 (Autumn 1981): 305–25; Rudolph and Thelin, The American College and University; Bill Ellis, A History of Education in Kentucky (Lexington: University Press of Kentucky, 2011); and Tom Eblen and Mollie Eblen, "Horace Holley and the Struggle for Kentucky's Mind and Soul," in Bluegrass Renaissance: The History and Culture of Central Kentucky, 1792–1852, ed. Daniel Rowland and James C. Klotter (Lexington: University Press of Kentucky, 2012), 204–21.

9. Two outstanding summaries of this period are Jurgen Herbst, From Crisis to Crisis: American College Government 1636–1819 (Cambridge, Mass.: Harvard University Press, 1982), and Margaret Sumner, Collegiate Republic: Cultivating an Ideal Society in Early America (Charlottesville: University of Virginia Press, 2014).

10. Accounts of Dwight's educational influences are found in John R. Fitzmier, New England's Moral Legislator: Timothy Dwight, 1752–1817 (Bloomington: Indiana University Press, 1998); Marc L. Harris, "Revelation and the American Republic: Timothy Dwight's Civic Participation," Journal of the History of Ideas 54 (July 1993): 449–68; R. Laurence Moore, "What Children Did Not Learn in School: The Intellectual Quickening of Young Americans in the Nineteenth Century," Church History 68 (March 1999): 42–61; Richard D. Shiels, "The Second Great Awakening in Connecticut: Critique of the Traditional Interpretation," Church History 49 (December 1980): 401–15; and Richard D. Birdsall, "The Second Great Awakening and the New England Social Order," Church History 39 (September 1970): 345–64.

11. Anne C. Rose, "Social Sources of Denominationalism Reconsidered: Postrevolutionary Boston as a Case Study," American Quarterly 38 (Summer 1986): 243–64.

12. Charles Alan Pilant, "Expressions of Nationalistic Sentiments in Early American Newspapers, 1776–1826," Ph.D. diss., Marquette University, 1989; Leon Jackson, "Jedidiah Morse and the Transformation of Print Culture in New England, 1784–1826," Early American Literature 34 (January 1999): 2–31; Michael J. Paulus Jr., "Archibald Alexander and the Use of Books: Theological Education and Print Culture in the Early Republic," Journal of the Early Republic 31 (Winter 2011): 639–69; Catherine O'Donnell Kaplan, The Republic in Print; Men of Letters in the Early Republic: Cultivating Forums of Citizenship (Chapel Hill: University of North Carolina Press, 2008); John Charles Nerone, The Culture of the Press in the Early Republic: Cincinnati, 1793–1848 (South

Bend, Ind.: University of Notre Dame, 1982); Jeffrey L. Pasley, *"The Tyranny of Printers":* *Newspaper Politics in the Early American Republic* (Charlottesville: University Press of Virginia, 2001).

1. "Great Truths"

1. Robert B. Gordon, *A Landscape Transformed: The Ironmaking District of Salis-bury, Connecticut* (Oxford: Oxford University Press, 2000), 19; Julia Pettee, *The Rev. Jonathan Lee and His Eighteenth Century Salisbury Parish: The Early History of the Town of Salisbury, Connecticut* (Winsted, Conn.: Dowd, 1957), 152.

2. Patricia U. Bonomin and Peter R. Eisenstadt, "Church Adherence in the Eighteenth-Century British American Colonies," *William and Mary Quarterly* 39 (April 1982): 250, 268–69; Brooks B. Hull and Gerald F. Moran, "The Churching of Colonial Con-necticut: A Case Study," *Review of Religious Research* 41 (December 1999): 167–68; *Acts and Laws of His Majesty's English Colony of Connecticut in New-England in America* (New London, Conn.: Timothy Green, 1750), 7, 107; Pettee, *Rev. Jonathan Lee,* 159–60, 147.

3. Gordon, *Landscape Transformed,* 29–30; Pettee, *Rev. Jonathan Lee,* 169–70.

4. The addition of the *e* to the name "Holley" is somewhat of a mystery. I. B. Holley believes Luther was the first to add the *e* in 1789 (I. B. Holley, "A New England Family: The Holleys of Connecticut," I. B. Holley Papers, 1965–2005, Special Collections, Ru-benstein Library, Duke University, Durham, N.C.). Horace inquired about the addition in 1819 (Horace Holley to Luther Holley, August 10, 1819, Holley Family Papers, CHS). Joseph Holly (1686–?), son of Increase Holly (1643–1726), moved to Sharon after selling inherited lands in Stamford, Connecticut. He had an initial allotment of eighty acres but sold it for a more favorable settlement (I. B. Holley, "A New England Family," 10, 12, 13; Caldwell, *Discourse,* 110–11).

5. Caldwell, *Discourse,* 108, 116; Horace Holley to Luther Holley, January 9, 1820, Holley Family Papers, CHS.

6. Luther Holley to Horace Holley, June 1, 1821, Holley Family Papers, CHS; Alfred Hall, "Taxation for the Support of Schools," *Connecticut Common School Journal and Annals of Education* 1 (April 1854): 114. Codes of 1650 made the education of children a responsibility of town trustees. Townships with more than fifty families were to hire a teacher of reading and writing; if there were more than one hundred families, city fathers were responsible for building and maintaining a grammar school and for seeing to it that instruction continued for three consecutive months. The minimum number of families needed to warrant school instruction was dropped to thirty in 1678 (Bernard Christian Steiner, *The History of Education in Connecticut* [Washington, D.C.: U.S. Government Printing Office, 1893], 27–28; Luther Holley to Horace Holley, June 1, 1821, Holley Family Papers, CHS; I. B. Holley, "A New England Family," 21–22).

7. David Benedict, *A General History of the Baptist Denomination in America. . . .* (London: Lincoln & Edmands, 1813), 546–47, quoted in I. B. Holley, "A New England Family," 546; Caldwell, *Discourse,* 108, 117; Luther Holley to Horace Holley, June 1,

1821, Holley Family Papers, CHS. See also John Lathrop's eulogy for Luther, "A Sermon, Preached at the Funeral of Mr. Luther Holley, Holley Family Papers," Salisbury Association (SA), Salisbury, Conn., 15.

8. Holley, "A New England Family," 22–25, 27; Gordon, *Landscape Transformed*, 33.

9. Richard L. Bushman, *The Refinement of America: Persons, Houses, Cities* (New York: Vintage Books, 1993), 404, 406, 28; James McLaughlan, "Classical Names, American Identities," in *Classical Traditions in Early America*, ed. John W. Eadie (Ann Arbor: University of Michigan Press, 1976), 85.

10. *Connecticut Journal* (New Haven), December 1790. Notable examples of works in this category include: James Forrester, *The Polite Philosopher* . . . (New York: Parker and Weyman, 1758); George Fisher, *The American Instructor* . . . (Worcester, Mass.: Isaiah Thomas, 1760); Abbe de Ancourt, *The Lady's Preceptor. Or, A Letter to a Young Lady of Distinction upon Politeness* . . . (London: J. Watts, 1743); Eleazar Moody, *The School of Good Manners* . . . (Boston: n.p., 1715); Philip Dormer Stanhope, *Principles of Politeness, and of Knowing the World* . . . (Portsmouth, N.H.: Melcher and Osborne, 1786).

11. *Connecticut Courant*, April 27, 1795; *Litchfield Monitor*, December 11, 1790.

12. Leverett Spring, *A History of Williams College* (Boston: Houghton Mifflin, 1917), 46, 52–53; *The Laws of Yale College* . . . (New Haven, Conn.: Yale College, 1800), 9; *Laws of Williams College* . . . (Williamstown, Mass.: Williams College, 1795), 5, 38; *The Laws of Rhode Island College* . . . (Providence: Rhode Island College, 1793), 3; David W. Kling, "The New Divinity and Williams College, 1793–1836," *Religion and American Culture* 6 (Summer 1996): 197.

13. *Laws of Williams College*, 10–18.

14. Thomas Fitch to Milton Holley, December 10, 1797; E. Hunt Mills to Milton Holley, August 29, 1797; Moses S. Curtis to Milton Holley, August 24, 1797: all in John Milton Holley Papers, 1793–1799, Williams College Archives and Special Collections (WC), Williamstown, Mass.

15. Calvin Durfee, *A History of Williams College* (Boston: A. Williams, 1860), 111; *Commencement at Williams-College, September 6, 1797* (Williamstown, Mass.: Williams College, 1797); *Commencement at Williams College, September 4, 1799* (Williamstown, Mass.: Williams College, 1799); "Address of the Students of Williams College to the President of the United States," in *A Williams Anthology: A Collection of the Verse and Prose of Williams College, 1798–1910* . . . , ed. Edwin Partridge Lehman and Julian Park (Williamstown, Mass.: n.p., 1910), 2–3; Adams quoted in *Gazette of the United States* (New York), July 10, 1798.

16. *Commencement at Williams College, September 6, 1797*, 19, 14, 22, 6, 16–17, 18, 19, 25, 23; Ephraim A. Judson to Milton Holley, April 20, 1796, John Milton Holley Papers, WC.

17. Myron Holley to Milton Holley, November 10, 1793; Thomas Fitch to Milton Holley, January 2, 1794; Milton Holley to Luther Holley, December 29, 1793: all in John Milton Holley Papers, WC.

18. Caldwell, *Discourse*, 119, 120 (quote from Mary); Sarah Holley to Milton Holley, March 23, 1797, John Milton Holley Papers, WC. The existence of Luther's store is attested to in Donna P. Hearn, *Dover* (Charleston, S.C.: Arcadia, 2008), 21.

19. Horace Holley to Milton Holley, January 1, 1797, Holley Family Papers, SA; Milton Holley to Horace Holley, April 21, 1797, John Milton Holley Papers, WC.

20. *The New Universal Letter-Writer* . . . (Philadelphia: D. Hogan, 1800), iii.

21. Thomas Fitch to Milton Holley, November 15, 1794, and Martin Field to Milton Holley, July 11, 1797, John Milton Holley Papers, WC.

22. Elijah H. Mills to Milton Holley, June 22, 1797, John Milton Holley Papers, WC.

23. Milton Holley to Myron Holley, November 11, 1798, John Milton Holley Papers, WC.

24. Horace Holley to Milton Holley, April 16, 1798, Holley Family Papers, SA; Myron Holley to Luther Holley, February 27, 1797, January 6 and April 22, 1798, John Milton Holley Papers, WC.

25. Milton Holley to Myron Holley, November 17, 1793, Holley Family Papers, SA.

26. Robert Dodsley, *Rhetoric and Poetry* (Boston: Thomas and Andrews, 1796), 42, 46, 50; *A Catalogue of Books, in the Library of Williams College* (Bennington, Vt.: Anthony Haswell, 1794), 12–14.

27. Sally Holley to Horace Holley, n.d., quoted in Caldwell, *Discourse*, 118. Horace's younger brothers Edward and Newman followed him to Yale, but his youngest brother, Orville, attended Harvard.

28. Nathaniel Willis, *The Complete Works of Nathaniel Willis* (New York: J. S. Redfield, 1846), 372; James Fenimore Cooper, *Satanstoe: Or, The Littlepage Manuscripts; a Tale of the Colony* (New York: D. Appleton, 1873), 27–28; Sarah Hale, *Traits of American Life* (Philadelphia: E. L. Carey and A. Hart, 1835), 165–66.

29. John C. Calhoun entered Yale in 1802 and described his classmates as "noble looking fellows" but was put off by the behaviors he witnessed in the commons: "human life in all its phases of incivility & selfishness unparalleled greediness" (John C. Calhoun to [?] Calhoun, 1802, in John C. Calhoun, *The Papers of John C. Calhoun*, vol. 1, ed. Robert L. Meriwether [Columbia: University of South Carolina Press, 1959], 5; also in Edmund Morgan, "Ezra Stiles and Timothy Dwight," *Proceedings of the Massachusetts Historical Society* 72 (October 1957–December 1960): 114, and Brooks Mather Kelley, *Yale: A History* (New Haven, Conn.: Yale University Press, 1999), 100–101. See also J. D. Wickham, "Yale College in the Second Decade of the Present Century," *University Magazine* 3 (April 1890): 48.

30. For some, Nathaniel Hale's legend begins with his studies of Hebrew at Yale: see, for example, George Lippard, "Sketch of Nathaniel Hale," in *Washington and His Generals; or, Legends of the Revolution* (Philadelphia: G. B. Zieber, 1847), 265. Student Edward Lamb was mythologized as the typical Yale man, sitting with stacks of books, reading by candlelight (Joseph Ingraham, *Charles Blackford, or The Adventures of a Student in Search of a Profession* . . . [Boston: Yankee Office, 1845], 3–4). Although college

attendance or the completion of a degree was by no means a prerequisite to political advancement, nearly half the delegates at the Constitutional Convention were former college students; graduates were similarly represented in the state conventions (Joseph F. Kett, *The Pursuit of Knowledge under Difficulties: From Self-Improvement to Adult Education in America, 1750–1990* [Stanford, Calif.: Stanford University Press, 1994], 11–12).

31. Kenneth Silverman, *Timothy Dwight* (Woodbridge, Conn.: Twayne, 1969), 20; Peter Kafer, "The Making of Timothy Dwight: A Connecticut Morality Tale," *William and Mary Quarterly* 47 (April 1990): 198–99; Kelley, *Yale*, 99.

32. Timothy Dwight, "An Essay on the Judgment of History Concerning America," *New-Haven Gazette, and the Connecticut Magazine*, April 12, 1787; Timothy Dwight, "Address on the Genius of Columbia to the Members of the Continental Convention," *American Museum* 1 (June 1787): 561–63.

33. Larry Tise, *American Counterrevolution: A Retreat from Liberty, 1783–1800* (Mechanicsburg, Pa.: Stackpole, 1998); *Columbia Herald*, October 18, 1787.

34. Benjamin Rush, *Essays, Literary, Moral, and Philosophical* . . . (Philadelphia: Thomas and William Bradford, 1806), 114–24; Timothy Dwight, *The Triumph of Infidelity* (Hartford: n.p., 1788), 17–18, 123.

35. Tise, *American Counterrevolution*, 385; Timothy Dwight, *Greenfield Hill* (New York: Childs and Swain, 1794), 168.

36. Timothy Dwight, *The True Means of Establishing Public Happiness* . . . (New Haven, Conn.: Green, 1795), 29.

37. Silverman, *Timothy Dwight*, 52.

38. Keith J. Hardman, *Seasons of Refreshing: Evangelism and Revivals in America* (Eugene, Ore.: Wipf and Stock, 1994), 112.

39. Silverman, *Timothy Dwight*, 104–5.

40. *Laws of Yale College*, 40.

41. Ibid., 13, 14.

42. Ibid., 9.

43. Ibid., 16–17.

44. David Field, *Brief Memoirs of the Members of the Class Graduated at Yale College in September, 1802* . . . (New Haven, Conn.: n.p., 1863), 7.

45. Benjamin Silliman, *An Address Delivered before the Association of the Alumni of Yale College, in New Haven, August 17, 1842* (New Haven, Conn.: B. L. Hamlen, 1842), 32–33.

46. Anson Phelps Stokes, *Memorials of Eminent Yale Men: A Biographical Study* . . . , vol. 1 (New Haven, Conn.: Yale University Press, 1864), 215–16.

47. *Laws of Yale College*, 11; Stokes, *Memorials of Eminent Yale Men*, 216.

48. Horace Holley to Luther Holley, February 9, 1800, Ravi D. Goel Collection on Yale, Manuscripts and Archives, Yale University, New Haven, Conn.

49. *Laws of Yale College*, 38; Kelley, *Yale*, 60.

50. Horace Holley to Milton Holley, March 16, 1800, Holley Family Papers, SA.

51. Kelley, *Yale*, 39; Stokes, *Memorials of Eminent Yale Men*, 208.

52. Horace Holley to Milton Holley, July 7, 1800, Holley Family Papers, SA.

53. Horace Holley to Milton Holley, November 25, 1800, Holley Family Papers, SA.

54. Ibid.

55. Horace Holley to Milton Holley, December 15, 1800, Holley Family Papers, SA.

56. Luther Holley to Horace Holley, December 30, 1799, quoted in Caldwell, *Discourse*, 122–23.

57. Luther Holley to Horace Holley, July 21, 1800, quoted in Caldwell, *Discourse*, 123–24.

58. Horace Holley to Milton Holley, July 7, November 1, and April 19, 1800, Holley Family Papers, SA.

59. Horace Holley to Milton Holley, April 19, 1800, Holley Family Papers, SA.

60. Milton Holley to Horace Holley, March 12, 1800, Holley Family Papers, SA.

61. Milton Holley to Myron Holley, January 4, 1800, Holley Family Papers, SA.

62. Horace Holley to Milton Holley, July 8, 1801, Holley Family Papers, SA.

63. Horace Holley to Milton Holley, June 30, 1802, Holley Family Papers, SA.

64. Horace Holley to Luther Holley, April 8, 1801, Holley Family Papers, CHS; Horace Holley to Milton Holley, November 1, 1800, Holley Family Papers, SA.

65. Horace Holley to Milton Holley, December 19, 1801, Holley Family Papers, SA.

66. Horace Holley to Milton Holley, December 19, 1801, and March 1, 1802, Holley Family Papers, SA.

67. Horace Holley to Milton Holley, March 8, 1801, Holley Family Papers, SA.

68. Horace Holley to Milton Holley, August 15, 1801, Holley Family Papers, SA.

69. Carol Winterer, *The Culture of Classicism: Ancient Greece and Rome in American Intellectual Life, 1780–1910* (Baltimore: Johns Hopkins University Press, 2002), 11.

70. James McLachlan, "Classical Names, American Identities," in *Classical Traditions in Early America*, ed. John W. Eadie (Ann Arbor: University of Michigan Press, 1976), 84.

71. James M. Farrell, "'Above All Greek, above All Roman Fame': Classical Rhetoric in America during the Colonial and Early National Periods," *International Journal of the Classical Tradition* 18 (September 2011): 428.

72. Horace Holley to Milton Holley, March 16, 1800, Holley Family Papers, SA.

73. Larry Tise, *Proslavery: A History of the Defense of Slavery in America, 1701–1840* (Athens: University of Georgia Press, 1990), 225–26.

74. Wayne K. Durrill, "The Power of Ancient Words: Classical Teaching and Social Change at South Carolina College, 1804–1860," *Journal of Southern History* 65 (August 1999): 473; Winterer, *Culture of Classicism*, 15.

75. Silverman, *Timothy Dwight*, 101.

76. *Gazette of the United States*, April 20, 1801.

77. *Impartial Observer* (Cooperstown, N.Y.), June 27, 1801.

78. *American Mercury* (Hartford, Conn.), October 6, 1803.

79. Horace Holley to Milton Holley, March 9, 1803, Holley Family Papers, SA.

80. *New England Palladium,* May 26, 1801.

81. *Gazette of the United States,* October 17, 1801.

82. Carol Sue Humphrey, *The Press of the Young Republic, 1783–1833* (Westport, Conn.: Greenwood Press, 1996), 67; Horace Holley to Milton Holley, April 19, 1800, Holley Family Papers, SA.

83. Horace Holley to Milton Holley, November 25, 1800, Holley Family Papers, SA.

84. Horace Holley to Milton Holley, October 5, 1801, Holley Family Papers, SA.

85. [Horace Holley], "An Extract from a College Exercise, Written in 1802," *Western Review and Miscellaneous Magazine* (Lexington, Ky.) 2 (April 1820): 190–91.

86. Horace Holley to Milton Holley, February 4, 1802, Holley Family Papers, SA; Milton Holley to Horace Holley, February 14, 1802, Holley Family Papers, SA.

87. Horace Holley to Luther Holley, February 22, 1802, Horace Holley Papers, Clements Library (CL), University of Michigan, Ann Arbor.

88. Luther Holley to Horace Holley, March 21, 1802, quoted in Caldwell, *Discourse,* 124–25.

89. Paine's essay was published in *Republican Watch Tower,* November 20, 1802.

90. Horace Holley to Luther Holley, November 22, 1802, Horace Holley Papers, CL.

91. Horace Holley to Sarah Holley, February 3, 1803, Holley Family Papers, SA.

92. Milton Holley to Horace Holley, February 13, 1803, Holley Family Papers, SA.

93. C. A. Goodrich, "Narrative of Revivals of Religion in Yale College, from Its Commencement to the Present Time," *Journal of the American Education Society* 10 (February 1838): 294.

94. Horace Holley to Milton Holley, November 22, 1802, Holley Family Papers, SA.

95. Goodrich, "Narrative of Revivals," 295.

96. Quoted in George P. Fisher, *Life of Benjamin Silliman . . . ,* 2 vols. (New York: Charles Scribner, 1866), 83.

97. *Connecticut Evangelical Magazine,* July 1802. Horace's membership in Yale's church is listed in his license to preach, January 7, 1804, Horace Holley Papers, TU.

98. Horace Holley to Sarah Holley, June 30, 1802, Crosby Family Papers, Family History Center, Salt Lake City, Utah.

99. Horace Holley to Sarah Holley, June 21, 1803, Horace Holley Papers, CL.

100. Horace Holley to Sarah Holley, June 21, 1803, Horace Holley Papers, CL; Luther Holley to Horace Holley, undated, quoted in Caldwell, *Discourse,* 132.

101. Horace Holley to Luther Holley, April 2 and June 8, 1803, Holley Family Papers, SA.

102. Horace Holley to Milton Holley, June 8, 1803, Holley Family Papers, SA.

103. Horace Holley to Milton Holley, June 29, 1803, Holley Family Papers, SA.

104. Horace Holley to Luther Holley, November 22, 1802, Horace Holley Papers, CL.

105. Senior year, which up to this point was a perfunctory and academically unchallenging year, became a rigorous and thoroughly enriching capstone of an education at Yale (Morgan, "Ezra Stiles and Timothy Dwight," 104).

106. Michael Bartanen and Robert Littlefield, *Forensics in America: A History* (Lanham, Md.: Rowman and Littlefield, 2014), 29.

107. Hugh Blair, *Lectures on Rhetoric and Belles Lettres*, 3 vols. (London: Strahan, Cadell, and Creech, 1787), 1:83, 299, 344, 412–41.

108. Timothy Dwight, *Sermons; by Timothy Dwight*, 2 vols. (New Haven, Conn.: Hezekiah Howe and Durrie and Peck, 1828), 1:302, 309, 311, 312.

109. Horace Holley to Luther Holley, March 14, 1803, Holley Family Papers, SA.

110. Horace Holley to Milton Holley, March 1, 1802, Holley Family Papers, SA.

111. Horace Holley to Milton Holley, February 4, 1802, Holley Family Papers, SA.

112. *Catalogue of the Connecticut Alpha of [Phi] B K, Yale College* (New Haven, Conn.: B. L. Hamlen, 1852), 12.

113. Horace Holley to Milton Holley, December 15, 1800, Holley Family Papers, SA.

114. *Catalog of the Society of Brothers in Unity, Yale College, Founded A.D. 1768* (New Haven, Conn.: T. J. Stafford, 1854), 3.

115. Christopher Grasso, *A Speaking Aristocracy: Transforming Public Discourse in Eighteenth-Century Connecticut* (Chapel Hill: University of North Carolina Press, 1999), 297–98.

116. Quoted in ibid., 397.

117. *Yale University Phi Beta Kappa Records,* quoted in ibid., 398 n. 16.

118. Horace Holley to Milton Holley, February 4, 1802, Holley Family Papers, SA.

119. Horace's oration before the Brothers was reprinted later, when he was at Transylvania, as "A Forensic Address, at an Evening Meeting of a Society of Young Men, on the Question, *Do the Pursuits of Ambition Contribute More to Happiness Than Those of Domestic Life?*" *Western Review and Miscellaneous Magazine* 2 (May 1820): 194–99.

120. William Hamilton Bryson, *Legal Education in Virginia, 1779–1979: A Biographical Approach* (Charlottesville: University Press of Virginia, 1982), 3.

121. Horace Holley to Luther Holley, June 19, 1803, Holley Family Papers, SA.

122. Horace Holley to Luther Holley, July 15 and June 19, 1803, Holley Family Papers, SA.

123. Horace Holley to Luther Holley, July 31, 1803, Holley Family Papers, SA.

124. Luther Holley to Horace Holley, July 13, 1803, quoted in Caldwell, *Discourse*, 129.

125. Horace Holley to Luther Holley, November 9, 1803, Holley Family Papers, SA.

126. Horace Holley to Luther Holley, August 3, 1803, Mary Holley Papers, TU.

127. *Federal Republican* (Elizabethtown, N.J.), September 27, 1803.

128. Horace Holley to Luther Holley, July 31, 1803, Holley Family Papers, SA. The coat may have been either "deep blue" or black, depending on the cloth available at the local tailor.

129. *American Mercury,* October 6, 1803.

130. Dwight, *Sermons,* 1:434.

131. *Connecticut Journal,* September 22, 1803.

132. Dwight, *Sermons,* 1:425, 43, 122, 432.

133. Caldwell, *Discourse*, 128.

134. Horace Holley to Milton Holley, December 12, 1803, Holley Family Papers, SA.

135. Horace Holley to Luther Holley, December 22, 1803, Holley Family Papers, SA.

136. Horace Holley to Luther Holley, December 28, 1803, Holley Family Papers, SA.

137. Horace Holley to Luther Holley, February 9, 1804, Holley Family Papers, SA.

138. Horace Holley to Luther Holley, January 20, 1804, Holley Family Papers, CHS.

139. Horace Holley to Luther Holley, February 9, 1804, Holley Family Papers, SA; Horace Holley to Peter Dewitt, February 8 and 24, 1804, Horace Holley Papers, CL.

140. Horace Holley to Luther Holley, February 9, 1804, Holley Family Papers, SA.

141. Horace Holley to Luther Holley, January 20, 1804, Holley Family Papers, CHS.

142. Luther Holley to Horace Holley, 1804, quoted in Caldwell, *Discourse*, 133.

143. Myron Holley to Horace Holley, October 12, 1804, Horace Holley Papers, TU.

144. Horace Holley to Sarah Holley, April 13, 1804, Mary Holley Papers, TU.

145. Horace Holley to Luther Holley, February 9, 1804, Holley Family Papers, SA.

146. Smith Lee, *Mary Austin Holley*, 4.

147. Ibid., 29.

148. Horace Holley to parents, n.d., Mary Holley Papers, TU.

149. Horace Holley to Luther Holley, December 3, 1800, Ravi D. Goel Collection on Yale, Yale University.

150. The poetic apology was published later: Horace Holley, "Lines Addressed to a Beautiful Young Lady by a Gentleman, Whom She Reproved for His Absence of Mind, Because He Spoke to Her by the Name of Another Young Lady Present," *Western Review and Miscellaneous Magazine* 1 (December 1819): 315–16.

151. Horace Holley to Luther Holley, August 25, 1804, Holley Family Papers, SA.

152. Mary Holley to Horace Holley, March 30, 1804, reprinted in *Western Review and Miscellaneous Magazine* 4 (June 1821): 314–15.

153. Horace Holley to Sarah Holley, April 13, 1804, Mary Holley Papers, TU.

154. Horace Holley to Luther Holley, April 11, 1804, Holley Family Papers, SA.

155. Horace Holley to Luther Holley, May 4, 1804, Holley Family Papers, SA; Horace Holley to Sarah Holley, June 18, 1804, Mary Holley Papers, TU.

156. Horace Holley to Luther Holley, August 14, 1804, Holley Family Papers, SA.

157. Horace Holley to Luther Holley, December 14, 1804, Holley Family Papers, SA.

158. Caldwell, *Discourse*, 127.

159. Horace Holley to Milton Holley, May 30, 1804, Holley Family Papers, SA.

160. Samuel Hopkins, "The Doctrine of Election," in *The Works of Samuel Hopkins...*, 2 vols., ed. Edwards Amasa Park (Boston: Doctrinal Tract and Book Society, 1854), 2:12.

161. Nathan Hatch, *The Democratization of American Christianity* (New Haven, Conn.: Yale University Press, 1989), 170–73.

162. Samuel Hopkins, *The System of Doctrines: Contained in Divine Revelation, Explained and Defended...*, 2 vols. (Boston: Thomas and Andrews, 1793), 2:228.

163. Joseph A. Conforti, "Samuel Hopkins and the New Divinity: Theology, Ethics,

and Social Reform in Eighteenth-Century New England," *William and Mary Quarterly* 34 (October 1977): 583.

164. Samuel Hopkins, *A Dialogue Concerning the Slavery of Africans* . . . (Norwich, Conn.: Judah P. Spooner, 1776), 549–50.

165. Samuel Hopkins, "The Slave Trade and Slavery," in *Works of Samuel Hopkins,* 2:619.

166. Paul Conkin, *The Uneasy Center: Reformed Christianity in Antebellum America* (Chapel Hill: University of North Carolina Press, 1995), 99.

167. Tise, *American Counterrevolution*, 141–42.

168. Kling, "The New Divinity at Williams College," 201, 204.

169. Caldwell, *Discourse*, 133.

2. "Term of Severe Trial"

1. Mary Holley to Horace Holley, June 16, 1805, Mary Holley Papers, TU.

2. Bradley also appears on the church payroll as a caretaker, paid thirty shillings in 1787 to "sweep and sand the meeting house for one year" (George H. Merwin, *Ye Church and Parish of Greenfield: The Story of an Historic Church in an Historic Town 1725–1913* [New Haven, Conn.: Tuttle, Morehouse & Taylor Press, 1913], 45).

3. Horace Holley to Mary Holley, June 6, 1805, transcript, Mary Holley Papers, TU.

4. Horace Holley to Mary Holley, June 12, 1805, and Mary Holley to Horace Holley, June 12, 1805, transcript, Mary Holley Papers, TU.

5. Horace Holley to Mary Holley, June 23, 1805, transcript, Mary Holley Papers, TU.

6. Mary Holley to Horace Holley, June 1805, transcript, Mary Holley Papers, TU; Milton Holley to Horace Holley, September 30, 1805, Holley Family Papers, SA.

7. Horace Holley to Mary Holley, June 1805, transcript, Mary Holley Papers, TU.

8. Andrew W. Robertson, "'Look on This Picture . . . and on This!': Nationalism, Localism, and Partisan Images of Otherness in the United States, 1787–1820," *American Historical Review* 106 (October 2001): 1264–66; Kevin M. Gannon, "Escaping 'Mr. Jefferson's Plan of Destruction': New England Federalists and the Idea of a Northern Confederacy, 1803–1804," *Journal of the Early Republic* 21 (Autumn 2001): 413–16; William F. Willingham, "Politics in Windham, Connecticut, during the Jeffersonian Era," *Journal of the Early Republic* 1 (Summer 1981): 134–35.

9. Williston Walker, *The Creeds and Platforms of Congregationalism* (New York: Scribner's, 1893), 447–48.

10. Merwin, *Ye Church and Parish*, 62.

11. *The Bee* (Hudson, N.Y.), December 24, 1805.

12. Ibid.

13. Horace Holley to Luther Holley, September 16, 1805, Holley Family Papers, SA.

14. Greenfield Hill or Northwest Society and Church, Records 1668–1878, vol. 2 of 3, 105–7, Fairfield (Area) Church Papers, 1782–2000, Fairfield Museum and History Center, Fairfield, Conn.

15. Horace Holley to Mary Holley, September 26, 1805, transcript, Mary Holley Papers, TU.

16. Horace Holley to Luther Holley, September 16, 1805, and January 15, 1806, Holley Family Papers, SA.

17. Mary Holley to Sarah Holley, March 6, 1806, Holley Family Papers, SA; Merwin, *Ye Church and Parish*, 63.

18. Horace Holley to Mary Holley, February 16, 1807, transcript, Mary Holley Papers, TU.

19. Horace Holley to Mary Holley, January 1, 1806, transcript, Mary Holley Papers, TU.

20. Mary Holley to Horace Holley, February 19, 1807, transcript, Mary Holley Papers, TU.

21. Horace Holley to Mary Holley, n.d., quoted in Caldwell, *Discourse*, 137.

22. Church records show forty-five adult members were added and another twenty-four were baptized (Greenfield Hill or Northwest Society and Church, Records 1668–1878, vol. 2 of 3, passim, Fairfield [Area] Church Papers).

23. Horace Holley to Luther Holley, November 2, 1807, Holley Family Papers, SA.

24. Horace Holley to Luther Holley, September 23, 1807, Holley Family Papers, SA.

25. Horace Holley to Milton Holley, May 2, 1808, Holley Family Papers, SA.

26. Horace Holley to Mary Holley, May 20, 1808, transcript, Mary Holley Papers, TU; see also Samuel Miller, *Memoir of the Rev. John Rodgers, D.D. . . .* (New York: Whiting and Watson, 1813), 278–80.

27. Mary Holley to Horace Holley, September 1808, transcript, Mary Holley Papers, TU; Horace Holley to Mary Holley, September 4, 1808, transcript, Mary Holley Papers, TU (Horace: "Send off furniture by water"—that is, by way of Long Island Sound).

28. Horace Holley to Mary Holley, October 9, 1808, Crosby Family Papers; Horace Holley to Luther Holley, September 20, 1809, Holley Family Papers, SA.

29. Horace Holley to Mary Holley, October 9, 1808, Crosby Family Papers; Mary Holley to Horace Holley, October 9, 1808, transcript, Mary Holley Papers, TU.

30. Mary Kupiec Cayton, "Who Were the Evangelicals? Conservative and Liberal Identity in the Unitarian Controversy in Boston, 1804–1833," *Journal of Social History* 31 (Autumn 1997): 86–87.

31. Ibid., 87.

32. Conrad Wright, "The Election of Henry Ware," in *The Unitarian Controversy: Essays on American Unitarian History* (Boston: Skinner House Books, 1994), 13–16; Peter S. Field, *The Crisis of the Standing Order: Clerical Intellectuals and Cultural Authority in Massachusetts, 1780–1833* (Amherst: University of Massachusetts Press, 1998), 124.

33. Horace Holley to Mary Holley, October 16, 1808, Crosby Family Papers.

34. Horace Holley to Mary Holley, October 13, 1808, Crosby Family Papers.

35. Horace Holley to Mary Holley, November 11, 1808, Mary Holley Papers, TU.

36. Horace Holley to Luther Holley, June 23, 1812, Holley Family Papers, CHS.

37. Horace Holley to Mary Holley, November 14, 1808, Mary Holley Papers, TU.

38. William Bentley Fowle, "Autobiography," 42, Massachusetts Historical Society, Boston.

39. Horace Holley to Mary Holley, January 26, 1809, Mary Holley Papers, TU.

40. Horace Holley to Mary Holley, February 6, 1809, Mary Holley Papers, TU.

41. Horace Holley to Mary Holley, February 15, 1809, Mary Holley Papers, TU.

42. Horace Holley to Mary Holley, February 6, 1809, Mary Holley Papers, TU.

43. "Order of Exercises at the Installation of Rev. Horace Holley," March 9, 1809, Horace Holley Papers, TU.

44. Joseph Eckley, "They Watch for Your Souls," in *A Sermon Delivered at the Installation of Rev. Horace Holley* (Boston: Belcher, 1809), 11, 13–16, 20, 23, 30, 34.

45. John Lathrop, "The Charge Given by Rev. John Lathrop, D.D.," in Eckley, *Sermon*, 40, 43–45.

46. John Kirkland, "The Right Hand of Fellowship by Rev. Kirkland," in Eckley, *Sermon*, 49–51.

47. Horace Holley to Milton Holley, March 9, 1809, Holley Family Papers, SA.

48. *Merrimack Intelligencer* (Haverhill, Mass.), March 11, 1809; *Commercial Advertiser*, March 14, 1809; *Spectator* (New York), March 15, 1809; *Boston Commercial Gazette*, April 10, 18, 1809; Eckley, *Sermon*.

49. *Boston City Directory for 1809* (Boston: Munroe, Francis, & Parker, 1809), cross-referenced with Ogden Codman, *Hollis Street Church, Boston: Records of Admissions, Baptisms, Marriages, and Deaths, 1732–1887*, transcribed by Robert J. Dunkle and Ann Smith Lainhart (Boston: New England Historic Genealogical Society, 1998).

50. *Boston City Directory for 1809*.

51. Jacqueline Barbara Carr, "A Change 'as Remarkable as the Revolution Itself': Boston's Demographics, 1780–1800," *New England Quarterly* 73 (December 2000): 585–89.

52. Ibid., 590–91; Nathaniel B. Shurtleff, *A Topographical and Historical Description of Boston* (Boston: Boston City Council, 1871), 139.

53. Carr, "A Change," 596; Heather S. Nathans, "Forging a Powerful Engine: Building Theaters and Elites in Post-revolutionary Boston and Philadelphia," *Pennsylvania History* 66 (1999): 114.

54. Codman, *Hollis Street Church*, passim (for ease of reading and locating information, data from this work was recompiled in another format, so no page numbers can be given for specific statistics).

55. Caldwell, *Discourse*, 144–46.

56. John Pierpont, *A Discourse Delivered in Hollis Street Church, Boston . . . Occasioned by the Death of Horace Holley L.L.D.* (Boston: Stephen Foster, 1827), 13–14.

57. Caldwell, *Discourse*, 148; George Leonard Chaney, *Hollis Street Church from Mather Byles to Thomas Starr King, 1732–1861* (Boston: G. H. Ellis, 1877), 29–30; James Spear Loring, *The Hundred Boston Orators, Appointed by the Municipal Authorities and Other Public Bodies, from 1770 to 1852* (Boston: John P. Jewett, 1852), 370–71.

58. Horace Holley to Mary Holley, August 30, 1810, Mary Holley Papers, TU.

59. Horace Holley to Mary Holley, September 3, 1810, Mary Holley Papers, TU.

60. Horace Holley to Mary Holley, August 21, 1810, Mary Holley Papers, TU.

61. Horace Holley to Luther Holley, March 13, 1809, Holley Family Papers, CHS.

62. Pierpont, *Discourse Delivered in Hollis Street Church,* 25–26; Chaney, *Hollis Street Church,* 128.

63. Caldwell, *Discourse,* 140–41.

64. Horace Holley to Luther Holley, April 10, 1810, Holley Family Papers, CHS.

65. Horace Holley to Luther Holley, October 4, 1810, Holley Family Papers, CHS.

66. Loring, *Hundred Boston Orators,* 371.

67. Horace Holley to Miles Day, April 10, 1810, Horace Holley Papers, TU.

68. Horace Holley to Milton Holley, February 24, 1810, Holley Family Papers, SA.

69. Field, *The Crisis of the Standing Order,* 47, 53, 68–70.

70. Horace Holley to Luther Holley, March 18, 1811, Holley Family Papers, CHS. The church continued to grow, and in 1811 Horace admitted thirty-eight new members into communion (Codman, *Hollis Street Church;* Chaney, *Hollis Street Church,* 31).

71. Horace Holley to Luther Holley, March 18, 1811, Holley Family Papers, CHS.

72. The list of those who might have objected to the views Horace expressed in his review of Ely's essay includes Samuel Smith, P. Wilson (professor of languages at Columbia College), John McNiece, George Faitoute, Philip Milledoler, G. A. Kuypers, Alexander McLeod, John B. Romeyn, Christian Bork, Thomas Hamilton, John Schureman, Stephan N. Rowan, Alexander Gunn, John M. Mason, Jacob Brodhed, James Mathews, John X. Clarke, and J. H. Livingston.

73. [Horace Holley], "Review . . . [of] 'A Contrast between Calvinism and Hopkinsianism,'" *General Repository and Review* (Cambridge, Mass.) 3 (April 1813): 330, 348.

74. Horace Holley to Sarah Holley, June 16, 1813, Holley Family Papers, CHS.

75. Codman, *Hollis Street Church,* no page.

76. Horace Holley to Milton Holley, May 3, 1809, Holley Family Papers, SA.

77. *Centennial Celebration of the Wednesday Evening Club . . .* (Boston: John Wilson and Son, 1878), 32.

78. Ibid., 142–44.

79. Conrad Wright, *The Transformation of Charity in Postrevolutionary New England* (Boston: Northeastern University Press, 1992), 52–64.

80. Horace Holley to Milton Holley, June 20, 1809, Holley Family Papers, SA.

81. Paul Goodman, "Ethics and Enterprise: The Values of a Boston Elite, 1800–1860," *American Quarterly* 18 (Autumn 1966): 438.

82. Ibid., 136; Horace Holley to Luther Holley, June 4, 1811, Holley Family Papers, CHS; *History of the Humane Society of Massachusetts . . .* (Boston: Samuel N. Dickerson, 1845), 32; Franklin Bowditch Dexter, *Biographical Sketches of the Graduates of Yale College* 6 vols. (New York: Holt, 1885–1912), 5:588.

83. *Repertory* (Boston), May 22, 1812; "An Act to Incorporate the Christian Moni-

tor Society," *Laws of the Commonwealth of Massachusetts* . . . , vol. 5 (Boston: State of Massachusetts, 1812), 613.

84. Horace became a member of the academy in November 1812 (*Memoirs of the American Academy of Arts and Sciences,* vol. 11 [Cambridge, Mass.: Wilson, 1888], 39; *Quinquennial Catalogue of the Officers and Graduates . . . 1636–1915* [Cambridge, Mass.: Harvard University Press, 1915], 12). Horace is not listed among the Athenaeum's subscribers, but his familiarity with the institution is attested to in his writings and correspondence (Horace Holley to Mary Holley, July 31, 1811, Mary Holley Papers, TU; Journal of Horace Holley, March 2, 1818, Horace Holley Papers, CL). Horace also had pronounced ties to Joseph Buckminster and William Emerson, two of the organization's founders. He delivered the funeral oration for Buckminster and in 1811 agreed to unite Hollis Street Church with Emerson's First Congregational Church. Horace's certificate of membership in the American Antiquarian Society is located in Horace Holley Papers, TU.

85. James Bowdoin, "A Philosophical Discourse, Publicly Addressed to the American Academy of Arts and Sciences," in *Memoirs of the American Academy of Arts and Sciences,* vol. 1 (Boston: Adams and Nourse, 1783), 2, 3, 5.

86. Ronald Story, "Class and Culture in Boston: The Athenaeum, 1807–1860," *American Quarterly* 27 (May 1975): 181–82.

87. E. Digby Baltzell, *Puritan Boston and Quaker Philadelphia: Two Protestant Ethics and the Spirit of Class Authority and Leadership* (New York: Free Press, 1979), 240.

88. Katherine Wolff, *Culture Club: The Curious History of the Boston Athenaeum* (Boston: University of Massachusetts Press, 2009), 2–3, 183.

89. Horace Holley and Isaac Bronson, "An Investigation of the Facts Relative to a Descent of Stones from the Atmosphere to the Earth, on the 14th of December, 1807, in the Towns of Fairfield, Weston, and Huntington, Connecticut . . . in a Memoir Addressed to Samuel L. Mitchill," *Medical Repository* 5 (1808): 418–21.

90. *Repertory,* December 14, 1812. Horace stated he was an avid reader of the *Connecticut Herald* (Horace Holley to Mary Holley, July 31, 1811, Mary Holley Papers, TU).

91. *Yankee* (Boston), June 5, 1812. The chaplaincy for the Massachusetts House required majority consent—Horace received 419 of 616 votes (*Weekly Visitor* [New York], June 6, 1812). Included on the Boston School Committee were Reverends William Channing and Charles Lowell; physicians Aaron Dexter, Thomas Welsh, and John C. Warren; and attorneys Charles Davis, John Heard, Peter O. Thatcher, Francis J. Oliver, William Smith, and William Welles (*A Volume of Records Relating to the Early History of Boston* . . . [Boston: Municipal Printing Office, 1906], 93).

92. This position was held previously by Thomas Baldwin, minister of Boston's Second Baptist Church and member of a number of charitable organizations. Baldwin was elected chaplain in 1800 (*Newport Herald,* June 6, 1800; Alden Bradford, *Biographical Notices of Distinguished Men in New England* . . . [Boston: S. G. Simpkins, 1842], 48–49).

93. Joseph M. Wightman, *Annals of the Boston Primary School Committee* . . . (Boston: Rand and Avery, 1860), 22.

94. Horace Holley to Mary Holley, September 30, 1812, Crosby Family Papers.

95. Stanley K. Schultz, *The Culture Factory: Boston Public Schools, 1789–1860* (New York: Oxford University Press, 1973), 11, 17, 22.

96. Ibid., 26; Wightman, *Annals,* 12–13.

97. Horace Holley to Milton Holley, February 16, 1809, Holley Family Papers, SA.

98. Horace Holley to Luther Holley, March 29, 1809, Holley Family Papers, CHS.

99. Horace Holley to Luther Holley, July 29, 1811, Holley Family Papers, CHS.

100. Fragments, Horace Holley Papers, Andover-Harvard Theological Library Manuscripts and Archives, Harvard Divinity School, Cambridge, Mass.

101. Marshall Foletta, *Coming to Terms with Democracy: Federalist Intellectuals and the Shaping of an American Culture* (Charlottesville: University Press of Virginia, 2001), 62–63, 68–69.

102. Solomon Aiken, *The Rise and Progress of the Political Dissension in the United States: A Sermon Preached in Dracutt, May 11, 1811* (Haverhill, Mass.: William B. Allen, 1811).

103. Horace Holley to Luther Holley, February 18, 1812, Holley Family Papers, CHS.

104. As remembered in Horace Holley to Mary Holley, September 23, 1812, Crosby Family Papers, emphasis in original.

105. Horace Holley to Mary Holley, September 30, 1812, Crosby Family Papers.

106. Horace Holley to Mary Holley, October 3, 1812, Crosby Family Papers.

107. Horace Holley to Mary Holley, September 20, 1814, Horace Holley Papers, TU.

108. Horace Holley to Mary Holley, October 3, 1814, Horace Holley Papers, TU.

109. Horace Holley to Mary Holley, September 20, 1814, Horace Holley Papers, TU; Mary Holley to Horace Holley, October 3, 1814, transcript, Mary Austin Holley Papers, Dolph Briscoe Center for American History (DBC), University of Texas, Austin.

110. Horace Holley to Mary Holley, October 5, 1814, Horace Holley Papers, TU.

111. Smith Lee, *Mary Austin Holley,* 81; Horace Holley to Sarah Holley, July 16, 1816, Crosby Family Papers.

112. Horace Holley to Luther Holley, April 14, 1814, and Luther Holley to Horace Holley, January 9, 1813, Crosby Family Papers.

113. Horace Holley to Luther Holley, April 14, 1814, and Horace Holley to Sarah Holley, July 16, 1816, Crosby Family Papers.

114. Horace Holley to Mary Holley, September 16, 1812, Crosby Family Papers.

115. Horace Holley to Sarah Holley, July 16, 1816, Crosby Family Papers.

116. The poem was printed later, when the family was in Kentucky. See [Horace Holley], "From a Husband to a Wife, on Seeing Their Daughter, a Little Girl, at Play," *Western Review and Miscellaneous Magazine* 3 (November 1820): 255.

117. Horace Holley to Mary Holley, July 25, 1811, Mary Holley Papers, TU.

118. Mary Holley to Horace Holley, July 27, 1811, Mary Holley Papers, TU; Mary Holley to Horace Holley, September 29, 1812, transcript, Mary Austin Holley Papers, DBC.

119. Horace Holley to Mary Holley, July 31, 1811, Mary Holley Papers, TU.

120. A comprehensive account of their time apart in this period is preserved in the following letters: Horace Holley to Mary Holley, July 25, 30, 31, 1811, Mary Holley Pa-

pers, TU; Mary Holley to Horace Holley, July 27, 1811, Mary Holley Papers, TU; Horace Holley to Mary Holley, August 3 and 6, 1811, Crosby Family Papers; Mary Holley to Horace Holley, August 20, 1812, Horace Holley Papers, TU; Horace Holley to Mary Holley, September 16, 21, 23, 1812, Crosby Family Papers; Mary Holley to Horace Holley, September 28, 29, 1812, transcript, Mary Austin Holley Papers, DBC; Horace Holley to Mary Holley, September 30 and October 3, 1812, Crosby Family Papers; Mary Holley to Horace Holley, October 5, 1812, transcript, Mary Austin Holley Papers, DBC; Mary Holley to Horace Holley, October 11, 1812, Mary Holley Papers, TU; Horace Holley to Mary Holley, October 13, 1812, Mary Holley Papers, TU; Mary Holley to Horace Holley, October 17, 1812, transcript, Mary Austin Holley Papers, DBC; Horace Holley to Mary Holley, September 20, 1814, Horace Holley Papers, TU; Mary Holley to Horace Holley, September 23, 25, 1814, transcript, Mary Austin Holley Papers, DBC; Horace Holley to Mary Holley, September 26, 1814, Mary Holley Papers, TU; Mary Holley to Horace Holley, September 29, 1814, Mary Holley Papers, TU; Horace Holley to Mary Holley, October 3 and 5, 1814, Horace Holley Papers, TU; Mary Holley to Horace Holley, October 12, 1814, Mary Holley Papers, TU.

121. Horace Holley to Mary Holley, September 26, 1814, Mary Holley Papers, TU.

122. M. [Mary Austin Holley], "Madame De Stael," *Western Review and Miscellaneous Magazine* 1 (September 1819): 124. "M." was one of Mary's signatures.

123. U. [Horace Holley], "To a Wife, Who Had Left the City for the Country in Spring on Account of Ill Health; Who Took with Her, among Other Books, the Works of Madam Roland and Madam De Stael, and Whose Favourite Amusement at Evening Was the Guitar," *Western Review and Miscellaneous Magazine* 1 (December 1819): 317–18. "U." was one of Horace's signatures.

124. Mary Holley to Horace Holley, October 5, 1812, transcript, Mary Austin Holley Papers, DBC.

125. M. [Mary Austin Holley], untitled poem, *Western Review and Miscellaneous Magazine* 1 (August 1819): 63–64.

126. M. [Mary Austin Holley], "Lines Written Immediately on First Beholding Niagara Falls; July 1815," *Western Review and Miscellaneous Magazine* 1 (September 1819): 127.

127. Caleb Hopkins Snow, *A History of Boston: The Metropolis of Massachusetts . . .* (Boston: Abel Bowen, 1828), 332.

128. *Columbian Centinel* (Boston), June 21, 1817. Horace attended the opening of Savage's museum and declared it superior to the Columbian Museum (Horace Holley to Mary Holley, July 31, 1811, Mary Holley Papers, TU).

129. *American Commercial Daily Advertiser* (Baltimore), May 1, 1817.

130. Marcus Whiffen and Frederick Koeper, *American Architecture*, vol. 1: *1607–1860* (Cambridge, Mass.: MIT Press, 1981), 110–12; Baltzell, *Puritan Boston and Quaker Philadelphia*, 324; Lawrence W. Kennedy, *Planning the City upon a Hill: Boston since 1630* (Boston: Thomson-Shore, 1992), 30–34.

131. Kentucky legislators John Breckinridge, John Brown, Valentine Peers, and

George Robertson sent sons to the College of New Jersey, and John Crittenden, Richard C. Anderson, and Thomas Todd enrolled sons in the College of William and Mary (Lewis Collins, *Historical Sketches of Kentucky* [Maysville, Ky.: J. A. and U. P. James, 1848], 138, 123, 322, 248, 169).

132. James Blythe, *A Portrait of the Times: Being a Sermon Delivered at the Opening of the Synod of Kentucky* (Lexington, Ky.: Thomas T. Skillman, 1814).

133. Joan Wells Coward, *Kentucky in the New Republic: The Process of Constitution Making* (Lexington: University Press of Kentucky, 1979), 62.

134. Lowell Harrison and James Klotter, *A New History of Kentucky* (Lexington: University Press of Kentucky, 1997), 77.

135. Ivan E. McDougle, *Slavery in Kentucky, 1792–1865* (Westport, Conn.: Negro Universities Press, 1970), 9.

136. *Kentucky Reporter,* May 29, 1815.

137. *Kentucky Gazette,* May 8, 15, 29, 1815; *Kentucky Reporter,* May 3, 1815.

138. Baldwin had preceded Horace as chaplain to the Massachusetts House of Representatives (*The Massachusetts Manual, or, Political and Historical Register . . . ,* vol. 1 June 1814–June 1815 [Boston: Charles Callender, 1814], 32).

139. James Prentiss to Thomas Baldwin, November 19, 1814, Horace Holley Papers, TU. It was later confirmed that Horace was first offered the position at Transylvania on the strength of Prentiss's recommendation (clipping, *Western Monitor* [Lexington], c. 1825, Horace Holley Scrapbook, 2834, TU).

140. Transylvania Board of Trustees, minutes of meeting, June 8, 1815, TU; *Kentucky Gazette,* July 3, 1815.

141. Richard Higgins of Lexington had donated four acres of land northwest of Lexington for these purposes. In 1818, Higgins sold this land for the sum of $1,000 to Spencer Cooper (County Deed Book R, January 2, 1818, p. 50, Fayette County Circuit Court).

142. *Kentucky Gazette,* June 26, 1815.

143. *Kentucky Gazette,* July 3, 1815.

144. *Western Monitor,* July 28, 1815.

145. *Kentucky Gazette,* October 2, 1815.

146. Ibid.

147. *Louisville Correspondent,* October 16, 1815.

148. Transylvania Board of Trustees, minutes of meeting, November 11, 1815, TU; Robert Davidson, *History of the Presbyterian Church in the State of Kentucky; with a Preliminary Sketch of the Churches in the Valley of Virginia* (New York: R. Carter, 1847), 299; Caldwell, *Discourse,* 197.

149. *Journal of the House of Representatives of the Commonwealth of Kentucky,* 1815, 203 (hereafter *Kentucky House Journal;* the publication data supplied for issues of this journal varied, sometimes including a volume number or a specific date or both, but all providing the year, so I have tried to make the presentation consistent by supplying only the year of the issue being cited).

150. *Kentucky House Journal,* 1815, 211, 208; Transylvania Board of Trustees, minutes of meeting, November 21, 1815, TU.

151. *Kentucky House Journal,* 1815, 201, 202, 203, 220.

152. However public these board meetings, it is clear that the terms of Blythe's resignation were worked out in private. At a subsequent meeting, the board agreed to provide free use of one room of the main building "on Sabbath evening for the instruction of female Africans." The schooling of girls and women was a true passion of Blythe's; in 1818, he established an independent seminary for young women. And on April 8 of that year, the board voted to pay $375 for prior service. The sum was "to be paid out of the funds of the University in consequence of his sallery [*sic*] being of late years in adequate to the support of his family" (Transylvania Board of Trustees, minutes of meetings, March 22 and April 8, 1816, TU).

153. Thomas Cooper to Frederick Ridgely, February 12, 1816, Miscellaneous Records, TU. Cooper later removed himself from consideration after learning of Transylvania's legislative troubles. His letter to the board on February 29, 1816, pronounced his great sorrow at the university's misfortunes, but at his stage of life, he said, he simply could not have such "uncertainty" (Dr. Thomas Cooper to John Beckly, February 29, 1816, Horace Holley Papers, TU).

154. Transylvania Board of Trustees, minutes of meeting, April 18, 1817, TU.

155. *Kentucky Gazette,* October 18, 1817.

156. *Kentucky Gazette,* October 4, 1817.

157. All reported in *Kentucky Gazette,* November 22, 1817.

158. *Journal of the Senate of the Commonwealth of Kentucky,* 1817–1818, 20, 21 (hereafter *Kentucky Senate Journal,* citing only the year of each issue).

159. John Brown had been formative in the creation of the state's first constitution and served three terms in the U.S. Senate; John Pope was both a state representative and U.S. senator; John Mason served in the House as a representative of Montgomery County; Robert Trimble was the district judge of Kentucky; Robert Wickliffe was a longtime member of the state legislature; Lewis Sanders was secretary of the commonwealth; Samuel Woodson was twice elected to Congress; Thomas Bodley won fame for his service in the War of 1812; and by 1817 Henry Clay had already served stints as Speaker of the U.S. House, negotiated the Treaty of Ghent, and founded the American Colonization Society (Collins, *Historical Sketches of Kentucky,* 632, 734, 144, 150, 285, 286).

160. *Kentucky Senate Journal,* 1817–1818, 36, 41; *Kentucky House Journal,* 1817–1818, 296.

161. *Kentucky House Journal,* 1816–1817, 16–18.

3. "The State of Society"

1. Journal of Horace Holley, February 3, 1818, Horace Holley Papers, CL.

2. As remembered in Horace Holley to James Freeman, March 18, 1818, James Freeman Papers, Harvard College Library, Harvard University, Cambridge, Mass.

3. Journal of Horace Holley, February 3, 1818, Horace Holley Papers, CL.

4. Ibid., February 18, 1818.

5. Mary Holley to Horace Holley, March 22, 1818, Horace Holley Papers, CL.

6. Horace Holley to Mary Holley, April 22, 1818, Horace Holley Papers, TU.

7. Horace Holley to Mary Austin Holley, April 9, 1818, Horace Holley Papers, CL.

8. Horace Holley to Mary Austin Holley, June 19, 1818, Horace Holley Papers, CL.

9. Horace Holley to Mary Austin Holley, April 2, 1818, Horace Holley Papers, CL.

10. Horace Holley to Mary Austin Holley, May 27, 1818, Horace Holley Papers, TU.

11. Horace Holley to Mary Austin Holley, March 18, 1818, Horace Holley Papers, CL.

12. Mary Austin Holley to Horace Holley, April 13, 1818, Mary Austin Holley Letters, Rare Books Library, University of Louisville (UL), Louisville, Ky.

13. James D. Watkinson, "Useful Knowledge? Concepts, Values, and Access in American Education, 1776–1840," *History of Education Quarterly* 30, no. 3 (1990): 352–53.

14. C. Dallett Hemphill, *Bowing to Necessities: A History of Manners in America, 1620–1860* (Oxford: Oxford University Press, 2002), 149.

15. C. S., "Letters from Boston," *The Ordeal: A Critical Journal of Politicks and Literature* 1 (1809): 234.

16. Samuel Lorenzo Knapp, *Extracts from a Journal of Travels in North America . . .* (Boston: Thomas Badger, 1818), 13.

17. Basil Hall, *Travels in North America . . .* , 3 vols. (Edinburgh: R. Cadell, 1830), 2:122.

18. John Adams to Thomas Jefferson, January 28, 1818, Thomas Jefferson Papers, Series 1, General Correspondence, 1651–1827, American Memory Project, Library of Congress, Washington, D.C., at http://hdl.loc.gov/loc.mss/mtj.mtjbib023087.

19. Horace Holley to Mary Austin Holley, March 31, 1818, Horace Holley Papers, CL; Horace Holley to Mary Austin Holley, April 22, 1818, Horace Holley Papers, TU.

20. Journal of Horace Holley, February 3, 1818, Horace Holley Papers, CL.

21. Ibid.

22. Ibid.

23. Ibid., February 18, 1818.

24. Bronson had coauthored an investigation of a meteor shower with Horace in 1807. See note 89, chapter 2.

25. Horace Holley to Mary Austin Holley, February 14, 1818, Horace Holley Papers, CL.

26. Journal of Horace Holley, February 9 and 18, 1818, Horace Holley Papers, CL.

27. Ibid., February 18, 1818.

28. Ibid., February 12, 1818.

29. Ibid., February 8, 1818.

30. Ibid., February 10, 1818.

31. Ibid.

32. Ibid., February 16, 1818.

33. Ibid.

34. Ibid.

35. Ibid., February 19, 1818.

36. Ibid., February 20, 1818.

37. Ibid.

38. Ibid.

39. Ibid.

40. John Maclean, *History of the College of New Jersey, from Its Origin in 1746 to the Commencement of 1854*, 2 vols. (Philadelphia: Lippincott, 1877), 2:41.

41. Journal of Horace Holley, February 25, 1818, Horace Holley Papers, CL.

42. Ibid., February 25, 1818.

43. Horace Holley to Mary Holley, March 5, 1818, Horace Holley Papers, CL.

44. Journal of Horace Holley, February 25, 1818, Horace Holley Papers, CL.

45. Ibid.

46. Horace Holley to Mary Holley, March 1, 1818, Mary Holley Papers, TU.

47. Journal of Horace Holley, February 25, 1818, Horace Holley Papers, CL; Horace Holley to Mary Austin Holley, March 1, 1818, Horace Holley Papers, TU.

48. Horace Holley to Mary Austin Holley, March 1, 1818.

49. Mary Holley to Horace Holley, February 24, 1818, Mary Austin Holley Letters, UL.

50. Horace Holley to Mary Holley, March 1, 1818, Horace Holley Papers, TU.

51. Journal of Horace Holley, March 7, 1818, Horace Holley Papers, CL.

52. Horace Holley to Mary Holley, March 10, 1818, Horace Holley Papers, CL.

53. Horace Holley to Mary Austin Holley, March 12, 1818, Horace Holley Papers, CL.

54. Ibid.

55. Horace Holley to Mary Austin Holley, March 18, 1818, Horace Holley Papers, CL.

56. Horace Holley to Mary Austin Holley, March 28, 1818, Horace Holley Papers, CL.

57. Horace Holley to Mary Austin Holley, March 13, 1818, Horace Holley Papers, CL.

58. Horace Holley to Mary Austin Holley, March 14, 1818, Horace Holley Papers, CL.

59. Charlene M. Boyer Lewis, *Elizabeth Patterson Bonaparte: An American Aristocrat in the Early Republic* (Philadelphia: University of Pennsylvania Press, 2012), 27–36.

60. Ibid., 41.

61. Horace Holley to Mary Austin Holley, March 12, 1818, Horace Holley Papers, CL.

62. Horace Holley to Mary Austin Holley, March 16, 1818, Horace Holley Papers, CL.

63. Journal of Horace Holley, March 19, 1818, Horace Holley Papers, CL.

64. Horace Holley to Mary Austin Holley, March 20, 1818, Horace Holley Papers, CL.

65. Horace Holley to Elizabeth Patterson Bonaparte, April 2, 1818, Elizabeth Patterson Bonaparte Papers, 1685–1879, Maryland Historical Society, Baltimore.

66. Ibid.

67. Horace Holley to Mary Austin Holley, March 13, 1818, Horace Holley Papers, CL.

68. Stephen F. Austin to Horace Holley, March 5, 1818, Horace Holley Papers, CL.

69. Horace Holley to Mary Austin Holley, April 5, 1818, Horace Holley Papers, CL.

70. Horace Holley to Mary Austin Holley, March 23, 1818, Horace Holley Papers, CL.

71. Horace Holley to Mary Austin Holley, March 25, 1818, Horace Holley Papers, CL.

72. Horace Holley to Mary Austin Holley, March 31, 1818, Horace Holley Papers, CL.

73. Horace Holley to Mary Austin Holley, April 2, 1818, Horace Holley Papers, CL.

74. Horace Holley to Mary Austin Holley, March 25, 1818, Horace Holley Papers, CL.

75. Horace Holley to Mary Austin Holley, April 3, 1818, Horace Holley Papers, CL.

76. Horace Holley to Mary Austin Holley, March 28, 1818, Horace Holley Papers, CL.

77. *Essex Register* (Salem, Mass.), April 11, 1818. See also *Columbian Centinel,* April 4, 1818; *Boston Commercial Gazette,* April 6, 1818; *Independent Chronicle and Boston Patriot,* April 11, 1818; *Litchfield Journal,* April 22, 1818.

78. Horace Holley to Mary Austin Holley, March 28, 1818, Horace Holley Papers, CL.

79. Ibid.

80. Horace Holley to James Freeman, April 2, 1818, Horace Holley Papers, TU.

81. Horace Holley to Mary Austin Holley, March 31, 1818, Horace Holley Papers, CL.

82. Horace Holley to Mary Austin Holley, April 5, 1818, Horace Holley Papers, CL.

83. Horace Holley to Mary Austin Holley, March 28, 1818, Horace Holley Papers, CL.

84. Horace Holley to Mary Austin Holley, April 2, 1818, Horace Holley Papers, CL.

85. Horace Holley to Mary Austin Holley, April 7, 1818, Horace Holley Papers, CL.

86. Horace Holley to Mary Austin Holley, March 26, 1818, Horace Holley Papers, CL.

87. Horace Holley to Mary Austin Holley, March 28, 1818, Horace Holley Papers, CL.

88. William Van Ness Bay, *Reminiscences of the Bench and Bar of Missouri . . .* (St. Louis: F. H. Thomas, 1878), 440.

89. Horace Holley to Mary Austin Holley, March 28, 1818, Horace Holley Papers, CL.

90. Horace Holley to Mary Austin Holley, April 6, 1818, Horace Holley Papers, CL.

91. Quoted in Horace Holley to Mary Austin Holley, March 22, 1818, Horace Holley Papers, CL.

92. Horace Holley to Mary Austin Holley, April 2, 1818, Horace Holley Papers, CL.

93. Horace Holley to Mary Austin Holley, April 10, 1818, Horace Holley Papers, CL.

94. Horace Holley to James Freeman, April 2, 1818, Horace Holley Papers, CL.

95. Horace Holley to Mary Austin Holley, April 8, 1818, Horace Holley Papers, CL.

96. Horace Holley to Mary Austin Holley, April 2, 1818, Horace Holley Papers, CL.

97. Ibid.

98. Horace Holley to Mary Austin Holley, April 10, 1818, Horace Holley Papers, CL.

99. Horace Holley to Mary Austin Holley, April 6, 1818, Horace Holley Papers, CL.

100. Ibid.

101. Horace Holley to Mary Austin Holley, April 2, 1818, Horace Holley Papers, CL.

102. Horace Holley to Mary Austin Holley, April 8, 1818, Horace Holley Papers, CL.

103. Ezra Stiles Ely, "An Inaugural Oration, Pronounced March 18, 1818," *Quarterly Theological Review* 3 (July 1818): 309.

104. Ezra Stiles Ely, "M'Chord's Essays," *Quarterly Theological Review* 2 (April 1818): 175.

105. Horace Holley to Mary Austin Holley, March 1, 1818, Mary Holley Papers, TU.

106. Horace Holley to Mary Austin Holley, April 15, 1818, Horace Holley Papers, CL. In addition to numerous other accomplishments, Bushrod Washington was a member of the American Colonization Society, an organization he cofounded with Henry Clay. It is likely that Clay provided a letter on Holley's behalf for the visit.

107. Horace Holley to Mary Austin Holley, April 15, 1818, Horace Holley Papers, CL.

108. Horace Holley to Mary Austin Holley, April 10, 1818, Horace Holley Papers, CL.

109. Thomas Jefferson to John Adams, May 17, 1818, Thomas Jefferson Papers, Series 1, General Correspondence, 1651–1827, American Memory Project, at http://www.loc.gov/resource/mtj1.050_0904_0905/.

110. John Adams to Thomas Jefferson, May 29, 1818, Thomas Jefferson Papers, Series 1, General Correspondence, 1651–1827, American Memory Project, http://www.loc.gov/resource/mtj1.050_0926_0929/.

111. Horace Holley to Mary Austin Holley, April 17, 1818, Horace Holley Papers, CL.

112. Mary Austin Holley to Horace Holley, February 7, 1818, Mary Austin Holley Letters, UL.

113. Mary Austin Holley to Horace Holley, March 5, 1818, Mary Austin Holley Letters, UL.

114. Mary Austin Holley to Horace Holley, March 22, 1818, Mary Austin Holley Letters, UL.

115. Mary Austin Holley to Horace Holley, February 14 and April 15, 1818, Mary Austin Holley Letters, UL.

116. Mary Austin Holley to Horace Holley, April 1, 1818, Mary Austin Holley Letters, UL.

117. Mary Austin Holley to Horace Holley, March 7, 1818, Mary Austin Holley Letters, UL.

118. Mary Austin Holley to Horace Holley, May 12, 1818, Mary Austin Holley Letters, UL.

119. Mary Austin Holley to Horace Holley, May 15, 1818, Mary Austin Holley Letters, UL.

120. Horace Holley to Mary Austin Holley, May 7, 1818, Horace Holley Papers, CL.

121. Ibid.

122. Horace Holley to Mary Austin Holley, May 21, 1818, Horace Holley Papers, CL.

123. Horace Holley to Mary Austin Holley, May 16, 1818, Horace Holley Papers, CL.

124. Horace Holley to Mary Austin Holley, May 21, 1818, Horace Holley Papers, CL.

125. Ibid.

126. Horace Holley to Mary Austin Holley, May 23, 1818, Horace Holley Papers, CL.

127. Ibid.

128. Horace Holley to Mary Austin Holley, May 25, 1818, Horace Holley Papers, CL.

129. Horace Holley to Mary Austin Holley, May 27, 1818, Horace Holley Papers, TU.

130. Horace Holley to Mary Austin Holley, May 25, 1818, Horace Holley Papers, CL.

131. Horace Holley to Mary Holley, May 27, 1818, Horace Holley Papers, TU.

132. Horace Holley to Mary Austin Holley, June 8, 1818, Mary Holley Papers, TU.

133. Ibid.

134. Horace Holley to Mary Austin Holley, June 11, 1818, Horace Holley Papers, CL.

135. Ibid.

136. Horace Holley to Mary Holley, June 15, 1818, Horace Holley Papers, TU.

137. *Lexington Reporter,* June 10, 1818.

138. Horace Holley to Mary Holley, May 25, 1818, Horace Holley Papers, CL.

139. Horace Holley to Mary Holley, June 15, 1818, Horace Holley Papers, TU.

140. Mary Holley to Horace Holley, June 25, 1818, Mary Austin Holley Letters, UL.

4. "A New Era of Literature"

1. Report of Hollis Street Church, August 24, 1818, Horace Holley Papers, TU.

2. *Kentucky Gazette,* June 26, 1818; *Independent Chronicle & Boston Patriot,* July 18, 1818.

3. *Invisible Rambler* (Boston), July 4, 1818; *Boston Commercial Gazette,* June 22, 1818.

4. Excerpt from "A Sketch of the Hollis Street Church," Andover-Harvard Theological Library Manuscripts and Archives; Hollis Street Church to Horace Holley, August 30, 1818, Horace Holley Papers, TU.

5. Codman, *Hollis Street Church,* passim.

6. Horace attempted to intervene in a dispute between Benjamin Bussey and his daughter (Horace Holley to Benjamin Bussey, December 28, 1821, Miscellaneous Collections No. 5, Andover-Harvard Theological Library Manuscripts and Archives).

7. See the first portrait in the illustrations gallery. Mary felt the portrait did not capture Horace's "best expression" (Mary Holley to Horace Holley, September 16, 1821, Mary Austin Holley Papers, DBC).

8. John Davis to Horace Holley, September 21, 1818, Horace Holley Papers, TU.

9. Joseph Story to Horace Holley, October 20, 1818, Horace Holley Papers, TU.

10. Boston School Committee to Horace Holley, September 29, 1818, Horace Holley Papers, TU.

11. Kentucky's reputation for Indian warfare gave rise to the term "dark and bloody ground." At negotiations for the Treaty of Sycamore Shoals in 1775—a deal that gave Colonel Richard Henderson's Transylvania Company rights to vast stretches of Kentucky land—Cherokee chief Dragging Canoe is said to have arisen, pointed north, and declared, "Bloody ground!" This story became written into the lore of Kentucky history and used to demonstrate the state's rough, dangerous, and untamed nature (Z. F. Smith, *The History of Kentucky: From Its Earliest Discovery and Settlement to the Present Date* ... [Louisville, Ky.: Prentice Press, 1901], 52; William Guthrie, *A New System of Modern Geography* ... (Philadelphia: Mathew Carey, 1794).

12. A contemporary of Henry Clay excused Clay's outlandish behaviors by remark-

ing that "he was a little given in his early days to such wild pranks, as your full-blooded Kentuckian is prone to" (*Harper's Magazine*, January 1853, 270).

13. Hugh H. Brackenridge, *Incidents of the Insurrection in the Western Parts of Pennsylvania, in the Year 1794* (Philadelphia: John M'Culloch, 1795), 61.

14. For an extended discussion of Burr's influences on the youth, see Joseph Fichtelberg, *Risk Culture: Performance and Danger in Early America* (Ann Arbor: University of Michigan Press, 2010), 186–216.

15. Harrison and Klotter, *A New History of Kentucky*, 94.

16. Norman C. Lord, "The War of 1812 on the Canadian Frontier: Letters Written by Sergt. James Commins, 8th Foot," *Journal of the Society for Army Historical Research* 18 (1939): 199–211.

17. Daniel Drake, *An Appeal to the Justice of the Intelligent and Respectable People of Lexington* (Cincinnati, Ohio: Looker, Reynolds, 1818), 18.

18. Benjamin Dudley, *To Dr. Drake* (Lexington, Ky.: n.p., 1818), 13–14.

19. Robert Peter and Johanna Peter, *Transylvania University: Its Origin, Rise, Decline, and Fall* (Louisville, Ky.: J. P. Morton, 1896), 100–101.

20. *Boston Commercial Gazette*, August 24, 1818; *Boston Recorder*, August 29, 1818; *Farmers' Cabinet* (Amherst, N.H.), August 29, 1818; *Portsmouth Oracle*, August 29, 1818.

21. Jefferson Davis remembered that Bishop had a "testy temper which frequently exploded in class" and that he on occasion beat recalcitrant students with a large wooden ruler (Varna Davis, *Jefferson Davis, Ex-president of the Confederate States of America. A Memoir by His Wife*, 2 vols. [New York: Belford, 1890], 24–25). Bishop's biographer is forced to admit that the two shared many allies (Rodabaugh, *Robert Hamilton Bishop*, 43).

22. Bishop first attempted to secure a position at the Presbyterian Chillicothe Academy; when this failed, he may have pursued an offer to begin a department for women (Rodabaugh, *Robert Hamilton Bishop*, 43).

23. Robert Bishop to Transylvania Board of Trustees, December 19, 1818, quoted in Peter and Peter, *Transylvania University*, 112. Bishop's salary of $1,200 was less than half of Horace's.

24. A student's description of Sharpe is included in Peter and Peter, *Transylvania University*, 110.

25. Ebenezer Sharpe to Transylvania Board of Trustees, n.d., printed in *Weekly Recorder* (Chillicothe, Ohio), October 30, 1818.

26. Horace Holley to James Freeman, November 11, 1818, James Freeman Papers.

27. Henry Clay to Horace Holley, September 8, 1818, in Henry Clay, *The Papers of Henry Clay, 1797–1852*, 11 vols., ed. James F. Hopkins et al. (Lexington: University of Kentucky Press, 1959–1992), 2:594–95.

28. Horace Holley to Henry Clay, September 15, 1818, in Clay, *Letters of Henry Clay*, 2:597–98.

29. *New-York Evening Post*, June 15, 1821; *Daily National Intelligencer* (District of Columbia), July 26, 1821.

30. As repeated in Horace Holley to James Freeman, November 11, 1818, James Freeman Papers.

31. Caldwell, *Discourse,* 199.

32. *Argus of Western America* (Frankfort, Ky.), December 4, 1818.

33. *Niles' Weekly Register* (Baltimore), October 24, 1818.

34. Ibid.

35. James Taylor to President James Monroe, n.d., in James A. Padgett, "The Letters of James Taylor to the Presidents of the United States," *Register of the Kentucky Historical Society* 34 (April 1936): 338.

36. *Weekly Recorder,* December 18, 1818.

37. *Weekly Recorder,* February 26, 1819.

38. Henry Clay to Horace Holley, December 9, 1818, in Clay, *Letters of Henry Clay,* 2:613–14.

39. *Western Monitor,* December 26, 1818.

40. *Western Monitor,* December 26, 1818.

41. *Lexington Gazette,* December 25, 1818.

42. Horace's inaugural address was later printed in the *Western Review and Miscellaneous Magazine* 1 (August 1819): 59.

43. Ibid., 58.

44. *Kentucky Gazette,* December 25, 1818.

45. Quoted in *Western Monitor,* December 26, 1818.

46. *Western Monitor,* January 16, 1819.

47. *Western Monitor,* January 9, 1819.

48. Ibid.

49. *Louisville Public Advertiser,* February 13, 1819.

50. Monies were to be paid directly from the "cashier" of the bank to the chairman of the Transylvania Board of Trustees (*Kentucky House Journal,* 1818–1819, 692–93).

51. *Kentucky House Journal,* 1818–1819, 621.

52. These three colleges were not created ex nihilo: Southern College was entitled to the holdings of Warren Seminary, Urania College to those of Barren County Seminary, and Western College to the land and monies of Christian Academy (*Kentucky House Journal,* 1818–1819, 737–39).

53. Joseph Story to Horace Holley, March 4, 1819, Horace Holley Papers, TU, referring to an earlier letter Horace had written.

54. Charles E. Rosenberg and William H. Helfand, *"Every Man His Own Doctor": Popular Medicine in Early America* (Philadelphia: Library Company of Philadelphia, 1998), 13.

55. *Lexington's First City Directory* (Lexington, Ky.: Joseph Charless, 1806); *Lexington's Second City Directory* (Lexington, Ky.: Worsley and Smith, 1818). As late as 1815, the town was without a dentist, so those in need of tooth pulling relied on the services of traveling practitioners (*Kentucky Gazette,* February 2, 1815). In 1818, E. Parmly an-

nounced that he would be in Lexington for the months of December and January. His dental practice was in his rented room "in the house occupied by Dr. Briggs opposite Keen & Lamphear's Hotel" (*Kentucky Gazette,* December 13, 1817).

56. Christianson, "The Conditions for Science," 313.

57. Frederick A. Wallis and Hambleton Tapp, *A Sesqui-centennial History of Kentucky,* 5 vols. (Hopkinsville, Ky.: Historical Record Association, 1945), 1:547–48. These methods were often less than adequate (Henry Burnell Shafer, *The American Medical Profession, 1783–1850* [New York: AMS Press, 1968], 20). One Kentucky doctor of this period admitted ignorance to the new names of medicines and admitted, "I write seldom and . . . I never saw the inside of a corpse" (William Ogden Niles, "Notes," *Niles' Weekly Register* 33 [1827], 92).

58. J. Wright, *Transylvania,* 79.

59. *Kentucky Gazette,* August 16, 1803.

60. Horace Holley to Benjamin Silliman, February 22, 1819, Horace Holley Papers, TU; Benjamin Silliman to Horace Holley, May 8, 1819, Horace Holley Papers, TU.

61. William Humphries to Samuel Brown, February 26, 1819, Samuel Brown Vertical File, TU.

62. Rafinesque's earliest biographer believed that Rafinesque and Clifford were much more than friends. Clifford was "the only man . . . [Rafinesque] ever loved," cherished more than any other man or woman (Richard Ellsworth, *The Life and Writings of Rafinesque* [Louisville, Ky.: J. P. Morton, 1895], 34–35).

63. Charles Boewe correctly doubts the long-standing assumption of Eric Christianson and others that Horace suggested or even agreed to Rafinesque's appointment. Although it is perhaps true that Horace did not know of Rafinesque personally, it is doubtful he was ever compelled to take him on (Charles Boewe, *The Life of C. S. Rafinesque, a Man of Uncommon Zeal* [Philadelphia: American Philosophical Society, 2011]).

64. *Philadelphia Medical Museum,* January 3, 1805, 359.

65. Charles Caldwell, introduction to *Medical Theses Selected from Inaugural Dissertations,* ed. Charles Caldwell (Philadelphia: Thomas and William Bradford, 1805–1806), vi, viii.

66. Thomas Horsfield, "An Experimental Dissertation on the Rhus Vernix, Rhus Radicans, and Rhus Glabrum . . . ," in Caldwell, *Medical Theses,* 122.

67. John Walker, "An Experimental Inquiry into the Similarity in Virtue between the Cornus Florida and Sericea . . . ," in Caldwell, *Medical Theses,* 301. There was a long-standing precedent to this idea. Peruvian Bark was used to some effect by Jesuit missionaries in the treatment of influenza.

68. Alexander May, "An Inaugural Dissertation on the Unity of Disease, as Opposed to Nosology," in Caldwell, *Medical Theses,* 215; Peter Miller, "An Essay on the Means of Lessening the Pains of Parturition," in Caldwell, *Medical Theses,* 346.

69. *Port-Folio* (Philadelphia), May 1817, 405; January 1815, 75; September 1816, 238; July 1815, 98; September 1816, 238.

70. *Port-Folio,* May 1814, 100.

71. Charles Caldwell, *Autobiography of Charles Caldwell* (Philadelphia: Lippincott, Grambo, 1855), 333.

72. Ibid., 334.

73. Ibid., 329.

74. F. L. M. Pattison, *Granville Sharp Pattison: Anatomist and Antagonist, 1791–1851* (Tuscaloosa: University of Alabama Press, 1987), 24, 52, 76, 90.

75. *Saint Louis Inquirer,* October 30, 1819.

76. Ibid.

77. *Plough Boy* (Albany, N.Y.), June 26, 1819; *Franklin Gazette* (Philadelphia), June 18, 1819.

78. *Western Monitor,* June 15, 1819.

79. *Western Monitor,* July 18, 1819.

80. *Kentucky Gazette,* March 18, 1819.

81. *Baltimore Patriot and Mercantile Advertiser,* July 23, 1819.

82. *Western Monitor,* July 27, 1819.

83. *Western Monitor,* July 6, 1819.

84. Henry Clay to Horace Holley, May 6, 1819, in Clay, *Letters of Henry Clay,* 2:690.

85. Horace Holley, sermon, May 30, 1819, Sermons of Horace Holley, Horace Holley Papers, TU.

86. Horace Holley, sermons, June 20 and 13, 1819, Sermons of Horace Holley, Horace Holley Papers, TU.

87. Horace Holley, sermon, June 6, 1819, Sermons of Horace Holley, Horace Holley Papers, TU.

88. Horace Holley, sermon, July 4, 1819, Sermons of Horace Holley, Horace Holley Papers TU.

89. *Weekly Recorder,* July 30, 1819; *Western Monitor,* August 10, 1819.

90. *Weekly Recorder,* October 6, 1819.

91. *Western Monitor,* August 10 and 17, 1819.

92. *Western Monitor,* August 24, 1819.

93. *Western Monitor,* August 17 and 31, 1819.

94. *Western Monitor,* August 31, 1819.

95. *Western Monitor,* August 24, 1819.

96. Willard R. Jillson, "Bibliography of Lexington, Kentucky: Designed to Portray the Changing Historical Scene from 1774–1946," *Register of Kentucky State Historical Society* 44 (July 1946): 171–72.

97. "Valedictory," *Western Review and Miscellaneous Magazine* 4 (July 1821): 383.

98. Peter S. Field, "The Birth of Secular High Culture: 'The Monthly Anthology and Boston Review' and Its Critics," *Journal of the Early Republic* 17 (Winter 1997): 578.

99. William Henry Venable, *Beginnings of Literary Culture in the Ohio Valley* (Cincinnati, Ohio: Robert Clarke, 1891), 58–59.

100. Advertisement for the *Western Review* in *The American* (New York), April 24, 1819.

101. Horace's original translation of *De l'Allemagne* appears in his letter to Mary dated September 26, 1814, Mary Holley Papers, TU.

102. [Horace Holley], "Doctissimo atque facundissimo," *Western Review and Miscellaneous Magazine* 1 (January 1820): 382–83.

103. Horace's "Free Translation an IDYL," found in the October 1819 issue of the *Western Review*, and a translation published as part of a multivolume collection of Gessner's works do not differ in any substantive way. There is also no mention of Horace's ever learning or translating German previous to this publication. Compare the poem translated in the *Western Review and Miscellaneous Magazine* 1 (October 1819): 191, and "Morning Song" in Solomon Gessner, *The Works of Solomon Gessner Translated from the German with Some Account of His Life and Writings*, 3 vols. (Liverpool, England: J. M'Creery, 1805), 2:207–8.

104. [Horace Holley], "Libraries," *Western Review and Miscellaneous Magazine* 1 (November 1819): 250–52.

105. *The Statute Law of Kentucky; with Notes, Praelections, and Observations on the Public Acts . . .*, 5 vols. (Frankfort, Ky.: State of Kentucky, 1809), 1:376.

106. [Horace Holley], "Bail," *Western Review and Miscellaneous Magazine* 1 (December 1819): 301.

107. [Horace Holley], "Trial by Jury," *Western Review and Miscellaneous Magazine* 1 (September 1819): 104–6.

108. [Horace Holley], review of Robert Walsh Jr., "An Appeal from the Judgments of Great Britain Respecting the United States," *Western Review and Miscellaneous Magazine* 1 (January 1820): 321–45.

109. In a letter to brother Orville, Horace later decoded the pennames as such: "B is Reverend Mr Burge, the Episcopalian minister of the town. . . . C is John D. Clifford, a merchant. . . . E is the editor. F is Mr Jenkins. . . . G and B G are Benjamin James. . . . H is Charles Humphrys Esqr. . . . I is Joseph C. Breckinridge Esqr. . . . C, D, is his brother John. . . . R, B, is Robert, a brother of the two preceding. . . . T is my signature in the Reviews, while U is for the Miscellany, the initials of Transylvania University. H, M, is Mary Holley" (Horace Holley to Orville Holley, February 25, 1820, Mary Austin Holley Letters, UL).

110. The use of pseudonyms was a step beyond the anonymous submissions that gave the appearance of corporate agreement—representing the editors' general opinion (Ellen Gruber Garvey, *Writing with Scissors: American Scrapbooks from the Civil War to the Harlem Renaissance* [London: Oxford University Press, 2012], 40–41; James Mussel, *The Nineteenth-Century Press in the Digital Age* [New York: Palgrave Macmillan, 2012], 38–40).

111. Jackson, "Jedidiah Morse," 23–24 n. 5.

112. *Carlisle Republican*, May 25, 1819.

113. *New-England Galaxy and Masonic Magazine* (Boston), September 10, 1819.

114. Nerone, *Culture of the Press,* 50.

115. It bears mentioning that Rafinesque's publications were not limited to the *Western Review;* throughout this same period, his articles on various natural subjects appeared in the *Cincinnati Literary Gazette*—for instance, on February 21 and May 3, 1824.

116. Constantine Rafinesque, "On the Different Lighturge Observed in the Western States," *Western Review and Miscellaneous Magazine* 1 (August 1819): 313–14; Constantine Rafinesque, "Botany of Kentucky," *Western Review* 1 (September 1819): 92–95.

117. Constantine Rafinesque, "Botany," *Western Review and Miscellaneous Magazine* 1 (November 1819): 228–30; Constantine Rafinesque, "Natural History," *Western Review* 1 (December 1819): 305–8.

118. Constantine Rafinesque, "Fishes of the Ohio River," *Western Review and Miscellaneous Magazine* 2 (January 1820): 355–66; Constantine Rafinesque, "Natural History," *Western Review* 1 (December 1819): 306.

119. Charles Caldwell, *An Inaugural Address* (Lexington, Ky.: Thomas Smith, 1819), 5, 9.

120. Ibid., 8.

121. Ibid., 10.

122. Ibid., 12.

123. J. W. Walker to Samuel Brown, December 19, 1819, Samuel Brown Papers, 1817–1825, Filson Historical Society, Louisville, Ky.

124. Edmund Clark to Horace Holley, September 8, 1819, Horace Holley Papers, TU.

125. Peter Stephen DuPonceau to Horace Holley, October 9, 1819, Horace Holley Papers, TU.

126. John Kirkland to Horace Holley, November 10, 1819, Horace Holley Papers, TU.

127. John Rowan to Horace Holley, November 11 and December 21, 1819, Horace Holley Papers, TU.

128. *Kentucky Senate Journal,* 1819, 17.

129. The summary was reported in the *Literary Cadet* (Cincinnati), January 13, 1820.

130. *Literary Cadet,* January 13, 1820; *Pittsburgh Gazette,* reprinted in *Kentucky Reporter,* February 23, 1820.

131. Governor John Adair, inaugural address (*Kentucky House Journal,* 1821, 264); the act in question was An Act Appropriating Fines and Forfeitures for the Purpose of Promoting Education.

132. The editor of the *New-England Galaxy* reprinted the story after commenting on the need to reform "these poor creatures [the Kentucky legislators] . . . and send them light from these regions" (*New-England Galaxy and Masonic Magazine,* February 11, 1820).

133. Henry Clay to Horace Holley, February 17, 1820, Horace Holley Papers, TU.

134. Horace Holley to Orville Holley, June 8, 1820, Horace Holley Papers, TU.

135. Horace Holley to Willard Phillips, March 26, 1820, Willard Phillips Papers, Massachusetts Historical Society, Boston.

136. *Western Monitor,* March 21, 1820.

137. *Western Monitor,* July 11, 1820.

138. Horace Holley to Orville Holley, October 14, 1820, Horace Holley Papers, TU.

139. *Kentucky Reporter,* July 12, 1820.

140. Mary Austin Holley to Orville Holley, December 5, 1820, Mary Austin Holley Papers, DBC.

141. *Kentucky Gazette,* August 18, 1803.

142. Caldwell first appears on the membership roster of the Philadelphia Medical Society as secretary in 1800 (*Constitutional Telegraph* [Boston], March 8, 1800).

143. Benjamin Smith Barton, *Collections for an Essay towards a Materia Medica of the United States. Read before the Philadelphia Medical Society . . .* (Philadelphia: Philadelphia Medical Society, 1798).

144. "An Act to Incorporate the Lexington Medical Society," in *Acts Passed at the First Session of the Thirtieth General Assembly for the Commonwealth of Kentucky* (Frankfort, Ky.: Kendall and Russell, 1821), 422–24.

145. James Sterrett to Elizabeth Sterrett, December 5, 1820, Miscellaneous Records, TU.

146. Three theses are mentioned in the *Lexington Public Advertiser* for March 15, 1820: Samuel Russell, "On Hepatitis"; William Jewell, "On the Topography and Diseases of Shepherdsville, Kentucky"; and Thomas Nelson, "On a Form of Fever, Denominated the 'Puking Sickness'" (Medical Thesis Collection, TU). These three are not found in extant collections, however.

147. James Sterrett, "On the Medical Topography of Bowling Green and Its Vicinity," thesis, Transylvania University, 1821, Medical Thesis Collection, TU, 24.

148. James Guild, "On Cholera Infantum," thesis, Transylvania University, 1821, Medical Thesis Collection, TU.

149. Theodore Elliott, "Typhus Fever," thesis, Transylvania University, 1821, and John Lancaster Jr., "On Phthisis Pulmonali," thesis, Transylvania University, 1821, Medical Thesis Collection, TU.

150. John O. Hodges, "On Hydrocephalus Internus," thesis, Transylvania University, 1821, Medical Thesis Collection, TU, 2–3.

151. Robert Gist, "On Digestion, with an Inquiry into the Nature and Treatment of Dyspepsia," thesis, Transylvania University, 1821, Medical Thesis Collection, TU, 2.

152. Guild, "On Cholera Infantum"; Reuben Berry, "On Dysentery," thesis, Transylvania University, 1821, Medical Thesis Collection, TU, 1.

153. *Lexington Public Advertiser,* March 15, 1820.

5. "Traces of Vast Design"

1. Diary of John James, John James Papers, Miami University Archives, Oxford, Ohio.

2. Population statistics are drawn from Harrison and Klotter, *A New History of*

Kentucky; Wade, "Urban Frontier"; and U.S. Bureau of the Census, "Table 5: Population of the 61 Urban Places: 1820," June 15, 1998 (Internet release date), https://www.census.gov/population/www/documentation/twps0027/tab05.txt. In 1821, Horace reckoned Lexington's population to be 5,267 (Horace Holley to Joseph E. Worcester, March 27, 1821, Worcester Family Papers, Massachusetts Historical Society). States and territories north of the Ohio River presented a more enticing alternative. In the same period, Ohio experienced an almost geometrical rate of expansion, its population increasing from 50,000 to more than 600,000 (Kim M. Gruenwald, *River of Enterprise: The Commercial Origins of Regional Identity in the Ohio Valley, 1790–1850* [Bloomington: Indiana University Press, 2002], 83–84).

3. Gruenwald, *River of Enterprise,* 127; Harrison and Klotter, *New History of Kentucky,* 102.

4. Friend, *Along the Maysville Road,* 232.

5. Diary of John James, John James Papers.

6. Ibid.

7. Ibid.; see also John H. James to Father, August 17, 1823, Family Letters 1814–1824, John James Papers.

8. *Literary Cadet,* January 13, 1820.

9. *Kentucky Reporter,* October 4, 1821; commencement announcement in *Western Monitor,* August 4, 1824.

10. *Kentucky Reporter,* April 30, 1821.

11. *The American Almanac and Repository of Useful Knowledge . . .* (Boston: Gray and Bowen, 1832), 164.

12. Kenneth Wheeler, *Cultivating Regionalism: Higher Education and the Making of the American Midwest* (DeKalb: Northern Illinois University Press, 2011), 12–13; Daniel Boorstein, *The Americans: The National Experience* (New York: Random House, 1965), 152–55.

13. Horace Holley to Luther Holley, January 1, 1820, Holley Family Papers, CHS.

14. *Pittsburgh Gazette,* reprinted in *Kentucky Reporter,* February 23, 1820.

15. *Literary Cadet,* January 13, 1820.

16. *Kentucky Reporter,* July 1, 1822.

17. For instance, news of Albert Harrison and Aylett Buckner's forensic on "who renders the most important services to his country; the Patriot Orator or the Patriot Warrior" was carried by the *Western Monitor,* February 13, 1819; the *Lexington Public Advertiser,* March 4, 1820; and the *Kentucky Reporter,* May 29, 1826.

18. Horace Holley to Orville Holley, February 22, 1821, Mary Austin Holley Letters, UL.

19. Clipping from *National Register,* May 15, 1819, Horace Holley Scrapbook, TU.

20. Horace Holley to Milton Holley, March 24, 1819, Holley Family Papers, CHS; Horace Holley to Orville Holley, December 19, 1820, Horace Holley Papers, TU; *Literary Cadet,* January 13, 1820, reporting slightly lower figures for 1820: 235 total students,

with 34 in the Medical Department; Horace Holley to Sarah Holley, December 22, 1822, Holley Family Papers, CHS.

21. Horace Holley to Milton Holley, March 15, 1821, Holley Family Papers, CHS. Another report estimated the total amount of savings for the state of Kentucky as a whole to be between $700,000 and $800,000 (*City of Washington Gazette,* April 25, 1821).

22. Horace Holley to Orville Holley, February 22, 1821, Mary Austin Holley Letters, UL.

23. A report in the *Woodstock Observer,* September 11, 1821, agreed with Horace and noted the following enrollment figures: Yale, 319; Harvard, 286; Transylvania, 282; Union, 264; Dartmouth, 146.

24. *Acts Passed at the First Session of the Thirtieth General Assembly for the Commonwealth of Kentucky,* 351–55.

25. *Kentucky Reporter,* January 21, 1822.

26. *Kentucky House Journal,* 1821, 162–64.

27. *Kentucky Reporter,* December 18, 1821.

28. Horace Holley to Samuel Brown, December 17, 1821, Samuel Brown Papers, Filson Historical Society.

29. Horace Holley to Benjamin Bussey, December 28, 1821, Miscellaneous Collections No. 5, Andover-Harvard Theological Library Manuscripts and Archives.

30. *Kentucky Reporter,* October 4, 1821.

31. *New Hampshire Sentinel* (Keene, N.H.), February 9, 1822, which also quotes Hardin.

32. Horace Holley to Mary Holley, February 7, 1822, Mary Austin Holley Letters, UL.

33. Horace Holley to Luther Holley, November 3, 1819, Holley Family Papers, CHS.

34. Mary Holley to Orville Holley, December 5, 1820, Mary Austin Holley Papers, DBC.

35. Horace Holley to Milton Holley, March 15, 1821, Holley Family Papers, CHS.

36. Horace Holley to Orville Holley, July 14, 1820, Horace Holley Papers, TU.

37. Horace Holley to Orville Holley, July 16, 1820, Mary Austin Holley Letters, UL.

38. Rodabaugh, *Robert Hamilton Bishop,* 43.

39. Mariano's death was somewhat mysterious. He was said, Mary later heard, to have died of a broken heart (Mary Holley to Horace Holley, August 6, 1821, Mary Holley Papers, TU).

40. Rafinesque's earliest biographer quotes from an unnamed intimate of the Holley household as saying that the two were close, at least for a time, sharing an interest in intellectual subjects (Ellsworth, *Life and Writings of Rafinesque,* 42 n.).

41. Horace Holley to Orville Holley, February 22, 1821, Mary Austin Holley Letters, UL.

42. Ibid.

43. Horace Holley to Mary Holley, November 5, 1821, Mary Austin Holley Letters, UL.

44. Horace Holley to Milton Holley, May 8, 1823, Holley Family Papers, CHS.

45. Horace Holley to Mary Holley, February 23, 1822, Mary Austin Holley Letters, UL.

46. Thomas Brown, *Lectures on the Philosophy of the Human Mind*, Vol 1 (Edinburgh: Glazier, Masters, 1820), 529.

47. Davis, *Jefferson Davis*, 23.

48. William Henry Harrison Jr. to John James, October 22 and 9, 1819, John James Papers.

49. *Literary Cadet*, January 13, 1820. The idea that Horace helped pioneer the "parallel course" system, with students able to select an alternate, nonclassical curriculum, has no basis in source evidence.

50. *Kentucky Reporter*, March 29, 1820.

51. Horace Holley to Professor James Kingsley, July 14, 1821, Kingsley Memorial Collection, Yale University Manuscripts and Archives, New Haven, Conn.

52. Margaret Newnan Wagers, *The Education of a Gentleman: Jefferson Davis at Transylvania, 1821–1824* (Lexington, Ky.: Buckley & Reading, 1943), 26.

53. *Kentucky Reporter*, July 1, 1822.

54. Only after a year's worth of tutoring at the hands of Jenkins was Davis able to pass through to the sophomore year (Davis, *Jefferson Davis*, 22).

55. George Jones, *Autobiography*, quoted in Wagers, *The Education of a Gentleman*, 24; Horace Holley to Luther Holley, March 27, 1823, Horace Holley Papers, TU.

56. James Morrison to Henry Clay, February 18, 1821, in Clay, *The Papers of Henry Clay*, 3:43–44; Horace Holley to Orville Holley, February 22, 1821, Mary Austin Holley Letters, UL.

57. *Cincinnati Literary Gazette*, May 15, 1824.

58. Charles Caldwell to James Buchanan, February 9, 1821, Charles Caldwell Papers, TU.

59. James Morrison to Henry Clay, February 18, 1821, in Clay, *Papers of Henry Clay*, 3:43–44.

60. Horace Holley to Orville Holley, February 22, 1821, Mary Austin Holley Letters, UL.

61. James Sterrett to Elizabeth Sterrett, December 5, 1820, Miscellaneous Records, TU.

62. Clipping from *Cincinnati Literary Gazette*, May 15, 1824, Mary Austin Holley Letters, UL.

63. Horace Holley to Orville Holley, June 8, 1820, Mary Austin Holley Letters, UL.

64. Horace Holley to Mary Austin Holley, November 5, 1821, Mary Austin Holley Letters, TU.

65. Horace Holley to Orville Holley, February 22, 1821, Mary Austin Holley Letters, UL.

66. Horace Holley to Luther Holley, January 24, 1819, Holley Family Papers, CHS.

67. Horace Holley to Orville Holley, December 19, 1820, Horace Holley Papers, TU.

68. Horace Holley to Luther Holley, March 2, 1819, Holley Family Papers, CHS.

69. Horace Holley to Luther Holley, July 15, 1821, Holley Family Papers, CHS; Horace Holley to Milton Holley, August 17 and October 27, 1821, Holley Family Papers, CHS.

70. Horace Holley to Luther Holley, July 15, 1821, Holley Family Papers, CHS.

71. Mary Holley to Orville Holley, December 5, 1820, Horace Holley Papers, TU. Despite the insistence of at least one historian (Frank Dunn, "Old Houses of Lexington," 54–55, manuscript typescript, n.d., Kentucky Room, Lexington Public Library), there is no evidence that Horace ever occupied 228 Market Street.

72. Horace Holley to Milton Holley, November 28, 1822, Holley Family Papers, CHS.

73. William Henry Harrison Jr. to John James, October 9, 1819, John James Papers.

74. *Lexington Public Advertiser,* August, 26, 1820.

75. Horace Holley to Milton Holley, March 23, 1822, Holley Family Papers, CHS.

76. Stephen W. Fackler, "John Rowan and the Demise of Jeffersonian Republicanism in Kentucky, 1819–1831," *Register of the Kentucky Historical Society* 78 (Winter 1980): 2–5.

77. Horace had been unwilling to come out publicly either for or against any party or candidate, fearing even to toast Henry Clay. However, he privately considered Clay of unparalleled political ability (Horace Holley to Orville Holley, June 8, 1820, Horace Holley Papers, TU).

78. Horace Holley to Luther Holley, July 15, 1821, Holley Family Papers, CHS.

79. Horace Holley to Luther Holley, August 27, 1822, Holley Family Papers, CHS.

80. On the carriage ride back from Boston, Horace, referring to the seeming lack of political enthusiasm along the road, said, "Our form of government will probably be found too democratical for our stability and ultimate prosperity" (Horace Holley to Luther Holley, October 2, 1822, quoted in I. B. Holley, "Transylvania University President Horace Holley's Carriage Journey from Connecticut to Kentucky in 1822," *Ohio Valley History* 3 [2003]: 65).

81. Horace Holley to Milton Holley, November 28, 1822, Holley Family Papers, CHS.

82. [Horace Holley], "Transylvania University and Good Oeconomy," *Western Review and Miscellaneous Magazine* 4 (March 1821): 93.

83. Horace Holley to Luther Holley, December 21, 1818, Holley Family Papers, CHS.

84. John Everett to Mary Holley, September 12 and 24, October 25, 1821, Horace Holley Papers, TU.

85. Mary Holley to Orville Holley, December 5, 1820, Mary Austin Holley Papers, DBC.

86. Horace Holley to Luther Holley, August 10, 1819, Holley Family Papers, CHS.

87. Horace Holley to Luther Holley, July 23, 1820, Holley Family Papers, CHS.

88. Horace Holley to Orville Holley, September 2 and October 14, 1820, Mary Austin Holley Letters, UL. One report of their visit to St. Louis published in the *St. Louis Enquirer* described Horace in glowing terms. "He is able," the report began, "not only

to see things as they are at present, but as they will be ten, fifty, and an hundred years hence" (clipping, n.d., Horace Holley Scrapbook, TU).

89. Horace Holley to Orville Holley, July 16, 1820, Mary Austin Holley Letters, UL.

90. Mary Holley to Horace Holley, June 27, 1821, trans., Mary Austin Holley Papers, DBC.

91. Mary Holley to Horace Holley, July 7, 1821, Mary Austin Holley Papers, DBC.

92. Mary Holley to Horace Holley, August 13, 1821, Horace Holley Papers, TU.

93. Mary Holley to Horace Holley, September 16, 1821, Mary Austin Holley Letters, UL.

94. Orville Holley to Mary Austin Holley, March 23, 1821, Horace Holley Papers, TU.

95. Mary Holley to Horace Holley, August 23, 1821, Mary Holley Papers, TU.

96. Mary Holley to Milton Holley, November 19, 1821, Holley Family Papers, CHS.

97. John Everett to Mary Holley, October 25, 1821, Horace Holley Papers, TU.

98. Union Philosophical Society to Horace Holley, April 8, 1822, Crosby Family Papers; Masons to Horace Holley, January 7, 1822, Crosby Family Papers.

99. Horace Holley to Milton Holley, October 27, 1821, Holley Family Papers, CHS.

100. Horace Holley to Benjamin Bussey, December 28, 1821, Miscellaneous Collections No. 5, Andover-Harvard Theological Library Manuscripts and Archives; Horace Holley to Mary Holley, February 7, 1822, Mary Austin Holley Letters, UL.

101. Horace Holley to Mary Holley, January 15, 1822, Mary Austin Holley Letters, UL.

102. Thomas G. Percy to Samuel Brown, February 15, 1822, Samuel Brown Papers, Filson Historical Society.

103. Horace Holley to Orville Holley, October 14, 1820, Mary Austin Holley Letters, UL.

104. Horace Holley to Orville Holley, February 22, 1821, Mary Austin Holley Letters, UL.

105. [William Hunt], "Valedictory," *Western Review and Miscellaneous Magazine* 4 (June 1821): 383–84.

106. Horace Holley to Mary Holley, January 8, 1822, Mary Austin Holley Letters, UL.

107. Horace Holley to Mary Holley, November 5, 1821, Mary Austin Holley Letters, UL.

108. Horace Holley to Milton Holley, October 27, 1821, Holley Family Papers, CHS.

109. Horace Holley to Mary Holley, January 15, 1822, Mary Austin Holley Letters, UL.

110. Horace Holley to Mary Holley, January 8, 1822, Mary Austin Holley Letters, UL.

111. Horace Holley to Mary Holley, January 15, 1822, Mary Austin Holley Letters, UL.

112. Horace Holley to Mary Holley, February 7, 1822, Mary Austin Holley Letters, UL.

113. Horace Holley to Mary Holley, February 23, 1822, Mary Austin Holley Letters, UL.

114. *Village Register* (Dedham, Mass.), August 2, 1822.

115. Horace Holley to Luther Holley, September 19 and 21, 1822, quoted in I. B. Holley, "Transylvania University President," 56, 57.

116. Letters to Luther Holley reveal that the party averaged more than thirty miles a day (I. B. Holley, "Transylvania University President," 62, 67).

117. Benjamin Waterhouse to Thomas Jefferson, September 14, 1822, Thomas Jefferson Papers, Series 1, General Correspondence, 1651–1827, American Memory Project, at https://www.loc.gov/item/mtjbib024450/.

118. Thomas Jefferson to Benjamin Waterhouse, October 15, 1822, Thomas Jefferson Papers, Series 1, General Correspondence, 1651–1827, American Memory Project, at https://www.loc.gov/item/mtjbib024464/. Waterhouse claimed Horace delivered a sermon while in Boston.

119. Horace Holley to Milton Holley, January 21, 1823, Holley Family Papers, CHS; Transylvania Board of Trustees, extract of minutes of meeting, April 7, 1823, reprinted in *Kentucky Senate Journal*, 1825, 155, 156.

120. Horace Holley to Luther Holley, June 20, 1823, Mary Austin Holley Letters, UL.

121. Horace Holley to Milton Holley, April 21, 1823, Holley Family Papers, CHS.

122. Henry Clay to Horace Holley, n.d. (c. June 1823), in Clay, *Papers of Henry Clay*, 3:424.

123. Horace Holley, *A Discourse Occasioned by the Death of Col. James Morrison* (Lexington, Ky.: John Bradford, 1823), 3.

124. Ibid., app. 31.

125. Ibid., 23–24, 19–20.

126. DeWitt Clinton to Horace Holley, September 14, 1823, Horace Holley Papers, TU.

127. Horace Holley to Milton Holley, July 12, 1823, Holley Family Papers, CHS.

128. Citizen, *Literary Pamphleteer*, vol. 1 (Paris, Ky.: n.p., 1823), 13–15.

129. McFarland became pastor of the church in 1820 until his death in 1828 (Robert Stuart Sanders, *Presbyterianism in Paris and Bourbon County, Kentucky, 1786–1961* [Louisville, Ky.: Dunne Press, 1961], 8).

130. Citizen, *Literary Pamphleteer*, 1:3, 4–5, 12, 13.

131. Ibid., 1:7, 9, 13, 15, 16.

132. A Christian Republican, *Literary Pamphleteer*, vol. 2 (Paris, Ky.: n.p., 1823), 1.

133. Ibid., 2:5–6.

134. A Friend to Truth, *Literary Pamphleteer*, vol. 3 (Paris, Ky.: n.p., 1823), 1.

135. Voltaire, *Literary Pamphleteer*, vol. 4 (Paris, Ky.: n.p., 1823), 8–10.

136. Article clipping, publication and date unknown, Horace Holley Scrapbook, TU.

137. "To the People of Kentucky," publication and date unknown, Horace Holley Scrapbook, TU.

138. A Friend to Truth, *Literary Pamphleteer*, 3:14–15.

139. Andrew Jackson to Horace Holley, February 27, 1822, in Andrew Jackson, *The Papers of Andrew Jackson*, vol. 5: *1821–1824*, edited by Sam B. Smith, Harriet Fason Chappell Owsley, Harold D. Moser, and Daniel Feller (Nashville: University of Tennessee Press, 1996), 154.

140. Horace Holley to Luther Holley, August 31, 1823, Crosby Family Papers.

141. Horace Holley to Luther Holley, September 7, 1823, Crosby Family Papers.

142. Horace Holley to Luther Holley, August 31, 1823, Crosby Family Papers; Citizens of Bowling Green to Horace Holley, August 31, 1823, Horace Holley Papers, TU; clipping from *Weekly Messenger*, n.d., Horace Holley Scrapbook, TU.

143. Citizens of Nashville to Horace Holley, August 9, 1823, Horace Holley Papers, TU.

144. Horace Holley to Luther Holley, August 14, 1823, Horace Holley Papers, TU.

145. Ibid.

146. Luther Holley to Horace Holley, September 14, 1823, Horace Holley Papers, TU.

147. Voltaire, *Literary Pamphleteer*, 4:8–9.

148. Fides, "Unitarian Deism," newspaper unknown, n.d. (c. August or September 1823), Horace Holley Scrapbook, TU; see also other articles denouncing the students and their addresses in the *Kentucky Reporter*, December 8 and 15, 1823.

149. Ultor [Horace Holley], no title, four-part series, *Kentucky Reporter*, n.d. (c. fall 1823), Horace Holley Scrapbook, TU. Horace claimed that he was "Ultor" later that year (Horace Holley to Milton Holley, December 7, 1823, Crosby Family Papers).

150. "Transylvania University," *Kentucky Reporter*, n.d. (c. 1823).

151. Fitzmier, *New England's Moral Legislator*, 45; *Christian Messenger* (Middlebury, Vt.), August 27, 1817. Of the forty-four college presidents in the United States in 1823, only three lacked a doctorate: James C. Young of Centre College, David Elliott of Washington College, and Samuel Eccleston of St. Mary's in Baltimore ("A Sketch of the Life and Character of President Dwight," in *American Almanac and Repository of Useful Knowledge*, 164, 5).

152. *Salem Gazette*, August 11, 1820; *Massachusetts Spy* (Boston), August 8, 1821.

153. Horace Holley to Samuel Wilson, May 25, 1823, Samuel Wilson Vertical File, Margaret L. King Library, University of Kentucky, Lexington.

154. Horace thought much less of Clay's sons, who attended Transylvania but did not have much potential (Horace Holley to Luther Holley, June 20, 1823, Mary Austin Holley Letters, UL; *New Hampshire Patriot & State Gazette*, September 2, 1822).

155. *Centinel of Freedom* (Rockville, Md.), October 23, 1821.

156. Notification of Horace's degree, received alongside the one conferred upon Postmaster General John McLean, was carried in newspapers around the country: *Massachusetts Spy*, October 19 and 22, 1823; *City Gazette* (Charleston, S.C.), October 24, 1823; *Hampden Journal and Advertiser* (Springfield, Mass.), October 22, 1823; *Salem Gazette*, October 17, 1823; *Rhode-Island America*, October 17, 1823; *Baltimore Patriot and Mercantile Advertiser*, October 11, 1823.

157. Horace Holley, "Rank, Duties, and Rewards of American Lawyers and Statesmen," Horace Holley Papers, TU.

158. Horace Holley to Samuel Wilson, May 25, 1823, Samuel Wilson Vertical File.

159. Horace Holley, "On the Interests of Learning and Humanity," sermon, August 1823, Horace Holley Papers, TU.

160. Horace Holley, introductory law lecture, delivered November 8, 1823, Horace Holley Papers, TU.

161. Horace Holley to Kentucky legislature, December 23, 1823, Horace Holley Scrapbook, TU.

162. Newspaper clipping, periodical and date unclear (c. 1823), Horace Holley Scrapbook, TU.

163. Collins's request is given in Henry Clay to Horace Holley, January 9, 1823, in Clay, *Papers of Henry Clay*, 3:351.

164. Jeremiah Day to Horace Holley, May 13, 1823, Horace Holley Papers, TU.

165. Michael Graziano, "The 'Peculiar Children' of the Nation: American Civil Religion at Antebellum West Point," Ph.D. diss., Florida State University, 2011, 23–26.

166. *Weekly Recorder*, April 10, 1818; *Christian Messenger*, January 28, 1818.

167. Roger L. Geiger, *The History of American Higher Education: Learning and Culture from the Founding to World War II* (Princeton, N.J.: Princeton University Press, 2014), 145.

168. *Providence Gazette*, March 15, 1823.

169. Thomas Jefferson Wertenbake, *Princeton, 1746–1896* (Princeton, N.J.: Princeton University Press, 1946), 176.

170. *Ohio Miscellaneous Museum* 4 (April 1822): 176.

171. *Theological Review and General Repository of Religious and Moral Information* 1 (April 1822): 274.

172. *Boston Recorder*, March 31, 1821.

173. *Washington Theological Repertory* 2 (April 1821): 287.

174. *Evangelical Witness* (Newburgh, N.Y.) 1 (April 1823): 425–26.

175. Horace Holley to Luther Holley, June 20, 1823, Mary Austin Holley Letters, UL; Horace Holley to Milton Holley, December 7, 1823, Holley Family Papers, CHS. Only Harvard possessed more students, 392 (*Rhode Island Religious Intelligencer*, November 14, 1823).

176. Horace Holley to Milton Holley, November 1, 1823, Holley Family Papers, CHS.

6. "A Time of Fruits and Flowers"

1. Horace Holley to Children, June 1, 1827, Horace Holley Papers, TU.

2. Mary Holley to Harriette Holley, May 6, 1827, Mary Holley Papers, TU.

3. Horace Holley to Milton Holley, May 9, 1827, Holley Family Papers, CHS.

4. Mary Ann Corlis to John Corlis, May 21, 1827, Corlis-Respess Family Papers, 1698–1984, Filson Historical Society; Dr. Benjamin Dudley to Mary Holley, May 15, 1827, Horace Holley Papers, TU.

5. Mary Ann Corlis to John Corlis, May 21, 1827, Corlis-Respess Family Papers, Filson Historical Society.

6. Caldwell, *Discourse*, 281.

7. Horace Holley to Children, July 19, 1827, Mary Austin Holley Letters, UL. Mary wrote to Harriette: "Your father is so bent on making money, that he is determined to

have an immediate income. All the little boys are to come to us as soon as we are fixed" (Mary Holley to Harriette Holley, June 26, 1827, Mary Austin Holley Letters, UL).

8. *Independent Chronicle and Boston Patriot*, March 12, 1825.

9. Philip Lindsley, inaugural address at Cumberland College, in *The Works of Philip Lindsley* (Philadelphia: Lippincott, 1859), 35.

10. Theodore Clapp to Horace Holley, June 9, 1825, Horace Holley Papers, TU.

11. In 1820, Jefferson worried about the future of the University of Virginia and in a letter to friend Joseph Cabell stated, "If our legislature does not heartily push our University, we must send our children for education to Kentucky or Cambridge. The latter will return them to us fanatics & tories [*sic*], the former will keep them to add to their population. If however we are to go a begging anywhere for our education, I would rather it should be to Kentucky than any other state, because she has more of the flavor of the old cask than any other" (Thomas Jefferson to Joseph C. Cabell, January 22, 1820, in Thomas Jefferson, *The Works of Thomas Jefferson, Federal Edition*, vol. 12 [New York: Putnam's, 1904–1905], at http://oll.libertyfund.org/titles/808#lf0054-12_head_061).

12. Thomas Jefferson to Horace Holley, April 5, 1825, Thomas Jefferson Vertical Files, TU.

13. Bunker Hill Monument Association to Horace Holley, April 12, 1825, Horace Holley Papers, TU.

14. George Fickner to Horace Holley, May 5, 1825, Horace Holley Papers, TU.

15. Jared Sparks to Horace Holley, December 8, 1825, Crosby Family Papers. Sparks wrote again in January 1827 to check the status of Horace's review, having received nothing from him (Jared Sparks to Horace Holley, January 23, 1827, Horace Holley Papers, TU). Horace never wrote one, and a review of *History of Kentucky* did not appear in the *North American Review* until 1832 (review of Henry Marshall, *The History of Kentucky*, *North American Review* 35 [July 1832]: 1–19).

16. *New Hampshire Sentinel*, April 2, 1824.

17. Jedidiah Morse and Sidney Morse, *A New System of Geography, Ancient and Modern: For the Use of Schools . . .* , 24th ed. (Boston: Richardson and Lord, 1824), 124.

18. William Channing Woodbridge and Emma Willard, *Universal Geography, Ancient and Modern. . .* (Hartford, Conn.: Oliver D. Cooke and Sons, 1824).

19. *Western Monitor*, August 22, 1820; Horace Holley to Luther Holley, June 20, 1823, Mary Austin Holley Letters, UL.

20. John Vaughan to Horace Holley, August 3, 1825, Horace Holley Papers, TU; George Fickner to Horace Holley, September 25, 1825, Horace Holley Papers, TU.

21. *New-York Evening Post*, March 9, 1824.

22. *Cincinnati Literary Gazette*, May 1824.

23. Clipping, *Western Monitor*, n.d., Horace Holley Scrapbook, TU.

24. Ibid.

25. John Breckinridge and Nathan Hall to John Bradford, April 16, 1824, Official Correspondence, TU.

26. Rodabaugh, *Robert Hamilton Bishop,* 46–47.

27. *A Plain Statement* (pamphlet) (Lexington, Ky.: n.p., January 1824), 3–4, 12–13.

28. Robert Bishop to Transylvania Board of Trustees, September 6, 1824, Crosby Family Papers.

29. Clipping, source unknown but most likely from the *Argus of the Western World,* February 4, 1824, Horace Holley Scrapbook, TU.

30. Clipping, date and publication unknown, Horace Holley Scrapbook, TU.

31. Clipping, *Argus of the Western World,* February 4, 1824.

32. William G. Hunt, clipping, publication unknown, March 5, 1824, Horace Holley Scrapbook, TU.

33. Mary Ann Corlis to John Corlis, May 3, 1824, Corlis-Respess Family Papers, Filson Historical Society.

34. *Boston Recorder,* March 20, 1824.

35. Lundsford P. Yandell to Wilson Yandel, December 24, 1824, Yandell Family Papers, 1837–1919, Filson Historical Society.

36. Horace Holley to Milton Holley, March 26, 1824, Holley Family Papers, CHS.

37. Quotes from "Dean Swift Turkish Spy," clipping, publication and date unknown, Horace Holley Scrapbook, TU.

38. Horace Holley to Luther Holley, June 2, 1824, Mary Holley Papers, TU.

39. Horace Holley to Milton Holley, December 22, 1824, Holley Family Papers, CHS.

40. *Report, on the Transylvania University, and Lunatic Asylum,* 10, Miscellaneous Records, TU.

41. *Cincinnati Literary Gazette,* October 23, 1824.

42. Horace Holley to Orville Holley, August 25, 1819, Mary Austin Holley Letters, UL.

43. Horace Holley, *The Advantages Arising from the Study of Law and Politics, in a Free Government, and Particularly in the United States, Nov. 8, 1824,* Horace Holley Papers, TU.

44. Clipping, unknown publication, March 12, 1825, Horace Holley Scrapbook, TU.

45. A complete list of the essays read at meetings of the Kentucky Institute can be found in the *Cincinnati Literary Gazette,* March 13, 1824. One of the first is Constantine Rafinesque's description of *Prenanthes opierins* and *opierine* as a "new kind of Opium" (*Cincinnati Literary Gazette,* July 10, 1824). On his way through Lexington, John James, the intrepid traveler from Cincinnati, was curious about the goings on at these meetings, but after meeting Drake, he was convinced that the institute was nothing more than a pompous dinner club (Journal of John James, John James Papers).

46. Nicholas Guyatt, "'The Outskirts of Our Happiness': Race and the Lure of Colonization in the Early Republic," *Journal of American History* 95 (March 2009): 986–1011.

47. Horace Holley to Mary Holley, April 17, 1818, Horace Holley Papers, CL.

48. Horace Holley to Mary Holley, July 23, 1824, Mary Austin Holley Letters, UL.

49. "The Second Annual Report of the American Society for Colonizing the Free

People of Colour in the United States . . . ," *Western Review and Miscellaneous Magazine* 1 (October 1819): 142–64. No author is named, but the sentiments, phrasing, and prose style strongly suggest Horace is the author.

50. Horace Holley to Orville Holley, December 19, 1820, Horace Holley Papers, TU.

51. Horace Holley to Mary Holley, August 28, 1824, Horace Holley Papers, TU.

52. Horace Holley to Milton Holley, July 7, 1825, Holley Family Papers, CHS.

53. Horace Holley to Harriette Holley Brand, July 28, 1824, Crosby Family Papers.

54. Horace Holley to Luther Holley, July 2, 1824, Mary Holly Papers, TU.

55. Horace Holley to Mary Holley, July 22, 1824, Mary Austin Holley Letters, UL.

56. Horace Holley to Mary Holley July 23, 1824, Mary Austin Holley Letters, UL.

57. Horace Holley to Mary Holley, August 2, 1824, Crosby Family Papers; Horace Holley to Mary Holley, August 4 and 10, 1824, Horace Holley Papers, TU.

58. Horace Holley to Benjamin Gratz, August 15, 1824, Horace Holley Papers, TU.

59. Horace Holley to Mary Holley, August 28, 1824, Horace Holley Papers, TU.

60. Horace Holley to Mary Holley, August 31, 1824, Horace Holley Papers, TU.

61. Jefferson's complaint is mentioned in Horace Holley to Mary Holley, September 6, 1824, Horace Holley Papers, TU.

62. Ibid. The salary figures for the University of Virginia change a bit in a letter Horace wrote to Milton, where he claims Jefferson offered to pay professors the equivalent of $4,000, including $1,500 in base salary plus housing and money from private lectures (Horace Holley to Milton Holley, September 6, 1824, Holley Family Papers, CHS).

63. Horace Holley to Milton Holley, October 7, 1824, Holley Family Papers, CHS.

64. "Interrogations Submitted to the Board of Trustees of the Transylvania University, 1824," Crosby Family Papers.

65. Attendance for only part of the school year was common but difficult to translate to legislators. Horace asked the state to consider the "aggregate of the present year," which he believed on par with past years (ibid., 14).

66. Ibid., 11–12.

67. Ibid., 4–5.

68. Ibid., 24.

69. *Argus of the Western World,* July 14, 28, 1824; Paul E. Doutrich, "A Pivotal Decision: The 1824 Gubernatorial Election in Kentucky," *Filson Club History Quarterly* 56 (1982): 14–29.

70. Doutrich, "A Pivotal Decision," 28.

71. Fackler, "John Rowan," 19–20; Frank F. Mathias, "The Relief and Court Struggle: Half-Way House to Populism," *Register of the Kentucky Historical Society* 71 (April 1973): 170–71.

72. Horace Holley to Milton Holley, February 14, 1825, Holley Family Papers, CHS.

73. *Statesman* (Newburyport, Mass.), March 18, 1825.

74. *Charlestown Courier,* April 5, 1825.

75. *Richmond Enquirer,* March 22, 1825.

76. *Pensacola Gazette*, April 23, 1825.

77. E. G. Swem, ed., *Letters on the Condition of Kentucky in 1825* (New York: C. F. Heartman, 1916), 39.

78. *American Mercury*, January 18, 1825.

79. "Dr. Fishback, and Transylvania University," *Western Luminary* (Lexington, Ky.), March 9, 16, 23, 30, 1825.

80. Horace Holley to Milton Holley, March 31, 1825, Holley Family Papers, CHS.

81. *Western Luminary*, January 5, 1825.

82. *Western Luminary*, January 19, 1825.

83. *Western Luminary*, February 2, 1825.

84. Clipping, *Western Monitor*, n.d., Horace Holley Scrapbook, TU.

85. Horace Holley, "An Anniversary Discourse, before the Kentucky Institute in the Chapel of Transylvania University," January 29, 1825, Horace Holley Papers, TU.

86. Horace Holley to Caroline Holley, December 31, 1824, Mary Austin Holley Letters, UL; Theodore Clapp to Horace Holley, June 9, 1825, Horace Holley Papers, TU; Mary Holley to Harriette Holley Brand, November 17, 1825, Mary Holley Papers, TU.

87. Horace Holley to Milton Holley, July 7, 1825, Holley Family Papers, CHS.

88. Horace Holley, "Address to Lafayette," May 25, 1825, Horace Holley Papers, TU. Lafayette later thanked Horace for his pleasantries and complemented him on helping to diffuse light throughout the West (General Marquis de Lafayette to Horace Holley, May 16, 1825, Horace Holley Papers, TU).

89. Ellsworth, *Life and Writings of Rafinesque*, 41.

90. Horace Holley to Milton Holley, September 12, 1825, Holley Family Papers, CHS.

91. J. Wright, *Transylvania*, 91.

92. Offers were made to notable attorneys Robert Trimble and John Boyal from Kentucky and Edward Livingston from Louisiana (Edward Livingston to Horace Holley, September 12, 1825, and August 3, 1826, Horace Holley Papers, TU; *Niles' Weekly Register*, December 10, 1825).

93. Horace Holley to Joseph Desha, October 27, 1824, Horace Holley Papers, TU.

94. Joseph Desha, address to the Kentucky legislature, printed in *Niles' Weekly Register*, December 3, 1825; quotes in the subsequent two paragraphs also come from this source.

95. *Kentucky Senate Journal*, 1825, 145–46.

96. *Independent Chronicle and Boston Patriot*, December 17, 1825.

97. Horace Holley to Transylvania Board of Trustees, December 23, 1825, Horace Holley Papers, TU.

98. Horace Holley to Milton Holley, March 8, 1826, Holley Family Papers, CHS; Horace Holley to Luther Holley, January 21, 1826, Holley Family Papers, CHS.

99. *Boston Commercial Gazette*, February 27, 1826.

100. *Alexandria Gazette*, March 21, 1826; *Baltimore Patriot and Mercantile Advertiser*, March 16, 1826; *Boston Commercial Gazette*, March 13, 1826; *Daily Georgian* (Savannah), March 30, 1826.

101. Horace Holley to Milton Holley, March 8, 1826, Holley Family Papers, CHS.

102. This feeling is evidenced in leading nineteenth-century European periodicals; see especially "Notions of the Americans," *Edinburgh Review* 98 (June 1829): 519. A feeling of inferiority stayed with Americans throughout the nineteenth century; see "English and American Universities Compared," *North American Review* 126 (March–April 1878): 217–37.

103. Horace Holley to Milton Holley, April 16, 1826, Holley Family Papers, CHS.

104. Horace Holley to Transylvania Board of Trustees, June 5, 1826, Horace Holley Papers, TU.

105. Horace sold his share of the family farm to Milton for $1,900 (Horace Holley to Milton Holley, May 9, 1827, Horace Holley Papers, TU).

106. Horace Holley to Milton Holley, May 29, 1825, Holley Family Papers, CHS; Horace Holley to Orville Holley, October 23, 1826, Horace Holley Papers, TU.

107. Horace Holley to Orville Holley, October 23, 1826, Horace Holley Papers, TU.

108. Ibid.

109. *Kentucky House Journal,* 1826, 15.

110. Horace Holley to Samuel Wilson, February 20, 1827, Horace Holley Papers, CL.

111. Horace Holley to Milton Holley, January 18, 1827, Holley Family Papers, CHS.

112. Horace Holley to Milton Holley, January 8, 1827, Holley Family Papers, CHS.

113. Clipping of advertisement in unknown paper, February 28, 1827, Horace Holley Scrapbook, TU.

114. Horace Holley to Milton Holley, January 8, 1827; Horace Holley to Orville Holley, February 4, 1827, Horace Holley Papers, TU.

115. Horace Holley to Orville Holley, February 4, 1827.

116. Benjamin Silliman to Horace Holley, March 14, 1827, Horace Holley Papers, TU.

117. Edward Everett to Horace Holley, April 18, 1827, Horace Holley Papers, TU; James Madison to Horace Holley, March 21, 1827, Unprocessed Holley Papers, TU; Horace Holley to James Madison, February 2, 1827, Unprocessed Holley Papers, TU.

118. U. U. Bouligny to Horace Holley, February 18, 1827, Mary Holley Papers, TU.

119. Henry Clay Jr. to Henry Clay, March 27, 1827, in Clay, *Papers of Henry Clay,* 6:365–66.

120. Henry Clay to Henry Clay Jr., April 2, 1827, in Clay, *Papers of Henry Clay,* 6:385.

121. Horace Holley to Transylvania Board of Trustees, January 10, 1827, Horace Holley Papers, TU. The trustees voted to approve Horace's resignation for the second Monday in March (resolution of Transylvania Board of Trustees, January 12, 1827).

122. *Rhode-Island Statesmen,* February 10, 1827; *Literary Cadet,* January 13 and February 10, 1827.

123. Transylvania University Records, 1827, TU.

124. Horace Holley to Milton Holley, January 18, 1827, Holley Family Papers, CHS.

125. Horace recalled parts of the speech in a letter to his brother Orville a week later (Horace Holley to Orville Holley, April 3, 1827, Horace Holley Papers, TU).

126. Henry Clay Jr. retold the story of the handkerchief years later, and Horace's nephew George Washington Holley recorded it in a letter (George Washington Holley to Milton Holley, January 29, 1830, Holley Family Papers, SA).

127. *Kentucky Reporter,* April 4, 1827.

128. *Kentucky Reporter,* March 21, 1827.

129. Mary Holley, "On Leaving Kentucky," March 1827, Mary Holley Papers, TU. Her poem was carried by at least one newspaper: *Daily National Intelligencer,* June 6, 1827.

130. Caldwell, *Discourse,* 273.

131. Horace Holley to Harriette Holley Brand, April 1, 1827, Mary Austin Holley Letters, TU.

132. Mary Holley to Harriette Holley Brand, April 8, 1827, transcript, Mary Austin Holley Papers, DBC.

133. Mary Holley to Harriette Holley Brand, April 9, 1827, Mary Holley Papers, TU.

134. *New-England Galaxy and Masonic Magazine,* August 17, 1827; the friend is quoted in Pierpont, *A Discourse Delivered in Hollis Street Church,* 7.

135. Caldwell, *Discourse,* 270.

136. Ibid., 269.

137. Edwin Whitfield Fay, *The History of Education in Louisiana* (Washington, D.C.: U.S. Government Printing Office, 1898), 31–32.

138. Timothy F. Reilly, "Parson Clapp of New Orleans: Antebellum Social Critic, Religious Radical, and Member of the Establishment," *Louisiana History* 16 (Spring 1975): 182.

139. John M. Sacher, *A Perfect War of Politics: Parties, Politicians, and Democracy in Louisiana, 1824–1851* (Baton Rouge: Louisiana State University Press, 2003), 26.

140. Quoted in Sidney J. Romero, "The Inaugural Addresses of the Governors of the State of Louisiana: Tweedledum-and-Tweedledee: Or Contrariwise?" *Louisiana History* 14 (Summer 1973): 231.

141. Henry Johnson, inaugural address, in *"My Fellow Citizens . . . ": The Inaugural Addresses of Louisiana's Governors,* ed. Sidney J. Romero (Lafayette: University of Southwestern Louisiana, 1980), 46.

142. Horace Holley to Milton Holley, May 9, 1827, Holley Family Papers, CHS.

143. Horace Holley to William T. Barry, May 22, 1827, Horace Holley Papers, TU.

144. Quoted in Caldwell, *Discourse,* 276–77.

145. Horace Holley to Children, June 1, 1827, Horace Holley Papers, TU.

146. Mary Holley to Harriette Holley Brand, June 26, 1827, Mary Austin Holley Letters, UL.

147. Mary Holley to Harriette Holley Brand, June 23, 1827, Mary Holley Papers, TU.

148. Horace Holley to unnamed correspondent, July 22, 1827, Mary Holley Papers, TU.

149. Horace Holley to Children, July 19, 1827, Horace Holley Papers, TU. It is likely that Horace's illness spread among members of the crew. When Mary and

Horace Jr. arrived in New York, the *Essex Register* for August 13, 1827, reported three other fatalities.

150. Mary Holley to Orville Holley, September 27, 1827, Horace Holley Papers, TU.

151. *New-England Galaxy and Masonic Magazine*, August 17, 1827; *Connecticut Herald*, August 14, 1827; *Newburyport Herald*, August 14, 1827; *Salem Gazette*, August 14, 1827.

152. Pierpont, *Discourse Delivered in Hollis Street Church.*

153. Eulogy for Horace Holley, Lexington, Ky., 1827, Horace Holley Scrapbook, TU.

154. Transylvania medical class to Charles Caldwell, September 4, 1827, in Caldwell, *Discourse*, iii–iv.

155. Mary requested Clay's assistance in early November 1827, and Clay responded a short time later (Mary Holley to Henry Clay, November 8, 1827, and Henry Clay to Mary Holley, November 10, 1827, in Clay, *Papers of Henry Clay*, 6:1267–68, 1249).

156. Mary Holley to Henry Clay, November 15, 1827, in Clay, *Papers of Henry Clay*, 6:1267–68.

157. Mary Holley to Orville Holley, September 27, 1827, Horace Holley Papers, TU.

158. Mary Holley to Charles Caldwell, February 18, 1828, Mary Holley Papers, TU.

159. Mary Holley to Milton Holley, January 10, 1828, Holley Family Papers, CHS.

160. Caldwell, *Discourse*, 180.

161. Clippings of reviews of Caldwell, *Discourse*, Horace Holley Scrapbook, TU.

Conclusion

1. Peter and Peter, *Transylvania University.*

2. Robert Peter and Johanna Peter, *The History of the Medical Department of Transylvania University* (Louisville, Ky.: J. P. Morton, 1905), 151.

3. *Morning Herald* (New Bern, N.C.), December 20 and 24, 1896.

4. *Lexington Herald*, June 13, 1907.

5. *Lexington Herald*, July 12, 1908.

6. *Lexington Herald*, February 6, 1911. The announcement gave Horace's birthday as February 13, but that day was a university holiday (*Lexington Herald*, August 13, 1905).

7. *Lexington Herald*, March 6, 1905.

8. "Why Students from the South Attend Yale," *Macon Telegraph*, September 10, 1906; "Harvard in the South," *Macon Telegraph*, September 23, 1906.

9. Bernard Bailyn, *Education in the Forming of American Society: Needs and Opportunities for Study* (Chapel Hill: University of North Carolina Press, 1960), 14.

10. Joyce Appleby, *Capitalism and a New Social Order: The Republican Vision of the 1790s* (New York: New York University Press, 1984), 36–37.

11. Kett, *Pursuit of Knowledge*, 11–12.

12. Gordon Wood, "Classical Republicanism and the American Revolution," *Chicago-Kent Law Review* 66 (1990): 25–27.

13. David C. Ward, *Charles Willson Peale: Art and Selfhood in the Early Republic*

(Berkeley: University of California Press, 2004), 107–10; Foletta, *Coming to Terms with Democracy,* 1–2; Linda K. Kerber, *Federalists in Dissent: Imagery and Ideology in Jeffersonian America* (Ithaca, N.Y.: Cornell University Press, 1970), 76.

14. Steven Watts, *The Republic Reborn: War and the Making of Liberal America, 1790–1820* (Baltimore: Johns Hopkins University Press, 1987).

Bibliography

Primary Sources

Manuscript Collections

Adair, Governor John. Official Correspondence File, 1822–1823. Kentucky Digital Libraries Association, Frankfort.

Andover-Harvard Theological Library Manuscripts and Archives. Divinity School, Harvard University, Cambridge, Mass.

Horace Holley Papers.

Miscellaneous Collections No. 5.

Catherine and Howard Evans Papers. Margaret L. King Library, University of Kentucky, Lexington.

Crosby Family Papers. Family History Center, Salt Lake City, Utah.

David M. Rubenstein Rare Book and Manuscript Library. Duke University, Durham, N.C.

Dunn, Frank. "Old Houses of Lexington." Manuscript typescript, n.d. Kentucky Room, Lexington Public Library.

Elizabeth Patterson Bonaparte Papers, 1785–1879. Maryland Historical Society, Baltimore.

Fairfield (Area) Church Papers, 1782–2000. Fairfield Museum and History Center, Fairfield, Conn.

Filson Historical Society, Louisville, Ky.

Bodley Family Papers.

Corlis-Respess Family Papers, 1698–1984.

Henry Clay Papers.

Samuel Brown Papers, 1817–1825.

Yandell Family Papers, 1837–1919.

Holley, I. B. "A New England Family: The Holleys of Connecticut." Unpublished manuscript. Papers of I. B. Holley, 1965–2005. Special Collections, Rubenstein Library, Duke University, Durham, N.C.

Holley Family Papers. Connecticut Historical Society, Hartford.

Holley Family Papers. Salisbury Association, Salisbury, Conn.

Horace Holley Papers. Clements Library, University of Michigan, Ann Arbor.

I. B. Holley Papers, 1965–2005. Special Collections, Rubenstein Library, Duke University, Durham, N.C.

James Freeman Papers. Harvard College Library, Harvard University, Cambridge, Mass.

John James Papers. Miami University Archives, Oxford, Ohio.

John Milton Holley Papers, 1793–1799. Williams College Archives and Special Collections, Williamstown, Mass.

Martha J. Lamb Papers. New-York Historical Society Manuscript Department, New York.

Mary Austin Holley Letters. Rare Books Library, University of Louisville, Louisville, Ky.

Mary Austin Holley Papers. Dolph Briscoe Center for American History, University of Texas, Austin.

Massachusetts Historical Society, Boston.

    F. L. Gay Papers.

    Fowle, William Bentley. "Autobiography."

    G. E. Ellis Papers.

    Horace Holley Vertical File.

    Jefferson Papers.

    J. C. Warren Papers.

    Norcross Family Papers.

    Washburn Family Papers.

    Willard Phillips Papers.

    Worcester Family Papers.

Samuel Wilson Vertical File. Margaret L. King Library, University of Kentucky, Lexington.

Thomas Jefferson Papers. American Memory Project, Library of Congress, Washington, D.C. At https://www.loc.gov/collections/thomas-jefferson-papers/about-this-collection/.

Transylvania University Special Collections and Archives, Lexington, Ky.

    Charles Caldwell Papers.

    Early Documents.

    Horace Holley Papers.

    Horace Holley Scrapbook.

    Joseph Buchanan Papers.

    Mary Holley Papers.

    Medical Thesis Collection.

    Miscellaneous Records.

    Official Correspondence.

    Samuel Brown Vertical File.

    Thomas Jefferson Vertical Files.

    Transylvania Board of Trustees, minutes of meetings.

    Transylvania University Records.

    Unprocessed Holley Papers.

Yale University Manuscripts and Archives, New Haven, Conn.
Anson Phelps Stokes Autograph Collection.
Kingsley Memorial Collection.
Ravi D. Goel Collection on Yale.

Periodicals and Journals

Connecticut
  American Mercury, Hartford
  Connecticut Courant, Hartford
  Connecticut Evangelical Magazine, Hartford
  Connecticut Herald, New Haven
  Connecticut Journal, New Haven
  Litchfield Monitor
  Litchfield Journal
  New-Haven Gazette, and the Connecticut Magazine
District of Columbia
  City of Washington Gazette
  Daily National Intelligencer
  Washington Theological Repertory
Florida
  Pensacola Gazette
Georgia
  Columbian Museum, Savannah
  Daily Georgian, Savannah
  Macon Telegraph
Kentucky
  American Republic, Frankfort
  Argus of the Western World, Frankfort
  Argus of Western America, Frankfort
  Guardian of Freedom, Frankfort
  Independent Gazetteer, Lexington
  Kentucky Gazette, Lexington
  Kentucky Palladium, Frankfort
  Kentucky Reporter, Lexington
  Lexington Gazette
  Lexington Herald
  Lexington Public Advertiser
  Lexington Reporter
  Louisville Correspondent
  Louisville Gazette

Louisville Public Advertiser
Western Review and Miscellaneous Magazine, Lexington
Western Luminary, Lexington
Western Monitor, Lexington
Western World, Frankfort
Maryland
    American Commercial Daily Advertiser, Baltimore
    Baltimore Patriot and Mercantile Advertiser
    Centinel of Freedom, Rockville
    Niles' Weekly Register, Baltimore
    Theological Review and General Repository of Religious and Moral Information, Baltimore
Massachusetts
    Boston Commercial Gazette
    Boston Recorder
    Boston Traveller
    Columbian Centinel, Boston
    Constitutional Telegraph, Boston
    Essex Register, Salem
    General Repository and Review, Cambridge
    Hampden Journal and Advertiser, Springfield
    Independent Chronicle and Boston Patriot
    Invisible Rambler, Boston
    Massachusetts Spy, Boston
    Merrimack Intelligencer, Haverhill
    Newburyport Herald
    New-England Galaxy and Masonic Magazine, Boston
    New England Palladium, Boston
    North American Review, Boston
    Repertory, Boston
    Salem Gazette
    Statesman, Newburyport
    Village Register, Dedham
    The Yankee, Boston
Missouri
    Saint Louis Inquirer
New Hampshire
    New Hampshire Patriot and State Gazette, Concord
    New Hampshire Sentinel, Keene
    Portsmouth Journal of Literature and Politics

Portsmouth Oracle
Farmers' Cabinet, Amherst
New Jersey
Federal Republican, Elizabethtown
New York
The American, New York
American Monthly Magazine and Critical Review, New York
The Bee, Hudson
Commercial Advertiser, New York
Evangelical Witness, Newburgh
Gazette of the United States, New York
Harper's Magazine, New York
Impartial Observer, Cooperstown
New-York Evening Post
Plough Boy, Albany
Republican Watch Tower, New York
Spectator, New York
Weekly Visitor, New York
Woodstock Observer
North Carolina
Morning Herald, New Bern
Ohio
Cincinnati Literary Gazette
Literary Cadet, Cincinnati
Ohio Miscellaneous Museum, Lebanon
Weekly Recorder, Chillicothe
Pennsylvania
Franklin Gazette, Philadelphia
Philadelphia Medical Museum
Carlisle Republican
Port-Folio, Philadelphia
Quarterly Theological Review, Philadelphia
Rhode Island
Newport Herald
Providence Gazette
Rhode-Island America, Providence
Rhode Island Religious Intelligencer, Providence
Rhode-Island Statesmen, Providence
Scotland
Edinburgh Review

South Carolina
  City Gazette, Charleston
  Columbia Herald
Vermont
  Christian Messenger, Middlebury
Virginia
  Alexandria Gazette
  Richmond Enquirer

Secondary Sources

Acts and Laws of His Majesty's English Colony of Connecticut in New-England in America. New London, Conn.: Timothy Green, 1750.

Acts of the Kentucky State Legislature, 1818–1819. Frankfort, Ky.: Kendall and Russell, 1819.

Acts Passed at the First Session of the Thirtieth General Assembly for the Commonwealth of Kentucky. Frankfort, Ky.: Kendall and Russell, 1821.

"Address of the Students of Williams College to the President of the United States." In *A Williams Anthology: A Collection of the Verse and Prose of Williams College, 1798–1910 . . .* , edited by Edwin Partridge Lehman and Julian Park, 2–3. Williamstown, Mass.: n.p., 1910.

Aiken, Solomon. *The Rise and Progress of the Political Dissension in the United States: A Sermon Preached in Dracutt, May 11, 1811.* Haverhill, Mass.: William B. Allen, 1811.

American Almanac and Repository of Useful Knowledge. Boston: Gray and Bowen, 1832.

Ancourt, Abbe de. *The Lady's Preceptor. Or, A Letter to a Young Lady of Distinction upon Politeness. . . .* London: J. Watts, 1743.

Appleby, Joyce. *Capitalism and a New Social Order: The Republican Vision of the 1790s.* New York: New York University Press, 1984.

Austin Hatcher, Mattie. *Letters of an Early American Traveller, Mary Austin Holley, 1784–1846.* Dallas: Southwest Press, 1933.

Bailyn, Bernard. *Education in the Forming of American Society: Needs and Opportunities for Study.* Chapel Hill: University of North Carolina Press, 1960.

Baker, Henry G. "Transylvania: A History of the Pioneer University of the West, 1780–1865." Ph.D. diss., University of Cincinnati, 1949.

Baltzell, E. Digby. *Puritan Boston and Quaker Philadelphia: Two Protestant Ethics and the Spirit of Class Authority and Leadership.* New York: Free Press, 1979.

Bartanen, Michael, and Robert Littlefield. *Forensics in America: A History.* Lanham, Md.: Rowman and Littlefield, 2014.

Barton, Benjamin Smith. *Collections for an Essay towards a Materia Medica of the United States. Read before the Philadelphia Medical Society.* Philadelphia: Philadelphia Medical Society, 1798.

Bay, William Van Ness. *Reminiscences of the Bench and Bar of Missouri. . . .* St. Louis: F. H. Thomas, 1878.

Beecher, Lyman. *Autobiography, Correspondence, Etc. of Lyman Beecher, D.D.* Vol. 1 of 2. Edited by Charles Beecher. New York: Harper and Brothers, 1865.

Benedict, David. *A General History of the Baptist Denomination in America.* . . . Boston: Lincoln & Edmands, 1813.

Birdsall, Richard D. "The Second Great Awakening and the New England Social Order." *Church History* 39 (September 1970): 345–64.

Blair, Hugh. *Lectures on Rhetoric and Belles Lettres.* 3 vols. Edinburgh: Strahan, Cadell, and Creech, 1787.

Blythe, James. *A Portrait of the Times: Being a Sermon Delivered at the Opening of the Synod of Kentucky.* Lexington, Ky.: Thomas T. Skillman, 1814.

Boewe, Charles. *The Life of C. S. Rafinesque, a Man of Uncommon Zeal.* Philadelphia: American Philosophical Society, 2011.

Bonomin, Patricia U., and Peter R. Eisenstadt. "Church Adherence in the Eighteenth-Century British American Colonies." *William and Mary Quarterly* 39 (April 1982): 268–69.

Boorstein, Daniel. *The Americans: The National Experience.* New York: Random House, 1965.

Borrowman, Merle. "The False Dawn of the State University." *History of Education Quarterly* 1 (June 1961): 6–22.

Boston City Directory for 1809. Boston: Munroe, Francis, & Parker, 1809.

Brackenridge, Hugh H. *Incidents of the Insurrection in the Western Parts of Pennsylvania, in the Year 1794.* Philadelphia: John M'Culloch, 1795.

Bradford, Alden. *Biographical Notices of Distinguished Men in New England.* . . . Boston: S. G. Simpkins, 1842.

Brown, Thomas. *Lectures on the Philosophy of the Human Mind.* Vol. 1. Edinburgh: Glazier, Masters, 1820.

Brubacher John S., and Willis Rudy. *Higher Education in Transition: A History of American Colleges and Universities, 1636–1968.* New York: Harper and Row, 1958.

Bryson, William Hamilton. *Legal Education in Virginia, 1779–1979: A Biographical Approach.* Charlottesville: University Press of Virginia, 1982.

Bushman, Richard L. *The Refinement of America: Persons, Houses, Cities.* New York: Vintage Books, 1993.

Caldwell, Charles. *Autobiography of Charles Caldwell.* Philadelphia: Lippincott, Grambo, 1855.

———. *A Discourse on the Genius and Character of the Rev. Horace Holley.* Boston: Hilliard, Gray, Little, and Wilkins, 1828.

———. *An Inaugural Address.* Lexington, Ky.: Thomas Smith, 1819.

———, ed. *Medical Theses Selected from Inaugural Dissertations.* Philadelphia: Thomas and William Bradford, 1805–1806.

Calhoun, John C. *The Papers of John C. Calhoun.* Vol. 1 of 28. Edited by Robert L. Meriwether. Columbia: University of South Carolina Press, 1959.

Carr, Jacqueline Barbara. "A Change 'as Remarkable as the Revolution Itself': Boston's Demographics, 1780–1800." *New England Quarterly* 73 (December 2000): 585–89.

Catalog of the Society of Brothers in Unity, Yale College, Founded A.D. 1768. New Haven, Conn.: T. J. Stafford, 1854.

A Catalogue of Books, in the Library of Williams College. Bennington, Vt.: Anthony Haswell, 1794.

Catalogue of the Connecticut Alpha of [Phi] B K, Yale College. New Haven, Conn.: B. L. Hamlen, 1852.

Catalogue of the Officers and Students of Dartmouth College. Concord, N.H.: Jacob B. Moore, 1825.

Catalogue of the Officers and Students of Transylvania University. Lexington, Ky.: T. Smith, 1825.

Cayton, Mary Kupiec. "Who Were the Evangelicals? Conservative and Liberal Identity in the Unitarian Controversy in Boston, 1804–1833." *Journal of Social History* 31 (Autumn 1997): 85–107.

Centennial Celebration of the Wednesday Evening Club. . . . Boston: John Wilson and Son, 1878.

Chaney, George Leonard. *Hollis Street Church from Mather Byles to Thomas Starr King, 1732–1861.* Boston: G. H. Ellis, 1877.

Channing, Steven A. *Kentucky: A Bicentennial History.* New York: Norton, 1977.

A Christian Republican. *Literary Pamphleteer.* Vol. 2. Paris, Ky.: n.p., 1823.

Christianson, Eric H. "The Conditions for Science in the Academic Department of Transylvania University, 1799–1857." *Register of the Kentucky Historical Society* 79 (Autumn 1981): 305–25.

Citizen. *Literary Pamphleteer.* Vol. 1. Paris, Ky.: n.p., 1823.

Clark, Thomas. *Kentucky, Land of Contrast.* New York: Harper & Row, 1968.

Clay, Henry. *The Papers of Henry Clay, 1797–1852.* 11 vols. Edited by James F. Hopkins et al. Lexington: University Press of Kentucky, 1959–1992.

Codman, Ogden. *Hollis Street Church, Boston: Records of Admissions, Baptisms, Marriages, and Deaths, 1732–1887.* Transcribed by Robert J. Dunkle and Ann Smith Lainhart. Boston: New England Historic Genealogical Society, 1998.

Collins, Lewis. *Historical Sketches of Kentucky.* Maysville, Ky.: J. A. and U. P. James, 1848.

Come, Donald R. "The Influence of Princeton on Higher Education in the South before 1825." *William and Mary Quarterly* 2 (October 1945): 359–95.

Commencement at Williams-College, September 6, 1797. Williamstown, Mass.: Williams College, 1797.

Commencement at Williams College, September 4, 1799. Williamstown, Mass.: Williams College, 1799.

Conforti, Joseph A. "Samuel Hopkins and the New Divinity: Theology, Ethics, and Social Reform in Eighteenth-Century New England." *William and Mary Quarterly* 34 (October 1977): 572–89.

Conkin, Paul. *The Uneasy Center: Reformed Christianity in Antebellum America.* Chapel Hill: University of North Carolina Press, 1995.

Cooper, James Fenimore. *Satanstoe: Or, The Littlepage Manuscripts; a Tale of the Colony.* New York: D. Appleton, 1873.

Coward, Joan Wells. *Kentucky in the New Republic: The Process of Constitution Making.* Lexington: University Press of Kentucky, 1979.

C. S. "Letters from Boston." *The Ordeal: A Critical Journal of Politicks and Literature* 1 (1809): 232–35.

Davidson, Robert. *History of the Presbyterian Church in the State of Kentucky; with a Preliminary Sketch of the Churches in the Valley of Virginia.* New York: R. Carter, 1847.

Davis, Varna. *Jefferson Davis, Ex-president of the Confederate States of America. A Memoir by His Wife.* 2 vols. New York: Belford, 1890.

Dexter, Franklin Bowditch. *Biographical Sketches of the Graduates of Yale College.* 6 vols. New York: Holt, 1885–1912.

Dodsley, Robert. *Rhetoric and Poetry.* Boston: Thomas and Andrews, 1796.

Doutrich, Paul E. "A Pivotal Decision: The 1824 Gubernatorial Election in Kentucky." *Filson Club History Quarterly* 56 (1982): 14–29.

Drake, Daniel. *An Appeal to the Justice of the Intelligent and Respectable People of Lexington.* Cincinnati, Ohio: Looker, Reynolds, 1818.

Dudley, Benjamin. *To Dr. Drake.* Lexington, Ky.: n.p., 1818.

Durfee, Calvin. *A History of Williams College.* Boston: A. Williams, 1860.

Durrill, Wayne K. "The Power of Ancient Words: Classical Teaching and Social Change at South Carolina College, 1804–1860." *Journal of Southern History* 65 (August 1999): 469–98.

Dwight, Timothy. *A Discourse on the Character of George Washington, Delivered at New Haven. . . .* New Haven, Conn.: Thomas Green and Son, 1800.

———. *Greenfield Hill.* New York: Childs and Swain, 1794.

———. *Sermons; by Timothy Dwight.* 2 vols. New Haven, Conn.: Hezekiah Howe and Durrie and Peck, 1828.

———. *The Triumph of Infidelity.* Hartford, Conn.: n.p., 1788.

———. *The True Means of Establishing Public Happiness. . . .* New Haven, Conn.: Green, 1795.

———. *Virtuous Rulers a National Blessing: A Sermon. . . .* Hartford, Conn.: Hudson and Goodwin, 1791.

Eaton, Clement. *The Growth of Southern Civilization, 1790–1860.* New York: Harper, 1961.

Eblen, Tom, and Mollie Eblen. "Horace Holley and the Struggle for Kentucky's Mind and Soul." In *Bluegrass Renaissance: The History and Culture of Central Kentucky, 1792–1852,* edited by Daniel Rowland and James C. Klotter, 204–21. Lexington: University Press of Kentucky, 2012.

Eckley, Joseph. *A Sermon Delivered at the Installation of Rev. Horace Holley.* Boston: Belcher, 1809.

Ellis, Bill. *A History of Education in Kentucky.* Lexington: University Press of Kentucky, 2011.

Ellsworth, Richard. *The Life and Writings of Rafinesque.* Louisville, Ky.: J. P. Morton, 1895.

"English and American Universities Compared." *North American Review* 126 (March–April 1878): 217–37.

Fackler, Stephen W. "John Rowan and the Demise of Jeffersonian Republicanism in Kentucky, 1819–1831." *Register of the Kentucky Historical Society* 78 (Winter 1980): 1–26.

Farrell, James M. "'Above All Greek, above All Roman Fame': Classical Rhetoric in America during the Colonial and Early National Periods." *International Journal of the Classical Tradition* 18 (September 2011): 415–36.

Fay, Edwin Whitfield. *The History of Education in Louisiana.* Washington, D.C.: U.S. Government Printing Office, 1898.

Felt Tyler, Alice. *Freedom's Ferment: Phases of American Social History to 1860.* Duluth: University of Minnesota Press, 1944.

Fichtelberg, Joseph. *Risk Culture: Performance and Danger in Early America.* Ann Arbor: University of Michigan Press, 2010.

Field, David. *Brief Memoirs of the Members of the Class Graduated at Yale College in September, 1802. . . .* New Haven, Conn.: n.p., 1863.

Field, Peter S. "The Birth of Secular High Culture: 'The Monthly Anthology and Boston Review' and Its Critics." *Journal of the Early Republic* 17 (Winter 1997): 575–609.

———. *The Crisis of the Standing Order: Clerical Intellectuals and Cultural Authority in Massachusetts, 1780–1833.* Amherst: University of Massachusetts Press, 1998.

Fisher, George P. *The American Instructor. . . .* Worcester, Mass.: Isaiah Thomas, 1760.

———. *Life of Benjamin Silliman. . . .* 2 vols. New York: Charles Scribner, 1866.

Fitzmier, John R. *New England's Moral Legislator: Timothy Dwight, 1752–1817.* Bloomington: Indiana University Press, 1998.

Flannery, Michael A. "The Significance of the Frontier Thesis in Kentucky Culture: A Study in Historical Practice and Perception." *Register of the Kentucky Historical Society* 92 (Summer 1994): 239–66.

Foletta, Marshall. *Coming to Terms with Democracy: Federalist Intellectuals and the Shaping of an American Culture.* Charlottesville: University Press of Virginia, 2001.

Forrester, James. *The Polite Philosopher. . . .* New York: Parker and Weyman, 1758.

Friend, Craig Thompson. *Along the Maysville Road: The Early American Republic in the Trans-Appalachian West.* Knoxville: University of Tennessee Press, 2005.

A Friend to Truth. *Literary Pamphleteer.* Vol. 3. Paris, Ky.: n.p., 1823.

Furness, William. *A Discourse Delivered on the Occasion of the Death of John Vaughan. . . .* Philadelphia: J. Crissy, 1842.

Gannon, Kevin M. "Escaping 'Mr. Jefferson's Plan of Destruction': New England Federalists and the Idea of a Northern Confederacy, 1803–1804." *Journal of the Early Republic* 21 (Autumn 2001): 413–44.

Garvey, Ellen Gruber. *Writing with Scissors: American Scrapbooks from the Civil War to the Harlem Renaissance.* London: Oxford University Press, 2012.

Geiger, Roger L. *The History of American Higher Education: Learning and Culture from the Founding to World War II.* Princeton, N.J.: Princeton University Press, 2014.

Gessner, Solomon. *The Works of Solomon Gessner Translated from the German with Some Account of His Life and Writings.* 3 vols. Liverpool, England: J. M'Creery, 1805.

Goodman, Paul. "Ethics and Enterprise: The Values of a Boston Elite, 1800–1860." *American Quarterly* 18 (Autumn 1966): 437–51.

Goodrich, C. A. "Narrative of Revivals of Religion in Yale College, from Its Commencement to the Present Time." *Journal of the American Education Society* 10 (February 1838): 289–310.

Gordon, Robert B. *A Landscape Transformed: The Ironmaking District of Salisbury, Connecticut.* Oxford: Oxford University Press, 2000.

Grasso, Christopher. *A Speaking Aristocracy: Transforming Public Discourse in Eighteenth-Century Connecticut.* Chapel Hill: University of North Carolina Press, 1999.

Graziano, Michael. "The 'Peculiar Children' of the Nation: American Civil Religion at Antebellum West Point." Ph.D. diss., Florida State University, 2011.

Green, Fletcher M. *The Role of the Yankee in the Old South.* Athens: University of Georgia Press, 1972.

Gruenwald, Kim M. *River of Enterprise: The Commercial Origins of Regional Identity in the Ohio Valley, 1790–1850.* Bloomington: Indiana University Press, 2002.

Guthrie, William, *A New System of Modern Geography....* Philadelphia: Mathew Carey, 1794.

Guyatt, Nicholas. "'The Outskirts of Our Happiness': Race and the Lure of Colonization in the Early Republic." *Journal of American History* 95 (March 2009): 986–1011.

Hackensmith, Charles William. "Ohio Valley Higher Education in the Nineteenth Century." *Bureau of School Service Bulletin* 45 (March 1973): 1–135.

Hale, Sarah. *Traits of American Life.* Philadelphia: E. L. Carey and A. Hart, 1835.

Hall, Alfred. "Taxation for the Support of Schools." *Connecticut Common School Journal and Annals of Education* 1 (April 1854): 113–18.

Hall, Basil. *Travels in North America....* 3 vols. Edinburgh: R. Cadell, 1830.

Hardman, Keith J. *Seasons of Refreshing: Evangelism and Revivals in America.* Eugene, Ore.: Wipf and Stock, 1994.

Harris, Marc L. "Revelation and the American Republic: Timothy Dwight's Civic Participation." *Journal of the History of Ideas* 54 (July 1993): 449–68.

Harrison, Lowell, and James Klotter. *A New History of Kentucky.* Lexington: University Press of Kentucky, 1997.

Hatch, Nathan. *The Democratization of American Christianity.* New Haven, Conn.: Yale University Press, 1989.

Hearn, Donna P. *Dover.* Charleston, S.C.: Arcadia, 2008.

Hemphill, C. Dallett. *Bowing to Necessities: A History of Manners in America, 1620–1860.* Oxford: Oxford University Press, 2002.

Herbst, Jurgen. *From Crisis to Crisis: American College Government 1636–1819.* Cambridge, Mass.: Harvard University Press, 1982.

History of the Humane Society of Massachusetts.... Boston: Samuel N. Dickerson, 1845.

Holley, Horace. *A Discourse Occasioned by the Death of Col. James Morrison.* Lexington, Ky.: John Bradford, 1823.

Holley, Horace, and Isaac Bronson. "An Investigation of the Facts Relative to a Descent of Stones from the Atmosphere to the Earth, on the 14th of December, 1807, in the Towns of Fairfield, Weston, and Huntington, Connecticut ... in a Memoir Addressed to Samuel L. Mitchill." *Medical Repository* 5 (1808): 418–21.

Holley, I. B. "Transylvania University President Horace Holley's Carriage Journey from Connecticut to Kentucky in 1822." *Ohio Valley History* 3 (2003): 53–72.

Hopkins, James F. *The University of Kentucky: Origins and Early Years.* Lexington: University Press of Kentucky, 1951.

Hopkins, Samuel. *A Dialogue Concerning the Slavery of the Africans....* Norwich, Conn.: Judah P. Spooner, 1776.

———. *The System of Doctrines: Contained in Divine Revelation, Explained and Defended.* ... 2 vols. Boston: Thomas and Andrews, 1793.

———. *The Works of Samuel Hopkins....* 2 vols. Edited by Edwards Amasa Park. Boston: Doctrinal and Book Society, 1854.

Hull, Brooks B., and Gerald F. Moran. "The Churching of Colonial Connecticut: A Case Study." *Review of Religious Research* 41 (December 1999): 165–83.

Humphrey, Carol Sue. *The Press of the Young Republic, 1783–1833.* Westport, Conn.: Greenwood Press, 1996.

Ingraham, Joseph. *Charles Blackford, or The Adventures of a Student in Search of a Profession....* Boston: Yankee Office, 1845.

Jackson, Andrew. *The Papers of Andrew Jackson.* Vol. 5: *1821–1824.* Edited by Sam B. Smith, Harriet Fason Chappell Owsley, Harold D. Moser, and Daniel Feller. Nashville: University of Tennessee Press, 1996.

Jackson, Leon. "Jedidiah Morse and the Transformation of Print Culture in New England, 1784–1826." *Early American Literature* 34 (January 1999): 2–31.

Jefferson, Thomas. *The Works of Thomas Jefferson, Federal Edition.* Vol. 12. New York: Putnam's, 1904–1905. At http://oll.libertyfund.org/titles/808#lf0054-12_head_061.

Jillson, Willard R. "Bibliography of Lexington, Kentucky: Designed to Portray the Changing Historical Scene from 1774–1946." *Register of Kentucky State Historical Society* 44 (July 1946): 151–86.

Judd, Romie D. *The Educational Contributions of Horace Holley.* Nashville, Tenn.: Cullom and Ghertner, 1936.

Kafer, Peter. "The Making of Timothy Dwight: A Connecticut Morality Tale." *William and Mary Quarterly* 47 (April 1990): 189–209.

Kaplan, Catherine O'Donnell. *The Republic in Print; Men of Letters in the Early Republic: Cultivating Forums of Citizenship.* Chapel Hill: University of North Carolina Press, 2008.

Kelley, Brooks Mather. *Yale: A History.* New Haven, Conn.: Yale University Press, 1999.

Kennedy, Lawrence W. *Planning the City upon a Hill: Boston since 1630.* Boston: Thomson-Shore, 1992.

Kerber, Linda K. *Federalists in Dissent: Imagery and Ideology in Jeffersonian America.* Ithaca, N.Y.: Cornell University Press, 1970.

Kett, Joseph F. *The Pursuit of Knowledge under Difficulties: From Self-Improvement to Adult Education in America, 1750–1990.* Stanford, Calif.: Stanford University Press, 1994.

Kling, David W. "The New Divinity and Williams College, 1793–1836." *Religion and American Culture* 6 (Summer 1996): 195–223.

Knapp, Samuel Lorenzo. *Extracts from a Journal of Travels in North America. . . .* Boston: Thomas Badger, 1818.

Lancaster, Clay. *Antebellum Architecture of Kentucky.* Lexington: University Press of Kentucky, 1991.

The Laws of the Commonwealth of Massachusetts. . . . Vol. 5. Boston: State of Massachusetts, 1812.

Laws of Rhode Island College. . . . Providence: Rhode Island College, 1793.

Laws of Williams College. . . . Williamstown, Mass.: Williams College, 1795.

Laws of Yale College. . . . New Haven, Conn.: Yale College, 1800.

Lewis, Charlene M. Boyer. *Elizabeth Patterson Bonaparte: An American Aristocrat in the Early Republic.* Philadelphia: University of Pennsylvania Press, 2012.

Lexington's First City Directory. Lexington, Ky.: Joseph Charless, 1806.

Lexington's Second City Directory. Lexington, Ky.: Worsley and Smith, 1818.

Lindsley, Philip. *The Works of Philip Lindsley.* Philadelphia: Lippincott, 1859.

Lippard, George. "Nathaniel Hale." In *Washington and His Generals; or, Legends of the Revolution,* 264–67. Philadelphia: G. B. Zieber, 1847.

Lord, Norman C. "The War of 1812 on the Canadian Frontier: Letters Written by Sergt. James Commins, 8th Foot." *Journal of the Society for Army Historical Research* 18 (1939): 199–211.

Loring, James Spear. *The Hundred Boston Orators, Appointed by the Municipal Authorities and Other Public Bodies, from 1770 to 1852.* Boston: John P. Jewett, 1852.

Maclean, John. *History of the College of New Jersey, from Its Origin in 1746 to the Commencement of 1854.* 2 vols. Philadelphia: Lippincott, 1877.

Marsden, George M. *The Soul of the American University: From Protestant Establishment to Established Nonbelief.* New York: Oxford University Press, 1994.

The Massachusetts Manual, or, Political and Historical Register. . . . Vol. 1. Boston: Charles Callender, 1814.

Mathias, Frank F. "The Relief and Court Struggle: Half-Way House to Populism." *Register of the Kentucky Historical Society* 71 (April 1973): 154–76.

McDougle, Ivan E. *Slavery in Kentucky, 1792–1865.* Westport, Conn.: Negro Universities Press, 1970.

McGlothlin, William J. "Rev. Horace Holley: Transylvania's Unitarian President, 1818–1827." *Filson Club History Quarterly* 51 (July 1977): 234–48.

McLachlan, James. "Classical Names, American Identities." In *Classical Traditions in Early America,* edited by John W. Eadie, 80–99. Ann Arbor: University of Michigan Press, 1976.

McVey, Frank L. *The Gates Open Slowly: A History of Education in Kentucky.* Lexington: University Press of Kentucky, 1949.

Memoirs of the American Academy of Arts and Sciences. Vol. 1. Boston: Adams and Nourse, 1783.

Merwin, George H. *Ye Church and Parish of Greenfield: The Story of an Historic Church in an Historic Town 1725–1913.* New Haven, Conn.: Tuttle, Morehouse & Taylor Press, 1913.

Miller, James L. "Transylvania University as the Nation Saw It: 1818–1828." *Filson Club History Quarterly* 34 (October 1960): 305–81.

Miller, Samuel. *Memoir of the Rev. John Rodgers, D.D.* . . . New York: Whiting and Watson, 1813.

Moody, Eleazar. *The School of Good Manners.* . . . Boston: n.p., 1715.

Moore, Arthur K. *The Frontier Mind.* Lexington: University Press of Kentucky, 1957.

Moore, R. Laurence. "What Children Did Not Learn in School: The Intellectual Quickening of Young Americans in the Nineteenth Century." *Church History* 68 (March 1999): 42–61.

Morgan, Edmund. "Ezra Stiles and Timothy Dwight." *Proceedings of the Massachusetts Historical Society* 72 (October 1957–December 1960): 101–17.

Morse, Jedidiah, and Sidney Morse. *A New System of Geography, Ancient and Modern: For the Use of Schools.* . . . 24th ed. Boston: Richardson and Lord, 1824.

Mussel, James. *The Nineteenth-Century Press in the Digital Age.* New York: Palgrave Macmillan, 2012.

Nathans, Heather S. "Forging a Powerful Engine: Building Theaters and Elites in Post-revolutionary Boston and Philadelphia." *Pennsylvania History* 66 (1999): 113–43.

Nerone, John Charles. *The Culture of the Press in the Early Republic: Cincinnati, 1793–1848.* South Bend, Ind.: University of Notre Dame Press, 1982.

The New Universal Letter-Writer. . . . Philadelphia: D. Hogan, 1800.

O'Callaghan, E. G. *Documentary History of New York.* Vol. 4. Albany, N.Y.: Charles Van Benthuysen, 1851.

Padgett, James A. "The Letters of James Taylor to the Presidents of the United States." *Register of the Kentucky Historical Society* 34 (October 1936): 318–46.

Pasley, Jeffrey L. *"The Tyranny of Printers": Newspaper Politics in the Early American Republic.* Charlottesville: University Press of Virginia, 2001.

Pater, Erra. *The Book of Knowledge: Treating of the Wisdom of the Ancients.* . . . Boston: John W. Folsom, 1787.

Pattison, F. L. M. *Granville Sharp Pattison: Anatomist and Antagonist, 1791–1851.* Tuscaloosa: University of Alabama Press, 1987.

Paulus, Michael J., Jr. "Archibald Alexander and the Use of Books: Theological Education and Print Culture in the Early Republic." *Journal of the Early Republic* 31 (Winter 2011): 639–69.

Peter, Robert, and Johanna Peter. *The History of the Medical Department of Transylvania University.* Louisville, Ky.: J. P. Morton, 1905.

———. *Transylvania University: Its Origin, Rise, Decline, and Fall.* Louisville, Ky.: J. P. Morton, 1896.

Pettee, Julia. *The Rev. Jonathan Lee and His Eighteenth Century Salisbury Parish: The Early History of the Town of Salisbury, Connecticut.* Winsted, Conn.: Dowd, 1957.

Pierpont, John. *A Discourse Delivered in Hollis Street Church, Boston . . . Occasioned by the Death of Horace Holley L.L.D.* Boston: Stephen Foster, 1827.

Pierson, George W. *A Yale Book of Numbers: Historical Statistics of the College and University 1701–1976.* New Haven, Conn.: Yale University Press, 1983. At http://oir.yale.edu/1701-1976-yale-book-numbers#A.

Pilant, Charles Alan. "Expressions of Nationalistic Sentiments in Early American Newspapers, 1776–1826." Ph.D. diss., Marquette University, 1989.

A Plain Statement (pamphlet). Lexington, Ky.: n.p., January 1824.

Quinquennial Catalogue of the Officers and Graduates . . . 1636–1915. Cambridge, Mass.: Harvard University Press, 1915.

Ramage, James A., and Andrea S. Watkins. *Kentucky Rising: Democracy, Slavery, and Culture from the Early Republic to the Civil War.* Lexington: University Press of Kentucky, 2011.

Reilly, Timothy F. "Parson Clapp of New Orleans: Antebellum Social Critic, Religious Radical, and Member of the Establishment." *Louisiana History* 16 (Spring 1975): 167–91.

Robbins, Thomas. *Diary of Thomas Robbins, D. D., 1796–1854.* 2 vols. Boston: Thomas Todd, 1886.

Robertson, Andrew W. "'Look on This Picture . . . and on This!': Nationalism, Localism, and Partisan Images of Otherness in the United States, 1787–1820." *American Historical Review* 106 (October 2001): 1263–80.

Rodabaugh, James. *Robert Hamilton Bishop.* Columbus: Ohio State Archeological and Historical Society, 1935.

Romero, Sidney J. "The Inaugural Addresses of the Governors of the State of Louisiana: Tweedledum-and-Tweedledee: Or Contrariwise?" *Louisiana History* 14 (Summer 1973): 229–53.

———, ed. *"My Fellow Citizens . . . ": The Inaugural Addresses of Louisiana's Governors.* Lafayette: University of Southwestern Louisiana, 1980.

Rose, Anne C. "Social Sources of Denominationalism Reconsidered: Post-revolutionary Boston as a Case Study." *American Quarterly* 38 (Summer 1986): 243–64.

Rosenberg, Charles E., and William H. Helfand. *"Every Man His Own Doctor": Popular Medicine in Early America.* Philadelphia: Library Company of Philadelphia, 1998.

Rudolph, Frederick, and John R. Thelin. *The American College and University: A History.* Athens: University of Georgia Press, 1990.

Rush, Benjamin. *Essays, Literary, Moral, and Philosophical.* . . . Philadelphia: Thomas and William Bradford, 1806.

Sacher, John M. *A Perfect War of Politics: Parties, Politicians, and Democracy in Louisiana, 1824–1851.* Baton Rouge: Louisiana State University Press, 2003.

Sanders, Robert Stuart. *Presbyterianism in Paris and Bourbon County, Kentucky, 1786–1961.* Louisville, Ky.: Dunne Press, 1961.

Schultz, Stanley K. *The Culture Factory: Boston Public Schools, 1789–1860.* New York: Oxford University Press, 1973.

Shafer, Henry Burnell. *The American Medical Profession, 1783–1850.* New York: AMS Press, 1968.

Shiels, Richard D. "The Second Great Awakening in Connecticut: Critique of the Traditional Interpretation." *Church History* 49 (December 1980): 401–15.

Shurtleff, Nathaniel B. *A Topographical and Historical Description of Boston.* Boston: Boston City Council, 1871.

Silliman, Benjamin. *An Address Delivered before the Association of the Alumni of Yale College, in New Haven, August 17, 1842.* New Haven, Conn.: B. L. Hamlen, 1842.

Silverman, Kenneth. *Timothy Dwight.* Woodbridge, Conn.: Twayne, 1969.

Smith, Z. F. *The History of Kentucky: From Its Earliest Discovery and Settlement to the Present Date.* Louisville, Ky.: Prentice Press, 1901.

Smith Lee, Rebecca. *Mary Austin Holley: A Biography.* Austin: University of Texas Press, 1962.

Snow, Caleb Hopkins. *A History of Boston: The Metropolis of Massachusetts.* . . . Boston: Abel Bowen, 1828.

Sonne, Niles. *Liberal Kentucky: 1780–1828.* New York: Columbia University Press, 1938.

Spring, Leverett W. *A History of Williams College.* Boston: Houghton Mifflin, 1917.

Stanhope, Philip Dormer. *Principles of Politeness, and of Knowing the World.* . . . Portsmouth, N.H.: Melcher and Osbourne, 1786.

Stark, James H. *Antique Views of ye Towne of Boston.* Boston: Photo-Electrotype Engraving, 1882.

The Statute Law of Kentucky; with Notes, Praelections, and Observations on the Public Acts. . . . 5 vols. Frankfort, Ky.: State of Kentucky, 1809.

Steiner, Bernard Christian. *The History of Education in Connecticut.* Washington, D.C.: U.S. Government Printing Office, 1893.

Stokes, Anson Phelps. *Memorials of Eminent Yale Men: A Biographical Study.* . . . Vol. 1. New Haven, Conn.: Yale University Press, 1864.

Story, Ronald. "Class and Culture in Boston: The Athenaeum, 1807–1860." *American Quarterly* 27 (May 1975): 178–99.

Sumner, Margaret. *Collegiate Republic: Cultivating an Ideal Society in Early America.* Charlottesville: University of Virginia Press, 2014.

Swem, Gregg, ed. *Letters on the Condition of Kentucky in 1825*. New York: C. F. Heartman, 1916.

Tise, Larry. *American Counterrevolution: A Retreat from Liberty, 1783–1800*. Mechanicsburg, Pa.: Stackpole, 1998.

———. *Proslavery: A History of the Defense of Slavery in America, 1701–1840*. Athens: University of Georgia Press, 1990.

U.S. Bureau of the Census. "Table 5: Population of the 61 Urban Places: 1820." June 15, 1998 (Internet release date). At https://www.census.gov/population/www/documentation/twps0027/tab05.html.

Venable, William Henry. *Beginnings of Literary Culture in the Ohio Valley*. Cincinnati, Ohio: Robert Clarke, 1891.

Voltaire. *Literary Pamphleteer*. Vol. 4. Paris, Ky.: n.p., 1823.

A Volume of Records Relating to the Early History of Boston. . . . Boston: Municipal Printing Office, 1906.

Wade, Richard. "Urban Life in Western America, 1790–1830." *American Historical Review* 64 (October 1958): 14–30.

Wagers, Margaret Newnan. *The Education of a Gentleman: Jefferson Davis at Transylvania, 1821–1824*. Lexington, Ky.: Buckley & Reading, 1943.

Walker, Williston. *The Creeds and Platforms of Congregationalism*. New York: Scribner's, 1893.

Wallis, Frederick A., and Hambleton Tapp. *A Sesqui-centennial History of Kentucky*. 5 vols. Hopkinsville, Ky.: Historical Record Association, 1945.

Ward, David C. *Charles Willson Peale: Art and Selfhood in the Early Republic*. Berkeley: University of California Press, 2004.

Watkinson, James D. "Useful Knowledge? Concepts, Values, and Access in American Education, 1776–1840." *History of Education Quarterly* 30, no. 3 (1990): 351–70.

Watts, Steven. *The Republic Reborn: War and the Making of Liberal America, 1790–1820*. Baltimore: Johns Hopkins University Press, 1987.

Wertenbake, Thomas J. *Princeton, 1746–1896*. Princeton, N.J.: Princeton University Press, 1946.

Wheeler, Kenneth. *Cultivating Regionalism: Higher Education and the Making of the American Midwest*. DeKalb: Northern Illinois University Press, 2011.

Whiffen, Marcus, and Frederick Koeper. *American Architecture*. Vol. 1: *1607–1860*. Cambridge, Mass.: MIT Press, 1981.

Wickham, J. D. "Yale College in the Second Decade of the Present Century." *University Magazine* 3 (April 1890): 48–49.

Wightman, Joseph M. *Annals of the Boston Primary School Committee. . . .* Boston: Rand and Avery, 1860.

Willingham, William F. "Politics in Windham, Connecticut, during the Jeffersonian Era." *Journal of the Early Republic* 1 (Summer 1981): 127–48.

Willis, Nathaniel. *The Complete Works of Nathaniel Willis*. New York: J. S. Redfield, 1846.

Winterer, Carol. *The Culture of Classicism: Ancient Greece and Rome in American Intellectual Life, 1780–1910.* Baltimore: Johns Hopkins University Press, 2002.

Wolff, Katherine. *Culture Club: The Curious History of the Boston Athenaeum.* Boston: University of Massachusetts Press, 2009.

Wood, Gordon. "Classical Republicanism and the American Revolution." *Chicago-Kent Law Review* 66 (1990): 13–38.

Woodbridge, William Channing, and Emma Willard. *Universal Geography, Ancient and Modern. . . .* Hartford, Conn.: Oliver D. Cooke and Sons, 1824.

Wright, Conrad. "The Election of Henry Ware." In *The Unitarian Controversy: Essays on American Unitarian History,* 1–16. Boston: Skinner House Books, 1994.

———. *The Transformation of Charity in Postrevolutionary New England.* Boston: Northeastern University Press, 1992.

Wright, John Dean. *Lexington, Heart of the Bluegrass.* Lexington: University Press of Kentucky, 1982.

———. *Transylvania: Tutor to the West.* Lexington: University Press of Kentucky, 1975.

Index

www.ingramcontent.com/pod-product-compliance
Lightning Source LLC
Chambersburg PA
CBHW030256100426
42812CB00002B/464